THE DEFENSE
MANAGEMENT
CHALLENGE

THE DEFENSE MANAGEMENT CHALLENGE

Weapons Acquisition

J. RONALD FOX

with James L. Field

HARVARD BUSINESS SCHOOL PRESS

Boston, Massachusetts

Harvard Business School Press

© 1988 by the President and Fellows of Harvard College
All rights reserved.
Printed in the United States of America
92 91 90 89 88   6 5 4 3 2

Library of Congress Cataloging-in-Publication Data

Fox, J. Ronald (John Ronald), 1929–
    The defense management challenge : weapons acquisition / J. Ronald
Fox with James L. Field.
      p.   cm.
    Includes bibliographies and index.
    ISBN 0-87584-187-2
    1. United States—Armed Forces—Procurement.   2. United States—
Armed Forces—Weapons systems.   I. Field, James L., 1954–
II. Title.
UC263.F69 1988
355.6'212'0973—dc19   88-1713
                                                                      CIP

CONTENTS

To
The Military Officers, Government Civilians,
and Industry Managers
Responsible for the Defense Acquisition Process

PREFACE

In 1984, I began a Harvard-sponsored study on managing large projects such as developing the North Sea oil fields, constructing the Trans-Alaska Pipeline, constructing nuclear power plants, and developing and producing defense and space programs. After interviewing managers and gathering and organizing information in 1984 and 1985, I concluded that the one-trillion-dollar five-year buildup of defense spending in the 1980s offered an unusual opportunity to reexamine the defense acquisition process. Therefore, during 1986 and 1987 I narrowed my focus to large projects related to defense.

Fifteen years earlier, from 1971 to 1973, I had conducted a study of defense development and production programs, interviewed government and industry managers, studied individual acquisition programs, and reviewed numerous reports and articles. That study culminated in the publication of *Arming America: How the U.S. Buys Weapons* (Harvard Business School, 1974). In 1986, I again interviewed government and industry managers, studied individual programs, and reviewed more than a hundred studies and reports and several thousand pages of congressional hearings on the defense acquisition process. My goal was to understand what had changed during the fifteen-year period.

I discovered that most of the problems reported in *Arming America* still existed; indeed some had become worse. The relationship between government and industry had deteriorated, costs had increased at a rate greater than in the rest of the economy, and reports of program technical shortfalls and inappropriate contractor cost charges had increased. By the mid-1980s, dissatisfaction with the defense acquisition process had spread throughout the Congress and across the country. As in the early 1970s, Congress, the press, and informed citizens demanded change, and government officials promised change.

My interest in defense development and production programs began in 1959 when I was a research associate with Prof. J. Sterling Livingston at the Harvard Business School. The following year Professor Livingston was awarded a contract to design and test a cost planning and control system for the Navy's Polaris program. I spent 1960 to 1962 as the project manager for developing and testing the Polaris cost-control system at two major defense contractor locations. In 1962, the Defense Department and the National Aeronautics and Space Administration (NASA) adopted our approach as a standard planning and control system. During the subsequent two years, I served as Deputy Assistant Secretary of the Air Force, visiting Air Force program offices and contractor facilities to review and appraise the management systems employed on large development and production programs.

In 1965, I returned to the Harvard Business School to teach a course entitled Project Management and Defense and Aerospace Marketing. In 1969, I took a two-year leave of absence to accept an appointment as Assistant Secretary of the Army, where I was responsible for procurement, installations, and logistics. In the last six months of that appointment, I served as chairman of a joint government-industry group conducting a study of defense contract financing and profit policy for the Secretary of Defense (Industry Advisory Council, Report to the Secretary of Defense by the Subcommittee to consider *Defense Industry Contract Financing,* June 11, 1971). For five years, during the mid-1970s, I left Harvard to found Fox Studios, Inc., a manufacturing firm. In 1978, I sold the firm and returned to Harvard to develop a course on business-government relations. That course resulted in a book of cases and notes titled *Managing Business-Government Relations* (Homewood, IL: Richard D. Irwin, 1984).

ACKNOWLEDGMENTS

Harvard Business School Associates Fellow James Field began working with me on this project in June 1986 after completing eight years' active duty with the U.S. Navy and the two-year Harvard MBA Program. Throughout the project, he has been a major contributor in collecting data, conducting interviews, and preparing drafts. His resourcefulness, good judgment, and tact in working with the Defense Department, congressional staffs, and defense contractors were invaluable.

My wife, Dorris, has been so deeply involved in this study that she comes close to qualifying as a third author. She has shown extraordinary ability as a research assistant, organizer, and provider of unceasing encouragement. Without her, the book would not exist.

Cynthia Mutti has been a masterful editor, while exercising wisdom, good humor, and persistence. Her penetrating questions and comments about the defense acquisition process have been of great help.

Without the cooperation, comments, and suggestions by many individuals who currently hold, or previously held, government and industry positions of responsibility in the acquisition process, this research would not be possible. In particular, I have benefited from the thoughtful insights of many members of the Procurement Roundtable.

General Charles Adsit, General James Cercy, Admiral Stephen Hostettler, Admiral Walter Locke, General Kenneth Meyer, Dr. Joseph Shea, Stephen Rowan, General James Stansberry, USAF (ret.), Michael Guthrie, Paul Bradburn, and Franklin Spinney, each spent valuable time discussing the acquisition process with us.

I am also indebted to David Acker, Alan Beck, Richard J. Bednar, Dr. Jacques Gansler, John T. Jones, Jr., and Leonard Sullivan, whose research and writing made significant contributions to the work.

Many others experienced in the acquisition process willingly gave of their time to discuss or to comment on draft chapters. They include:

Colonel Robert Drewes, General William Eicher, USA (ret.), O. S. Hiestand, David Westerman, Robert C. Moot, Dr. John Morgan, Thomas D. Morris, Frank Sanders, Charles Enwright, Robert Bowes, George Rabstejnek, William D. Brown, Paul J. Kern, L. Kirk Lewis, Richard Stubbing, John G. Zeirdt, and John Cataldo. I am also grateful to the many others from the Defense Department and defense contractor firms who have contributed to this study. In particular, I wish to cite General Henry A. Miley, USA (ret.), Robert J. Stohlman, and General Frank Hinrichs, USA (ret.) — friends, advisers, and experts in the acquisition process, who served as valuable contributors and critics.

Michael Stevenson from the Harvard Business School Library, and W. Scott Slocum, a graduate of the School, were especially helpful and resourceful in gathering research materials. Mary Schumacher, a Harvard research associate and talented writer, read early drafts and made valuable suggestions for improving the research and the presentation of the material.

Theresa Morales, in addition to her heavy secretarial and administrative responsibilities, has made major contributions in arranging interviews and cheerfully gathering and organizing thousands of notes from interviews, reports, and articles on the acquisition process. It is difficult to imagine this project without her dedicated assistance and resourceful, everpresent support.

I am very grateful to Barbara Ankeny and Natalie Greenberg of the Harvard Business School Press who demonstrated considerable talent and patience in their suggestions on the content, organization, and format of the manuscript. I also extend special thanks to Susan Oleksiw, whose considerable professional editing skills helped prepare the final manuscript.

These acknowledgments would be incomplete without expressing appreciation to John McArthur, Dean of the Harvard Business School, to Professor Thomas McCraw, and Kathryn May of the Division of Research, for their continuing support and encouragement.

Although many in government, industry, and academia have contributed significantly to this work, I have enjoyed complete freedom with respect to what is said and left unsaid. The fact that an individual is cited in the acknowledgments does not imply endorsement of the findings or recommendations of this study.

J. Ronald Fox

Boston, Massachusetts
March 1988

THE DEFENSE
MANAGEMENT
CHALLENGE

INTRODUCTION

This volume examines the roles of government personnel in the acquisition process: congressmen and senators, Secretaries and Assistant Secretaries, senior military officers and civilians in the Pentagon, program managers and contracting officers, and military officers and civilians at all management levels. A second volume will deal with several additional aspects of the acquisition process: planning, methods of procurement, cost estimating, the source selection process, preparing a negotiation objective, types of contracts, profit policy, indirect costs, and program control.

I have written the current volume for government and industry policy makers and for practitioners in the defense acquisition process. I have attempted to present the sometimes complex technical subject matter in a way that is understandable to the informed lay person. Although the terms *program management* and *project management* are often used synonymously, I tend to restrict usage to *program management*. Some writers make the distinction that programs are large projects, but that convention is not widely accepted, and I have not adopted it.

The term *acquisition* gained popularity in the 1980s over the terms *defense procurement* and *defense R&D management,* which were used more frequently in the 1960s and 1970s. Where I have used the term *acquisition* I mean the process of developing and producing defense systems — usually weapon systems.

Chapter 1 provides the context and background. It describes the size and complexity of defense R&D and procurement, includes a description of the steps in the acquisition process, and introduces the problems and topics discussed more extensively throughout the remainder of the

book. Following this chapter, the focus is narrowed to the major play-
ers. Chapter 2, "Congress and the Weapons Acquisition Process," ex-
plores the role of Congress, how it has changed during the past fifteen
years, and how it contributes to serious schedule and cost problems.
Chapter 3, "The Pentagon," examines the senior Defense Department
decision makers and describes their organization and interaction with
each other, with lower management levels, and with contractors. Chapter 4, "Program Management," describes the actual versus planned role
of government program managers and contracting officers, briefly comparing their roles with those in industry program management. Chapter
5, "Careers in Acquisition Management," explains how military officers — the key managers in the process — are assigned, trained, developed, promoted, and retired. Chapter 6, "Civil Servants in the Defense
Acquisition Work Force," describes the limited career opportunities,
training, and evaluation system for the thousands of civil servants assigned to the process. Chapter 7, "Government Representatives at
Contractor Plants," examines the problems and opportunities of government personnel (military officers and civil servants) assigned to contractor plants to fulfill the work of the government program office. The
final chapter reviews the ideas introduced throughout the book and
summarizes the analyses and recommendations.

I have great appreciation for the magnitude and challenge of managing the defense acquisition process and great respect for many in government and industry who devote their careers to it. In this book I do
not challenge the premise that the United States needs a strong defense.
I reject the view that defense spending should be cut indiscriminately. I
served four years as a naval officer and four more years as an appointed
civilian in the Pentagon. I have been a manager in a defense contractor
firm and have devoted several years of my academic career to studying
the management of government-sponsored programs (usually defense
and space) with industry.

I differ, however, with the view held by a number of government
personnel that responsibility for cost control of weapons acquisition
programs can be delegated to contractors or to fixed-price contracts.
If one purchases standard items — cars, trucks, or other commercial
products — a fixed-price contract is usually an appropriate substitute
for day-to-day management of the project. If one purchases a large cus-
tom-made R&D or production program, however, where changes in
schedules, costs, and specifications occur as frequently as once a week
(or, more likely, once a day), a fixed-price contract is inappropriate and

therefore no substitute for day-to-day evaluations and negotiations between the buyer and the seller. Defense development and production programs are in the latter category. Government managers are needed to play major roles in shaping the effectiveness and efficiency of the acquisition process.

Some readers will approach this book predisposed to believe there are major management problems in the acquisition process, and others will be predisposed to believe there are few problems. I have not attempted to weigh the positive and negative features of various methods of managing the process or to assign blame or praise. My goal is to point the way to improving the management of the billions of dollars spent annually on defense R&D and production programs. Defense acquisition contains much that is right, including the ingenuity of government and industry engineers and the excellence of many of its products. There is also much that is wrong, resulting in a longer and more expensive process than is necessary. This book attempts to explain why.

— 1

THE DEFENSE ACQUISITION PROCESS:
AN OVERVIEW

> Management and employees of companies that contract with the Defense Department assume unique and compelling obligations to the people of our Armed Forces, the American taxpayer, and our nation. They must apply (and be perceived as applying) the highest standards of business ethics and conduct.
>
> President's Blue Ribbon Commission on Defense Management,
> *A Quest for Excellence,* June 1986, p. 77.

The U.S. Defense Establishment

The U.S. Department of Defense (DOD) is by far the largest and most complex business organization in the world. It operates more than fifty-four hundred installations worldwide and executes more than fifteen million contracts per year (more than sixty thousand per day).[1] It also develops and produces the most sought-after weapons and equipment in the free world.

The Defense Department provides full or partial employment to almost ten million Americans: 2.2 million active military personnel, 1.0 million civilian DOD employees, 1.9 million part-time reservists, 1.5 million military retirees, and 3.2 million private-sector employees. Thus, nearly 10 percent of the U.S. work force can attribute all or part of its income to the Defense Department. Among full-time DOD employees are tens of thousands of military and civilian personnel who work on multibillion-dollar weapons and equipment development and produc-

TABLE 1.1.   Defense Outlays

Fiscal Year	% of GNP	% of Total Federal Outlays
1950	4.9	27.4
1955	9.1	51.3
1960	8.2	45.0
1965	6.8	38.7
1970	7.8	39.4
1975	5.6	25.5
1980	5.0	22.5
1981	5.2	23.0
1982	5.8	24.5
1983	6.2	25.4
1984	6.0	25.9
1985	6.2	25.9
1986	6.4*	26.8*
1987	6.2*	27.0*

*Projected

SOURCE: Office of the Assistant Secretary of Defense (Comptroller), "National Defense Budget Estimates for Fiscal Year 1988 and Fiscal Year 1989," May 1987.

tion programs. They include contracting officers, program managers, plant representatives, engineers, cost estimators, pricing specialists, auditors, inspectors, and their superiors up the chain of authority to the Secretary of Defense.[2]

The defense budget is described in various ways. *Total Obligational Authority* (TOA) refers to the value of the congressionally approved defense program for each fiscal year, regardless of the financing method (which could include balances available from prior years, other resources available from prior years, or resources available from the sale of items in inventory). *Budget Authority* (BA), on the other hand, refers to the value of annual new authority to incur obligations. *Outlay* refers to an expenditure or a check issued. Defense outlays are often presented in terms of a percentage of the gross national product (GNP) or of total federal outlays (see table 1.1).

The defense budget is distributed among the military services and a variety of smaller defense agencies, although not equally. In the 1980s, the Army share of the Budget Authority has been approximately 30 percent less than the share for either the Air Force or the Navy (see table 1.2).[3]

In 1963, 47 percent of the total federal budget was devoted to

TABLE 1.2. DOD's Budget Authority by Component ($ in Millions)

	FY 1985	FY 1986	FY 1987
Army	74,270	73,128	75,297
Navy	99,015	96,113	95,693
Air Force	99,420	94,870	94,637
DOD Agencies	13,126	15,520	17,952
DOD-wide	970	1,759	1,352
Total	286,801	281,390	284,931

SOURCE: Office of the Assistant Secretary of Defense (Comptroller), "National Defense Budget Estimates," May 1987.

national defense and 45 percent to social programs and entitlements. In 1986, 28 percent of the unadjusted budget was devoted to defense and 57 percent to entitlements (see chart 1.1).[4]

Nearly $130 billion is spent each year on defense research and development and on production of weapons systems and equipment (see table 1.3). In addition, approximately $45 billion is spent on military construction, highly classified programs, supplies and equipment, operations and maintenance, and some nuclear weapons development.[5]

CHART 1.1. Total Federal Outlays

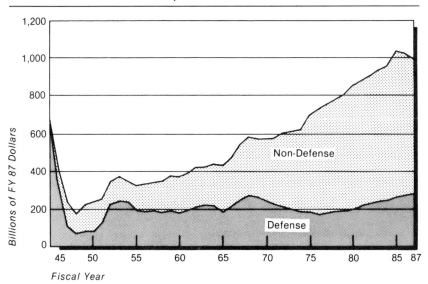

SOURCE: Secretary of Defense Annual Report to the Congress, Fiscal Year 1987, February 5, 1986, p. 99.

TABLE 1.3.   Defense Acquisition

Purchases of Defense Research and Development (R&D)	
Service	($ in millions) FY 1987
Army	4,772
Navy	9,382
Air Force	15,191
Defense Agencies	7,172
Defense Test and Evaluation	150
Defense Operational Test and Evaluation	57
Total	36,724
Purchases of Weapons and Equipment in Production (Procurement)	
Army	15,870
Navy	32,877
Air Force	34,463
Other	2,637
Total	85,847

SOURCE: Office of the Assistant Secretary of Defense (Comptroller), "National Defense Budget Estimates," May 1987.

From World War II until the 1970s, military research and development constituted by far the largest single share of the total federal R&D effort. In 1960, for example, the Defense Department's R&D budget was $5.6 billion, of a total federal R&D budget of $8.7 billion, or 64.4 percent.[6] By 1987, the U.S. defense R&D budget had risen to $37 billion, accounting for 65 percent of the total federal R&D budget of $57 billion ($37 billion is more than ten times the 1987 defense R&D in France, Germany, or the United Kingdom and one hundred times that of Japan).[7]

Between fiscal years 1980 and 1987, the DOD annual Budget Authority almost doubled, from $143 billion to $281 billion, with its total exceeding $1 trillion during that period. This sharp increase contributed to rising deficits and aroused public concern over the ways defense dollars were being spent. With increasing pressures to reduce the federal deficit, the challenge facing Congress was how to contain rising defense budgets while maintaining sufficient military strength to protect national security interests.[8]

MAJOR WEAPON SYSTEMS

The acquisition mission of the Defense Department is to contract for and oversee the development and production of weapon systems and equipment on time and at a reasonable cost. In pursuit of this mission, DOD engages tens of thousands of prime contractors — including most of the major firms in the United States — and hundreds of thousands of suppliers and subcontractors.[9]

Since the late 1950s and early 1960s, at the time of the Peck and Scherer (Harvard Business School) study of the weapons acquisition process, the major products of the defense industry have been described as weapon systems. The term *weapon systems* — or often *major weapon systems* or *major programs* — refers to technically complex items such as aircraft, missiles, ships, and tanks. A weapon system includes not only the major item of equipment itself but the subsystems, logistical support, software, construction, and training needed to operate and support it. Subsystems can include power plants; armaments; equipment for guidance and navigation, ground support, test and checkout, maintenance facilities, communications, and training; spare parts; and technical data (including operating and maintenance handbooks and parts catalogs).

One result of the amorphous nature of the term *weapon system* is that there is no general agreement among DOD, the Congress, the Office of Management and Budget, and the General Accounting Office on what is and is not included in a cost estimate. Two or more organizations (e.g., Office of the Secretary of Defense [OSD], a military service, or Congress) preparing separate cost estimates for the same weapon system can make different assumptions about the development program, spare parts, logistics, training, or any of a variety of associated hardware and service costs. Hence, the same weapon system can be identified with widely differing cost estimates at different times.

During the 1980s, increasing percentages of the defense budget were devoted to major weapon systems. In 1986, nearly one hundred major defense systems were at various stages of development and production. Total programs included thousands of jet fighters, bombers, and transport aircraft; one hundred new combat and support vessels; and thousands of tanks and cannon-carrying troop transports and strategic and tactical missiles. The total cost of the hundred major systems was estimated to exceed $750 billion, or more than the gross national product of most countries of the world.[10]

During much of the past three decades, constant-dollar unit costs for major defense systems have grown much faster than constant-dollar total budgets for these systems. The result has been the purchase of smaller quantities of new systems, delayed modernization, and shrinking capabilities.[11] DOD analysts reported that the Army spent in 1983 about the same amount of money ($2 billion in 1983 dollars) on new tanks that it had spent thirty years ago, but the number of tanks purchased declined 90 percent, from nearly 7,000 to about 700. In 1951, the Air Force ordered 6,300 fighter planes at a cost of $7 billion in 1983 dollars. In 1984, they spent approximately $11 billion to build 322 planes — 95 percent fewer. Of course, weapon systems have become much more capable over the past three decades; but even granting greater capability, the trends in increasing costs and declining output are significant.[12]

Major weapon systems development and production programs are technologically advanced and complex. Indeed, they are often designed to achieve performance levels never before realized, using many components and some materials never before used in military applications. Production is characteristically low volume, with the final cost of a major system frequently running into billions of dollars. This substantial expenditure of time and money occurs in an environment of rapidly evolving technology and unexpected changes in priorities for individual programs. This predicament creates an environment of uncertainty and risk for buyer and seller alike, exacerbated by the unpredictability of technical performance, development time, and cost.[13]

Military aircraft illustrate the complexity of modern weapon systems. The Air Force F-15 fighter, for example, has had 585,000 parts designed, fabricated, assembled, and tested by more than 22,000 people. These parts include 4,200 feet of tubing, 20 miles of wiring, 475 castings, and 437 forgings.[14] The fuel-control system alone in a modern fighter jet such as the F-15 has more than 5,000 parts. For every hour logged in the air by an F-15, the Air Force spends an average of fifty-three hours in maintenance on the ground. The amount of electronics equipment in a modern fighter aircraft is astounding. An Air Force general captured the essential change: "In the past, the Air Force used to buy airplanes and add electronics. Today the Air Force buys computers and puts wings on them."[15] Forty percent of the funds for DOD aircraft are spent on electronics equipment.

The management of business operations and technical development programs becomes more complex as technology advances. It is virtually impossible for any one individual — or any one contractor — to comprehend every aspect of the research, engineering design, and production stages of a major acquisition program. These programs usually extend for ten years or more, during which time many thousands of components must be designed and manufactured to work together as a unit. Individuals and firms involved in defense work become increasingly specialized, as does the equipment employed. Coordination of the many operations of acquisition is itself a major Defense Department activity.

HISTORICAL PERSPECTIVE

Despite the significant problems plaguing the acquisition process, few would challenge the statement that U.S. defense weapons and equipment are among the best in the world. Throughout the past thirty years, the defense industry has attracted outstanding scientists and engineers. The industrial firms that design and produce weapon systems are among the largest in the country. The managers of these firms are highly trained and experienced technical experts who understand the rewards and penalties inherent in the process, and usually produce profits for defense firms. It is no surprise that their firms are considered prudent investments by many sophisticated investors, including large pension trusts and mutual funds.[16]

Since the earliest days of our nation, the military forces have relied on private enterprise to supply the material, equipment, and services needed in peace and war. Although the government has always manufactured some war materials — especially ammunition — at no time have the armed forces been fully independent of the private sector in meeting their needs. Food, clothing, and ordinary necessities have always been supplied by contract. Ordnance and ships also have been supplied primarily by private industry, although government shipyards and arsenals have played an important role.[17]

Before and during World War II, the defense industry was usually compared with a typical manufacturing industry, such as the auto industry. The emphasis was on simplicity, reliability, and producibility. Since the late 1950s, however, the industry has been compared with a custom design and development industry, where contracting plays a major role. R. Jameson uses the housing industry for a simple analogy:

The housing contractor hires an architect and before the first board is cut, unless he has another development down the road, the contractor has to reduce the architect's effort to part time, or get the customer to agree to keep the architect on the payroll full time while the job requires the architect part time. The same thing follows with the carpenters, electricians, plumbers and roofers. In the aerospace business, a major effort is made by one or more firms to obtain a contract to develop and produce a defense program. Some preliminary design is accomplished, some computer modeling, and some independent research and development (R&D). Usually a large engineering team is amassed to demonstrate to the military buyers that the company has the capability in place to do the job. If the contract award is delayed, as is often the case, this high-cost team can stand virtually idle for months. In the absence of a rigorous determination to keep costs low, costs to the company and to the Government for these programs can be astronomical.[18]

Following a decline in the business of major defense companies after World War II, in the 1950s there was an expansion in the development and production of weapons and equipment. By the close of the decade, the trend was away from long production runs to more research, development, testing, and evaluation.[19]

Emphasis was placed on the development and production of weapon systems that incorporated the most advanced technological innovations. Toward the close of the 1950s, heavy reliance was placed on sole-source procurement. By 1960, for instance, a majority of the contract awards made by the military services were noncompetitive, and more than 40 percent were cost-plus-fixed-fee contracts.[20]

David Acker, a senior faculty member of the Defense Systems Management College, has characterized the defense acquisition environment of the 1950s.

Money was authorized to develop almost any new defense system that appeared capable of giving the United States a performance advantage over any potential adversary. Such considerations as "should-cost," "design-to-cost," and "life-cycle cost" were not uppermost in the minds of defense planners until the late 1950's. Both development and production were carried out under cost-reimbursement contracts. In this environment, production costs did not pose a major constraint on engineering design. When a design was discovered to be impractical in production — or to be inoperative in field use — it was modified in accordance with government-funded engineering changes. . . .

The lack of a well-organized and integrated DOD financial management system, along with the practice of "piecemeal" procurement, led to unstable employment in the defense industry and the emergence of a transient work force. Many of the contractors being challenged to develop and produce defense systems on the outer fringes of technology found it difficult to create and maintain smoothly functioning program management teams.[21]

The RAND Corporation reports that before the 1960s there was no formal DOD acquisition policy, largely because the Secretary of Defense did not have the authority to enforce such a policy. When the Department of Defense was established, in 1947, it was by design a loose confederation of the three military departments, and the Secretary of Defense was limited to providing general direction to those departments.[22]

The first Secretary of Defense, James Forrestal (1947–1949), lost no time in recommending that "the statutory authority of the Secretary of Defense should be materially strengthened . . . by making it clear that the Secretary of Defense has the responsibility for exercising direction, authority and control over the departments of the National Military Establishment."[23] That power was only slowly granted, however, and throughout the 1950s the individual services generally ran their own acquisition programs with very little interference by OSD, each service buying the weapon systems suitable for the kind of conflict it envisioned. The higher military budgets, resulting from the increased international role of the United States following the Korean War, presented this decentralized decision-making system with a twofold challenge: (1) efficient management of the first peacetime defense industry in U.S. history and (2) effective coordination of military R&D efforts.[24]

The Department of Defense Reorganization Act of 1958 authorized the Defense Secretary to assign the development, production, and operational use of weapon systems to any military department or service. Although this legislation provided the groundwork for the expanding role of OSD in the management of defense acquisition programs, the authority to direct and control DOD was not fully exercised until 1961, when Robert McNamara, a former Ford Motor Company executive, became Secretary of Defense. He believed in active management from the top, choosing to play a role in all aspects of programs rather than wait for problems to be brought to his attention.[25]

During Secretary McNamara's first year in office, he decided to centralize authority and planning for the defense establishment at the OSD level and to decentralize operations. He achieved the centralization of the planning and operational decisions during his term of office, but not the decentralization of operations.[26]

Another change in government management of the acquisition process during the late 1950s was the emergence of program management. Development and production for a particular program, formerly managed by several officials within each military service, were combined into one enterprise, known as a program (or project) management office, or, simply, program office. This change was made to smooth the transition from engineering to production and to allow for the consideration of such issues as operational support and maintenance during the early design phases. The concept of the program office meant that the development and production of a major weapon system was to be managed by a program manager, who answered to the commander of a government buying organization. Since the 1960s, each military service has organized its acquisition activities into system commands (materiel organizations), each of which oversees the activities of a number of program offices.[27]

The program manager for each major defense program is assisted by government personnel (and in the Air Force often by systems engineering contractors) with varying degrees of expertise in such areas as engineering, contracting, logistics, and testing. In addition, before a program office can engage in business with private industry, a contracting officer must become involved. Only contracting officers are authorized to execute contracts with industrial firms; they have a mandate to comply with government policy and to ensure fairness in government-business practices.[28]

DOD program offices are responsible for ensuring that the acquisition of major defense systems is accomplished efficiently and effectively.[29] Surprisingly, however, DOD provides its contractors with very few incentives to control and reduce costs. In fact, through its profit policy and source selection process, it often inadvertently does just the opposite — rewards cost increases and penalizes cost reductions.

For each weapon system, the military services usually contract with one firm (a prime contractor) for system design and integration functions. With limited exceptions (e.g., government-furnished equipment), the prime contractor directs subordinate contractors (subcontractors), who develop and produce particular subsystems and components, which the prime contractor brings together to produce a totally integrated defense weapon system.[30]

Most major defense programs have repeated setbacks before a success is achieved. How does a defense manager adapt to a job that has so much built-in frustration? Most of those who remain in the Defense Department are, by temperament, unfailingly optimistic. In dealing with inquiries from Congress, the press, or the public, most government (and industry) managers minimize the significance of performance failures, cost overruns, and schedule changes. Their progress reports and predictions are invariably positive, no matter what setbacks their programs actually experience. The gap between prediction and performance engages public attention only when there are significant increases in cost or problems in technical performance. This disparity is, however, a fact of daily life.

DEFENSE ACQUISITION VERSUS COMMERCIAL BUSINESS OPERATIONS

In the commercial marketplace, two exchanges occur when goods are produced: income is drawn from those who buy the goods, and is paid to the producers. The creation of purchasing power is matched by the sale of goods, the receipts from which absorb the purchasing power. But a government purchase — civilian or military — completes only half of the two-way transaction. Charles Schultze, former chairman of the President's Council of Economic Advisors, points out that in the defense business, although the government pays income to the producers, it does not then resell those goods in the marketplace. Consequently, it does not absorb an equivalent amount of income and purchasing power. Because the extra income earned in production is not absorbed by the sale of an added supply of goods in the market, the government must levy taxes to absorb the added purchasing power created when goods are produced for it. Although the government need not cover every dollar of its purchases by taxes, large-scale failure to absorb the added purchasing power — that is, large-scale budget deficits — can cause inflation and high interest rates. Under these conditions, purchasing power has been added to the system but not reabsorbed.[31]

In sum, government purchases do not add to market supply in the economic sense of the term. Hence, taxes must be levied. The military nature of the goods, however, is largely irrelevant to economic consequences. If the government bought massive amounts of food, clothing, and houses and distributed them free of charge, it would add nothing to the economic supply of goods in the country. Inflation would result, no matter how "useful" the goods in question.

Mr. Schultze criticizes the frequently heard proposition that the lower share of defense spending in the economy of Japan (and to a lesser extent, Germany) compared with that of the United States is an important reason for Japan's higher rate of productivity growth. A variant of this argument holds that the Japanese have gained a competitive edge on the United States in world markets because of their low defense spending. Both propositions are questionable. If the U.S. defense share of the GNP were to be at the expense of investment instead of consumption, reduction of investment might indeed lower U.S. productivity and competitiveness. But there is no economic reason, in principle, why the United States cannot alter the tax system so that it provides revenue to support defense spending by depressing consumption instead of investment. Indeed, if the United States does otherwise, the resulting fall in investment has to be recognized as a conscious choice and not a characteristic result of defense spending. In any event, Mr. Schultze points out that in the postwar period there is little evidence that the business investment spending share of GNP followed changes in the defense spending share of GNP, which ranged between 5 and 10 percent.[32]

Hence, there is nothing inherent in defense spending that leads to inflation or lowers productivity, and that should therefore prevent the United States from maintaining the spending level it believes necessary for national security, so long as it is willing to pay for increased defense spending through higher taxes.

The rules of the game in the defense business differ markedly from those in the commercial marketplace. Many authors have sought to describe the unusual business environment of the defense industry. Defense scholar Robert Art points out that in the classic theory of industrial capitalism, the business firm is characteristically autonomous. Corporate management is the formal decision maker regarding what it will produce, the method of production, quantity, price, and distribution. Moreover, in the commercial marketplace, the pressures of competition compel participants to minimize costs, to a greater or lesser degree, on behalf of profits, which, in turn, are the basis for further investment by private industrial management.[33]

In analyzing the defense acquisition process, the classical concepts of the industrial firm do not apply: price is usually not an overriding factor;

product and quantity are determined, not by the management of the firm, but by governmental authority; and competition normally focuses on proposed design rather than the physical product, and on promises of performance rather than the performance itself. The supplier often holds a monopoly and the purchaser holds a monopsony (i.e., one buyer only).[34]

GOVERNMENT PROCUREMENT REGULATIONS

The regulations governing business operations of the Defense Department and private industry have increased markedly since World War II. In 1947, the Armed Services Procurement Regulation (ASPR) numbered approximately 125 pages; in 1987, Federal Acquisition Regulation (FAR) and Defense Acquisition Regulation (DAR), the successors to ASPR, constituted several large volumes, totaling approximately 1,200 pages, with new pages added each month.[35]

Despite their size, these volumes do not cover all procurement requirements. The Office of the Secretary of Defense and the military services supplements them with directives or instructions. In the early 1970s, an officer in the program control division of the Air Force F-15 aircraft project reported: "There are 1,282 directives affecting the systems management process during the concept formulation phase of a major defense program." In other words, a team planning a weapon system must conform to over twelve hundred directives concerning all phases of the acquisition process, including, for example, integrated logistics support, reliability, configuration management, parts numbering, milestone reporting, cost estimating, monthly budgeting, performance measurement, training, and maintenance, as well as other matters of varying importance. Since the early 1970s, the quantity and detail of these government regulations have increased, becoming more burdensome for government and industry managers alike.

David Acker points out that in early 1965, industry leaders asked to be released from a number of government-imposed management systems. Contractors, through their industry associations, voiced concern about the proliferation of reporting requirements imposed on defense systems programs. They deemed this proliferation to be inconsistent with fixed-price or incentive contracting, questioning how the customer (i.e., DOD) could direct and approve contractor actions without seriously weakening either the contract incentives or warranties. Other industry representatives argued that when the government chooses to exercise detailed management of a program, the customer should share the financial success or failure of the contractor's performance.[36] They had a point. If the Defense Department wants to impose detailed controls on contractors, fixed-price and incentive contracts make little sense. Even in the absence of detailed controls, the use of these contracts for development programs with many uncertainties (requiring frequent contract changes) is counterproductive.

The Defense Acquisition Process

PARTICIPANTS IN THE ACQUISITION PROCESS

The major participants in the acquisition process are Congress, the Office of Management and Budget (OMB), the Office of the Secretary of Defense (OSD), the Office of the Service Secretary, the service headquarters staff, the military service materiel commands (the location of the program management offices), and industry. Until these groups reach a consensus, nothing is accomplished. In some instances, the executive branch (through OSD and a military department) advocates a particular program, but faces serious opposition in Congress. The MX missile is an example of a system that has lacked a consensus on deployment since the program began in the mid-1970s. In other instances, the administration and Congress agree to adopt one system, but industry exerts what influence it has with particular congressional members to obtain certain favorable decisions on another system.[37] The C-5B/C-17 aircraft decision in 1982 is an example. Sometimes a military service and OSD no longer advocate procurement of a system, yet Congress dictates further procurement, as in the case of the 1979–1981 purchase of the A-7D aircraft for the Air Force. At other times, a military service advocates a system opposed by OSD (e.g., the Army's DIVAD program) or vice versa (e.g., the Navy's F-111 aircraft program). In many instances, traditional areas of responsibility are blurred. For example, Congress has become more involved in specifying program technical requirements, as when it imposed a weight restriction on the new Small ICBM. There also has been conflicting direction, as when the House and Senate differed on the need for a second production source for the Army's M-1 tank engine in 1983.[38]

Each of the participants in the acquisition process exercises an oversight responsibility to ensure that laws and regulations are observed and programs pursued efficiently. Consequently, there are numerous oversight and monitoring agencies. The executive branch has the Justice Department and the Office of Management and Budget; the Department of Defense and each military service has an independent inspector general and auditing office; and Congress uses the General Accounting Office (GAO) for program audits and assessment, the Congressional Budget Office for budget and program cost estimates, and the Congressional Research Service and Office of Technology Assessment for analyses. Industry has its legal resources, Washington representatives, and industry associations to protect its interests. The government manager of a major systems acquisition program must be sensitive to all participants' positions and their vested interests.[39]

DEFINING NEW DEFENSE SYSTEMS

As new defense systems emerge over a period of years and improvements are made to existing systems, a large group of people in Congress, OSD, and the military services establish priorities among major acquisitions. Not only do the decision makers in this group change frequently, but so do the perceptions of the conditions on which acquisition judgments are based. An individual acquisition program, therefore, is usually subjected to frequent changes in funding, schedules, and technical performance requirements.[40]

The changes are caused by many variables, including altered perceptions of

- the current security threat;
- the future threat;
- the capability against the current threat;
- the best weapon mix to meet the current threat;
- the best mix of systems that can be acquired, given the available funding; and
- congressional support.[41]

The defense program manager (who is required, under the current system, to devote a significant amount of time to promoting his program) often views this large group of decision makers as an impediment to rapid completion of the program. Overseers within the higher-level decision-making groups, reviewing a large number of complex systems on a regular basis, may easily lose sight of the uniqueness and importance of individual systems. A funding cut of a few million dollars can be disastrous to a program manager, whereas to a congressman it represents much less than .0001 percent of the defense budget and an even smaller portion of the total federal budget.[42]

The DOD budget, sent to Congress each year, is the result of a complicated consensus-building exercise. Literally hundreds of organizational units within the Defense Department contribute to decisions and their justifications. Each unit has its "staffed" positions and rebuttals representing its perspective on the myriad questions needing resolution in the course of developing plans, programs, and priorities. Each unit has written operational procedures and regulations governing the flow of information and (especially) paper work that punctuates the process. Finally, the unit position from previous years is known and offered as a starting point; most changes are therefore incremental.[43]

Congress authorizes and appropriates funds for all defense programs. As it has become much more directly involved with the technical details of the acquisition process, it has, throughout the 1980s, made numerous additions or amendments to authorization and appropriation bills, specifying constraints on and objectives for many weapon system programs.

The lack of satisfactory information appears to be one of the reasons Congress delves into the daily management of the acquisition process and changes funding levels throughout the life of a program.[44] There are three primary reasons why this information may not be forthcoming from the Defense Department.

1. The complexity, advanced technology, and first-of-a-kind nature of many weapon systems preclude precise estimates of schedules, costs, or technical performance. There is frequently disagreement over how much information should be given to Congress.
2. When there is no general agreement on a well-defined mission need, program managers, their staffs, and higher headquarters cannot state confidently how effective a weapon will be. Decision makers at all levels become indecisive, and the program stretches out.
3. Program managers or their superiors may worry that program funding will be curtailed and promotions may not be forthcoming if problems are candidly portrayed.[45]

CONGRESSIONAL AUTHORIZATION AND APPROPRIATION

The contracting authority of DOD and other federal agencies is closely tied to congressional appropriations. Appropriations are made for a specified period of time and are usually stated in maximum dollar amounts, which are often amended one or more times a year.

There are three main types of appropriations: no-year, multiple-year, and annual (single-year). No-year appropriations remain available for obligation until expended, and multiple-year appropriations are available for a specific time, such as two or three years. Annual appropriations are available for obligation only during the current fiscal year, unless otherwise specified by law. Multiple-year appropriations are the most prevalent form of congressional funding for the R&D and production phases of acquisition programs, and annual appropriations are used for operating expenses of federal agencies.

Subject to the availability of multiyear appropriated funds, Congress occasionally authorizes a government agency to execute a contract for more than one year's requirements for an R&D or production program in the hope of achieving schedule and cost economies.[46] In these cases, parties to the contract are released from their mutual obligations only upon completion or termination of the contract. In contrast, a single-year contract (with options for extension beyond one year) allows the government the choice of extending the contract beyond one year, but it does not guarantee to the contractor that it will do so. Not knowing whether the contract will be renewed, the contractor usually has little inducement to make cost-reducing investments.

Congress budgets funds for an acquisition program into separate appropriations (e.g., procurement, construction, or research, development, test, and evaluation [RDT&E] for each military service, and there are prohibitions against transferring funds from one account to another to accommodate unexpected short-term exigencies.

Reprogramming within or among appropriations is permissible within thresholds (in 1987, $10 million for procurement and $4 million for RDT&E) if certain conditions are met. If thresholds are exceeded, DOD must return to Congress for reprogramming or a supplemental appropriation.

The net result of the congressional funding process is an operating budget with limited management reserves. Almost every program is underfunded, not overfunded. And the buying organizations also lack discretionary reserves. Reserves, if identified in the budget so that congressional staff members can find them, are spotlighted, renamed slush funds, and deleted. These actions, in reality, punish prudent management.[47]

The complete absence of management reserves might be less significant if perfect short-term planning were possible. In the main, however, program budget estimates are prepared six to twelve months before their submission to the Congress. Congress then spends a year deciding how much and where to increase or decrease requested program funding (usually with little awareness of the resulting imbalances across program phases). It is then often two years before the appropriated funds are actually "outlaid." Hence, the funding requirements are from three to four years out of date when it comes time to spend the money.

STAGES IN THE ACQUISITION PROCESS

The acquisition of a weapon system is a two-stage process. The first stage, development, includes planning, research, testing, and evaluation; the second is production. Stage one is summarized below in the order in which it generally occurs.

1. DOD identifies a security threat or defense operational mission. (A military service within DOD would normally take the lead in this and each of the following steps.)
2. DOD, usually with assistance from defense contractors, designs an engineering development program to meet the mission need and draws up an acquisition strategy and budget.
3. Congress authorizes and appropriates funds for the program.
4. The administration releases funds for the planned program.
5. DOD and interested contractors develop detailed technical approaches to the program (often simultaneously with steps 1 and 2).
6. DOD prepares a contract statement of work, with formal or informal assistance from contractors.
7. DOD issues requests for proposals (RFPs) to interested contractors and arranges preproposal conferences for bidders.
8. Contractors submit proposals to DOD, where they are evaluated.
9. DOD selects one contractor (or more), and the parties sign a contract for development of the weapon system.
10. The contractor begins work under the contract and each party

initiates negotiated changes and modifications where required or deemed desirable (often as many as several changes a week, usually negotiated with the government monthly).
11. The contractor delivers items to DOD for testing and evaluation while the work is in progress.

The formal acquisition process normally begins with a threat analysis, which evolves into an operational requirement. For example, if the Marine Corps defines a mission need (i.e., response to a threat) for a new landing craft with access to a larger percentage of the world's beaches and with a higher speed than that of existing landing craft, a military requirement for such a product would be established. If the Navy determines that the Soviets have made certain submarine advances, the Navy then defines the need to counter with an antisubmarine warfare helicopter with certain capabilities; that is then established as an operational requirement. Both requirements would reflect the estimated capabilities of potential adversaries.

There is often an earlier informal acquisition process that has its origin in defense laboratories or defense contractor firms, where engineers conceive of a new device or a new subsystem. Representatives of a firm may approach a military service, describe how the device or subsystem will enhance the defense capability of the service, and then help the service prepare the justification and RFP to conduct a more formal study of the idea. This assistance nurtures the idea until it evolves into a military requirement.[48]

A defense firm wishing to obtain a contract to develop a new weapon system must become involved in the program two to four years before a formal RFP is issued, or it is unlikely to qualify as a prospective contractor. This involvement generally means assisting the buying service in defining elements of the planned weapon system. The cost of this initial work generally becomes part of overhead costs (e.g., bid and proposal [B&P] expense or independent research and development [IR&D] expense), which the Defense Department usually reimburses in part or in full. After several firms have completed this work, the sponsoring service generally has sufficient information to request Budget Authority in the annual request of the department.

The acquisition process then proceeds from definition of the requirement to concept exploration, from demonstration and validation to full-scale development, and finally to production.

The basic DOD Directive (DODD) on major systems acquisition, 5000.1, describes four key decisions and four phases of activity in the DOD acquisition process:[49]

a. *Milestone 0 Decision:*   Approval or disapproval of a mission need and entry into the concept exploration/definition phase.

    Phase 0:   Concept exploration: solicitation and evaluation of alternative system design concepts.

b. *Milestone I Decision:*   Approval or disapproval to proceed into the concept demonstration/validation phase.

    Phase I: Demonstration and validation.

c. *Milestone II Decision:*   Approval or disapproval to proceed into the full-scale development phase and, as appropriate, low-rate initial production.

    Phase II: Full-scale development.

d. *Milestone III Decision:*   Approval or disapproval to proceed into the full-rate production and initial deployment phase.

    Phase III: Production and initial deployment.

e. *Milestone IV Decision:*   Encompasses a review one to two years after initial deployment to ensure that operational readiness and support objectives are being achieved and maintained during the first several years of the operations support phase.

The Milestone 0 decision determines mission need and approves program initiation and authority to budget for a new program. Normally a concept exploration/definition phase follows this approval.

At Milestone I, a system concept paper (SCP), prepared by the responsible military service, identifies key areas of technical risk to be reduced through research and development. Reductions are expected to be validated through testing and evaluation before Milestone II. The SCP

- summarizes the results of the concept exploration before Milestone I;
- describes the DOD acquisition strategy (including identification of concepts to be included in the demonstration and validation phase) and reasons for elimination of other concepts; and

- establishes goals, thresholds, and threshold ranges (as appropriate) to be met and reviewed at the next milestone.

Phase I ends with Milestone II, approval (or, rarely, disapproval) to proceed with full-scale development. The timing of the decision is flexible, depending on the acquisition strategy adopted at Milestone I. At Milestone II, all significant risks are expected to have been resolved, the technology is in hand, and only engineering (as opposed to experimental) efforts remain.

When a military service determines that a program is ready for full-scale development, the Secretary of the service requests approval of a document called the decision coordinating paper (DCP), formerly known as the development concept paper.

The DCP provides program information essential to the decision-making process: a statement of direction from the Secretary of Defense, a description of the overall program, the need for the program, design alternatives, program schedule and acquisition strategy, and issues affecting the Secretary's milestone decisions. The DCP annexes include program goals and thresholds, resource requirements, and projected life-cycle costs.[50] The responsible military service prepares the DCP after reaching agreement with OSD on an outline. The Office of the Under Secretary of Defense for Acquisition has the primary responsibility for reviewing the DCP and for recommending its approval or disapproval to the Secretary of Defense.

Phase 0. Concept Exploration. During this phase, the DOD component develops an acquisition strategy, including identification of the best concepts to be carried into the concept demonstration/validation phase for further development, and reasons for elimination of alternative concepts. Broad program cost, schedule, and operational effectiveness goals and thresholds are established.

Phase I. Demonstration/Validation. During this phase, the government program manager and his staff are expected to accomplish a variety of tasks relevant to the technical issues. They seek to verify preliminary design and engineering, prepare cost estimates, analyze trade-off proposals, prepare a formal requirements document, and validate the concept for the next phase, full-scale development. Hardware prototypes are often used to demonstrate the feasibility of the system, subsystem, components, and support equipment. Plans for testing and evaluating the system are updated. The program management office also seeks to ensure that the risks have been identified and are acceptable and that realistic alternatives have been established. Performance estimates are reviewed for their consistency with the risks involved.

There are six criteria for obtaining a decision to proceed to engineering development (Milestone II).

1. Demonstrable engineering, rather than experimental, effort.
2. Definition of the mission and performance requirements.
3. Selection of the best-perceived technical approaches.
4. A thorough trade-off analysis.
5. Comparison of the cost effectiveness for the proposed weapon system and competing systems within DOD, concluding that the proposal is feasible.
6. Credible and acceptable cost and schedule estimates.

In practice, paper studies and analyses often substitute for essential system development and testing. As a result, uncertainties that could be eliminated or reduced in the research and exploratory development phases are often carried into advanced engineering development or operational systems development, where unresolved technical problems are significantly more expensive and troublesome to correct. In addition, when exploratory development and testing do not take place, the new technology that could improve weapon capability is often lost. Were all six prerequisites conscientiously fulfilled, the acquisition process would suffer fewer false starts, although the program could be delayed by many months. In the name of military urgency, a blanket approval to proceed with engineering development is sometimes requested and granted.

Phase II. Full-scale Development. In the development phase, the system (including training devices, computer resources, and other items necessary for its support) is expected to be fully developed, engineered, fabricated, and tested. (Defense has normally delegated Milestone III, the decision to proceed with production of a major weapon system, to the service Secretary, unless thresholds established at Milestone II have been crossed or the public or the Congress is greatly concerned about, for example, persistent technical problems or cost increases.)

Phase III. Full-rate Production and Initial Deployment.   During the final phase, the service trains operational units, produces and distributes equipment, and provides logistical support. Product improvements are later introduced, as required.

Theoretically, if a weapon system developed by a contractor is not satisfactory in terms of performance or cost, it will not enter production. The department could reject the system and negotiate a contract with another company to develop a replacement system. Then the second company would negotiate contract changes, develop a system, and deliver it for government testing. In practice, however, when a weapon system performs unsatisfactorily, DOD normally arranges an accommodation with the company already under contract. Such accommodations have been made in a substantial number of defense programs, including the F-111 fighter aircraft, the C-5A giant transport aircraft, the MK-48 torpedo, and the TACFIRE battlefield electronic control system.

When a weapon system tests satisfactorily (which may be to standards the same as or lower than those previously planned), the production stage of the acquisition process begins. In theory, steps two through eleven of the development stage are repeated for the production stage because a contractor other than the initial development firm might submit a more attractive (i.e., more feasible or less costly or both) bid and win the production contract. Normally, however, the company that developed the weapon system is awarded the first (and often subsequent) production contracts. Potential cost savings from competition may therefore not be realized because of the impracticality of introducing a second source or because of a sense of urgency; a second bidding procedure requires time and money. In addition, both the development contractor companies and the military services often argue persuasively that the expertise (acquired during the development program) required for the first production contract cannot realistically be transferred from one contractor to another because so many modifications to the design are made during initial production engineering. The policy of awarding production contracts before prototypes are completely tested makes it even more difficult to award the initial production contract to any firm other than the developer. For obvious reasons, the development contractor encourages this overlap between development and production.

There is good reason for the impatience of the military to proceed to production. The beginning of the acquisition process — DOD's planning and congressional budget hearings — can last from twelve to twenty-four months, or longer. Further, more than half the DOD procurement account (for items other than ammunition) is not spent until three or more years after Congress appropriates the funds. From initial planning to expenditure of funds for production, there can be a time lag of eight years.

THE TRANSITION BETWEEN PHASES

In practice, the line between phases of the acquisition process is frequently blurred because of the iterative nature of development and initial production. Indeed, it has been management of the transition from one phase to the next that has posed significant problems for senior defense managers over the years.[51]

A major weapon system can be granted exemptions from some phases of the full process. For example, a system judged not to require a full concept exploration, which can happen with a follow-on to an existing system, may go directly to the demonstration and validation phase or combine concept exploration with demonstration and validation in a single effort before full-scale development. Milestone reviews may also be skipped or delayed if there are no distinct concept exploration and demonstration and validation phases.

As a system moves through the acquisition process, a program management office assumes responsibility for identifying, monitoring, and solving problems that affect schedule, cost, and technical performance. At each milestone, reviewers appraise the sources of risk and the progress achieved toward reducing it.

Program appraisal has many possible approaches. Usually, one or more technical experts identify particular components of a system being developed and then describe or rate the risk associated with each component. Their ratings reflect the level of risk and sometimes the consequences of potential technical problems for the cost, schedule, or performance of the overall system.[52]

Prolongation of the acquisition process is a common occurrence. The amount of time spent on nine weapon system programs ranged from eleven to almost twenty years (see table 1.4).[53]

The lengthy acquisition process (seven to ten years, or longer) for major weapon systems is a central problem, and produces other acquisition problems. The 1986 Packard Commission pointed out three typical hazards.

TABLE 1.4. Time Spent at Each Phase of the Acquisition Process (in years)

System	Defense Acquisition Milestones				
	0	I	II	III	
	Concept Development	Demonstration and Validation	Full-scale Development	Production & Initial Deployment[a] Capability	Total Years
Phalanx	6.5	5.5	1.5	1.7	15+
Sea Launch Cruise Missile	3.7	3.0	4+	1.5	12+
Captor	3.5	7.0	3.5	4.0	18
Patriot	5.0	4.5	8+	2.0	19.5+
Roland	3.5	[b]	4.3	[c]	—
Stinger	7.0	—	4.0	2.0	13
F-16	2.0	3.0	2.7	[c]	—
A-10	4.5	2.0	3+	1.7	11+
EF-111A	7.5	5.0	—	4.7	17+

[a] Represents time consumed from approval of production to delivery of the quantity required for initial operation capability.
[b] The technology was subsequently purchased from NATO countries.
[c] Classified for security reasons.
SOURCE: U.S. General Accounting Office, "Can the United States Major Weapon Systems Acquisition Process Keep Pace with the Conventional Arms Threat Posed by the USSR?" GAO/PSAD/GP, May 27, 1980, pp. 6, 8.

- It leads to unnecessarily high costs of development. Time is money, and experience argues that a ten-year acquisition cycle is clearly more expensive than a five-year cycle.
- It leads to obsolete technology at the time of deployment.
- It aggravates the concern that is one of its causes. Users, knowing that the equipment designed to meet their requirements is fifteen years away, make extremely conservative (i.e., high) threat estimates. Because long-term forecasts are uncertain at best, users tend to err on the side of overstating the threat.[54]

SELECTING A CONTRACTOR

The government source selection process includes preparation and issuance of an RFP and the selection of one or more contractors. The RFP requests whatever information is needed to select contractors capable of accomplishing the development or production program. Included within the RFP, and available to contractors when preparing their proposals, are the technical, managerial, and cost criteria against which the proposals are to be evaluated.[55]

The Secretary of a military service designates a senior official (sometimes the Secretary himself) to be the source selection authority (SSA), and three or more people are assigned to serve as members of a Source Selection Advisory Council (SSAC). After a military service has issued an RFP to prospective contractors and the contractors have responded with their (multivolume) proposals, it convenes a temporary committee called the Source Selection Evaluation Board (SSEB).[56] The time and effort spent in the evaluation vary widely, but a period of six months or more is typical for major acquisition programs.

Most contractor proposals for the development of complex weapon systems are subdivided into the areas of technical, management, and cost information corresponding with the evaluation criteria. In evaluating the technical information, for example, the SSEB normally identifies a number of key technical items that are further divided into factors, with chairmen assigned. Factor chairmen evaluate each proposal according to their specialty. On large proposals there can be more than eighty factors and the total number of source selection personnel may exceed two hundred. Factor scores are tallied to arrive at an item score; item scores are tallied to arrive at an area score. Evaluation of the cost area does not include scoring.

The SSEB then prepares and submits an evaluation report to the SSAC. If the SSAC decides to assign weights (their use is not mandatory) to areas of contractor proposals, the weights must be assigned before receiving contractor proposals. After analyzing the SSEB's findings and applying any weights, the SSAC prepares a report for the SSA. The report may or may not recommend a specific contractor, depending on the SSA's preferences. The SSA then selects the winning contractor or contractors based on (1) comparative evaluations of proposals, (2) costs, (3) risk assessment, (4) past performance, (5) contractual considerations, and (6) surveys of contractor capabilities.[57]

During the source selection process, government personnel at times, often through suggestions to improve the quality of all proposals, disclose the technical and design approaches of a company, as described in its proposal, to other prospective contractors to allow them to consider incorporating the proposal's better or less costly features (or both) into their own proposals. Industry generally considers this practice, known as technical leveling, unethical, particularly because it has no counterpart in the commercial marketplace. The possibility for technical leveling to influence unduly the ultimate selection of a contractor is obvious.

Problems in the Defense Business

Within two years of the beginning of major increases in defense spending in the early 1980s, news reports began to describe the purchase of unreasonably high-priced items by the Defense Department. The most frequently cited examples were $437 hammers, $659 ashtrays, $640 toilet seats, $3,046 coffee makers, $1,000 plastic stool caps, $9,000 wrenches, and $748 duckbill pliers. These allegations caused many Americans to question DOD's management capability as well as the integrity of the defense industry. Although television, radio, and print media repeatedly contained reports of these high-priced items, they rarely — if ever — explained that the high prices frequently had to do with the allocation of overhead costs and the rigor of military requirements as much as or more than they had to do with implied contractor overcharges.

Government regulations require that overhead costs (i.e., costs associated with more than one program) be distributed in equal percentage among a contractor's products. Under this system, prices for small items are often artificially inflated and those for large items artificially reduced. Overhead costs have to be absorbed one way or another, but if the allocation system results in pricing anomalies and is not adequately understood or explained by the media, the public is misled.

Exacerbating the situation, these news reports usually implied that the Defense Department had overlooked the high prices; only the efforts of enterprising reporters, legislators, or whistle blowers had discovered them. In reality, most of the high-cost problems were discovered by DOD in its internal reviews. The unsung heroes in the news stories were DOD's own auditors.

In some cases the news reports contained outright distortions, by omission. The $3,046 coffee maker was designed for the huge C-5A aircraft, which carries as many as 365 people. Major airlines have purchased similar coffee makers for $3,107. The $640 toilet seat cover was, in fact, a large molded plastic cover for the entire toilet system of a P-3 aircraft.[58]

It is dismaying to examine the rationale behind the inaccurate or incomplete reporting by the news media, or even the theatrics of a congressman or senator displaying duckbill pliers on a television news program while expressing outrage at the implied unconscionable prices charged by defense contractors. In most cases, the promoters of these news reports either failed to take the time to examine the facts, or recognized an opportunity to use sensationalism (and entertainment) as a means to attract the attention of large numbers of the public.[59]

Possibly some who promoted the reports were well intentioned but simply ill prepared or poorly informed. Judging from the prevailing tone, however, one can assume that publication of these issues was seen by many as an opportunity to discredit efforts to achieve a defense buildup or to discredit those who voted to increase the defense budget.[60]

News reports of the high-priced items were in part counterproductive for another reason: they served to distract DOD, Congress, and the public from the less sensational but far more serious cost problems of the defense acquisition process. Numerous researchers and presidential commissions during the past twenty-five years have concluded repeatedly that opportunities exist to save tens of billions of dollars per year by improving the acquisition process. The studies repeatedly urged Congress and the Defense Department to correct five basic deficiencies:

1. Setting requirements for the most sophisticated systems attainable, often irrespective of cost;
2. Underestimated schedules and costs of major programs, distorting the decision-making process for the allocation of the national budget;
3. Changes in program and contract requirements caused by changes in military user preferences, leading to annual or more frequent changes in program funding levels, initiated by Congress and DOD itself;
4. Lack of incentives for contractors and government personnel to reduce program costs; and
5. Failure to develop sufficient numbers of military and civilian personnel with training and experience in business management and in dealing with industrial firms to oversee the development and production of enormous, highly technical industrial programs.

CONTROLLING SCHEDULES AND COSTS

Notwithstanding the large budget increases in recent years, major defense programs have repeatedly experienced significant schedule delays and cost increases. Schedules have been extended by about 33 percent in approximately one-half of the programs. Again, more than nine in ten programs exceed initial cost estimates, and the average increase in cost for the majority has been more than 50 percent, *excluding* the effects of quantity changes and inflation.[61]

A review of the history of major weapons procurement reveals that inaccurate cost estimates have been the rule for many years. The Peck and Scherer study, based on twelve major weapon programs of the 1950s, concluded that development costs were generally significantly higher than originally estimated.[62] Production costs also tended to exceed original estimates by significant margins. These systems also experienced schedule delays, which averaged 36 percent beyond the projected time for completion. In the 1960s, cost increases continued to occur on major systems. No systems were found that had been completed at the cost projected, and none was found to have cost less than predicted.[63]

Whereas the 1960s and 1970s saw numerous cases of defense acquisition cost problems, the 1980s saw a remarkable increase. On March 17, 1981, President Reagan sent a memorandum to Secretary of Defense Weinberger that stated, in part:

> We were concerned, as I am sure you were, to learn of the significant cost growth in a number of Defense programs . . . we need to make certain that the increase does not also signal program management weaknesses or technical problems in the Defense programs.[64]

Among the weapon systems with significant cost increases up to 1981 were:

- Navy's Aegis Cruiser program, $8.4 billion increase
- Navy's current submarine, frigate, and destroyer programs, $42 billion increase
- Navy's Trident program and Air Force's F-16 program, $33 billion increase
- Navy's 5-inch Guided Projectile program, more than $300 million increase
- Navy's Tomahawk Cruise Missile program, $450 million increase
- Navy's frigate (FFG-7) program, $5 billion increase
- Army's heavy-tank (M-1) program, $13 billion increase
- Army's UH-60A helicopter program, $4.7 billion increase[65]

In 1983, a DOD Inspector General's report found that of some 15,000 spare engine parts studied, the cost of 65 percent had increased by more than 50 percent between 1980 and 1982, and the cost of 4,000 of the parts (27 percent) had increased by 500 percent or more.[66] During the period 1983 through 1987 hundreds of news articles appeared reporting cost increases, inappropriate charges, and other problems associated with the defense acquisition process. The Appendix contains a sampling of reports of thirty-two of these articles.

EFFECTS OF DEFENSE COST PROBLEMS

The media reports of cost increases and mischarges during the 1980s led to widespread criticism of DOD and the defense industry by both Congress and the public, but in this instance the criticism was different. It now came from strong supporters of the Defense Department as well as from the usual critics in Congress and among the public.

As early as 1981, former Rep. Joseph P. Addabbo (D-NY), who presided over the Defense Appropriations Subcommittee, stated:

> We must give a strong message to the Defense Department that the old way of doing business will not be tolerated. . . . Unless we demonstrate we are getting a handle on cost overruns, we'll lose what appears to be a consensus to rebuild our military forces.[67]

Sen. William S. Cohen (R-ME), a leading Republican on the Senate Armed Services Committee, made the same point:

> We've got to be more responsible in the way that we spend defense dollars, just as we've got to be more responsible in the way we spend dollars on social programs.[68]

In early 1982, Sen. Barry Goldwater (R-AZ), then Chairman of the Senate Armed Services Committee, and Sen. Howard Metzenbaum (D-OH), then a senior Democrat on the same committee, joined forces in expressing their concerns to Defense Secretary Caspar Weinberger about inefficiencies in defense spending:

> waste and inefficiency have over the years become a way of life for too many in the Department [of Defense]. The Nation cannot afford to permit this situation to perpetuate itself any longer.[69]

When these two respected senators took the Senate floor and joined forces to offer sharp criticism of DOD, many in the department and in the defense industry became concerned. In eight sharply worded speeches, the two accused DOD of endangering the nation's defense and squandering its assets with interservice bickering. "If the United States has to go to war anytime soon," charged Senator Goldwater, "these problems will cause Americans to die unnecessarily. Even more, they may cause us to lose the fight."[70]

In 1985, Senator Goldwater, along with Sen. Sam Nunn (D-GA), one of the most knowledgeable and respected defense experts in the Senate, issued a lengthy report critical of the Defense Department. The report highlighted the problems of cost increases and cost mischarges and concluded that DOD was in a mess, that U.S. combat readiness was in a lamentable state, and that the correlation between spending a lot of money and acquiring better defense did not exist. The report also blamed the Congress for meddling with the defense budget and thereby contributing heavily to waste and inefficiency.[71]

In mid-1985, Sen. Charles Grassley (R-IA) expressed similar criticism of the acquisition process.

> I and others here in Congress have charged that the defense industry is fat, wasteful, poorly managed, and consequently contributes to an erosion of our national defense. Now I plead guilty to having called the defense industry the new generation of welfare queens, and I intend to verify this, right or wrong, through strictly empirical data and analysis.[72]

Again in 1985, House Armed Services Committee Chairman Les Aspin (D-WI) launched a series of hearings addressing the question: What have we received for a trillion dollars? He was referring to the trillion-dollar defense spending total for the first half of the 1980s. Mr. Aspin's answer: Not enough. In a twenty-five-page report, the Wisconsin Democrat cited "skimpy improvements in the U.S. defense posture despite the huge increases in defense spending over the years."

The Pentagon dismissed Mr. Aspin's charges as "uninformed and inaccurate," and Defense Secretary Weinberger continued to assert that there was nothing basically wrong with the military establishment. "If a thing ain't broke," he repeatedly argued, "don't fix it."[73]

Not surprisingly, the dissatisfaction in Congress with defense spending and management mirrored the increasingly vocal dissatisfaction among the general public. In March 1985, a *Business Week*/Harris survey revealed that 70 percent of Americans were convinced that defense contractors routinely overcharge the Pentagon. The respondents

also thought, by a three-to-one margin, that the congressional committees in charge of military programs "are so influenced by defense contractors that they won't crack down on wasteful spending." And 56
percent thought that Defense Secretary Weinberger was doing at best a
"fair" and at worst a "poor" job of managing the Pentagon's budget.
Only 4 percent gave him an "excellent" rating.[74]

In analyzing the poll, *Business Week* concluded that the public was
unhappy enough to want dramatic action. By a margin of 57 percent to
36 percent, those surveyed would bar any company found to have over-
charged the Pentagon from receiving any new defense contracts. Approximately 60 percent would cancel "some or all" of the offending
company's existing contracts. Americans would also like to see anyone
found guilty of fraud go to jail, "no matter how important they are."
Most of the respondents thought that the costs of defense programs
were inflated because of design changes to defense systems while they're
being built.

In 1986, another national survey, conducted under the auspices of
the President's Blue Ribbon Commission (the Packard Commission) on
Defense Management, found that the general public held "professional
military personnel" in very high esteem. The public placed the military,
on a scale of zero to one hundred, in the range of eighty, along with
doctors, ministers, and other professional people with high status and
recognition. On the other hand, "the defense industry was down at 25
percent, and in some of the detailed questions the public indicated that
they thought half of the defense budget was being wasted by the defense
industry."[75]

The Packard Commission survey revealed also that many Americans
thought defense contractors customarily placed profits above legal and
ethical responsibilities. The commission drew the following conclusions
from the survey:

- Americans consider waste and fraud in defense spending a very serious
  national problem and one of major proportions. On average, the
  public believes almost half the defense budget is lost to waste and
  fraud.
- Americans believe that fraud (illegal activity) accounts for as much loss
  in defense dollars as waste (poor management).
- Although anyone involved in defense procurement is thought likely to
  commit fraudulent and dishonest acts, Americans widely perceive defense contractors as especially culpable for fraud in defense spending.
- In overwhelming numbers, Americans support imposition of the

severest penalties for illegal actions by contractors — including more criminal indictments — as a promising means to reduce waste and fraud.

Nine out of ten Americans believe that the goal of reduced fraud and waste also could be served through development and enforcement of strict codes of conduct. They are almost evenly divided, however, on whether defense contractors can be expected to live up to codes they develop for themselves.[76]

The commission's survey made clear that Americans think inefficiency in DOD spending to be a problem of major proportions. They consider "waste and fraud in federal spending for national defense" second in seriousness only to the budget deficit when asked to rate a selected list of national problems. The list included unemployment, inflation, the nuclear arms race, fairness of the federal income tax system, effectiveness of the U.S. military as a fighting force, and waste and fraud in federal spending for domestic programs. Close to two-thirds of those polled thought there was more waste and fraud in defense spending than was the case ten to twenty years ago, more than at present in nondefense federal spending, and more than at present in private business spending.[77]

In response to the reported cost problems, congressional members adopted a fragmented approach to reform, introducing a large number of bills designed to impose new requirements on DOD and the defense industry. In 1984, members of Congress introduced more than 150 bills related to improving the defense acquisition process. In 1985, they introduced another 140 bills, many of which were accompanied by numerous press conferences, public expressions of outrage, and assertions that the new legislation would plug a few more holes in the dike.[78] In 1986, once again, members of Congress introduced more than 100 bills concerning defense acquisition.

The Defense Department also responded to the concerns about defense spending. From 1984 to 1987, the DOD issued new directives and instructions regarding defense procurement. This effort, however, was not as effective in bringing about change as one might expect. The profusion of new laws, directives, and instructions, combined with the limited training and experience of the personnel assigned to manage the acquisition process, means in fact that practices in the field are usually different from the laws and regulations on the books. In reality, it may take one to three years to implement the latest laws and regulations, and even longer to foster the perspective and skills needed to implement new regulations effectively. Even the task of discarding the old laws and regulations from reports and legal binders and replacing them with new material is a major one.[79] Regardless of the changes in rules and regulations, it is the lack of skills and commitment to dealing with industrial cost-control problems that remains a matter of critical concern.

Controlling Acquisition Costs

In a comprehensive report titled "Impediments to Reducing the Costs of Weapon Systems," the General Accounting Office (GAO) outlined several aspects of the acquisition process that contribute to the cost of large defense programs. Most of the following discussion is based on those portions of the report confirmed by our own interviews and research.

FUNDING INSTABILITY

In the commercial world, company managers normally control funding levels, ensuring predictable levels over a number of years. In the government, annual congressional review of the DOD budget and changing priorities, whether political or military, often mean a change in funding levels on a major program one or more times a year. Pentagon and congressional cutbacks or delays in approving funds frequently disrupt the development or production process, thereby increasing the ultimate cost of a weapon system. In particular, funding uncertainty makes long-term production planning extremely difficult and decreases the probability that contractors will benefit from any attempt to reduce production costs or to increase productivity or both. Because increasing and decreasing labor resources is easier than acquiring and disposing of capital investments to cope with fluctuating business volume, defense contractors may elect not to invest in labor-saving equipment. As a result, production costs remain high.[80]

THE BASIS FOR PROFITS

The bulk of major defense systems acquisition money is expended through contracts. Once the contracting parties agree on the estimated costs, profit is negotiated largely as a percentage of these costs.[81]

Unfortunately, this method of contracting also provides little incentive for contractors to reduce costs; in fact, it often encourages higher costs. For the past twenty-five years, studies by DOD, the Logistics Management Institute (LMI), the General Accounting Office, and many others have concluded that changes in the method by which profits are earned are necessary to motivate contractors to reduce costs. In the late 1970s and 1980s, OSD has directed DOD negotiators to place more weight on invested capital and less on cost in the negotiation of profit. In fact, however, there has been only a minimal shift away from cost-based profit determination. It is not yet clear whether this is because of limited potential benefits to the contractors or the lack of implementation skills by government personnel. Although the Defense Department has devised various theoretical incentives for cost reduction, the costs actually incurred on the prior contract usually serve as the baseline for negotiating costs of follow-on contracts. Thus, a cost-based profit structure discourages the acquisition of plant and equipment or any other actions by management that could lower the overall acquisition costs to the government.[82]

SOCIOECONOMIC PROGRAMS, GOVERNMENT CONTROLS, AND RED TAPE

One of the most common complaints from defense contractors has been that doing business with the government is difficult, time consuming, and costly, particularly when compared with commercial practices. Indeed, there is no doubt that government procurement practices are complex, time consuming, and costly. Two factors are the perceived need by government to protect its interests and to provide safeguards for the proper expenditure of public funds.[83]

In addition, the government may seek to use the procurement process to help accomplish its socioeconomic objectives. Eligibility for government contracts thus depends on compliance with regulations designed to promote a variety of social objectives:

Maintaining employee health and safety
Protecting the environment
Supporting small business
Supporting minority businesses and employment programs
Maintaining wage-level supports
Aiding the economy and protecting domestic business

Encouraging NATO standardization
Rehabilitating prisoners
Providing employment for the handicapped[84]

LIMITED RATES OF PRODUCTION

In the commercial sector of the U.S. economy, production volume is determined by company management based on production efficiency and market analyses. In the case of defense systems, however, production rates are dictated, often indirectly, by constraints set by the Congress, OMB, OSD, and the military services. Major weapon systems, subject to annual review, are often revised numerous times. Again, either Congress, OSD, or the military services can (and often do) dictate that production of items be extended at a low rate to ensure that an active industrial base, that is, an in-place production capability, is maintained.[85]

Uneconomical production rates of new DOD hardware can also result from concurrent development and production, dictating that a limited production rate be maintained until the hardware has been tested and proved effective. Both new and standard hardware may also be produced at a limited rate because sufficient funds are not available in the DOD budget to produce a greater number in a given year. Whatever the reason for limiting production to less than the optimal rate, the result is a loss of productivity and an increase in the cost of major weapon systems. For example, a study of the F-14A aircraft procurement concluded that a reduction of sixty-six in the number to be procured and an increase in the time during which they would be produced has raised the estimated program cost by $2.3 billion — about 38 percent.[86]

LIMITATIONS OF GOVERNMENT PROGRAM MANAGERS

The acquisition of large defense development and production programs poses one of the most challenging management problems in the world. Controlling and reducing costs is difficult in any industry, but even more so in larger and more complex industrial development and production programs. Costs rise in all organizations unless managers and their staffs are determined to control or reduce them. Yet the Army, the Navy, and, to a lesser extent, the Air Force provide only limited industrial management training for military officers whom they assign to key managerial positions in major acquisition programs. Army and Navy officers assigned to acquisition programs often have extensive combat arms experience (e.g., as pilots, ship captains, armor commanders), but little or no advanced training and experience in the planning and control of industrial development and production programs.

A procurement system with few cost-reduction incentives, directed by government managers with limited industrial management experience, understandably will have significant cost problems. Given the variety of factors described in the preceding paragraphs, we would be surprised if defense programs did not have significant cost increases.

Efforts to Improve the Acquisition Process

Since the early 1960s, many studies analyzing the defense weapons acquisition process have noted its strengths, its deficiencies, and its needed reforms. From 1960 to 1987 there were twelve major studies, not including many excellent studies by the General Accounting Office (see table 1.5).[87]

TABLE 1.5.   Studies of the Defense Acquisition Process, 1960–1987

Report by	Initiated by	Issued
Peck and Scherer (Harvard Business School)	Authors	1962, 1964
Blue Ribbon Defense Panel (Fitzhugh Commission)	President	1970
Commission on Government Procurement	Congress	1972
J. R. Fox (Harvard Business School)	Author	1974
Military services and Secretary of Defense	DOD	1974–1975
Defense Resource Board	DOD	1979
Department of Defense Resource Management Study	President	1979
Jacques Gansler	Author	1980
Special Panel on Defense Procurement Procedures	House Armed Services Committee	1982
Grace Commission	President	1983
Georgetown Center for Strategic and International Studies	Center	1985
Blue Ribbon Commission on Defense Management (Packard Commission)	President	1986

SOURCE: U.S. General Accounting Office, "DOD Acquisition: Strengthening Capabilities of Key Personnel in Systems Acquisition," GAO/NSIAD–86–45, p. 128.

Despite the large number of studies and the similarity of their findings, problems of cost growth remain significant. Virtually all attempts to implement improvements have fallen short of their objectives. It is increasingly evident that barriers to improving the acquisition process derive, not from a lack of ideas, but from the difficulties encountered by senior government managers (in Congress as well as in the Defense Department) in identifying and changing counterproductive government and industry incentives. There seems to be little hope of solving the chronic problems if the usual attempts at reform are tried once again. A more comprehensive approach is required — an approach based on a better understanding of how and why the defense business works the way it does and how government and industry incentives reinforce the seemingly intractable problems.[88]

To explain the acquisition problems and opportunities of the late 1980s, I will discuss the previous attempts at reform.

During the Kennedy and Johnson administrations (1960–1968), in response to numerous cost overruns of the 1950s and early 1960s, OSD discouraged cost-plus-fixed-fee contracts in favor of fixed-price and incentive contracts. In the early 1960s, Secretary McNamara and his management team developed and implemented a number of sensible improvements. One was the planning, programming, and budgeting system (PPBS), which provided the Secretary and the President with an organized approach to major program decisions and to the allocation of resources within DOD, though it was not designed to have a major impact on the acquisition process. Another was the creation of the Office of Systems Analysis, to perform cost-effectiveness studies; the services were encouraged to do the same. Despite these significant improvements in DOD management, the government continued to reward cost increases and to penalize cost reductions.[89]

The McNamara team also developed and implemented, to greater or lesser degrees, a wide variety of acquisition organizations and techniques, including the Defense Supply Agency, Defense Contract Administration Service, Defense Contract Audit Agency, increased competition, incentive contracting, network planning and scheduling, total package procurement (TPP), and the development concept paper (DCP).[90]

TPP required simultaneous bidding, on a fixed-price basis, for both the first (development) and second (production) stages as a means of preventing a winning contractor (for the first stage) from facing little or no competition for the second stage. It was applied on such systems as the Lockheed C-5A cargo plane, the General Dynamics F-111 fighter aircraft, and the Grumman F-14A Tomcat fighter aircraft. All of these had large cost overruns, and TPP was judged to be ineffective for two reasons: (1) DOD introduced or allowed numerous changes in the programs, thereby obscuring any incentives for cost control and accountability for cost growth; and (2) DOD was either unwilling or unable to enforce the fixed-price contracts. Military services, reluctant to incur delays by shifting to a new contractor, did not want to enforce provisions of the TPP technique for fixed-price contracts. In 1966, Secretary McNamara abandoned the TPP concept.

This failure in procurement reform prompted Congress in 1969 to appoint the Commission on Government Procurement (soon followed by the Nixon administration's Blue Ribbon Panel on Defense Procurement, in 1970) to identify the causes of weapons cost overruns and to propose new methods of cost control.[91]

In the mid to late 1960s, Secretary McNamara's office issued several additional acquisition policies and directives. These included:

- Planning procedures for integrated logistics support for systems and equipment (the integration of supply and maintenance considerations and planning into the systems engineering and design process);
- Procedures for proposal evaluation and source selection;
- Procedures for improved quality assurance (the enforcement of technical criteria governing the quality of material, data, supplies, and services);
- Information systems for planning and control of schedules and costs;
- Value engineering (a program to eliminate or modify unessential equipment features and thus to minimize costs);
- Technical data management (procedures for doing business when contractor-prepared data are required by managers in various functional areas, e.g., engineering, procurement, and quality control);
- Configuration management (technical and administrative procedures to (1) identify and document functional and physical characteristics of a configuration item, (2) control changes to those characteristics, and (3) record and report change processing and implementation status);
- Work breakdown structure framework (WBS) (product-oriented family trees used to subdivide large programs into their parts; they comprise hardware, software, services, and work tasks that result from engineering efforts during development and production of defense systems or equipment); and

- Defense standardization (a program to control product proliferation).[92]

Unfortunately, the level of managerial training and development for DOD acquisition managers, from the program office to higher levels of the Pentagon, fell far short of the level of sophistication required to implement the new policies and directives effectively and identify and reverse policies that rewarded cost increases and penalized cost reductions.

During the Nixon and Ford administrations (1968–1976), Defense Secretary Melvin Laird and Deputy Defense Secretary David Packard returned some autonomy to the individual services but maintained OSD involvement in program decisions.[93] The Packard monitoring process required that there be a "contract" between OSD and the procuring military department. The contract was the development concept paper (DCP), which established the criteria for program review.[94] The DCP became known as a decision coordinating paper in 1971.

Deputy Secretary Packard established the Defense Systems Acquisition Review Council (DSARC) to advise him of the status of each major defense system and to allow for careful evaluation before proceeding from one program phase to the next. DSARC membership included most of the senior DOD managers, the composition of the individual councils depending on the specific program and its phase of development or production. In 1972, Mr. Packard formed a second group, the Cost Analysis Improvement Group (CAIG), to provide OSD staff with independent program cost estimates to present to the DSARC and to determine uniform DOD cost-estimating standards.[95] Equally important, Mr. Packard sought ways to limit the expensive practice of putting a weapon system into production before completing its development. This reform, called fly-before-buy, entailed the development of prototypes and competitive fly-offs before choosing a contractor and entering production.[96] As sensible and constructive as Deputy Secretary Packard's initiatives were, there were significant cost increases in weapon development and production programs during the 1970s.

In May 1970, Mr. Packard issued a memorandum citing additional ways by which the acquisition of major defense systems could be improved.[97] The memorandum served as the basis for DOD Directive 5000.1, "Acquisition of Major Defense Systems" (the first of a number of directives and associated instructions in the 5000 series). The memorandum and directive set forth Mr. Packard's view that "successful development, production, and deployment of major defense systems are primarily dependent upon competent people, rational priorities, and clearly defined responsibilities." Program managers were to be given adequate authority to make major decisions, recognition and rewards for good work, and more opportunity for career advancement. As constructive as this directive was, it produced few encouraging changes within the military services. Reassignments for additional tours of duty to program management positions were rare, except in the case of nonrated (nonflying status) officers in the Air Force. Promotion to the several hundred flag officer (i.e., general or admiral) positions in the Army, Navy, and Air Force continued to be based largely on experience and performance in combat arms assignments. There was little or no accountability for cost growth on acquisition programs.

Other attempts to reform the acquisition process have been short-lived or implemented superficially. During 1969 and 1970, for example, the President's blue ribbon defense panel studied the Pentagon and stressed the need for, among other reforms, an independent weapons testing office. But despite the prodding of then Secretary Laird and Deputy Secretary Packard, a bureaucratic war of attrition gradually devoured the initiative. Thirteen years later, disturbed by the number of weapons incapable of meeting their technical performance goals, Congress overruled vehement Pentagon objections and legislated into being an independent weapons testing office. It took another two years for Secretary Weinberger to appoint somebody to head it.[98]

The same panel reexamined other problems that had accompanied hardware development for several years, including major cost increases, schedule delays, and failures in technical performance. The panel concluded that the causes were largely failures of management, that officers serving as program managers generally lacked any special training or expertise in their duties, were rotated at short intervals (often at critical points in their programs), usually had no assignment overlap with their predecessors, and saw little potential for career advancement in program management.[99]

In December 1972, a congressionally appointed Commission on Government Procurement presented its report. Among its principal findings and recommendations were these:

- Congress was ill equipped to evaluate performance, costs, and schedules for new defense systems programs in the context of national security objectives and priorities.

- Congress should establish an Office of Federal Procurement Policy, to be headed by a Presidential appointee, to oversee procurement policies and systems throughout the government.
- Congress should consolidate all statutory procurement regulations into a single statute.
- DOD should upgrade the acquisition force by establishing an institution to provide necessary education and services.
- DOD should reduce the management and administrative layers between policy makers and program offices.
- Congress should have greater visibility in the acquisition process to exercise its responsibilities, i.e., provide the information needed to make key program decisions and commitments.

Pentagon officials adopted the position that DOD was already moving in the direction recommended in the commission's report.[100]

Given the earlier failure of total package procurement (TPP) to control costs, Mr. Packard returned to cost reimbursement and incentive contracting. He reduced sole reliance on documented studies for concept definition and contractor selection, replacing paper studies with hardware testing and prototyping.

Mr. Packard left the Defense Department in 1971. Near the time of his departure, he expressed disappointment at the department's resistance to improvements in the acquisition process. He had wanted to apply the lessons of his success with Hewlett-Packard Company, which he frequently described as finding good men for the job of program manager, assigning them, and then leaving them alone — to the defense acquisition process. Mr. Packard and his predecessors during the McNamara tenure assumed that the military and civilian career development systems would provide sufficient people with the required skills in industrial management. Unfortunately, that did not happen.

In 1976, the Office of Federal Procurement Policy (part of OMB) published Circular A-109, which required mission area analysis (MAA) in the early stages of the acquisition process and more competition throughout the process. Nevertheless, its implementation by successive defense secretaries often encountered resistance from contractors and the military services.[101]

Under A-109 requirements, the acquisition cycle began with a military service determination of a need for a particular system to perform a mission. The service then prepared a mission-need statement (MNS), which expressed the need in terms of operational requirements rather than performance specifications or system characteristics. To acquire control over this portion of the acquisition cycle, OSD added a new Milestone Zero. When a service identified a mission need, it submitted a MNS for approval by the Secretary of Defense before the exploration of systems could begin.[102]

During the Carter administration (1976–1980), Defense Secretary Harold Brown (formerly Director of Defense Research and Engineering) sought to regain some of the authority in weapons acquisition Mr. Packard had relinquished to the services. Secretary Brown also issued a formal requirement to comply with OMB Circular A-109 for MAA and MNS.[103]

In 1979, the Defense Resource Board completed a study of the acquisition process. It focused on the use of MNS, schedule compression, multiple technologies in one weapon system, improved incentives for program managers, and greater consideration of life-cycle costs. The recommendations in the report were never acted upon, and a new administration was elected in November 1980.

In 1981, President Reagan's Defense Secretary, Caspar Weinberger, expressed interest in reforming the acquisition process. Whereas his predecessor Secretary Brown had sought to tighten control over key aspects of the process, Secretary Weinberger implemented what he called controlled decentralization, whereby subordinate line executives, especially service program managers, were to be held accountable for executing policy decisions made by the Secretary after consultation with his top civilian and military advisers. Secretary Weinberger acted on the conviction that cost-overrun problems and hardware that failed to perform as planned were made worse by previous attempts at detailed, centralized control, especially by the senior civilian research and engineering advisers in the Defense Department.

The second Weinberger modification to the Packard policies was a streamlining of DSARC's formal milestones, from four to two. The review processes of individual services, however, retained four decision milestones (called SSARCs — Service Systems Acquisition Review Councils), and OSD continued to hold informal reviews at each of the previous four milestone decision points.[104]

Early in the Reagan administration (1981), Secretary Weinberger and Deputy Secretary Frank Carlucci instituted a set of thirty-two reforms (the Carlucci initiatives) to the acquisition process. The more significant initiatives called for more multiyear procurement contracts, greater competition in contracting, stabilized programs, more realistic budgeting, and more fixed-price contracts.[105]

The Carlucci initiatives were intended to reduce weapons cost and development time, and improve weapons support and readiness. Although they did not address all the major causes of growth in weapons cost, many dealt with longstanding problems, the correction of which would do much to lower costs. Once again, however, the underlying principles were not new. For the preceding ten years, similar measures had been urged — and many tried — but few significant improvements had been made.[106]

DOD experienced a number of problems implementing the Carlucci initiatives. In July 1986, five years after their introduction, more than half of a GAO sample of fifty-four program managers (who had been in their jobs more than two years) thought that the initiatives had made little or no difference in the acquisition process. The GAO survey suggested that the senior-level commitment to change had not filtered down to the program management level.[107]

The GAO study concluded that DOD had once again "not carried through with its action plans on most of the Carlucci initiatives" and was "not monitoring actions to ensure that results were being achieved." It did add, however, that "although DOD has made some progress in implementing the program, implementation has not been completed, and, consequently, results have not been fully achieved."[108]

The core idea of the Carlucci initiatives is that overregulation thwarts efficiency and increases costs. The principle is sound to a certain point, after which problems arise, according to critics. Some decentralization may increase efficiency — provided that David Packard's "good men" are properly trained and can be held responsible for their program's performance — but initiatives such as reduced oversight of fixed-price contracts make industry less accountable to senior DOD management, as well as to Congress and the public.[109]

My analysis agrees with that of defense analyst Gordon Adams, who points out that the defense initiatives of the early 1980s, which collectively sought increased "up-front" spending and more "realistic" budgeting, were reforms that attempted to streamline an inefficient procurement system without attacking the real sources of cost overruns. For example, if the cost data from industry are not strictly and independently verified by DOD program managers or auditors, many of the Carlucci initiatives could have precisely the opposite result from the one intended. Specifically, "more realistic" (i.e., higher) estimates of costs and inflation, longer-term contracts, greater reliability, and more test items could result in large budget increases. These reforms, by themselves, could provide contractors with less incentive to control and to minimize costs while providing DOD with a rationale to accept rising costs as "more realistic." In short, the Carlucci initiatives could have made a great deal of sense, but only if the Defense Department had created incentives for cost reduction and had sufficient numbers of personnel skilled in managing large industrial programs.[110]

Retrospective

Most of the proposed solutions to defense management problems in the past have been undermined in one of two ways. The first is the lack of continuity. When a Pentagon official adopts a new control system, there is a flurry of activity, and for a year or two progress is made. Then the sponsoring military or civilian official leaves the Pentagon, a new official takes over and shifts the focus to other activities, and the old problems begin to surface again.[111]

The second is the tendency to apply quick-fix solutions to reduce budgets for a particular program. An attempt is made to find an easy solution — for example, a funding stretchout or a new contract form such as total package procurement on the C-5A cargo plane, the Tacfire Program, or the AH-64 Helicopter — in the misguided hope that quick-fixes, by themselves, will substitute for better trained, experienced, and more capable program management personnel.

Many of the so-called centralized *or* decentralized approaches to improvements in the acquisition process could succeed if experienced managers — military and civilian — at each level, from the program office to OSD, understood the process, were committed to achieving its objectives, were deeply involved in the process for most of their careers, and were rewarded for achieving improved performance. As it is, many defense managers often have little understanding of the desired improvements or lack a commitment to implementing them, resulting in implementation that is superficial or frustrates the goals of the improvement program (e.g., imposing expensive reporting requirements on contractors in the hope that vast amounts of detailed data will alone achieve cost control).

Few people have been as dedicated to improving the acquisition process as David Packard. Although he did not forget what had proved successful for him at Hewlett-Packard, there were crucial differences between that company and the government. At Hewlett-Packard, large numbers of career professionals are skilled in managing development and production programs and highly motivated to reduce costs to produce profits. In the Defense Department, acquisition managers normally incur penalties, not rewards, for failing to expend the entire budget. At Hewlett-Packard, it is easy to identify the good people — their divisions make the most money. In government, a successful agency is expected to increase, not decrease, its budget year after year. Therefore, the "good people" are those who spend all the money allotted in one year and can justify an increase for the next year, while incurring the least amount of opposition.[112]

In 1986, the latest presidential panel on defense, the Packard Commission, characterized the defense acquisition process as expensive, inefficient, and cumbersome. It observed that "the increasing complexity of the process means unnecessary delays are incurred in acquiring needed goods and supplies and that higher costs are paid for what is acquired." In brief, the Packard Commission concluded that "the defense acquisition process is not being operated and managed effectively, and that this is having a disastrous effect on the cost and efficiency of the system."[113]

As a result of the paper work required by the various defense acquisition initiatives of the past, the program management task of researching, interpreting, and applying the various rules and regulations to the numerous contracts issued each year requires large government and contractor staffs. The problem, as the Packard Commission observed, is that much of the work performed by those who review the proposals, plans, contracts, reports, and legal documents is now unproductive and costly.[114] To address this and the other major problems, the Packard Commission made four major recommendations:

- Create a new Under Secretary of Defense for Acquisition, a person who would take charge of procurement, research, development, and testing of all weapon systems.
- Create acquisition executives (AEs) in each service, people who will report directly to the new DOD Under Secretary, as well as to their service Secretary (or who may be the service Secretary) reporting to the Secretary of Defense.
- Create program executive officers (PEOs) reporting directly to AEs. Each PEO will oversee a group of program managers.
- Give the chairman of the Joint Chiefs of Staff more authority and create a vice-chairman, who, along with the new Under Secretary, will be part of a Joint Requirements Management Board, which will estab-

lish requirements for new weapons and approve or reject them at each step along the path to production.

The problem with any recommendation that rests on DOD reorganization is that the underlying counterproductive incentives usually remain unchanged. The Defense Department has grown accustomed to reorganizations; they occur at least once every four years. As a DOD acquisition manual states,

> The central cry heard in the halls of the Pentagon when things go wrong is reorganize, restructure the management system. Some think that if enough organizational boxes or enough people are moved, the problem will go away. Of course, it doesn't, yet those responsible for creating the organizational mess think so. Consequently, we are left with a legacy that only grows worse with time. Why is this the case? Most probably because it is the path of least resistance.[115]

After twenty-seven years of initiatives to improve the acquisition process, it is increasingly evident that any changes must include careful and consistent implementation if they are to succeed. If a commission does not speak explicitly and directly about the problems in implementing its recommendations, it may be well intentioned and perceptive, but it is unlikely to be effective.

In considering improvements to the acquisition process, one may do well to remember that there is no sovereign power in Washington; instead, there are many independent powers. It is easier to block the policy initiatives of others than to translate one's own initiatives into action.[116]

Acquisition reforms up to 1987 have tended to attack the symptoms of cost increases, not their causes, and at best have been only partially implemented. They have left the basic negative incentives for government and industry personnel largely undisturbed.

Notes

1. Office of Management and Budget, Executive Office of the President, *Management of the United States Government, Fiscal Year 1988* (Washington, D.C.: Government Printing Office, 1987), p. 83.
2. Ibid. See also Richard A. Stubbing, *The Defense Game* (New York: Harper & Row, 1986), pp. xiii, 89, 90; and "U.S. Defense Acquisition: A Process in

Trouble," Center for Strategic and International Studies, Georgetown University, March 1987.

3. Office of the Assistant Secretary of Defense (Comptroller), "National Defense Budget Estimates," 1987.

4. "American Defense Preparedness Association Annual Meeting, April 24, 1986," *National Defense,* July-August 1986.

5. National Science Foundation, "International Science and Technology Update 1986," Directorate for Scientific, Technological, and International Affairs, Division of Science Resources Studies, Washington, D.C., p. 85.

6. Office of Management and Budget, *Special Analyses of the Budget of the U.S. Government, Fiscal Year 1972* (Washington, D.C.: Government Printing Office, 1971), p. 273.

7. National Science Foundation, "International Science and Technology Update 1986," Directorate for Scientific, Technological, and International Affairs, Division of Science Resources Studies, Washington, D.C.; and Office of Management and Budget, *Special Analyses of the Budget of the U.S. Government, Fiscal Year 1988* (Washington, D.C.: Government Printing Office, 1987). See also Colleen A. Preston, "Improving the Acquisition Process — The Role of Congress," paper prepared for the Defense Acquisition Study, Center for Strategic and International Studies, Georgetown University, 1986, pp. 1–2; and "How to Reform the Pentagon's Wasteful Ways," *Business Week,* May 27, 1985.

8. Office of the Assistant Secretary of Defense (Comptroller), "National Defense Budget Estimates," May 1987.

9. David Packard, "Management of America's National Defense," *AEI Memorandum,* Winter 1987.

10. Major systems are those requiring more than $200 million in research and development or $1 billion in production. Department of Defense Directive (DODD) 5000.1, "Acquisition of Major Defense Systems," March 12, 1986, p. 6; U.S. General Accounting Office, "DOD Acquisition: Strengthening Capabilities of Key Personnel in Systems Acquisition," GAO/NSIAD–86–45, May 1986, p. 2; Department of Commerce, *Statistical Abstracts of the United States* (Washington, D.C.: Government Printing Office, 1986); and *International Financial Statistics Yearbook, 1986* (Washington, D.C.: International Monetary Fund, 1986).

11. Office of Management and Budget, Executive Office of the President, *Management of the United States Government, Fiscal Year 1988* (Washington, D.C.: Government Printing Office, 1987). See also Franklin C. Spinney, *Defense Facts of Life: The Plans/Reality Mismatch* (Boulder, CO: Westfield Press, 1985), p. 121.

12. J. Ronald Fox, "Revamping the Business of National Defense," *Harvard Business Review,* September-October 1984, pp. 63–64.

13. Leonard Sullivan, Jr., "Characterizing the Acquisition Process," paper prepared for the Defense Acquisition Study, Center for Strategic and International Studies, Georgetown University, January 1986, p. E-6.

14. Artemis March, "Note on the Aerospace Industry and Industrial Moderniza-

tion," Harvard Business School 0–687–009, under the supervision of Associate Professor David A. Garvin.

15. Rick Atkinson and Fred Hiatt, "Military in a Fix," *Washington Post,* August 18, 1985.

16. "Dangers in the Big Buildup," *Time,* March 22, 1982, p. 50.

17. Richard J. Bednar and John T. Jones, Jr., "The Role of the DOD Contracting Officer," Draft Report of the American Bar Association (ABA) Section of Public Contract Law, Ad Hoc Committee, John E. Cavanagh, Chairman, January 11, 1987, p. 23.

18. R. Jameson, *Armed Forces Journal,* January 6, 1969.

19. David D. Acker, "The Maturing of the DOD Acquisition Process," *Defense Systems Management Review,* Summer 1980, p. 14.

20. Charles J. Hitch, "Evolution of the Department of Defense," in Richard Head and Eavin J. Rokke (eds.), *American Defense Policy,* 3d ed. (Baltimore: Johns Hopkins University Press, 1973), p. 347.

21. David D. Acker, "The Maturing of the DOD Acquisition Proccss," *Defense Systems Management Review,* Summer 1980, p. 14.

22. Hitch, "Evaluation of the Department of Defense," p. 347.

23. *First Report of the Secretary of Defense, 1948* (Washington, D.C.: Government Printing Office, 1948), p. 3.

24. Staff Report to the Senate Committee on Armed Services, "Defense Organization: The Need for Change," October 16, 1985, p. 530.

25. Alain Enthoven and K. Wayne Smith, *How Much Is Enough?* (New York: Harper & Row, 1971), p. 32.

26. Acker, "The Maturing of the DOD Acquisition Process," pp. 14–17.

27. DODD 5000.1, p. 1 (see note 10).

28. U.S. General Accounting Office, "DOD Acquisition: Strengthening Capabilities of Key Personnel in Systems Acquisition," GAO/NSIAD–86–45, May 1986, p. 10.

29. DODD 5000.1, p. 1.

30. U.S. General Accounting Office, GAO/NSIAD–86–45, p. 10.

31. Charles L. Schultze, "Economic Effects of the Defense Budget," *The Brookings Bulletin,* Fall 1981. Schultze is a Senior Fellow in the Brookings Economic Studies program and a former chairman of the Council of Economic Advisors.

32. Ibid.

33. Robert J. Art, "Bureaucratic Politics and American Foreign Policy: A Critique," *Policy Sciences,* December 1973, cited by Paul M. Bradburn, "Strategic Postures in the Military Aircraft Industry: A Comparison of Two Companies," paper prepared at Massachusetts Institute of Technology, June 1986, p. 16.

34. Bradburn, "Strategic Postures," p. 8.

35. *Code of Federal Regulations,* Title 48, Federal Acquisition Regulations System (Washington, D.C.: General Services Administration, 1984), and U.S. Department of Defense, *Defense Acquisition Regulation* (Washington, D.C.: Government Printing Office, 1986).

36. Acker, "The Maturing of the DOD Acquisition Process," pp. 26–28.

37. Defense Systems Management College, "Acquisition Strategy Guide," July 1984, pp. 2–3.

38. Ibid.

39. Ibid.

40. U.S. General Accounting Office, "Can the United States Major Weapon Systems Acquisition Process Keep Pace with the Conventional Arms Threat Posed by the USSR?" GAO/PSAD/GP, May 27, 1980, pp. 23–24.

41. Ibid.

42. Ibid.

43. Bradburn, "Strategic Postures," pp. 54–69.

44. For example, see U.S. General Accounting Office, "Need for More Accurate Weapon System Test Results to Be Reported to the Congress," GAO/PSAD–79–46.

45. U.S. General Accounting Office, GAO/PSAD/GP, May 27, 1980, pp. 23–24.

46. Comptroller General of the United States, "Impediments to Reducing the Costs of Weapon Systems," Report to the Congress, November 8, 1979, pp. 5–24. The 1986 Defense Authorization Act required that multiyear contracts could not be entered into unless the results of negotiation confirmed that a savings of at least 10 percent would result. If a nonrecurring cancellation ceiling of more than $20 million was to be incurred, prior congressional approval would be required before the contract could be signed.

47. Sullivan, "Characterizing the Acquisition Process," p. E-6.

48. Background Information, Senior Steering Group, Defense Acquisition Study, November 7–8, 1985, pp. 8.9 to 8.10.

49. DODD 5000.1. See also U.S. General Accounting Office, GAO/PSAD/GP, September 1, 1987, pp. 1–3.

50. Acker, "The Maturing of the DOD Acquisition Process," pp. 35–37.

51. G. K. Smith and E. T. Friedmann, "An Analysis of Weapon System Acquisition Intervals, Past and Present," RAND Report R-2605-DR&E/AF, November 1980, pp. 2–6.

52. U.S. General Accounting Office Report, "Technical Risk Assessment," GAO/EMD 86-5, April 1986.

53. U.S. General Accounting Office, GAO/PSAD/GP, May 27, 1980, pp. 6, 8.

54. President's Blue Ribbon Commission on Defense Management, *A Quest for Excellence,* Final Report to the President, June 1986, p. 47.

55. Bradburn, "Strategic Postures," pp. 54–69.

56. Ibid.

57. Air Force Regulation 70-15.

58. William F. Buckley, Jr., "The Defense Bilkers," *Washington Post,* August 20, 1985.

59. "Flying by Their Seat," *The Wall Street Journal,* July 29, 1985.

60. Colleen A. Preston, "Congress and the Acquisition Process: Some Recommendations for Improvement," *NCMA Journal,* Summer 1986, pp. 1–2.

61. U.S. Senate, testimony of Norman Augustine, President of Martin Marietta and former Under Secretary of the Army, hearing before the Committee on Governmental Affairs, "Acquisition Process in the Department of Defense," October 21 and 27, and November 5, 1981, pp. 85, 86; and Jacques S.

Gansler, "Program Instability: Causes, Costs, and Cures," paper prepared for the Defense Acquisition Study, Center for Strategic and International Studies, Georgetown University, March 1, 1986.

62. M. J. Peck and F. M. Scherer, *The Weapons Acquisition Process: An Economic Analysis* (Boston: Division of Research, Harvard Business School, 1962), pp. 429–430. Cited by the U.S. House of Representatives, Committee on Government Operations, "Inaccuracy of Department of Defense Acquisition Cost Estimates," November 16, 1979, p. 4.

63. Report of the Acquisition Cycle Task Force, Defense Science Board, 1977 Summer Study, March 15, 1978, p. 68. Cited by the U.S. House of Representatives, Committee on Government Operations, p. 4.

64. President Ronald Reagan, "Defense Program Cost Growth," unpublished memorandum to the Secretary of Defense, March 17, 1981. See also Lt. Col. John R. Power, Jr., "A Cost Growth Primer," *Concepts,* Spring 1982, p. 93.

65. SAR Program Acquisition Cost Summary, December 31, 1980, Procurement Programs (P-1), March 10, 1981, as reported in the *New York Times,* July 26, 1981.

66. DOD report cited by Walter S. Mossberg, "Probe Says Navy, Air Force Are Subjected to Steep Price Boosts on Jet Engine Parts," *The Wall Street Journal,* July 12, 1983. See also "Cost Bombshells," *Time,* July 23, 1983, p. 16. Cited in Stubbing, *The Defense Game,* pp. 209–210.

67. "Congress Braces for an Assault on Defense," *New York Times,* November 8, 1981.

68. Ibid.

69. Gordon Adams, with Paul Murphy and William Grey Rosenau, *Controlling Weapons Costs: Can the Pentagon Reforms Work?* (New York: Council on Economic Priorities, 1983), p. 21.

70. "Drums along the Potomac," *Time,* October 21, 1985, p. 34.

71. "Don't Ignore These Pentagon Critics," *Business Week,* October 28, 1985, p. 130.

72. U.S. Senate, statement of Sen. Charles E. Grassley, before the Subcommittee on Administrative Practice and Procedure of the Committee on Armed Services, "Agency Flow of Information," July 23 and 24, 1985, p. 2.

73. "Drums along the Potomac," p. 34.

74. *Business Week*/Harris Poll reported in *Business Week,* March 25, 1985, p. 73.

75. David Packard press conference on *A Quest for Excellence* (see note 54), by the President's Blue Ribbon Commission on Defense Management, Washington, D.C., July 2, 1986.

76. President's Blue Ribbon Commission on Defense Management, *A Quest for Excellence,* June 1986, pp. 76–77.

77. Ibid.

78. John C. Yoder and Jan Horbaly, "Department of Defense Procurement Alternatives," paper prepared for the Defense Acquisition Study, Center for Strategic and International Studies, Georgetown University, March 17, 1986, pp. 11–12.

79. Ibid.

80. Comptroller General of the United States, "Impediments to Reducing the

Costs of Weapon Systems," Report to Congress, November 8, 1979, pp. 5–24.

81. The following pages are based on the Comptroller General of the United States, "Impediments to Reducing the Costs of Weapon Systems," November 8, 1979, pp. 5–24. The comments in this report are as relevant in the late 1980s as they were in 1979.

82. Ibid.

83. Ibid., pp. 18–19.

84. Ibid., pp. 5–24.

85. Ibid.

86. Ibid.

87. U.S. General Accounting Office, GAO/NSIAD–86–45, "Strengthening Capabilities of Key Personnel in Systems Acquisition," May 1986, p. 128.

88. Fox, "Revamping the Business of National Defense," pp. 63–64 (see note 12).

89. Background Information, Senior Steering Group, Defense Acquisition Study, Center for Strategic and International Studies, Georgetown University, November 7–8, 1985.

90. U.S. Senate, testimony of Laurence E. Lynn, Professor of Public Policy, Harvard University, hearing before the Committee on Governmental Affairs, October 21 and 27, and November 5, 1981, pp. 133–135.

91. Adams, *Controlling Weapons Costs,* pp. 19–20.

92. Acker, "The Maturing of the DOD Acquisition Process," pp. 31–32.

93. See note 89.

94. Acker, "The Maturing of the DOD Acquisition Process," pp. 35–37.

95. Staff Report to the Senate Committee on Armed Services, "Defense Organization: The Need for Change," October 16, 1985, p. 532.

96. Adams, *Controlling Weapons Costs,* pp. 19–20.

97. David Packard, "Policy Guidance on Major Weapon Systems Acquisition," May 28, 1970, a memorandum to the Secretaries of the military departments, Director of Defense Research and Engineering, Assistant Secretaries of Defense, and others.

98. John M. Barry, "Congress Wrestles the Pentagon on Procurement," *Dun's Business Month,* August 1985, p. 39.

99. Blue Ribbon Defense Panel, Report to the President and Secretary of Defense on the Department of Defense, December 1972, pp. v, 62, 79; cited in William D. Brown, Paul J. Kern, L. Kirk Lewis, and John G. Zeirdt, "Acquisition Management — The Role and the Reality," National Security Program Report, John F. Kennedy School of Government, Harvard University, June 1987.

100. Acker, "The Maturing of the DOD Acquisition Process," pp. 41–43.

101. U.S. Senate, testimony of Laurence E. Lynn, pp. 133–135 (see note 90).

102. G. K. Smith and E. T. Friedmann, RAND Report R-2605-DR&E, pp. 5–6.

103. Background Information, Defense Acquisition Study (see note 89).

104. Kosta Tsipis and Penny Janeway (eds.), *Review of U.S. Military Research and Development* (Washington, D.C.: Pergamon-Brassey's, 1984), pp. 14–15; and

Bradburn, "Strategic Postures," pp. 45–53; and U.S. Senate, testimony of Laurence E. Lynn, pp. 133–135 (see note 90).

105. Background Information, Defense Acquisition Study (see note 89).
106. Robert Foelber, "Cutting the High Cost of Weapons," The Heritage Foundation, Washington, D.C., March 16, 1982, pp. 5–6.
107. U.S. General Accounting Office, "DOD's Defense Acquisition Improvement Program: A Status Report," GAO/NSIAD–86–148, July 1986, p. 14.
108. Ibid., pp. 12–13.
109. Adams, *Controlling Weapons Costs,* p. 36.
110. Ibid., pp. 32–33.
111. Fox, "Revamping the Business of National Defense," pp. 63–64.
112. "The Pentagon: Waste Probers Faulted," *Boston Globe,* July 27, 1986, pp. 73–74.
113. President's Blue Ribbon Commission on Defense Management, *A Quest for Excellence,* June 1986, cited in Yoder and Horbaly, "Department of Defense Procurement Alternatives," pp. 7–10.
114. Ibid.
115. U.S. Department of Defense Manual 4245.7M, *Transition from Development to Production,* Assistant Secretary of Defense (A&L), September 1985, pp. 1–3.
116. Robert J. Art, "Bureaucratic Politics and American Foreign Policy: A Critique," *Policy Sciences,* December 1973, cited by Bradburn, "Strategic Postures," p. 8.

2

CONGRESS AND THE
WEAPONS ACQUISITION PROCESS

Article II of the Constitution stipulates that "the President shall be Commander-in-Chief of the Army and Navy of the United States." Yet the so-called "War Power" clauses of the Constitution (Article I, Section 8, Clauses 11–14) give to Congress the authority "to declare war," "to raise and support Armies," "to provide and maintain a Navy," and "to make rules for the government and regulation of the land and naval forces." This separation of powers makes clear that although the Founding Fathers granted the President the authority to command the armed forces, it was their intent to reserve for Congress the authority to determine the size of those forces and the kind and number of weapons and equipment produced for their use.

Before the Department of Defense can spend money for research, development, or production of weapon systems, Congress must authorize specific weapons programs and appropriate funds to pay for each authorized program. Two separate pieces of legislation are required. First, in its annual defense authorization bill, Congress determines which new programs from among those proposed by DOD will be initiated and which existing programs will be continued. Then, in its annual defense appropriations bill, Congress grants to DOD the authority to pay out funds or to contract ("obligate" funds). Although funding levels stipulated in the authorization bill for approved weapon systems may be reduced or increased in the appropriations bill, funds may not be appropriated for unauthorized weapon systems. Nor may Defense Department officials — military or civilian — initiate or continue unauthorized programs. During the course of the fiscal year, DOD may, however, ask Congress to authorize new programs or renew lapsed ones and to change appropriations for programs already authorized.

The Congressional Committee System

Congress fulfills most of its major constitutional responsibilities through its system of standing (permanent) committees, a brief outline of which, as it relates to the defense acquisition process, is included here.

During the 99th Congress (1984–1986), there were sixteen standing committees in the Senate and twenty-one in the House of Representatives.[1] There were also four joint Senate-House standing committees (Library, Printing, Taxation, and Economic) and several select and special committees of the House and Senate.

Senate	House of Representatives
Agriculture, Nutrition, and Forestry	Agriculture
Appropriations	Appropriations
Armed Services	Armed Services
Banking, Housing, and Urban Affairs	Banking, Finance, and Urban Affairs
Budget	Budget
Commerce, Science, and Transportation	District of Columbia
Energy and Natural Resources	Education and Labor
Environment and Public Works	Energy and Commerce
Finance	Foreign Affairs
Foreign Relations	Government Operations
Governmental Affairs	House Administration
Judiciary	Judiciary
Labor and Human Resources	Merchant Marine and Fisheries
Rules and Administration	Post Office and Civil Service
Small Business	Public Works and Transportation
Veterans' Affairs	Rules
	Science and Technology
	Small Business
	Standards of Official Conduct
	Veterans' Affairs
	Ways and Means

SOURCE: See note 1.

Most of the committees perform their work in subcommittees. The 99th Congress had a total of 84 subcommittees in the Senate and 143 subcommittees, panels, or task forces in the House.[2] Typically, Senate and House committees with identical titles will nevertheless be organized differently. For example, the Armed Services committees (SASC and HASC) comprised sixteen subcommittees and panels between them, each with a different functional title.[3]

Armed Services Subcommittees

Senate	House
Military Construction	Military Personnel and Compensation
Strategic and Theater Nuclear Forces	Research and Development
Preparedness	Seapower and Strategic and Critical
Sea Power and Force Projection	Materials
Manpower and Personnel	Procurement and Military Nuclear
Defense Acquisition Policy	Systems
	Investigations
	Readiness
	Morale, Welfare, and Recreation (MWR) Panel
	Military Installations and Facilities
	Defense Policy Panel
	Grace Commission Panel

Each committee and subcommittee studies its area of responsibility through research conducted by members or their staff assistants or both and by holding hearings. At least once a year, each committee prepares legislation or recommendations for consideration by the full membership of the House or Senate or the two combined.

In early January, the President submits his State of the Union message and federal budget to Congress; after this and before the end of the fiscal year, September 30, Congress must authorize and appropriate defense funds for the next fiscal year, October 1 to September 30. The Defense Department submits its budget request (as part of the President's budget) to Congress, where it is referred to the Senate and House Armed Services committees and the Appropriations committees.

Although authorization and appropriation of defense funds are closely allied, there is, in theory, a good reason for dealing with them in separate committees. Ideally, members of HASC and SASC, the committees that authorize defense programs, have specialized knowledge and expertise concerning national defense; military operations; weapons requirements, technology, and production; and DOD operations. They should therefore be able to evaluate DOD budget requests based on their own in-depth understanding of defense needs as well as the research provided by their staffs.

House and Senate Appropriations committees, on the other hand, must reconcile requests from all federal agencies with the total funds that Congress will make available for the next fiscal year. Concerned with the best possible use of tax money, each of twenty-six subcommittees must study its own programs. Members of the Defense Appropriations subcommittees, in theory, have not only a broad understanding of national defense needs but also a capacity to analyze the management of existing programs and the accuracy of current budget proposals.

Each subcommittee reports to the full (House or Senate) Appropriations Committee, whose members then measure and compare the nation's health, education, defense, transportation, and other needs to produce a budget that will reflect the combined needs. In fact, although the full committees often change dollar amounts assigned to controversial weapons programs, in aggregate dollars most bills reported out of the Defense Appropriations subcommittees are sent intact to the House or Senate floor.

In addition, early in the calendar year, House and Senate Budget committees draft a budget resolution to provide Congress with spending targets for the next three fiscal years. At the time the committees were established (1974), it was hoped that a single guiding budget resolution would improve coordination between the authorization and appropriations processes, resulting in a more efficient and timely budgetary process. Unfortunately, since the resolutions are nonbinding, they have little effect on Congress.

Each year other House and Senate committees conduct investigations and hold hearings related to the defense acquisition process. These committees include Governmental Affairs, Government Operations, Budget, Small Business, Energy and Commerce, and the Joint Economic Committee.

In each session of Congress, the majority party is awarded a majority of the seats on each committee and subcommittee. The minority party is traditionally represented in approximate proportion to its numerical strength in the House or Senate. For instance, during the 99th Congress, when the Republicans controlled the Senate and the Democrats the House, the Senate Armed Services Committee comprised ten Republicans and nine Democrats, whereas the House Armed Services Committee comprised twenty-six Democrats and twenty Republicans.[4] Senators usually serve on three or four joint or standing committees, although a few belong to as many as five. Most representatives serve on only two joint or standing committees and, in some cases, three or four.[5] Although responsibility for committee assignments rests with the full House and Senate, party caucus or congressional leaders of each party determine actual membership. Senators and representatives actively pursue assignment to the more powerful and influential committees, such as Armed Services, Appropriations, and Foreign Affairs. Such major committees receive enough media attention to ensure for their members consistent public exposure, one of several key factors shaping committee preferences.

The chairman of each committee, chosen annually, is always a member of the majority party and, traditionally, the senator or representative with the longest uninterrupted service on the committee. In 1985, this tradition was broken when Les Aspin (D-WI) replaced a more senior member as HASC chairman after an acrimonious contest that symbolized to many the coming to power of a younger generation in the House. Although their power has been diminished somewhat in recent years, chairmen still exercise considerable authority within their respective committees. The primary source of their power stems from the right of origination, that is, control over the committee agenda. Chairmen decide whether and when to hold hearings on particular issues and determine the style and pace of individual hearings. They also have the right to represent their committee on the House or Senate floor. To some degree, chairmen also exercise control over committee activity through appointment of committee staff.

The Nature of Federal Defense Budgeting

Before examining the hearings conducted by the Armed Services and Appropriations committees, the concept of budgeting, as it applies to federal agencies, should be considered. It is a subject often misunderstood by the layman, who associates the term *budget* with a plan or schedule for spending money that he already has or has a commitment to receive. The use of the word by the federal government refers not only to a plan or schedule to spend money but also to annual requests to Congress for federal agency funds. During annual congressional budget hearings, employees of each federal agency present and defend their funding requests; that is, they attempt to "sell" Congress on the need for a specified amount of money for use in the following fiscal year. As such, the budgeting function within federal agencies is comparable to the marketing function in commercial firms. The success of the marketing, or budgeting, activity has a major impact on the amount of money that will be made available for the activities of the firm, or federal agency. The Defense Department is naturally sensitive to the subtleties of the budgeting process and is engaged year round in some phase of preparation for congressional budget hearings.

At any given time, the Defense Department is actually involved with three defense budgets. It is (1) obligating, or placing under contract, the money appropriated by Congress for the current fiscal year; (2) preparing for congressional hearings or presenting testimony before congressional committees for the defense budget for the next fiscal year; and (3) planning and preparing a budget request for the fiscal year two years hence. For example, in March 1986, the department was expending funds from the 1986 fiscal year budget, presenting testimony to House and Senate committees for the requested 1987 fiscal year budget, and planning and preparing the 1988 fiscal year budget.

The annual defense budget presented and defended before congressional committees develops during the twelve- to eighteen-month period before congressional debate and passage of legislation. Involved in the planning and preparation are Army, Navy, Air Force, and Marine Corps military and civil service staffs; Army, Navy, and Air Force Secretaries and Assistant Secretaries and their staffs; and the Secretary and Assistant Secretaries of Defense and their staffs. These officials determine defense needs by identifying emerging threats to national security and assessing the resources, in personnel and equipment, required to counter and defeat these threats. Because it takes many years to translate weapons requirements into weapons in the field, the Defense Department attempts to define its needs as many as twenty years in advance. This long-term projection poses serious problems for the Office of the Secretary of Defense (OSD) and the services, because threats, and therefore needs, often change as rapidly as weapons technology evolves.

Program requests, many initiated by operational units in the field, are submitted for review and revision to successively higher levels of management within the military services before they reach OSD. During this refining process, the services and OSD must evaluate competing requests for funds, making cutbacks of some programs inevitable. Because there is always a limit on the amount of money Congress will appropriate, the Defense Department, in an effort to begin as many programs as possible, often sets optimistically low cost estimates for proposed programs, and forecasts optimistically high levels of future appropriations. Only much later does it become clear that these programs will require more money than was originally estimated. Described as having a "bow wave" effect on future funding levels, the underestimation of initial costs exacerbates the difficulties associated with long-term planning.

Over the years, this foot-in-the-door technique, also referred to by a Senate Armed Services Committee member as the camel's-nose-under-the-tent syndrome, has proved highly successful; each year more new programs are begun than are likely to be completed. Moreover, history shows that once a program is funded, Congress can usually be prevailed upon, for reasons discussed later in this chapter, to maintain it, despite performance irregularities or increases in schedules and costs. In 1971, Sen. Thomas McIntyre (D-NH), then Chairman of the Senate Subcommittee on Defense Research and Development, commented on the foot-in-the-door approach:

> We have been unable to either eliminate or substantially affect a single program getting ready to emerge from the far end of the pipeline. I have discovered, much to my own frustration, that the present viewpoint seems to be that we are committed to a system's ultimate production as soon as we have sunk virtually any money into it. This is an attitude we will have to change.[6]

More than a decade later, Congress was still having difficulty controlling the fate of individual programs. By one estimate, in 1982 there were so many programs in progress that the equivalent of 2.3 times current spending levels was required to move all the programs in development to the production stage, and 3 times current spending levels was required to complete all programs in production. Consider the following comments by two congressmen in 1985:

> *Sen. Dan Quayle (R-IN):* From a political point of view, Congress cannot and does not cut procurement programs.[7]
>
> *Rep. Dave McCurdy (D-OK):* Once it gets into the procurement stage, a system develops a life of its own. There is no way you can make much of a difference except on the margins.[8]

Unwilling to cancel programs after money has been spent on development, yet reluctant to set priorities among them or devote valuable staff time to early screening, Congress has kept a host of programs alive by approving proposed Pentagon budgets that reduce either the tempo of development or rate of production so as to distribute available funds among as many programs as possible. Some programs are deferred, others are extended (i.e., stretched out, in DOD parlance). For instance, instead of canceling the Air Force's C-17 cargo plane, Congress agreed with DOD to buy fewer of the planes each fiscal year.[9]

Juggling production rates causes program instability, however, and quickly raises the per-unit cost of each weapon purchased. In 1984, Congress paid a $3 billion premium to contractors when it agreed to stretch out twenty-two weapons programs.[10] The F-15 aircraft production stretch-out, which occurred over a three-year period, resulted in a $2 billion increase in program costs, which meant that eighty-three fewer aircraft were purchased for the same amount of money.[11] In a January 1987 edition of the "MacNeil/Lehrer News Hour," Secretary of Defense Caspar Weinberger and Sen. Sam Nunn (D-GA), SASC Chairman, discussed program stretch-outs.

> *Senator Nunn:* I think that when you see the programs stretched out that are already being stretched out, you are seeing one of the fundamental problems with our defense budget. And that is that we've got too many weapon systems being produced, and we're not producing any of those weapon systems — or many of them — at efficient rates. That is colossal waste. When you take all the coffeepot scandals and all the hammers and all of those things we read about and worry about and add them all together and multiply them by 10,000, you don't have the kind of waste in dollars that you do when you stretch too many weapon systems and, therefore, don't produce any of them — or many of them — at efficient rates. That's where the real waste and fat is.

> *Mr. MacNeil:* Mr. Secretary, why are you stretching out so many programs, adding to the cost, say, of an M-1 tank $300,000 per item, of a Black Hawk helicopter $1.3 million per item, instead of simply cancelling some programs?

> *Secretary Weinberger:* Because we need them, and we are stretching them out because Congress won't give us enough money. It's just that simple. The most efficient rates of production are the ones that we requested in earlier budgets that have been rejected. And we have had two years now in which we have gone down in real terms — not just stayed level or anything of the kind, but gone down two years running. And that's a very dangerous thing to do in this kind of world, when the Soviets do nothing but continue to go up.[12]

"Cut insurance" is another budgetary technique. In this case, instead of understating individual program costs to maximize the number of programs approved, DOD inflates the costs of selected programs to ensure that even after expected congressional cuts, desired funding levels will remain intact. Although used with the best of intentions, cut insurance undermines DOD's credibility in the eyes of Congress and the usefulness of its budget as a planning tool.

AUTHORIZATION HEARINGS

The Armed Services committees' hearings on authorization, usually begun in February, are divided into two parts. Initially, each committee schedules "posture hearings" during which military and civilian officials at the highest levels of the Pentagon set the stage for more detailed budget requests. Their statements include descriptions of past and present Defense Department performance, plans for the future, and overall defense policies and goals. Congressional attendance at posture hearings is usually much higher than at any subsequent hearing. Testimony is given by the Secretary of Defense, the chairman of the Joint Chiefs of Staff, and the Secretaries and chiefs of staff for each military service. Although posture hearings are closed to the public, an unclassified version of the Defense Secretary's statement is available through the Government Printing Office.

During the second phase of authorization hearings, specific budget requests are presented and discussed in detail. Testimony is given by Assistant Secretaries of Defense and of the Army, Navy, and Air Force, as well as by the Deputy Chiefs of Staff. During the authorization hearings, as well as later during the appropriations hearings, congressional committees and subcommittees consider separately the R&D and procurement programs of each service.

Pentagon officials who testify during committee hearings require three or more weeks of intensive preparation. An Assistant Secretary, for example, is expected to present budget proposals for his service's acquisition programs. In preparation, he must review twenty-five to fifty major programs and be ready to discuss their current status, their importance to the service, their funding requirements, and the effects on the service if specific ones are not authorized. A Secretary or Assistant Secretary is accompanied by a senior officer (a general or an admiral) from his branch of the service who has spent substantial time during the previous year preparing for the hearings and learning about performance on all service programs. Assistant Secretaries and senior military officers are also accompanied by several military and civilian specialists who are prepared to answer technical questions congressional committee members raise.

An Assistant Secretary presents his statement in summary form. He presents total budget requests for individual programs (e.g., aircraft, missiles, ships, ammunition, tactical vehicles, and combat vehicles), compares current estimates with previous budgets, explains budget needs, and may discuss controversial programs in detail. During this testimony, which could last a few hours or a few days, committee members can question witnesses at any time.

In 1959, Public Law 86–149 increased congressional control over the acquisition process by requiring that a specific authorization accompany the appropriation of funds for aircraft, missiles, and naval vessels. Since then, periodic amendments to the original law have broadened and strengthened congressional control over the process. Currently, the law reads thus:

(a) No funds may be appropriated for any fiscal year to or for the use of any armed force or obligated or expended for —

    (1) procurement of aircraft, missiles, or naval vessels;

    (2) any research, development, test, or evaluation, or procurement or production related thereto;

    (3) procurement of tracked combat vehicles;

    (4) procurement of other weapons; [Essentially this covers heavy, medium, and light artillery; antiaircraft artillery; rifles; machine guns; mortar; small-arms weapons; and any crew-fired piece using fixed ammunition.]

    (5) procurement of naval torpedoes and related support equipment;

    (6) military construction;

    (7) the operation and maintenance of any armed force or of the activities and agencies of the Department of Defense (other than the military departments);

    (8) procurement of ammunition; or

    (9) other procurement by any armed force or by the activities and agencies of the Department of Defense (other than the military departments);

unless funds therefore have been specifically authorized by law.[13]

In fiscal year 1987, of the $302.3 billion in Budget Authority requested by the Defense Department, $224.6 billion, or 74.3 percent, required authorization.[14]

The House and Senate pass separate defense authorization bills upon completion of the hearings of the Armed Services committees. A joint Senate-House conference committee, appointed by the respective legislative bodies, reconciles differences between the two bills, and both houses then adopt the compromise defense authorization bill.

APPROPRIATIONS HEARINGS

Hearings by Defense Appropriations subcommittees usually begin in early February, simultaneously with authorization hearings. The witnesses are, for the most part, the same officials who either have appeared or will appear before the Armed Services committees, and they usually present similar testimony. This means that the Secretary of Defense, the chairman of the Joint Chiefs of Staff, the Assistant Secretaries of Defense, chiefs of staff and their deputies, Secretaries and Assistant Secretaries of the military services, and other military and civilian officials (often including program managers) within the Defense Department may give very similar testimony before four standing committees. In 1986, beginning on February 20 and ending on August 7, the Senate Defense Appropriations Subcommittee alone held twenty-five hearings on the 1987 fiscal year budget request, producing more than 7,300 pages of transcript, the unclassified portion constituting a six-volume public record of testimony.[15]

Because the House originates all bills for raising revenue, it customarily takes the lead over the Senate on the appropriations bill. After the subcommittee completes its bill, the full House Appropriations Committee considers and votes on it. If it passes, the bill then goes to the House floor for more consideration and debate, where, after passage, it goes to the Senate. The Senate Defense Appropriations Subcommittee then writes its own version, using the House bill as a point of departure. After the Senate version works its way through the full Appropriations Committee and the full Senate, in much the same manner as in the House, a joint Senate-House Conference Committee prepares a compromise bill. Both houses eventually pass it, and the Defense Department can make its plans for the coming fiscal year.

The 1987 defense appropriations bill was divided into sixty-two accounts distributed under nine titles.[16]

TITLE: I   Military Personnel
II   Operations and Maintenance
III Procurement
IV Research, Development, Test, and Evaluation
V   Special Foreign Currency Program
VI Space Transportation System
VII Chemical Agents and Munitions Destruction Defense
VIII Related Agencies
IX General Provisions

Sixteen accounts were listed under Title III — Procurement.[17]

> Aircraft Procurement, Army
> Missile Procurement, Army
> Procurement of Weapons and Tracked Combat Vehicles, Army
> Procurement of Ammunition, Army
> Aircraft Procurement, Navy
> Weapons Procurement, Navy
> Shipbuilding and Conversion, Navy
> Other Procurement, Navy
> Coastal Defense Augmentation
> Procurement, Marine Corps
> Aircraft Procurement, Air Force
> Missile Procurement, Air Force
> Other Procurement, Air Force
> Procurement, Defense Agencies
> National Guard and Reserve Component Equipment
> Defense Production Act Purchases

Appropriations for Title II, Operations and Maintenance, must be obligated within one year, for Title III, Procurement, within three years, and for Title IV, R&D, within two years. Procurement and R&D are not mutually exclusive accounts, however. At least 10 to 15 percent of the work on major programs can be identified with either category. Tasks such as tooling, building prototypes, production engineering, and testing are periodically redefined by the Defense Department and defense contractors, who often base their decisions on the availability of funds in one category or the other. For many defense programs, funds in the gray area can amount to more than $100 million.

During the fiscal year, unforeseen military requirements or specific program changes sometimes make it necessary for the Defense Department to obtain additional funds or to move existing funds from one program to another. One option is to request supplementary appropriations from Congress. A second option, reprogramming, involves shifting funds from one item within an appropriations account to another item within the same account. A third option, called a transfer of funds, involves shifting money between different appropriations accounts.

Reprogramming is loosely defined as "the reapplication of resources," or "the use of funds for purposes other than those originally contemplated by Congress at the time of appropriations."[18] An example would be a shift of funds from the Harpoon Missile program to the Phoenix Missile program within the Weapons Procurement, Navy, account. Defense Department reprogramming guidelines stipulate that funds should not be shifted unless they are moved to higher-priority items. There are four types of reprogrammings, only two of which require either congressional approval or prior notification. At least four, and sometimes six, committees or subcommittees are involved in each congressional review. In a recent study, the General Accounting Office described reprogramming as "a cumbersome process within both DOD and the Congress because of the many levels of review and the wide variety of congressional committee review procedures."[19] Most congressional staff members believe, however, that the review process is an important oversight tool, and that reprogramming requests notify the committees of problems and changes in the budget. In addition, the burdensome review process discourages DOD from beginning new projects or changing the scope of programs without congressional review. During a five-year period, from fiscal year 1981 to fiscal year 1985, the Defense Department reprogrammed $29.1 billion, or 2.7 percent, of the $1.1 trillion Congress approved for defense programs.[20]

The third option, the transfer of funds between appropriations accounts, is prohibited without authority from Congress, which usually grants it within a ceiling specified in the annual Defense Appropriations Act. An example of transferring funds would be a shift from Aircraft Procurement, Army, to Missile Procurement, Army. The Defense Department Appropriations Act for 1986 limited the transfer of funds to $950 million. The Appropriations Act for 1987 increased this limit to $1.1 billion, with the stipulations that a transfer may not be used except for higher-priority items and that the Secretary of Defense notify Congress "promptly" of all transfers.[21] Twice a year, the Defense Department must submit to Congress a report showing the cumulative effects of all transfer and reprogramming changes on each appropriations account.

Congressional Management of the Defense Process

Congress has ultimate responsibility for determining the reasonableness of DOD requests for human and material resources and ensuring that DOD, in turn, efficiently manages the resources it does in fact receive. Toward the end of the Vietnam War, though, many observers concluded that Congress was no longer fulfilling either of these critical responsibilities with distinction. Because of the rapid increase since 1950 in the size and complexity of the Defense Department, its budget, the acquisition process, and weapon systems, Congress no longer had the technical abilities required to make independent and sound decisions involving billions of dollars.

Many congressmen were simply overwhelmed and intimidated by the magnitude of the Pentagon's requests, the new concepts and vocabulary associated with high-technology warfare, and the web of financing arrangements between the government and contractors. Other congressmen devoted more of their limited time to nondefense issues and never gained a working knowledge of the Defense Department's policies and practices. It was usually easier to defer to the judgment of military "experts," the explanations of Pentagon officials, the advice of lobbyists, and the recommendations of congressional staffs.

Many HASC and SASC members, reluctant to wade through the briefing material gathered by staffs, were often unprepared for hearings, therefore choosing to ask as few questions as possible to conceal their unfamiliarity with the issues being discussed. Many of the questions they did ask were prepared by members of their staffs, who had often solicited these questions from the Pentagon in order to give the hearings a semblance of substance and their bosses a semblance of expertise. Rarely did these planted questions raise controversial issues.

Pentagon witnesses new to the congressional committee process were often discouraged on discovering that some committee members were unprepared to discuss their programs. More experienced witnesses, however, learned to take advantage of the lack of interest, skirting issues that might have compromised their budget requests. A program might have been behind schedule or not performing as predicted, but Pentagon and industry witnesses were unlikely to mention such problems if committee members did not raise them. When these problems could no longer be ignored, some members were quick to blame the Defense Department for lack of candor but rarely questioned their own limited ability and interest to evaluate complicated and expensive programs.

In most cases, while attempting to present honest testimony, Pentagon officials were unable to explain, in terms comprehensible to laymen, the complex reasons for program difficulties or the steps that would lead to solutions. Very often, the Pentagon had decided that program problems were temporary and that forthright discussion would lead only to a cutback or cancellation of funds. If a branch of the military believed a program to be essential to the service and therefore to national defense, it would withhold problems from Congress as long as possible.

To make matters worse, in 1971 congressional committees were severely understaffed and, for the most part, staff members had little technical background. Congress limited the Senate and House Armed Services committees to fourteen and thirteen staff members, respectively, yet expected them to analyze more than seventy-five major defense programs totaling $70 billion.[22] Efforts by some committee chairmen to increase their staffs were resisted by congressmen who felt that too much money was already being spent for analysis and investigation. In addition, staff members were not granted ready access to information held by the Pentagon. In short, congressional staffs were unsatisfactory advisers because they had limited ability to

assess the validity of testimony given by Defense Department witnesses at congressional hearings;

assess the credibility of the enemy threat, as defined by the Defense Department;

perform the analyses required to determine whether weapons would perform as advertised;

judge whether program costs and schedules were reasonable; and

perform an analysis to determine whether a program's cost growth was justified at expected rates.[23]

The combined effect of these individual shortcomings was a wide gap between the theory and the reality of congressional control over the level and use of resources appropriated to the Defense Department.

Despite all the hearings, debates, and publicity, Congress exercised little control over the size or content of budgets. From 1950 to 1970, congressional reductions of DOD-submitted budgets often amounted to less than 2 percent. Between 1961 and 1971, reductions were always less than 5 percent, except in 1970, when growing opposition to the Vietnam War prompted a 7 percent reduction. Of the seventy-five defense programs for which funds were requested in 1971, more than half were approved as requested or with increases, and only seven received no funding at all.[24]

Fifteen years later, Congress could no longer be criticized for failing to involve itself vigorously in DOD affairs. Instead, it was widely criticized for doing just the opposite and "micromanaging" the system, becoming involved in the day-to-day activities of the department.

In testimony before the Senate Armed Services Committee in 1985, the president of the Machinery and Allied Products Institute succinctly defined congressional micromanagement as a practice whereby Congress was "overdefinitive in its legislation and . . . overproductive in terms of the number of [procurement reform] bills that are generated."[25] Before the same committee, Gen. Lawrence Skantze, commander of the Air Force Systems Command, provided a similar definition by stating that "congressional micromanagement of DOD acquisition activities occurs when legislation goes beyond broad policy guidance and invokes specific requirements affecting individual contract and program management actions."[26] Many in Congress, however, refused to believe they were guilty of excessively detailed management. They felt their critics were condemning them for attempting to solve a host of well-documented, seemingly implacable problems that few would deny had been plaguing the acquisition process for more than two decades. Others acknowledged that micromanagement was inappropriate and that some of the criticism was valid, yet disagreed with the defense industry and the Pentagon over which legislation and actions constituted micromanagement and which did not. Depending on where one stood, micromanagement was either a serious impediment to the establishment of an efficient acquisition process or an essential ingredient to the establishment of reasonable program costs.

Although it is difficult to determine at what point an appropriate level of managerial involvement ends and micromanagement begins, by 1986 a wide variety of measures seemed to indicate that Congress, in both its oversight and legislative capacities, was managing the DOD acquisition process in too much detail. Consider some of the administrative burdens the Pentagon and the defense industry experienced as a result of congressional actions.

In contrast to 1970, when approximately twenty-six committees and subcommittees (House and Senate Armed Services and Appropriations) were primarily involved with defense review, in 1985 ninety-six committees and subcommittees wrote defense legislation or heard testimony from defense witnesses, or both.[27]

The number of congressional staff members involved in defense matters matched the increase in the number of committees and subcommittees involved. For example, since 1959, the number of Senate office buildings has tripled, although the number of senators has remained the same. In contrast to the fourteen and thirteen staff members who, in 1970, worked on the Senate and House Armed Services committees, respectively, by 1986 these staffs had increased to twenty-nine and forty-one, respectively. In addition, eighty-two and sixty-three staff members were assigned to the Senate and House Appropriations committees, respectively.

During an eight-month period in 1983, Congress managed to hold 407 review hearings and listen to more than 5,000 hours of testimony from 1,200 defense officials.[28] During the entire year, the military received 84,148 written queries from Capitol Hill and 592,150 phone calls.[29]

During 1983, a single Pentagon staff (Office of the Chief of Naval Operations) prepared 37 formal reports at the request of Congress, answered 2,900 requests for information from members of Congress, testified at 100 separate hearings, submitted 4,500 written replies to questions for the *Congressional Record,* and gave 245 briefings.[30]

In support of the 1984 budget request alone, the Pentagon wrote 21,753 pages of supporting documents (a 300 percent increase since 1970). In addition, 1,306 Defense Department witnesses provided 2,160 hours of testimony.[31]

The 1985 budget request contained 1,890 separate line entries for procurement and 897 program requests for R&D.[32] A joint Senate-House conference committee eventually authorized 92.5 percent and 94.4 percent of the Budget Authority requested by the administration for procurement and R&D, respectively.[33] Nevertheless, the

HASC and SASC together changed 440, or 23.3 percent, of the procurement line entries and 317, or 35.3 percent, of all R&D programs.[34]

In 1985, the Pentagon was able to identify 458 congressional reporting requirements stemming from prior years' defense authorization and appropriation bills and their accompanying reports. To fulfill these requirements in fiscal year 1985, the Pentagon submitted to Congress an estimated 24,000 pages of documentation.[35] The SASC reported that between 1970 and 1985, the number of reports Congress required of the Defense Department increased by 1,000 percent.[36]

Reporting requirements range from one-time studies to reports whose submission is contingent on a previously specified "triggering event." An example of the latter is the Nunn amendment, named after its author, Sen. Sam Nunn (D-GA), which requires

> the Secretaries of the Army, Navy and Air Force to make special reports to Congress whenever a major system exceeds established cost thresholds. If, by the end of a quarterly fiscal period, the unit cost of a system (adjusted for inflation) grows 15 to 25 percent over its initial projected unit cost, the service secretary must submit an explanation for the cost increase to Congress within 30 days or face a cutoff of all funds for the affected program. If the acquisition unit cost growth is greater than 25 percent, the service secretary has 60 days to submit to Congress both a detailed explanation of program costs and a report from the Secretary of Defense stating that the weapon system is essential to national security, that there are no alternatives to the acquisition program, that the new unit-cost projections are reasonable and that the program is being managed adequately. If any of these stipulations are not met, Congress may cut off funds.[37]

Although many of the reports and studies prepared by the Defense Department at the request of Congress can be considered necessary and valuable, the benefits of some are questionable when compared with the costs of preparation. For instance, consider 2 of the 107 additional reporting requirements included in the 1986 Authorization Act.

> Section 1456. Defense Industrial Base for Textile and Apparel Products
> (a) Capability of Domestic Textile and Apparel Industrial Base — The Secretary of Defense shall monitor the capability of the domestic textile and apparel industrial base to support defense mobilization requirements.

(b) Annual Report — The Secretary shall submit to Congress not later than April 1 of each of the five years beginning with 1986 a report on the status of such industrial base. Each such report shall include:

(1) an identification of textile and apparel mobilization requirements of the Department of Defense that cannot be satisfied on a timely basis by the domestic industries;

(2) an assessment of the effect any inadequacy in the textile and apparel industrial base would have on a defense mobilization; and

(3) recommendations for ways to alleviate any inadequacy in such industrial base that the Secretary considers critical to defense mobilization requirements.

Report and Demonstration Project Concerning the Sale of Certain United States Meat in Military Commissaries Overseas

(a) Feasibility Study and Demonstration Project — The Secretary of Defense shall study the feasibility of providing beef, pork, and lamb produced in the United States for sale in American Military Forces' commissaries located overseas in volumes equivalent to beef, pork, and lamb secured for sale from non–United States producers. Such study:

(1) shall be carried out in consultation with the Secretary of Agriculture; and

(2) shall include a demonstration project in which beef, pork, and lamb produced in the United States shall be stocked in three commissaries at Air Force bases in Europe and in three commissaries located at Army bases in Europe for a six-month period in volumes equivalent to beef, pork, and lamb secured for sale from non–United States producers; such United States–produced products shall, to the best of the Secretary's ability, be compared with non–United States produced red-meat products offered for sale in the commissary system.

(b) Report — Not later than one year after the date of the enactment of this Act, the Secretary of Defense shall submit to Congress a report on the results of such study and the findings and conclusions of the Secretary under such study. Such report shall include any views provided by the Secretary of Agriculture.[38]

Purportedly used only for informational purposes, such reports have become popular in Congress in part because of their usefulness in eliciting an unambiguous response from the Defense Department on highly controversial issues.

But congressional "over-oversight," characterized by an immense appetite for information, was only part of the micromanagement issue.[39] A second part involved detailed restrictions and directions that Congress wrote into its defense legislation and committee reports. By 1970 standards, the defense legislation produced in 1986 constrained to a significant degree the authority of executive branch officials to manage their agencies independently. The reform statutes were not only detailed but also often poorly worded and constructed, resulting from a legislative process based on compromise. Obscure legislative language, in turn, impeded the Defense Department in translating statutes into regulations embodying congressional intent. According to Ms. Colleen Preston, counsel for the Procurement Policy Panel of the House Armed Services Committee,

> the process by which Congress addresses issues itself almost bodes against clear definitive statements. . . . This is so because no one person has the authority to make a decision, but instead resolution is achieved through compromise and consensus. That process is appropriate and successful in resolving policy issues, but unsuitable for directing practical applications of a policy. Specifically, when Congress is unable to reach a consensus or agreement on a particular solution, it leaves a term undefined or a provision unclear so that neither side's solution is precluded. This leaves the executive branch in a position of interpreting the provision, usually without adequate legislative history to guide it. The door is thus open for various committees to attempt to influence the regulatory implementation process in the hopes of achieving an implementation more akin to their view of the most appropriate solution.[40]

Ms. Preston went on to explain the results of such legislation.

> As various parties challenge regulatory implementation of legislation, courts are faced with deriving the "intent of Congress" from often quickly drafted committee or conference reports and member statements . . . which . . . may or may not represent what Congress believed it was adopting. More often than not, particularly with legislative provisions not specifically considered in committee, there is little, if any, legislative history. Because the courts cannot avoid having to reach a decision . . . it is they who ultimately define the real parameters of the legislation.[41]

In addition, many pieces of reform legislation were simply not practical because they attempted to impose a uniform requirement for all programs, despite a cardinal rule of procurement that no two programs are exactly alike, and therefore program decisions and requirements must be made and enforced on a case-by-case basis. Ms. Preston described such legislation.

An example is the requirement [10 U.S.C. 2403, Weapon System Warranties] to warranty performance, workmanship and materials on all products supplied by a company, but then the Government [breaks out] for competition the spares going into that system. As most people are aware, once an owner replaces a part in a product purchased from other than an authorized dealer, or has it repaired by someone other than the manufacturer, all warranties are voided.[42]

Title IX of the 1986 DOD authorization act, entitled "Procurement Policy Reform and Other Procurement Matters," contains what may be the best examples of legislative micromanagement. The following list of sections under Title IX indicates the broad range of issues Congress addressed and the depth to which it was involved in virtually every aspect of the defense acquisition process.

Part A: Program Management Matters:
Sec. 911. Regulations relating to allowable costs.
Sec. 912. Multiple sources for major defense acquisition programs.
Sec. 913. Minimum percentage of competitive procurements.
Sec. 914. Regulations to control prices that may be paid for spare parts.
Sec. 915. Should-cost analyses.
Sec. 916. Limitations on progress payments.
Sec. 917. Cost and price management in defense procurement.
Sec. 918. Contracted advisory and assistance services.
Sec. 919. Revision and extension of Procurement Technical Assistance Cooperative Agreement program.

Part B: Procurement Personnel Matters:
Sec. 921. Post-Government service employment bars on senior defense officials.
Sec. 922. Improved reporting and disclosure for former employees of the Department of Defense; prevention of conflicts of interest.
Sec. 923. Requirements relating to private employment contracts between certain Department of Defense officials and defense contractors.
Sec. 924. Management of Department of Defense procurement personnel.
Sec. 925. Assignment of principal contracting officers.

Part C: False Claims, Debarment, Burden of Proof, and Related Matters:
Sec. 931. Increased penalties for false claims in defense procurement.

Sec. 932. Prohibition on felons convicted of defense-contract-related felonies and penalty on employment of such persons by defense contractors.

Sec. 933. Burden of proof in Government contract dispute resolution.

Sec. 934. Reimbursement, interest charges, and penalties for overpayments.

Sec. 935. Subpoenas of defense contractor records.

A closer inspection of the text of almost any section provides ample evidence of the great detail Congress included in its procurement reform legislation. Consider the following passages.

> (3) The testing . . . shall be carried out in 5-ton trucks configured in the M939 validated technical data package of the Army and shall include tests to determine:
>
> > (a) whether the engine is durable after testing in a mission profile for at least 20,000 miles; and
> >
> > (b) whether the performance reliability of the engine for high ambient temperature cooling, cold starting, deep water fording, grade climbing, and noise is acceptable.
>
> * * *
>
> (c) AH-64 Apache Helicopters — The Secretary of the Army may not obligate funds appropriated or otherwise made available for a fiscal year after fiscal year 1985 for procurement of AH-64 Apache attack helicopters until the Director of the Defense Contract Audit Agency reports to the Secretary that the contractor for such helicopter has demonstrated to the satisfaction of the Director:
>
> > (1) that the contractor has implemented an effective and reliable system of internal accounting controls; and
> >
> > (2) that the contractor has accumulated documentation (including journals, vouchers, invoices, and expense data) to support the contractor's final submission for settlement of indirect expenses for calendar years 1979 through 1983 and that such documentation is available to the Director.[43]

Causes of Congressional Micromanagement

In medicine, knowing the symptoms of a disease is of little help to the patient; the doctor must identify the disease itself before prescribing a cure. The same holds true for Congress's oversight and legislative micromanagement; identifying and measuring the problem are simply not enough. To solve it, one must understand the forces that drive it.

Micromanagement did not develop overnight. It began gradually, when American involvement in the Vietnam War was ending. Traditionally, in times of war, Congress closes ranks and supports whatever steps the President and his administration take to end hostilities on favorable terms. There is usually a spirit of bipartisanship on defense and foreign policy issues, at least to some degree, in the early stages of a conflict. Only after cessation of hostilities does Congress fully resume its scrutiny of executive branch activities.

Public opinion on the war in Vietnam broke this traditional pattern of congressional behavior. As the war persisted, most in Congress became increasingly skeptical of the way the military was conducting it. By 1972, the military had lost much of its credibility in the eyes of the American public, the media, and Congress. The Watergate affair accelerated the erosion of faith in the honesty and integrity of the executive branch of government. In response, in 1974, the public elected to Congress many who wore their skepticism of "big government" like a badge of honor.

During the mid-1970s, this skepticism and lack of trust in the executive branch led to a gradual increase in congressional resources devoted specifically to oversight. A major investment was made in expanding the size of committee staffs. Acknowledging this growth, a senior Navy official confirmed in 1978 that since the end of the Vietnam War, committee staff members had become "a relatively new and terribly important part of the Washington decision-making community."[44] The expansion of committee staff was accompanied by a similar expansion in the size and number of congressional research and investigative agencies: the General Accounting Office, the Office of Technology Assessment (established in 1972), the Congressional Budget Office (1974), and the Congressional Research Service. In 1986 these agencies employed over twenty-five hundred people.[45] The mushrooming of committee and supporting agency staff gave Congress many of the analytical capabilities it needed to challenge seriously the Pentagon and offset to some degree the dominance of the executive branch based on knowledge and a command of facts, a dominance that had existed since the tenure of Defense Secretary Robert McNamara (1961–1968).

In 1980, the American public elected Ronald Reagan to the presidency and provided his administration with a mandate to rebuild

America's defenses. Congress authorized money for what was to become the nation's largest peacetime military buildup. Given what Defense Secretary Weinberger has called "an aversion in our democratic system to peacetime spending on defense," continued public support for large defense budgets was fragile.[46] Therefore, if the administration was to continue its defense buildup throughout the 1980s as planned, it would have to preserve the public perception of efficient and wise Defense Department spending of tax dollars.

In 1984, this perception was shattered when the media began to report on overpriced spare parts. In response to constituency pressure and damaged professional pride, Congress decided it had to act to restore the integrity of a defense establishment riddled by "waste, fraud, and abuse." Consider these statements from members of Congress:

> In my district all the people running against me are holding up a hammer and saying that it costs $600.
>
> * * *
>
> What have you [addressed to a collective group of defense "experts"] done to correct fraud, waste, and abuse in the procurement process? They [his constituents] don't write to the Defense Department, they write to me, and I have to do something or I don't get reelected.
>
> * * *
>
> The drumbeat of news stories about $600 ashtrays and $700 toilet seats is symptomatic of an utter failure of the Defense Department to exercise proper oversight of Pentagon procurement contracts and the failure of all of us in the House to perform oversight responsibility.[47]

Congressional action could have taken the form of selective additional committee oversight or legislative reform, or a combination of the two. In the long term, Congress would have to use a judicious mixture of oversight and legislation to fulfill its constitutional responsibilities. Yet in the short term, it chose to emphasize legislative reform. In contrast to careful oversight, which is a lengthy, often tedious, and reactive measure that generally reviews events after they have occurred, legislation is a quick, active measure of reform that serves as tangible evidence of a member's ability to do the job.

Assigned the task of drafting procurement reforms at a time when the public was demanding action, staff members eagerly and aggressively began to change the system by legislative fiat. The ensuing detailed, prescriptive statutes, when combined with increased congressional demands for information, resulted in charges of congressional micromanagement. In 1986, Russell Murray II, special counsel to the House Armed Services Committee, wrote:

> Such detailed legislation is clearly the product of the Congressional staff; few elected members would have the time to become sufficiently versed in programmatic details to be able to draft such specific language. The merits of such legislation are certainly open to debate.[48]

The roots of micromanagement of DOD activities can also be traced to a federal spending disparity. By 1985, although the defense budget represented only about 26 percent of total federal outlays, it accounted for nearly 65 percent of total discretionary spending (i.e., money Congress could control without reducing benefits already promised) during a period of record budget deficits.[49] Therefore, many in Congress believed they had little choice but to analyze and regulate defense activities in greater detail in the hope of realizing potential savings. Unquestionably, the historical reluctance by the President and Congress to interfere with the growth of major domestic entitlement programs, the discretionary nature of defense spending, and the persistence of the federal budget deficit provide valuable clues to how long the Defense Department can expect such intensified scrutiny by Congress.

The Consequences of Micromanagement

Although some reform legislation and selected oversight initiatives may well prove beneficial to the operation of the DOD acquisition process, by 1987 it was evident that increased congressional involvement in DOD activities had also created or exacerbated a number of system inefficiencies. Ironically, in attempting to reform a management process many members believed to be fundamentally flawed, congressmen and their staffs — though generally well intentioned — often left new and equally serious problems in their wake.

One undesirable effect of micromanagement was the further obfuscation of accountability. Instead of laying the groundwork for a more effective management system in which decision makers would be held more accountable for their actions, the vast majority of reform legislation led to so many additional checks, balances, and layers of review that decisions remained too often a product of the bureaucracy, not of individuals. Further complicating the issue of accountability, some congressional staff members prepared legislation directing the execution of selected program actions but were not held responsible for ensuing difficulties.

Other undesirable consequences included the reduction of managerial autonomy and the emergence of incentives that discouraged individual initiative and encouraged defense managers to concentrate more on process and procedure than on results. Instead of creating an environment in which able managers could freely exercise their judgment and authority, Congress was telling many of them in excruciating detail how to manage their programs. Some, fearful of making an error while congressional overseers and the press were in search of trouble, deferred action until convinced that there was documentation to justify every decision. The safest path had become strict adherence to regulatory detail, regardless of the results achieved. In 1986, addressing the problem as it affected contracting officers, Senator Nunn, then the leading Democrat on the Senate Armed Services Committee, noted:

> Congress has become 535 individual program managers who are micro-managing the Department [of Defense] at an alarming rate. . . . I am not convinced that all the changes we have made are positive. For example, we have imposed countless requirements on the procurement process which have resulted in huge lists of things that contracting officers must check off before they can approve a project. If the contracting officers check all of those boxes, they feel they have done their job. Unfortunately, nowhere on the list is a box marked "Common Sense." Consequently, it is no wonder that significant acquisition problems exist.[50]

Micromanagement also resulted in a slower and, in some areas, a costlier procurement process. As a general rule, the more complicated and abundant the regulations and layers of review, the greater the time required to obtain approval to perform even relatively simple tasks. Furthermore, as the number of people involved in a decision increases, the more likely it is that someone will erect a bureaucratic roadblock to impede an initiative's progress or say no and quash it outright. In either case, time and, ultimately, technological advantage in time of war are squandered. Similarly, the cost of doing business often increases when the government requires industry to comply with a new regulation, perform another internal audit, design a more sophisticated measurement system, or prepare an additional report.

Finally, micromanagement could not avoid diminishing the mutual trust and good will so important to the working relationship between Congress, the Defense Department, and industry. On the one hand, Congress viewed micromanagement — to the extent that it acknowledged its existence — as a necessary and natural response to the Defense Department's failure to manage properly its own affairs. Indeed, some members believed it to be especially necessary because of the high levels of defense spending in the mid-1980s, which they considered out of step with the fiscal realities posed by large federal deficits. Pentagon and defense industry officials, on the other hand, viewed micromanagement as politically motivated and equivalent to a vote of "no confidence" in their honesty and professional abilities.

In the mid-1980s, an atmosphere of uncertainty, frustration, and apprehension pervaded the Pentagon and its contracting base, for each new day brought with it additional regulations and concerns that more errors would be uncovered by either the press or congressional auditors, investigators, and overseers. By 1986, the logjam of procurement legislation awaiting implementation had become so great that Pentagon and defense industry officials pleaded with Congress for a moratorium on further reform legislation. Congress responded by appealing for greater professionalism by all personnel involved in the acquisition process. Understandably, morale and confidence declined further.

Hidden Costs of Micromanagement

A critical analysis of the decision by Congress to pursue a hands-on approach to procurement reform would be incomplete if the intended benefits of detailed legislation and additional oversight were weighed only against the undesirable consequences described above. A thorough understanding of the costs requires consideration also of what exactly was sacrificed, compromised, or ignored when the decision was made, in the name of reform, to move in the direction of micromanagement.

By justifying — and later maintaining support for — its role as micromanager, Congress sacrificed broad public support for a continued defense buildup. Although the media first eroded public confidence in the defense establishment with "horror stories" about spare parts, Congress played a major role in transforming this erosion into a landslide.[51] Instead of putting the issue into proper perspective, some in Congress chose instead to soothe the outrage of constituents (the vast majority of whom were unfamiliar with the intricacies of the acquisition process) by responding to their demands for major and immediate reform. This acquiescence, in turn, required reinforcing popular misconceptions, which also served to legitimatize an activist role born of political pressure. In short, Congress had to verify that a sickness existed before advocating its cure. In the mid-1980s, each time a member of Congress appeared on the evening news to proclaim the passage of a new reform or to disclose another instance of alleged contractor corruption, public disillusionment with the entire defense budget increased. Eventually, the American public considered appeals for procurement reform and requests for larger military budgets as mutually exclusive.

Once members discovered that key reformers were all but guaranteed valuable media exposure, cases of micromanagement increased, as did the deterioration of committee discipline and the compromise of the committee system itself. Turf battles erupted between the traditional defense-oriented committees and committees wanting to share the spotlight. The challengers claimed the incumbents, because of a close association with the Defense Department and contractors, were incapable of challenging them or making difficult decisions. Especially criticized were the Armed Services committees, whose key staff members sometimes moved on to assume influential positions in the Pentagon. Therefore, new blood was required to reform the Defense Department, leading individual congressmen to seek platforms to expand their involvement.

A case in point is the Military Reform Caucus (MRC), cofounded in 1981 by Sen. Gary Hart (D-CO) and Rep. G. William Whitehurst (R-VA) after a number of congressmen pledged their mutual interest in and active support for reforms spelled out by Senator Hart in a *Wall Street Journal* article.[52] By 1986, the MRC comprised 133 members, 29 from the Senate and 104 from the House (70 Democrats and 63 Republicans).[53] Although the MRC had no office space, no permanent staff, and no telephone number, it made it possible for every member of Congress, if he or she so desired, to establish a reputation as a procurement reform expert. Not surprisingly, the MRC joined in the contest for turf with nearly one hundred other committees and subcommittees.

The harm resulting from the breakdown of committee discipline was all too evident. The weakening of the role of the Senate and House Armed Services committees reduced the influence of DOD's essential congressional advocates. Committees new to the issues of procurement introduced laws inconsistent with the established laws in this area. As more people and committees became involved with defense matters, the defense authorization and appropriations processes became more complicated than ever. In 1986, more than a hundred floor amendments were attached to the defense authorization bill in the House. Disputes over individual line-item amounts in the defense budget fueled a growing rivalry between the Armed Services committees and the Defense Appropriations subcommittees. Furthermore, efforts by the Armed Services committees to write line-item authorizations for a growing percentage of the defense budget resulted in schedule delays, obliging defense appropriations subcommittees, mindful of their own scheduling demands, to proceed without an authorization bill. The Packard Commission wrote:

> DOD now finds itself involved in a new congressional budgeting phenomenon in which the Appropriations Committees have funded programs that the Armed Services Committees have not authorized. In fiscal year 1986, the DOD Appropriations Act included over 150 line items, valued at $5.7 billion, that were authorized at a lower level or were not authorized at all. As of this date [June 1986], the fiscal year is more than half over but DOD cannot obligate funds nor conclude contract negotiations for almost $6 billion [worth] of programs while the disagreement continues between congressional committees.[54]

The result: legislative inefficiency that has forced Congress to use continuing appropriations bills for every fiscal year since 1978. Although congressional staff members are quick to point out that continuing appropriations bills are harmless because they provide the Defense Department with enough information for planning purposes, others strongly disagree. Again, the 1986 Packard Commission, commenting on the environment created by this practice:

> defense managers and defense procurement personnel around the world must implement late congressional decisions after the fiscal year has started. They are confronted with numerous changes that alter and delay their program plans, schedules, and contract decisions. This instability, in turn, spreads outward to the defense industry, whose investment and production plans must be hastily adjusted annually as a result of late congressional appropriations.[55]

Regardless of how much the uncertainty and instability in the acquisition process are directly attributable to continuing appropriations bills, their repetitive use is strong evidence of the inability of Congress to accomplish one of its primary responsibilities: the orderly and timely passage of sound legislation. The following excerpt from the *Washington Post* illustrates how far the defense legislative process had deteriorated by September 1986.

The big decisions on the new [FY1987] defense budget will not be made by the House and Senate Armed Services Committees, lawmakers acknowledged, but by the Appropriations Committees and the members of the House and Senate as they shape the continuing resolutions. They said it appears unlikely that a defense authorization bill will clear Congress this year.

. . . Rep. Samuel S. Stratton [D-NY], a senior Democrat on the House Armed Services Committee, said, "We've been worried about becoming irrelevant for some time. And this year it looks like it is coming closer to that."[56]

Although Congress eventually (on November 14, 1986) passed a defense authorization bill for fiscal year 1987, the experience was so unsettling and distasteful that the Chairmen and select members of the Senate Armed Services and Appropriations committees felt compelled to sign a four-page coordinating document, entitled "Basis of Agreement," to minimize future committee differences.

Enmeshed in detail, Congress ignored one of its primary responsibilities: the oversight and determination of overall defense policy and priorities. Key legislators agreed that instead of involving itself in line items, Congress should have decided the fundamental question of how to allocate national resources among competing interests and conducted oversight to ensure that the nation gets what it asked and paid for. Consider the following statements:

Sen. Sam Nunn (D-GA), Chairman of the Senate Armed Services Committee: We are spending most of our time looking at the grains of sand on the beach, and we are not looking at the ocean or looking over the horizon.[57]

Rep. Les Aspin (D-WI), Chairman of the House Armed Services Committee: We should oversee policy, and we should assert ourselves when we think things have gotten screwed up.[58]

Packard Commission: The present method of budget review, involving duplicative effort by numerous congressional committees and subcommittees, centers on either the minutiae of line items or the gross dollar allocation to defense, and [it] obscures important matters of strategy, operational concepts, and key defense issues.[59]

Sen. Barry Goldwater (R-AZ), Chairman of the Senate Armed Services Committee from 1984 to 1986: The budget process distorts the nature of congressional oversight by focusing primarily on the question of how much before we answer the key questions of what for, why, and how well.[60]

Finally, instead of directing the actions of DOD officials and managers, Congress might have been more effective had it developed incentives for the Defense Department to use to attract and retain more experienced and talented people. In the long term, the additional burdens and loss of managerial autonomy attributable to micromanagement provide little encouragement to good managers to remain in DOD and discourage those with proven records in industry from entering the department for a tour of duty. This loss of talent may be the largest hidden cost resulting from micromanagement.

A Serious Misconception

One of the arguments used most often to justify congressional micromanagement is that the Defense Department is incapable, because of structural inefficiency and internal rivalries, of efficiently managing and reforming itself. Therefore, Congress must assume control. Because the Constitution grants Congress the authority to manage the Defense Department — and the acquisition process if it so desires — the only question remaining concerns the degree to which it should prudently immerse itself in the detail. The argument for doing so is based in part on a serious misconception held by proponents of micromanagement: Congress, as a body, is somehow more able to achieve objective reform and less likely to mismanage the acquisition process than the Department of Defense. This misconception could very well be the result of the considerable dedication and integrity found in many who have served as members and Chairmen of the House and Senate Armed Services committees.

Frequently forgotten, however, is that Congress is "inefficient" by design, as demonstrated by the inherent rivalry in a two-party system electing members every two years. In addition, because of its political nature and busy agenda, Congress is not simply reluctant to act promptly on difficult issues; it is often unable to act, even on matters of grave importance.

A review of defense appropriations bills since 1980 emphasizes that, in its own way, Congress is as imperfect a manager as the agency it attempts to manage. In what is disparagingly referred to as pork barrel politics, many members of Congress (often in response to labor union and industry requests) initiate or perpetuate the expenditure of funds on programs or facilities of only marginal value to create or save jobs, and their popularity, in their districts.

Torn between what is best for their constituents and what is best for national security, many in Congress are no more equipped to make objective and detached decisions on resource allocation than is the Department of Defense, whose decision-making integrity is often considered to be compromised by its close relations with its contractors.

Following are comments on, and examples of, pork barrel politics since 1980:

Defense Secretary Harold Brown complained that congressional pressure forced him to keep open military bases of marginal value. His estimate of the amount wasted: $1 billion per year.[61]

In 1982, a House Armed Services subcommittee authorized $300 million for work at bases, against the wishes of the Pentagon.[62] The 1984 budget appropriated $910,000 for a new roadway at a base the Pentagon had wanted to close since 1964.[63]

In 1983, a Congressman from New York serving on a defense appropriations subcommittee added $361 million to the budget to purchase 20 attack planes — manufactured in his district — that the Air Force regarded as outmoded.[64]

In 1983, despite Senate support for the Army's push to complete a $3.1 billion tank engine contract, the House successfully pushed through legislation prohibiting the establishment of a second source. Commented a congressman: "We talk a good game about accountability and independence . . . but as far as actually letting go, we've got a lousy record."[65] Referring to congressmen in general, the Navy's Competition Advocate General stated that: "For the most part, competition is great in every district but theirs."[66]

In 1984, Congress added $4.6 billion for weapons and equipment never requested by the Defense Department.[67]

During the first Reagan administration, when John Tower (R-TX), Chairman of the Senate Armed Services Committee from 1980 to 1984, asked legislators to propose military spending cuts in their states in order to reduce the federal deficit, only two members suggested specific cuts while others argued against any cuts at all.[68]

Despite the inefficiencies and waste attributable to pork barrel politics, on Capitol Hill the practice is considered little more than a matter of perception, and the epithet is rarely used. Protecting and promoting the interests of constituents is seen as an important part of a congressman's job, and many are willing to contribute to a colleague's good fortune, as long as their turn is next. It is a fact of life in American politics that defense contracts mean many jobs, and the creation or protection of these jobs usually results in reelection. In 1986 the *Boston Globe* described the enormous impact that defense spending can have on a political career and a state economy.

> With the unemployment rate in Massachusetts among the lowest in the nation, the question of who deserves the credit will be hotly debated in the coming campaign for statewide office.
>
> Democrats point to the industrial parks, the training programs for welfare recipients, and the favorable climate for business growth created by the Dukakis Administration.
>
> Republicans talk about the way the Reagan Administration has cut taxes and harnessed inflation, increasing capital investment by business and protecting the purchasing power of consumers.
>
> Both parties will be wrong. Far more than anything else, the economic surge in Massachusetts in recent years has been the result of the rapid rise of defense spending.
>
> Without it, the commonwealth would be in the economic doldrums. This is the dirty little secret of the Massachusetts economy: Far more than most states, our prosperity depends upon war and the preparation for war.
>
> Between fiscal years 1979 and 1985, the military poured more than $42 billion in prime defense contracts into Massachusetts. The yearly value of awards won by Massachusetts firms rose by 156 percent — from $3 billion to $7.7 billion. The upward march has been steady — about $700 million more each year.
>
> While prime contractors do not produce all the equipment in the weapon systems for which they are responsible, a hefty share of what they subcontract goes to firms within the state. In addition, Massachusetts companies produce military equipment for prime contractors in other parts of the country.
>
> One way or the other, defense contracts provide employment directly to almost 175,000 workers in the commonwealth — in defense plants, the companies that service them, and in the research labs of our universities.
>
> These jobs generate activity in the rest of the economy that provides employment for 260,000 more. Since total state employment is more than three million, military work, in one way or another, is the source of jobs for at least one out of every seven workers.[69]

During the late 1970s, defense contractors recognized that the promise of jobs could be used as a lever to gain congressional support not only for marginally valuable programs but also for politically volatile and unpopular ones. For instance, the manufacturer of the B-1 bomber, Rockwell International Corporation, spread the work among 5,200 subcontractors in 48 states and 400 congressional districts.[70] Only thirty-five representatives and four senators failed to obtain jobs for their constituents from this project.[71] During the mid-1970s, when the merits of the B-1 were under attack, Rockwell International Corporation paid a consultant $110,000 for a report (to be used by itself and the Air Force) detailing how the program would affect each state and district.[72] Consider this statement by former Rep. Joseph Addabbo (D-NY), Chairman of the House Defense Appropriations Subcommittee and an opponent of the bomber:

> Rockwell is the best. I've had many members say: "I have a plant with x number of jobs, and I just can't vote against that." In effect, they've used Congressmen from those states as lobbyists.[73]

Noted a defense security analyst:

> Why, despite the rhetoric, can we assume that even dovish politicians will vote for potentially aggressive weapon systems whenever their votes are crucial for passage — even strategic nuclear weapons? The answer: jobs.[74]

In his often-quoted 1961 farewell address to the nation, President Eisenhower warned the public to "guard against the acquisition of unwarranted influence . . . by the military-industrial complex." In the 1980s, however, many believe that the warning would be more applicable against unwarranted influence from a "congressional-industrial" complex. In a 1978 *Wall Street Journal* article, Kenneth Bacon explained the new partnership's origins.

> . . . probably the main reason for the change is that contractors are realizing that "there's less to go around" in the Pentagon budget, Mr. Stempler [Defense Secretary Harold Brown's assistant for congressional relations] says.
> The Pentagon is buying smaller numbers of increasingly expensive weapons. For example, 20 years ago the military bought about 3,000 airplanes a year; this year it's purchasing only 530. A prime reason for the cutback is that today's fighters cost between $10 million and $20 million each.

As a result, despite increasing defense budgets, there are fewer major contracts. For contractors, Mr. Stempler says, this means "if they miss the brass ring one time, they've got to wait a long time for it to come around again."

But rather than wait, many go to Capitol Hill, hoping to persuade Congress to give them what the administration hasn't.

The other major reason many contractors say they have stepped up congressional lobbying efforts is that the Pentagon has made it more difficult for them to get the ear of admirals and generals.

"It's not so much that we've found Congress so much more accessible, it's just that we've found Defense Department people less accessible" in the wake of . . . scandals, one contractor says.

A top Pentagon official says that "the social contacts that existed" between contractors and the military "have simmered down." But "there's nothing in the law that says a contractor can't wine and dine a congressional committee staffer," he notes. "Some staffers probably haven't bought a lunch in the last decade."[75]

Whether reelection justifies the practice of pork barrel politics is, however, secondary. The primary question is whether it is in the best interests of the nation for Congress to attempt detailed management of the acquisition process, given the amount of political obligation carried by each House and Senate member. Clearly, a double standard exists. For instance, during the 1984 session, Congress successfully discredited the Defense Department on the issue of "graft and corruption" in the acquisition process, while at the same time some of its members advertised their power to influence the process, as did this senator from Pennsylvania in an open letter to contractors in his state:

Let me know if you are bidding on government contracts. I have been influential in gaining award of these contracts, but you must let me know if you want me to help.

Regardless of how much reform legislation Congress passes to isolate the Pentagon from undesirable influences threatening the integrity of its decision-making process, the quality of decisions will suffer if partisan politics remains unrestrained to defeat that integrity. Whereas political compromise and "favors" are useful tools for eliminating extremes in the authorization and appropriations processes, their use is questionable in managing the details of the acquisition process. How in the future do we want to select among competing weapon systems: by the number of jobs created in powerful members' districts or on the merits of the weapon systems themselves? The inevitable result of the propensity of Congress for increased involvement in issues better resolved by the Defense Department is "bad" micromanagement, according to Russell Murray II:

> While all micromanagement is objectionable in principle on grounds of poaching on the preserves of the executive branch, micromanagement is objectionable in practice only when it's *bad* micromanagement — "bad" in the sense that it would result in a worse outcome than if the Pentagon had been left to its own devices, however faulty they might be.[76]

The Future Role of Congress

The interest on Capitol Hill in micromanagement may have diminished when the final report of the Packard Commission, released in June 1986, characterized the recent reform activities of Congress as largely ineffective and counterproductive. In the foreword, Mr. Packard wrote:

> Congress must resist its inveterate tendency to legislate management practices and organizational details for DoD. Excellence in defense management will not come from legislative efforts to control and arrange the minutest aspects of DoD's operations. Congress can more usefully contribute by concentrating on larger, often neglected issues of overall defense posture and military performance.[77]

Although legislative reform efforts continued, the commission's official reprimand sent an implicit — yet powerful — message to Congress that continued or increased micromanagement would be met by growing criticism. Instead of serving as an instrument of constructive change, micromanagement had become one more problem plaguing the acquisition process.

Hoping to initiate debate on the subject and reduce the detail of congressional activity, the Packard Commission addressed the issue of the future role of Congress in the acquisition process.

> Biennial budgeting, authorization and appropriation of major programs not annually but only at key milestones, and a focus on strategy and operational concepts instead of line items are among the most important changes

that could be made to improve defense planning. They would enhance the congressional role in framing good national security policy.[78]

Each of the commission's recommendations advised Congress — in relative terms — to detach itself from the procurement process and shift its attention away from detail toward a broader, more beneficial purview. Given the heated political environment surrounding the defense budget and the complexity of defense issues, however, it has been extremely difficult for Congress to implement the commission's recommendations and voluntarily exercise the administrative discipline required to shift its focus and reduce its scrutiny of the procurement process. Historically, bureaucrats tend not to surrender any of their powers and privileges.

The issue of biennial budgeting illustrates how political reality inhibits implementation of an otherwise sound management practice. The Packard Commission summarized the many benefits that theoretically would accrue from a two-year defense budget cycle:

> . . . promote stability by providing additional time to do a better job — to think through military planning options, to evaluate results of current and prior-year execution of the defense budget, and to ensure that each phase of the cycle has the attention needed.
> . . . allow DOD to pay more attention to programming, the second phase of the Planning, Programming, and Budgeting System (PPBS), where individual defense programs are put together, refined, and compared to each other to respond to defense needs.
> . . . allow the Executive and Legislative Branches of government to spend one of the two years on a necessarily, but generally ignored, evaluation process.
> . . . help the Services to better manage their programs, and Congress to stick to its deadlines and schedules. Having spent a year reviewing ongoing activities, Congress should be able to begin earlier and move faster in the appropriation year.
> . . . stop the yearlong chaos of budget-making that we now have, or at a minimum, allow it to happen only every two years rather than annually. This would surely provide a greater degree of stability over a longer period of time.[79]

Convinced by the sheer logic of the arguments in favor of biennial budgeting, the Armed Services committees included the following section in the 1986 Department of Defense Authorization Act, a year before the commission's final report was released:

Sec. 1405. Two-year Budget Cycle for the Department of Defense

(a) Finding — The Congress finds that the programs and activities of the Department of Defense could be more effectively and efficiently planned and managed if funds for the Department were provided on a two-year cycle rather than annually.

(b) Requirement for Two-year Budget Proposal — The President shall include in the budget submitted to the Congress pursuant to section 1105 of title 31 United States Code, for fiscal year 1988 a single proposed budget for the Department of Defense and related agencies for fiscal years 1988 and 1989. Thereafter, the President shall submit a proposed two-year budget for the Department of Defense and related agencies every other year.[80]

Technical objections to biennial budgeting were few, and the Packard Commission easily dismissed the most popular.

> One of the major arguments against biennial budgeting is that it builds too much inflexibility into the system. National security objectives and priorities, however, ordinarily do not change appreciably from year to year, nor should military strategy or the military force structure change radically over a two-year period. In addition, the appropriate tools needed to make any changes required in the second year of budget execution are already in existence. Current reprogramming, supplemental appropriations, and budget amendment procedures are more than adequate to address the need. Reprogramming thresholds and transfer limitations within program categories should be reviewed by both Congress and DOD in a biennial budget context and additional flexibility should be provided if needed. Recisions and deferrals are also techniques that can be used when necessary.[81]

Valid technical objections, however, only partly affect the future of biennial budgeting. Objections based on political considerations matter most, and, unfortunately, these are powerful:

Elected to the House for only two-year terms, 435 representatives view the annual authorizations and appropriations process as their most powerful tool for controlling the Defense Department. Shifting to a two-year budget cycle would have the practical effect of cutting in half their influence and input.

Allowing biennial budgeting only for the Defense Department would penalize the other federal agencies, whose budgets each year would be exposed to the budget resolution and efforts to trim the federal deficit.

Because the defense budget represents approximately 65 percent of discretionary spending in the entire federal budget, congressmen advocating domestic programs would find it unacceptable that in half of the two-year period, defense spending would be untouchable. (Alternatively, defense advocates would have only half the opportunities to raise defense spending.)

Because many in Congress believe that the Defense Department today is unable to manage a $300 billion budget properly, Congress is unlikely to reward it with a two-year appropriation for more than $600 billion.

Privately, congressional staff members also claim that biennial budgeting will not lead to more constructive and selective oversight by Congress, simply because its members will remain as busy as ever with nondefense issues, which, by comparison, could suddenly appear to be more pressing than defense issues. They add that biennial budgeting will not help Congress meet its legislative schedules, for like most people, Congress can often procrastinate, making its most difficult decisions at the last possible moment.

Although the Packard Commission was encouraged by the action of the Armed Services committees in supporting biennial budgeting, it grudgingly acknowledged the overriding persuasion of the political objections:

> We are mindful, however, that for some years the President has, at congressional direction, provided requests for two-year defense authorizations, but only the first year of each of these requests has ever been acted upon.[82]

Political realities discussed throughout this chapter, like those obstructing the implementation of biennial budgeting, will impede the efforts of congressmen who agree with the Packard Commission that micromanagement must cease if the acquisition process is to improve. Reformers who attempt to redefine the role of Congress by redirecting its energies will have to deal directly with a mentality of some on Capitol Hill best characterized by the following comment of a staff member:

> Congress will stop micromanaging when the Defense Department stops mismanaging.

The dangers inherent in expecting a rapid improvement in congressional management of the acquisition process are probably best understood after considering this timeless passage, written in 1946 by then Under Secretary of State Dean Acheson:

> Then we turn to processes of government at both ends of Pennsylvania Avenue. The problem is the same; the manifestation different. Our machinery was devised for a government which was thought of as soldier, policeman, umpire. It is actually engaged in functions of management — and has to be. To do this Congress must lay down in many fields the general principles and rules which shall govern, leaving to others the administrative details.
>
> This takes all the time and study which all the five hundred-odd members can give. But no sooner is a general statute enacted than Congress becomes involved in the very administrative detail which it knows it cannot handle. A special investigating committee is set up to go into every last act of the administrative agency; or, if this is not done, the appropriation committees will spend weeks, and often months, attempting to direct administration through the qualifying or withholding of funds.
>
> And not content with the troubles which the Lord sends, the Congress adds to them by the practice of putting a time limit on legislation, so that it has to regurgitate and chew its cud annually or biannually. This is useful to an obstacle race, but not as an improvement in modern democratic method.[83]

Notes

1. *Congressional Directory,* 99th Congress, 1985–1986, Senate Print 99–39 (Washington, D.C.: Government Printing Office), pp. 271–383.
2. Ibid.
3. Ibid., pp. 275–276, 306–308.
4. Ibid., pp. 275, 306.
5. Ibid., pp. 387–418.
6. *Washington Post,* March 15, 1971.
7. Steven V. Roberts, "Billions for Defense: The Spending Debate," *New York Times,* May 17, 1985.
8. Ibid.
9. Ibid.
10. Evan Thomas and Bruce van Voorst, "Drums along the Potomac," *Time,* October 21, 1985, pp. 34–36.
11. U.S. Senate, hearing before the Task Force on Selected Defense Procurement Matters of the Committee on Armed Services, "Defense Procurement Process," September 20, 1984, Part 2, p. 155.

12. "MacNeil/Lehrer News Hour," January 12, 1987.
13. 10 U.S.C. 138 (a).
14. Department of Defense Appropriations Bill for 1987, Senate Report 99–446, September 17, 1986, p. 19.
15. Ibid., p. 4.
16. Ibid., pp. 2–3.
17. Ibid., p. 3.
18. U.S. General Accounting Office, "Budget Reprogramming, Department of Defense Process for Reprogramming Funds," GAO/NSIAD–86–164BR, July 1986, p. 1.
19. Ibid.
20. Ibid., p. 14.
21. U.S. House of Representatives, "Making Continuing Appropriations for Fiscal Year 1987," Report 99–1005, October 15, 1986, p. 108.
22. J. Ronald Fox, *Arming America: How the U.S. Buys Weapons* (Boston: Division of Research, Harvard Business School, Harvard University, 1974), p. 130.
23. Criteria established from *Arming America* and David D. Acker, "The Maturing of the DOD Acquisition Process," *Defense Systems Management Review*, Summer 1980, pp. 67–68.
24. Fox, *Arming America*, p. 126.
25. U.S. Senate, testimony of Charles W. Stewart, President of Machinery and Allied Products Institute, hearing before the Subcommittee on Defense Acquisition Policy of the Committee on Armed Services, "Implementation of the 1984 Defense Procurement Legislation," October 17 and 29, and November 7 and 13, 1985, p. 343.
26. U.S. Senate, testimony of Gen. Lawrence Skantze, USAF, Commander, AFSC, hearing before the Subcommittee on Defense Acquisition Policy of the Committee on Armed Services, "Implementation of the 1984 Defense Procurement Legislation," October 17 and 29, and November 7 and 13, 1985, p. 121.
27. Jacques S. Gansler, "Program Instability: Causes, Costs, and Cures," paper prepared for the Defense Acquisition Study, Center for Strategic and International Studies, Georgetown University, March 1, 1986, pp. 18–19.
28. Glenn Pascall, *The Trillion Dollar Budget* (Seattle: University of Washington Press, 1985), p. 145.
29. Gregory A. Forredal, "Military-Congressional Complex," *The Wall Street Journal*, August 8, 1985.
30. Edward N. Luttwak, *The Pentagon and the Art of War* (New York: Simon and Schuster, 1985), p. 130.
31. Gansler, "Program Instability," pp. 18–19.
32. U.S. Senate, hearing before the Committee on Armed Services, October 17 and 29, and November 7 and 13, 1985, pp. 121–123.
33. Office of the Assistant Secretary of Defense (Comptroller), "DOD Congressional Action on FY85 Appropriations Request," October 12, 1984.
34. U.S. Senate, hearing before the Committee on Armed Services, October 17 and 29, and November 7 and 13, 1985, pp. 121–123.
35. Ibid.
36. Ibid., p. 545.

37. Gordon Adams, with Paul Murphy and William Grey Rosenau, *Controlling Weapons Costs: Can the Pentagon Reforms Work?* (New York: Council on Economic Priorities, 1983), pp. 57–58.

38. Department of Defense Authorization Act for 1986, Senate Report 99–118, July 29, 1985, pp. 181, 187.

39. The term *over-oversight* is used by Glenn Pascall, *The Trillion Dollar Budget,* p. 145.

40. Colleen A. Preston, "Improving the Acquisition Process — The Role of Congress," paper prepared for the Defense Acquisition Study, Center for Strategic and International Studies, Georgetown University, 1986, p. 23.

41. Ibid., p. 24.

42. Ibid., p. 25.

43. Department of Defense Authorization Act for 1986, pp. 21–23, 27, 31.

44. "The New Power Elite in Defense," *Business Week,* March 27, 1978, pp. 90–92.

45. Theodore J. Crackel, "Pentagon Management Problems: Congress Shares the Blame," *Heritage Backgrounder,* January 22, 1985.

46. Tom Donnelly, "Weinberger, Mavroules Warn Defense Funding, Image Enhancement Are Linked," *Defense News,* November 3, 1986.

47. *Armed Forces Journal,* August 1985, p. 42.

48. Russell Murray II, "Congressional Actions to Improve the Defense Acquisition Process," paper, prepared for the Defense Acquisition Study, Center for Strategic and International Studies, Georgetown University, February 19, 1986, pp. 11–14.

49. This calculation assumes that in fiscal year 1985 nondiscretionary federal outlays totaled $571.9 billion, the sum of the following functional accounts: health ($33.5 billion); Medicare ($65.8 billion); income security ($128.2 billion); Social Security ($188.6 billion); VA benefits ($26.4 billion); and net interest ($129.4 billion). Discretionary spending totaled $407.2 billion, the sum of thirteen miscellaneous accounts, the largest of which was Defense ($252.8 billion). Office of Management and Budget, *Special Analyses of the Budget of the U.S. Government, Fiscal Year 1987* (Washington, D.C.: Government Printing Office, 1986), Special Analysis A, Table A-4, p. A-8.

50. *Government Executive,* March 1986, p. 20.

51. Leonard Sullivan, Jr., "Characterizing the Acquisition Process," paper prepared for the Defense Acquisition Study, Center for Strategic and International Studies, Georgetown University, January 1986, pp. G-1 to G-4.

52. Gary Hart, "The Case for Military Reform," *The Wall Street Journal,* January 23, 1981.

53. David C. Morrison, "Caucusing for Reform," *The Wall Street Journal,* June 28, 1986.

54. President's Blue Ribbon Commission on Defense Management, *A Quest for Excellence,* Final Report to the President, June 1986, p. 22.

55. Ibid.

56. "Shuttle Funding Sought from Pentagon Savings," *Washington Post,* September 11, 1986.

57. Steven V. Roberts, "Billions for Defense: The Spending Debate," *New York Times,* May 17, 1985.
58. Ibid.
59. President's Blue Ribbon Commission on Defense Management, *A Quest for Excellence,* June 1986, p. xviii.
60. Ibid.
61. *U.S. News & World Report,* June 26, 1978, p. 8.
62. Pascall, *The Trillion Dollar Budget,* p. 139.
63. Robert A. Little, "Pentagon Bogs Down in Its War on Waste," *U.S. News & World Report,* June 4, 1984, pp. 73–76.
64. Ibid.
65. John M. Barry, "Congress Wrestles the Pentagon on Procurement," *Dun's Business Month,* August 1985, pp. 38–41.
66. "Competition: A Pentagon Battlefield," *New York Times,* May 12, 1985.
67. Little, "Pentagon Bogs Down in Its War on Waste," pp. 73–76.
68. Ibid.
69. "Defense Spending Spurs the State Economy," *Boston Globe,* August 17, 1986.
70. Orr Kelly, "The B-1: When Pentagon, Politicians Joined Hands," *U.S. News & World Report,* July 11, 1983, pp. 34–35.
71. Pascall, *The Trillion Dollar Budget,* p. 104.
72. Kelly, "The B-1," pp. 34–35.
73. Ibid., pp. 34–35.
74. Pascall, *The Trillion Dollar Budget,* p. 139.
75. Kenneth H. Bacon, "The Congressional-Industrial Complex," *The Wall Street Journal,* February 14, 1978.
76. Murray, "Congressional Actions to Improve the Defense Acquisition Process," pp. 11–14.
77. President's Blue Ribbon Commission on Defense Management, *A Quest for Excellence,* June 1986, p. xiii.
78. Ibid., p. xviii.
79. Ibid., pp. 25–26.
80. Department of Defense Authorization Act for 1986, p. 168.
81. President's Blue Ribbon Commission on Defense Management, *A Quest for Excellence,* June 1986, pp. 25–26.
82. Ibid., p. 25.
83. Dean Acheson, Department of State Press Release No. 397, Address to the Graduates of Bryn Mawr College, Bryn Mawr, PA, June 11, 1946.

__3__

THE PENTAGON

There are no other jobs in the world quite like those needed to manage a 300 billion dollar-a-year philanthropy (no profit-and-loss statement, just war avoidance) that operates a three-trillion-dollar depreciating investment, with three million full-time employees — under the watchful eye of 550 inexperienced politicians with their thousands of enthusiastic staffers.

Leonard Sullivan, Jr., "Characterizing the Acquisition Process," paper prepared for the Defense Acquisition Study, Center for Strategic and International Studies, Georgetown University, January 1986, p. F-6.

The Department of Defense: Size and Organization

The Defense Department consists of two parts, the operating forces and the supporting establishment. Unified commands comprise components of two or more services. Specified commands usually comprise forces from one service, but they can include units and representatives from other services as well. The ten CINCs (commanders in chief) of the unified and specified commands have full operational charge of the forces assigned to them. They are responsible to the President and the Secretary of Defense for accomplishing their assigned military missions. For operational purposes, combat units of the military services are assigned to the unified and specified commands.

Unified Commands

European Command — Stuttgart-Vaihingen, Germany
Pacific Command — Honolulu, Hawaii
Atlantic Command — Norfolk, Virginia
Southern Command — Panama
Special Operations Command — MacDill AFB, Florida
Central Command — MacDill AFB, Florida
Space Command — Colorado Springs, Colorado

Specified Commands

Aerospace Defense Command — Colorado Springs, Colorado
Strategic Air Command — Omaha, Nebraska
Military Traffic Management Command — Scott AFB, Illinois

The military chain of command runs from the President to the Secretary of Defense and, through the Joint Chiefs of Staff (JCS), to the CINCs. Orders to the CINCs are issued by the President or the Secretary of Defense, or by the JCS on authority and direction of the Secretary of Defense.[1]

The military departments (Army, Navy, Marine Corps, and Air Force) are responsible for supporting the assigned forces, that is, for recruiting, training, R&D, procurement, supply, and maintenance. In the mid-1980s, Congress aggressively moved to clarify and emphasize this separation of mission by strengthening the CINCs and their operational commander, the chairman of the JCS.

The men and women at the highest levels of DOD management fall into three categories: (1) civilians nominated by the President and approved by the Senate; (2) senior career military officers (Army, Marine Corps, and Air Force generals and Navy admirals); and (3) senior career civil service personnel. They manage the activities of more than three million defense employees (see table 3.1).

More than 165,000 DOD employees, both civilian and military, manage the vast array of R&D, procurement, and logistics programs. Nearly all of these people, subject to oversight by the Office of the Secretary of Defense (OSD), work for the Army, Navy, Air Force, or Defense Logistics Agency (DLA). The executive office of the President, including the Office of Management and Budget (OMB), provides further oversight, particularly concerning the President's defense budget. The Congress (as noted in the preceding chapter) authorizes and appropriates funds for each of the more than twenty-seven hundred specified

TABLE 3.1. Department of Defense Personnel

Component	Military	Civilians	Total
OSD	513	1,380	1,893
Army	781,609	457,285	1,238,894
Navy	572,791	357,676	930,467
Air Force	608,036	270,242	878,278
Marine Corps	197,075	*	*
Defense Agencies	13,348	98,348	111,696
Total	2,173,372	1,184,931	3,161,228

*Marine Corps civilians are included with Navy civilians.
SOURCE: *Defense,* September-October 1986.

procurement and R&D line items and plays a major role in overseeing acquisition programs.[2]

This chapter examines the senior decision makers in the Pentagon: their roles; their motivations; and their responses to pressure, criticism, and conflict in the initiation, funding, development, and administration of defense acquisition programs. Subsequent chapters analyze the roles of government program managers, contracting officers, and government representatives at contractor plants.

To understand defense acquisition, managers must understand the environment in which defense acquisition decisions are made. New defense managers, at all levels, often need from six to twelve months or more to master the intricacies of department policy and protocol — for example, how information is channeled, altered, or restricted; how decisions are affected by conflicting and often changing military-civilian priorities; how DOD and defense contractors interact; how DOD is influenced by Congress and the press; which management techniques are officially sanctioned; how cost controls are applied or avoided; and how change can be effected. Some managers function comfortably within the system and introduce changes that improve the procurement process. Others never find their way through the maze of ritual, tradition, and paper.

The Secretary of Defense, a presidential civilian appointee, is the highest-ranking official in DOD. The Secretary's immediate staff consists of twenty-three people, nominated by the President and approved by the Senate:

one Deputy Secretary
two Under Secretaries
twelve Assistant Secretaries
General Counsel
Director, Program Analysis and Evaluation
Director, Defense Research and Engineering
Director, Operational Test and Evaluation
Director, Small and Disadvantaged Business Utilization
Advisor, U.S. Mission to NATO
Assistant to the Secretary (Intelligence Oversight)
Inspector General

These officials range from level I (cabinet secretary) to level V (advisers and assistants); compensation set by Congress in 1987 was level I, $86,200; level II, $75,000; level III, $73,600; level IV, $72,300; and level V, $68,700. The total number of staff members of OSD in 1987 was approximately two thousand.[3]

The President also appoints Secretaries of the Army, Navy, and Air Force, with statutory authority and responsibility for their services. Each service Secretary, who reports directly to the Secretary of Defense, has a chief assistant, called the Under Secretary of the Army, Navy, or Air Force, and two or three Assistant Secretaries. These civilian officials are all appointed by the President (with the advice of the Defense Secretary) and approved by the Senate. Each service Secretary has a staff of several hundred military and civilian personnel.[4]

Several DOD agencies also are involved in the acquisition process. For example, DLA is responsible for central purchasing of the thousands of smaller items the services use. DLA reports to the Assistant Secretary of Defense for Production and Logistics and is responsible also for the contract administration services performed by the Defense Contract Administration Service (DCAS), discussed in chapter 7.

Another DOD agency with an important role in the acquisition process is the Defense Contract Audit Agency (DCAA), responsible for auditing defense contracts. The Director of DCAA reports to the Assistant Secretary of Defense (Comptroller); however, it is the DOD Inspector General who sets audit policy.

Civilian control of the military has been an absolute and unquestioned principle throughout U.S. history. The June 12, 1776, Declaration of Rights of Virginia sets forth this principle: "In all cases the military should be under strict subordination to and governed by civil power." The Constitution incorporated this principle, giving both the President and the Congress power and responsibilities to ensure civilian supremacy. Despite the importance of the concept of civilian control, it remains ill defined in the late 1980s, as it has been for decades.

The policy of civilian control of all U.S. military activity is weakened by the brief tenure of most civilian appointees. The range is from a few months to seven years; the average, less than three years. Appointees come from a wide variety of backgrounds; among them have been lawyers, business executives, bankers, public accountants, engineers, and teachers. The basis for their selection varies. Some are thoroughly trained and experienced in the field they will oversee within DOD: procurement, personnel, R&D, or financial management. Some have had no relevant experience but have been loyal to the President's political party. The short-term focus of many defense officials (as well as the short-term focus of Congress) predisposes them to a quick-fix approach to problems — more warranties on contract performance, more fixed-price contracts, more incentive contracts, more reporting systems — rather than to the structural reforms needed for lasting improvements.

The Secretary of Defense and Secretaries of the Army, Navy, and Air Force select civilians and military officers to fill senior positions on their staffs. The White House staff (of the party in office) usually exerts considerable pressure to base civilian selections on political rather than professional credentials. In recent decades, according to most government and industry observers, the Defense Department has had fewer "political" Secretaries and Assistant Secretaries than other federal departments. At any one time in the 1960s and 1970s, perhaps ten or fewer of the thirty-five senior civilians within the Pentagon have been strictly political appointees. In the 1980s, however, difficulties in attracting qualified civilians to government service have resulted in a significant number of DOD appointees with little experience in the fields for which they are responsible. This problem was discussed in the 1985 Senate Armed Services Committee (SASC) staff report on defense organization:

> In many instances, the defense management credentials of senior OSD officials seem to have been given low priority in their selection by the Executive Branch. In many cases, political debts [often to members of Congress] were apparently the pivotal consideration.[5]

DISINCENTIVES FOR PROSPECTIVE CIVILIAN APPOINTEES

A major problem in recruiting qualified senior managers to serve in DOD is the federal regulation that requires senior defense appointees to divest themselves of all stocks, bonds, and interests in profit-sharing plans of any firm with defense contracts worth more than $25,000 per year. Although many private industry managers are well qualified for defense positions, most are either unwilling or unable to endure the fishbowl environment, subsequent employment regulations, and tax liabilities associated with the liquidation of their holdings or loss of stock options, or both. The purpose of the regulations (avoiding conflicts of interest) is entirely sound; the problem is that the financial and career penalties can be a powerful deterrent to some well-qualified candidates. Consequently, Assistant Secretary positions are sometimes vacant for several months. Russell Murray II, counsel for the House Armed Services Committee and former Assistant Defense Secretary, has cited a number of problems associated with restrictions on civilian appointees. For example, to many, accepting a senior government position means the loss of all of one's private-sector perquisites and often at least half of one's private-sector salary. By the same token, leaving a government position can often mean doubling of salary, a company automobile, a generous expense account, and other attractive forms of compensation. Compensation can be an especially important consideration for the most marketable professionals — those at the peaks of their careers, at a time when they face the mounting costs for their children's education or the care of elderly parents.[6]

Federal employees and retired military officers are subject to numerous restrictions on what they may or may not do once they have left government (see table 3.2). Officials still in government service are prohibited from dealing with matters in which they, or prospective private employers with whom they are negotiating, have a financial interest.

Similarly, Mr. Murray is concerned about the limiting effects of such legislation on a prospective employee's opportunities. For example, DOD must warn anyone it is trying to hire from the aircraft industry that on eventually leaving the govenment, employment with any aircraft manufacturer with whom he or she has dealt in an official capacity may not be allowed.[7]

Mr. Murray also notes that some members of Congress have persistently attacked any perquisites enjoyed by senior Pentagon employees (e.g., access to private dining rooms, government limousines or free parking, and large offices) as wasteful and undeserved luxuries. But such perquisites have been modest at best when compared with the fringe benefits widely provided in private industry. In view of the restrictions placed on senior government employees (mediocre pay; prohibitions against accepting gifts, meals, or even honoraria; public disclosure of all assets and sources of income, including those of one's immediate family; and restrictions on postgovernment employment), Congress should not only refrain from attacking reasonable perquisites but also consider whether it might be in the government's interest to encourage them as at least partial compensation for the more demanding aspects of DOD employment.[8]

Yet another difficulty for Pentagon appointees lies in dealing with a sensationalistic press. Richard Allen, former director of the National Security Council, has noted that competition among the Washington media for air time and space is so great that reporters often lose sight of the facts they are reporting. The media's willingness to publish leaks and the views of "anonymous" sources leads to reports that are grossly unfair to the subjects of the leaks and serve only the questionable goals of the person supplying the information to the media.

The Washington press has a tendency to place allegations directed at highly placed people on the front page. The standards they apply to officials are so rigorous that even a hint of behavior that appears not in accordance with those standards can lead to sensationalistic charges. When it becomes clear that the charges were incorrect or exaggerated, the item pertaining to the error or exaggeration — if it appears at all — is usually buried in an obscure corner, far removed from the front page.

Gerald Rafshoon, communications adviser to former President Carter, commented:

> Today, the emphasis is on what will dazzle and shock. There is a need to rebuild the sense of responsibility on the part of the press.
>
> Whatever the shortcomings of the capital's news media, public officials soon learn that there is no alternative to learning to live with an institution whose power was described this way by author Douglass Cater in his book *The Fourth Branch of Government:* "The press decides which of those words and events [that occur in Washington daily] shall receive the prompt attention of millions and which, like timber falling in a deep and uninhabited forest, shall crash silently to the ground."[9]

TABLE 3.2. The Revolving Door: Current Postemployment Disqualifications and Certain Related Provisions

Statute	Provisions
18 U.S.C. 207(a)	Permanently bans representation to the government of any person on any "particular matter involving a specific party" in which a former executive branch employee "participated personally and substantially" while in government.*
18 U.S.C. 207(b)(i)	Bans for two years representation to the government of any person on any particular matter over which a former executive branch employee exercised "official responsibility" while in government.*
18 U.S.C. 207(b)(ii)	Bans for two years representation by a former "senior employee" of the executive branch, through his "personal presence at any formal or informal appearance" before the government, of any person on any particular matter in which such former employee personally and substantially participated while in government.*
18 U.S.C. 207(c)	Bans for one year representation by a former "senior employee" of the executive branch of any person to his former agency on any particular matter before or of substantial interest to that agency.*
18 U.S.C. 208	Prohibits an employee of the executive branch from participating "personally and substantially" as such in any "particular matter" in which any person with whom he is "negotiating" or has any "arrangement" concerning postgovernment employment has a financial interest.*
18 U.S.C. 281	Prohibits retired military officers from representing any person in the sale of anything to the government through their former department.*
18 U.S.C. 283	Bans for two years following retirement participation by military officers in prosecution of claims against the United States involving their former department.*
18 U.S.C. 801	Prohibits payment of compensation to military officers engaged, within three years after retirement, "in selling, or contracting or negotiating to sell, supplies or war materials" to DOD or other agencies.
18 U.S.C. 2397	Requires reporting by certain military personnel and civilian officials of DOD of employment by defense contractors occurring within two years prior or subsequent to government service.**

TABLE 3.2.   (Continued)

Statute	Provisions
18 U.S.C. 2397a	Requires reporting by military personnel and civilian officials having procurement responsibilities in DOD of "contacts" regarding postgovernment employment opportunities with certain defense contractors.**
18 U.S.C. 2397b, Section 931	Prohibits, for two years, compensation from a defense contractor with whom a DOD employee performed a procurement function with that contractor for more than a majority of the preceding two years, or was the primary representative of DOD in the negotiation of a contract in excess of $10,000,000 with that contractor.**

*Violation punishable by fine or imprisonment, or both.
**Violation subject to administrative penalty up to $10,000.
SOURCE: President's Blue Ribbon Commission on Defense Management, *A Quest for Excellence,* Final Report to the President, June 1986, p. 98.

In short, industry managers see financial restrictions, the need to sever relationships with industry, and the Washington environment as significant barriers to government service. Roy Anderson, then chief executive officer of Lockheed Corporation, stated in a Senate hearing in January 1985:

> The current regulations significantly restrict the number of available candidates to choose from for key positions. The greatest impediment in recruiting from business and industry is the current prohibition against a leave of absence. A person must quit to enter government service, which means forfeiture of retirement and other benefits for a position which is most frequently temporary in tenure.
>
> Divestiture requirements positively inhibit recruiting. In addition, several other factors make entry into Government service unattractive to industry personnel, such as: no provision for relocating the candidate and family; possible restrictions on the employee after leaving government service; and the depressed salary level of key positions as compared to similar levels of responsibility outside government.[10]

Thomas G. Pownall, the chief executive officer of Martin Marietta Corporation, presented testimony on the same problems:

> Industry can and does attract many talented retired military and civilian personnel who are able to make significant contributions without en-

croachment upon conflict rules and regulations. On the other hand, I do detect considerable difficulty in attracting industry personnel into key government appointed positions because of postgovernment employment restrictions. I earnestly believe there is little or no abuse and that current rules are harmful to the overall best interests of good management in government. Further restrictions may serve to deprive us all of the valuable service these people can contribute.[11]

These statements highlight how restrictions and inconveniences impede DOD recruiting of highly skilled, experienced managers, thereby hindering attainment of a high level of businesslike performance in DOD, a level that could and should match the best of U.S. industry.

SENIOR MILITARY POSITIONS IN THE PENTAGON

In addition to the civilian Under Secretary and Assistant Secretaries, the military chiefs of staff report to the civilian Secretary of each service. The President appoints each chief of staff, who becomes the senior military officer in his service and senior military adviser, to the President and the Secretary of Defense, for that service. The President also appoints (with the approval of the Senate) a chairman of the Joint Chiefs of Staff from one of the services. Individual chiefs of staff report through the chairman of the JCS to the Secretary of Defense as well as directly to the Secretaries of their respective services. The office of the JCS employs approximately two thousand military and civilian personnel and is responsible for directing the operations of combat forces.

Civilian appointees in the service secretariats have their counterparts in the service military staffs. As described by the Senate Armed Services Committee staff:

> These military officers are involved in both the process that generates requirements and in monitoring acquisition activities for the Service Chiefs. In the Navy, the Deputy Chiefs of Naval Operations are primarily formulators of requirements. In the Army and Air Force, the formulation of military requirements is conducted primarily by commands in the field but ultimately is reviewed and coordinated for the Service Chief by the appropriate Deputy Chiefs of Staff. All of these offices are responsible for monitoring the activities of the buying commands on behalf of the Service Chiefs.[12]

Each military chief of staff is served by several thousand military and civilian personnel. A military officer working for a Chief of Staff also serves the Secretary of his service. Although the Defense Secretary is the senior official within the Pentagon, officers receive their military promotions based on evaluations by their military superiors, including their chief of staff. This fact is especially significant whenever the goals of the Secretary or Assistant Secretaries of a service and the chief of staff differ.

The total number of flag officers (generals and admirals) serving in the U.S. military throughout the world is more than a thousand (Army 398, Navy 252, Marine Corps 65, and Air Force 338).[13] Military assignments, including those on the Pentagon staff, normally rotate every three years or less, which is, coincidentally, about the average term of office for senior civilian appointees. There is at least one significant difference between civilian and military staffs, however. When military officers leave the Pentagon, they remain in the service. Secretaries and Assistant Secretaries return to positions outside the federal government. The long-term commitment of career military officers is to their service and to military values. Civilian appointees assume authority for relatively short periods of time, among conflicting service rivalries and military-civilian priorities. Although military officers can rotate after two or three years, the "military point of view" remains relatively stable, whereas political administrations change and civilian appointees come and go, often creating an inconsistent civilian approach.

At times there is conflict between civilian and military loyalties. An extreme example was given by a colonel who had been assigned to the staff of an Assistant Secretary to develop a military personnel information system. With this system, the Assistant Secretary felt he would be able to take a more active role in the assignment of career officers within his area. Just before beginning his new assignment, the colonel's military superior informed him, "the Chief of Staff does not want to see this information system developed," and instructed him to work so slowly that the Assistant Secretary would not achieve his objective. He also reminded him that his future depended on his military superiors, not the civilian secretariat. At the end of a year and a half, the Assistant Secretary left the Pentagon to return to industry. The project was then placed directly under the control of the deputy chief of staff and was completed without providing information that could affect assignments and promotions.

Another group of career officials with vested interests that sometimes conflict with those of presidential appointees are the senior civil servants. They hold ranks of senior executive service (SES-1, SES-2, SES-3, and SES-4), comparable to the ranks of military generals and admirals. They work throughout DOD, in OSD and in the offices of the service Secretaries, the Assistant Secretaries, and the military chiefs of staff. Unlike the military officers or civilian appointees, they often remain at their jobs for ten to fifteen years, or longer, and are therefore an important source of continuity within the Defense Department. There are currently six SES salary rates, set by the President at the same time that annual comparability increases are authorized for the general pay schedule. In 1986, the rates for these levels were ES-1, $61,296; ES-2, $63,764; ES-3, $66,232; ES-4, $68,700; ES-5, $70,500; ES-6, $72,300.[14]

It would be inappropriate and untrue to leave the topic of civilian-military conflict with the implication that conflict is the normal mode of behavior. Some service Secretaries earn the respect of both their military and civil service counterparts and subordinates. Many military officers and civil servants are loyal to the agendas of their appointed civilian superiors. But there is sometimes suspicion and guarded interaction between the staffs of the chief of staff and the appointed civilian secretariat. When senior military officers perceive their civilian superiors as unprepared for their jobs or deficient in defending a major system supported by a military chief of staff (e.g., a manned bomber or aircraft carrier), the civilian is likely to find it difficult to obtain information.

INTERSERVICE RIVALRY

James Forrestal, the first Secretary of Defense, once commented: "The peacetime mission of the Armed Services is to destroy the Secretary of Defense." If a Defense Secretary is to succeed at his job, he must gain and maintain the support of the military services; yet he has limited power to hire, fire, or promote members of the military services.[15] Richard Stubbing, a defense expert and former OMB official, stated:

> The consequence is that the first loyalty of officers is to their service, not to the Secretary. Thus, the Secretary of Defense faces a difficult task in attempting to lead defense in new directions with a team of subordinates over whom he has little direct control. Finally, the long-established and close working relations between the military and the Congress suggest an "end run" approach.[16]

The problem is not a new one for the Defense Department. In 1956, President Dwight Eisenhower described in a letter to Everett E. Hazlett his problem in dealing with the department.

So far as I am personally concerned, I should say that my most frustrating domestic problem is that of attempting to achieve any real coordination among the Services. Time and again I have had the high Defense officials in conference — with all the senior military and their civilian bosses present — and have achieved what has seemed to me general agreement on policy and function — but there always comes the breakdown. The kindest interpretation that can be put on some of these developments is that each service is so utterly confident that it alone can assure the nation's security that it feels justified in going before the Congress or the public and urging fantastic programs. Sometimes it is by no means the heads of the Services that start these things. Some subordinate gets to going, and then a demagogue gets into the act and the Chief of the Service finds it rather difficult to say, "No, we could not profitably use another billion dollars."[17]

Hence, a technique for dealing with unwanted change becomes a device for maintaining the appearance of agreement while avoiding any action that might bring about the change in question. A fundamental constraint for the Defense Secretary is that he can order a change but he has little power to mandate performance or interservice cooperation. The Defense Department, like all large bureaucracies, has more management by negotiation than many critics appreciate. Making choices among rival service systems is very difficult for the Defense Secretary, and consolidating the various military programs represents a major challenge.

As former Assistant Secretary of Defense Alain Enthoven explained in the early 1970s:

> The Secretary has the legal power to curtail, transfer, or abolish programs, but these options have been used sparingly. The Secretary may want a consensus at top military levels before revising important military programs. The Secretary can "ramrod" an occasional order, but if it is unpalatable to the bureaucracy, it may be diluted at lower levels, or "outwaited" and reversed when the Secretary's term is up.

> Secretary McNamara, who closely supervised the F-111 aircraft joint program from the start of his term, contended with considerable opposition and deep conflict in biservice requirements all through weapon development. One month after he left office, the decision was made to cancel the Navy version. The Air Force continued to develop the F-111, and the Navy went on to develop the F-14.

> The F-111 program failure has haunted joint programming and people's opinions of joint programs ever since. It showed that a Secretary of

Defense, however "strong," cannot always get the services to do what they strongly oppose.[18]

In the Pentagon, as in most other organizations, formal authority is often insufficient to accomplish a challenging goal. Unless a Secretary of Defense can convince the services of the desirability of his objectives, the informal network, if not the formal one, will limit his success.

Responsibilities for Defense Acquisition

An analysis of the defense acquisition process must consider the various layers of management affecting the process. These include, in ascending order, the program manager and the contracting officer, the commander of the buying command division, the systems command headquarters, the military service headquarters staff, the service secretariat, OSD, OMB, and Congress. Each layer within DOD has its staff and its advocates for engineering, manufacturing, producibility, maintainability, streamlining specifications, competition, reliability, small-business interests, minority business interests, and several other topics. In addition, the Defense Contract Audit Agency (DCAA), the Inspector Generals of the services and OSD, and advisory groups oversee the operations of a program manager. The structure demonstrates that bureaucracies thrive on shared responsibilities, not on individual autonomy and responsibility.[19]

At the highest level of the Pentagon, the Under Secretary of Defense for Acquisition, a new position created in 1986, serves as the principal assistant for acquisition management to the Secretary of Defense and the Deputy Secretary (see chart 3.1). He supervises all acquisition matters, including research and development; production; logistics; command, control, communications, and intelligence activities (concerning acquisition); and procurement. Reporting to this Under Secretary are:

Director of Defense Research and Engineering
Assistant Secretary of Defense for Research and Technology
Assistant Secretary of Defense for Production and Logistics
Assistant Secretary of Defense for Command, Control, Communications, and Intelligence
Assistant to the Secretary of Defense for Atomic Energy
Director of Small and Disadvantaged Business Utilization

CHART 3.1. Office of the Secretary of Defense

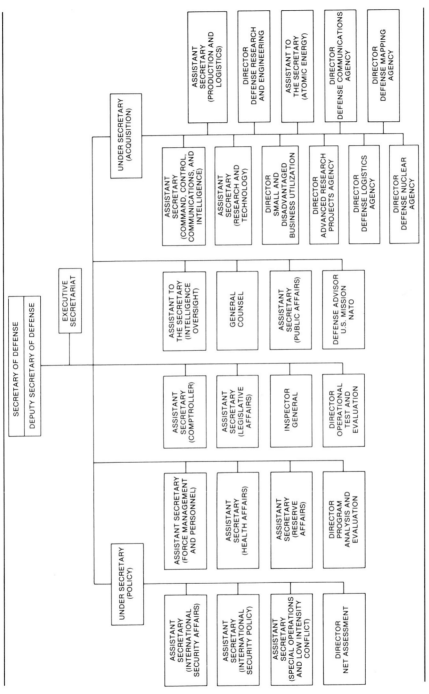

SOURCE: *Defense Almanac*, September/October 1987, Department of Defense.

Also reporting to this Under Secretary are the Defense Advanced Research Projects Agency, Defense Communications Agency, Defense Logistics Agency, Defense Mapping Agency, and the Defense Nuclear Agency.

The Director of Operational Test and Evaluation reports directly to the Secretary and Deputy Secretary of Defense, separated by statute from the Under Secretary to achieve greater objectivity.

For the first time in DOD history, almost all facets of acquisition, from acceptance of the military requirements through delivery of the product and its field support, are centered in one person whose primary function is acquisition. Previously, the focal point was the Deputy Secretary of Defense, whose other duties included the overall management of DOD. The new Under Secretary makes recommendations to the Secretary and Deputy Secretary on matters pertaining to acquisition programs, including the allocation of resources to them.[20]

The legislation creating the new Under Secretary position defined the term *acquisition* in two ways: First, it includes "procurement, research and development, logistics [supply and maintenance], developmental testing, and contract administration," and, second, it includes "contracting, logistics, quality control, program management, systems engineering, production, and manufacturing."[21] This definition broadened considerably the meaning of *acquisition,* which had previously been limited to the management of research and development, procurement, contracting, and contract administration.

The Director of Defense Research and Engineering serves as the chief scientific technical adviser on military requirements. The director's office is staffed for, and charged with, settling conflicts on technical and operating requirements that the services cannot resolve independently. Multiservice agreement on OSD-directed changes, however, is difficult to achieve if one service or another perceives a threat to its mission "ownership." The office also is generally responsible for minimizing duplication in weapon systems, supporting standardization, and furthering joint programs.[22]

The office of the Assistant Secretary of Defense for Production and Logistics was created for two reasons. First, it combines the acquisition elements of logistics (such as spare parts procurement) with the acquisition of major weapon systems. Second, it permits a senior defense official to focus on all acquisition program and policy questions, without being unduly diverted by the development of military requirements and their accompanying scientific and technical issues.

Reporting to this Assistant Secretary are five Deputy Assistant Secretaries for Procurement, Production Support, Spare Parts, Logistics, and Installations.

In 1987, the Under Secretary of Defense for Acquisition began to establish a uniform acquisition management process in the military services. The first step was creating the position of acquisition executive (AE) within each service. The AEs oversee one or more program executive officers (PEOs), who in turn oversee a cluster of program managers (see chapter 4). The AEs report both to the service Secretary and the Under Secretary.

As former Assistant Secretary of Defense Leonard Sullivan points out, the structure is even more complicated than it appears. None of the OSD positions described above has exclusive line management responsibility for acquisition, maintenance, and support of weapon systems. The military departments have this responsibility. Thus, for example, the commander of the Air Force buying organization — the Air Force Systems Command — reports to the Air Force chief of staff, who in turn reports to the Secretary of the Air Force.[23]

Within the military services, the major responsibility for acquisition, maintenance, and support of weapons lies with the materiel commands. These are the five systems commands of the Navy (see chart 3.2), the Army Materiel Command (see chart 3.3), and the Air Force Systems Command and the Logistics Command (see chart 3.4).

NAVY ACQUISITION ORGANIZATION

The Secretary of the Navy serves as the Navy acquisition executive. The commanders of the Navy systems commands are the Navy PEOs. The Navy systems commands were assembled under the Naval Material Command until 1985, when it was abolished.* The five systems commands (Naval Sea Systems Command [NAVSEA], Naval Air Systems Command [NAVAIR], Space and Naval Warfare Systems Command [SPAWAR], Naval Facilities Engineering Command [NAVFAC], and Naval Supply Systems Command [NAVSUP]), all located in the Washington, D.C., area, were then directed to report to the Chief of Naval Operations.[24] Most functions of the previous Naval Material Command

---

*By tradition, the Navy uses the English spelling (material) but retains the French pronunciation used by the Army and Air Force for materiel.

CHART 3.2.   Chain of Command for Navy Acquisitions

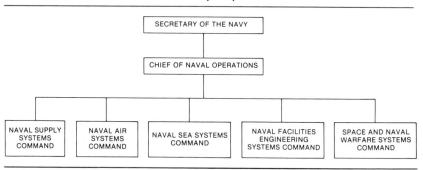

SOURCE: Office of the Assistant Secretary of Defense (Comptroller).

headquarters were transferred to the five systems commands, and the three-star commanders of NAVSEA, NAVAIR, SPAWAR, NAVFAC, and NAVSUP were designated program executive officers. The buying commands manage their major programs through program managers, who, in theory, report directly to the three-star commanders. In reality, the program managers have an intermediate supervisor, usually a two-star admiral, below the level of the three-star commander.[25]

CHART 3.3.   Chain of Command for Air Force Acquisitions

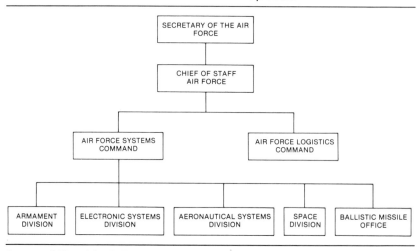

SOURCE: Office of the Assistant Secretary of Defense (Comptroller).

AIR FORCE ACQUISITION ORGANIZATION

The Under Secretary of the Air Force serves as the Air Force acquisition executive. In acquisition matters he is assisted by the Assistant Secretary for Acquisition (formerly the Assistant Secretary for Research, Development, and Logistics, combining the R&D offices in the headquarters military staff with the Air Force secretariat). The Air Force Systems Command with headquarters at Andrews Air Force Base, Maryland, includes five divisions: the Armament Division at Eglin Air Force Base, Florida; the Ballistic Missile Office at Norton Air Force Base, California; the Electronic Systems Division at Hanscom Air Force Base, Massachusetts; the Aeronautical Systems Division at Wright Patterson Air Force Base, Ohio; and the Space Division at the Los Angeles Air Force Station, California. It also includes laboratories and miscellaneous agencies. The commander of the Air Force Systems Command serves as a PEO, as do the five product division commanders and other senior general officers, each reporting to the Air Force chief of staff and to the Under Secretary of the Air Force and the Under Secretary of Defense for Acquisition.[26] Each Air Force program manager reports to a PEO.

The fact that PEOs report to the AE may suggest that the Air Force Systems Command headquarters is removed from the decision-making process. But the command continues to wield considerable power through its control over the allocation of funds and personnel to the various weapons-buying commands and its continuing responsibility for administering acquisition and contracting policies and operating its test ranges.[27]

The Air Force and Navy have responded to the new Under Secretary of Defense for Acquisition by stating that they comply with the new organization structure, albeit with virtually the same structure they had been using in the past.

ARMY ACQUISITION ORGANIZATION

The Army has taken a different approach. The Under Secretary of the Army is the acquisition executive. Army PEOs are usually brigadier generals, each of whom reports to a major general commanding one of the divisions of the Army Materiel Command, as well as to the AE.

The Army Materiel Command, with headquarters in Arlington, Virginia, includes six primary buying divisions: the Aviation Systems Command (AVSCOM) at St. Louis, Missouri; the Tank-Automotive

CHART 3.4. Chain of Command for Army Acquisitions

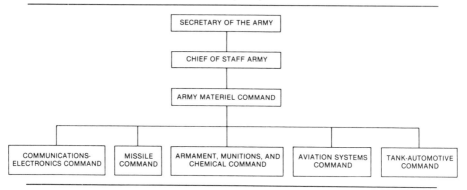

SOURCE: Office of the Assistant Secretary of Defense (Comptroller).

Command (TACOM) at Warren, Michigan; the Missile Command (MICOM) at Huntsville, Alabama; the Communications-Electronics Command (CECOM) at Fort Monmouth, New Jersey; the Armament, Munitions, and Chemical Command (ARMCOM) at Rock Island, Illinois; and the Laboratory Command (LABCOM) at Adelphi, Maryland. It also includes laboratories and miscellaneous agencies. Army program managers report directly to a PEO. Both are attached to commodity commands because they continue to rely on the commands for functional support through the matrix management concept.

At the Army headquarters in the Pentagon, the Office of the Deputy Chief of Staff for Research, Development, and Acquisition has been combined with the Office of the Assistant Secretary for Research, Development, and Acquisition to consolidate the Army acquisition hierarchy.

DIFFUSE RESPONSIBILITIES

Throughout the 1970s and 1980s, many people, inside and outside government, have been critical of the diffuse responsibilities for the acquisition process. Former Assistant Defense Secretary Leonard Sullivan summarized these views:

> In the long run, there is no substitute for having a professional leader in full charge. DOD has never gone beyond naming the most "convenient" appointee as "Acquisition Executive" (AE) and expecting him to carry that burden and an extra duty and without a professional staff. The result has been that the "Developer" has generally: doubled as the "Buyer"; bought near the leading edge of technology; paid lip-service at best to affordability; and ignored the downstream consequences of his actions.[28]

Regarding management style, Secretary Weinberger announced soon after his appointment his intention to grant the services a relatively free hand in setting military priorities and making program decisions. Echoing the views of many in the military services, Secretary Weinberger argued that civilians — in OSD, OMB, and Congress — had been meddling far too much in military decisions and undermining the defense program through excessively detailed management. Defense expert and former OMB official Richard Stubbing states that Secretary Weinberger attempted to solve this problem by focusing his attention outside the Pentagon:

> Weinberger's only serious managerial initiatives have been directed outside the Pentagon, toward defense contractors who produce defective or overpriced goods. Spare-parts purchases, in particular, have received attention following a series of "horror stories" since 1983 showing routine items bought at astronomical prices. Late in 1983 Weinberger announced reforms for buying spare parts. He and his staff have also been more willing at times to challenge defense contractors that perform poorly or overcharge the government on major weapon contracts. Several large firms — including General Dynamics, Raytheon, Hughes, General Electric, Texas Instruments, McDonnell Douglas, Electric Boat, Rockwell, and Avco — have been publicly taken to task since 1980, some having their contracts temporarily suspended for poor workmanship or overcharging and others being threatened with new rounds of competition (though each contractor has retained its sole-source status).[29]

THE DEFENSE ACQUISITION BOARD (DAB) AND THE DEFENSE SCIENCE BOARD (DSB)

The Under Secretary of Defense for Acquisition is supported by two major boards: the Defense Science Board (DSB) and the Defense Acquisition Board (DAB). The primary function of the DSB is to canvass the needs and opportunities for radically new weapon systems prompted by new scientific knowledge. The DAB, created in 1987 with a structure similar to the former Defense Systems Acquisition Review Council (DSARC) it replaced, has a much larger mission. It provides advice and information to the Under Secretary of Defense for Acquisition at Milestones 0 (begin concept exploration), I (begin concept demonstration/ validation), II (full-scale development), and III (full-scale production) and any special reviews of defense programs. The DAB has responsibility for

defining and validating new system requirements,
cost/performance trade-offs,
alternatives to new R&D starts, and
full-scale development and high-rate production recommendations in
  joint and major programs.

In addition, the DAB provides a forum for addressing issues such as broader acquisition improvement concerns, early commitment to programs, and increased program stability. Although DAB membership changes from time to time, in late 1987 there were ten permanent DAB members:

Under Secretary of Defense for Acquisition (Chair)
Vice-Chairman, Joint Chiefs of Staff (Vice Chair)
Service Acquisition Executive, Army
Service Acquisition Executive, Navy
Service Acquisition Executive, Air Force
Assistant Secretary of Defense (Comptroller)
Assistant Secretary of Defense (Production and Logistics)
Assistant Secretary of Defense (Program Operations)
Director of Defense Research and Engineering
Director of Program Analysis and Evaluation

Participating, as appropriate, in DAB reviews are the Deputy Under Secretaries of Defense (for Strategic and Theater Nuclear Forces and for Tactical Warfare Programs); Assistant Secretaries of Defense (for Command, Control, Communications, and Intelligence and for Atomic Energy); Director of Operational Test and Evaluation; Deputy Assistant Secretary of Defense for Procurement; Director, Defense Intelligence Agency; Director, Weapons Support Improvement Group; and Chairman, Cost Analysis Improvement Group.

The Goldwater-Nichols Defense Reorganization Act of 1986 provided the combat commands' CINCs (i.e., the unified and specified commands) with the opportunity to influence acquisition plans to ensure support for strategies and tactics. Before 1986, the Joint Chiefs of Staff had sought similar influence but were not successful, for a number of reasons, including staffing limitations and the absence of a clear mission assignment. The Joint Chiefs are now part of the acquisition process through representation on the Defense Acquisition Board. The

Under Secretary of Defense for Acquisition is Chairman and the Vice-Chairman of JCS is Vice-Chairman of the Board.[30]

The Under Secretary may request ad hoc advisers, such as the Deputies for International Programs and Technology and for Research and Advanced Technology, to participate in DAB reviews that entail issues requiring their expertise.

The Under Secretary convenes formal DAB meetings to facilitate the decision-making process. As long as a program is managed within the schedule, cost, and technical performance thresholds established at Milestone II, further DAB review is often not required. If thresholds are crossed, the Director of Defense Research and Technology and the Assistant Secretary of Defense for Production and Logistics are notified, and they decide whether or not a less formal program review or another DAB review will be required.[31]

ACQUISITION RESPONSIBILITY AT THE SERVICE SECRETARIATS

Throughout the 1960s and the early 1970s, the Army, Navy, and Air Force each had four Assistant Secretaries, who shared responsibility for the acquisition process: Research and Development (R&D), Installations and Logistics (I&L), Financial Management (FM), and Manpower and Reserve Affairs (M&RA). In 1977, at the beginning of Defense Secretary Harold Brown's administration, OSD told each military service that it had to eliminate one Assistant Secretary position. The Air Force combined R&D and I&L, and the Army and Navy combined FM and I&L, resulting in a markedly decreased emphasis on procurement. Moreover, most R&D Assistant Secretaries were not familiar with procurement. In the words of one senior defense official:

> The organizational changes in OSD have been a disaster for procurement. They have been chained to R&D. Their interest is not in procurement. R&D is the tail that wags the dog.

In 1987, the secretariat of each military department included one or more Assistant Secretaries to provide oversight of that department's acquisition activities. The Army had an Assistant Secretary for Research, Development, and Acquisition, one for Installations and Logistics, and one for Financial Management; the Navy had one for Shipbuilding and

Logistics and one for Research, Engineering, and Systems; the Air Force had one for Acquisition. Each of these officials, with a staff, shared responsibility with the service Secretary for acquisition matters.

Each Assistant Secretary in the military services reports to his OSD counterpart as well as to his own service Secretary, who is his immediate superior. Because both of his superiors report to, and are directed by, the Secretary of Defense, an Assistant Secretary may seek the support of his service Secretary when conflicts arise with his OSD counterpart, or vice versa.

The Assistant Secretaries in the services and in OSD share responsibility for oversight of government and contractor cost control, which means that one or more Assistant Secretaries oversee direct cost-control activities for acquisition programs and work with the buying organizations and defense contractors; or no one Assistant Secretary takes responsibility, each assuming that one of the others has done the necessary work. Both the military service and the OSD Assistant Secretaries frequently make public statements about the need for cost accountability in defense programs. Most of them, however, are reluctant to insist on cost-control procedures comparable to those used in private industrial management. There are at least four reasons for their ambivalence.

First, most Assistant Secretaries want to acquire the weapons and equipment needed, on schedule and for the lowest reasonable cost. At the same time, each is directed to build or maintain an industrial base that will meet tomorrow's uncertain defense needs. Restraining or lowering contractor costs means reducing (or restraining the increase in) the number of employees in a contractor's plant. Such an action supports the first objective but endangers the second. Indeed, during periods of declining defense spending, contractors frequently visit congressional and Pentagon offices to plead for additional business, each claiming that their plant capability is vital to national defense needs. Some military officers support this contention, as do senators and congressmen within whose districts employment is affected. The problem is that in periods of budget austerity, the military services compete with each other and with all other demands for federal funds.

Second, an Assistant Secretary considers himself the chief spokesman for the programs of his service within his own areas of responsibility. A military service expects an Assistant Secretary to champion its programs before Congress and to obtain as much financial support as possible. If he frequently fails to obtain the level of funding requested, he will lose the support of senior military officers and may then find it almost impossible to gain access to important information. (Within the Pentagon, the withholding of information is one of the most effective weapons in any person's arsenal.)

Even the Secretary of Defense may subscribe to the view that civilian appointees are spokesmen for the military. Lawrence Korb, while a faculty member at the U.S. Coast Guard Academy, conducted an extensive study of the Secretary's role and his relationship to the military staff. In an article in the *Naval War College Review,* Mr. Korb reported:

> Secretary Laird also sees himself as the Department of Defense advocate before the Congress and the public. His public statements do not emphasize the waste and inefficiency in the Pentagon. Rather, Laird points out that present defense spending is at "rockbottom." . . . The Chiefs see the Secretary as the "defender of Defense." They expect him to protect their services from the onslaughts of those who want to reduce defense spending drastically.[32]

Third, an Assistant Secretary has such a large area of responsibility that concentrating on other important tasks while neglecting the unpopular though equally important job of controlling costs can be readily justified. (One Assistant Secretary commented that his job was not to improve efficiency but to keep his service out of trouble.)

Fourth, an Assistant Secretary with little experience in industrial practices and business management usually does not know how to begin to control acquisition program costs.

THE DEVELOPER

In research and development, senior officials have somewhat different responsibilities and priorities from those of their counterparts in procurement and financial areas of defense management. R&D officials advocate new technology, initiate new development programs, and petition OSD and Congress for program funds. Most of them have excellent technical backgrounds, but few have significant training in business management. Nevertheless, in addition to their other duties, they are responsible for the efficient management of their programs as performed by industry. In reality, however, cost-versus-effectiveness analyses and periodic cost-performance correlations are far less important to them than the advancement of weapons technology. Periodic status reports prepared by contractors and government laboratories for senior officials seldom contain much information on cost and performance. According to one official, cost-performance measurement problems are seldom considered during program evaluation sessions; virtually all discussion centers around the challenging technical problems. Whether the level of direct or indirect costs is appropriate or excessive is simply not a consideration until the program is threatened by higher government or congressional officials who may oppose additional funds to cover cost growth.

Leonard Sullivan described this problem, in January 1986, in comments to the Georgetown University Defense Acquisition Study Group.

> To this day, DDR&E is populated with technicians who have virtually no experience with production problems, no knowledge of cost drivers, and no interest in the downstream training and logistic support problems flowing from their developments.
>
> This entire generation of [DOD's] defense industry technologists has been virtually immune from considerations of both acquisition and operational costs — and routine production line problems, for that matter. It is a particularly interesting phenomenon because it did not appear to infect their commercial counterparts who successfully improved automobiles, televisions, washing machines, private and commercial aviation, and now calculators, computers, and other stunning market-sensitive technologies.
>
> Nevertheless, there are few, if any, corporate laboratory directors who are also the corporate buyers, or the last word on capital investment planning. It is equally inappropriate to assume that a scientific background and laboratory experience is sufficient to produce a competent acquisition executive.
>
> The developer often has a somewhat exaggerated idea of what is fully within the technological state of the art. He is likely to overstate "requirements" in an effort to present himself with an interesting challenge. . . . He tends to believe that if it can be made, it should be. He can inevitably develop elaborate "requirements" for any new idea he has conjured up.
>
> He is also likely to believe that his product is fully ready for production well before all the operational "bugs" have surfaced and been eliminated. These are considered to be "details" which will work themselves out as production goes on. This excess optimism has plagued industrial developers and finally resulted in a congressional mandate for a separate OT&E office within DDR&E: not exactly a vote of confidence in the Director of Research and Engineering![33]

Of all senior Pentagon appointees, those assigned to R&D positions most frequently identify with the contractor's point of view. Before the mid-1980s, most of them came to DOD from defense-oriented laboratories or companies, and returned to those employers on leaving government service. The report of the 1970 Blue Ribbon Panel on Defense Management included an analysis of the careers of 101 directors, assistant directors, and other professional personnel in Director of Defense Research and Engineering.[34] Of them, 31 (30 percent) had accepted employment with one of the hundred defense contractors, but 16 of these 31 were merely returning to their former employers. A comparable analysis was made for 124 Secretaries, Under Secretaries, and Assistant Secretaries who had served in the Pentagon since 1958. Of these 124, only 10 (8 percent) had accepted a position with one of the hundred largest defense contractors upon their departure. From these figures the commission concluded:

> It should be emphasized that there is no record or evidence of attempts by former presidential appointees or former officials in DDR&E to exercise influence in the awarding or administration of contracts. DDR&E is a focal point in determining what kinds of weapons systems are developed, and, therefore, to a certain extent, by what contractors. Familiarity with this process would provide an insight into the direction of future weapons requirements which could be of value to a defense contractor. If the dominant consideration is avoiding any potential use of influence, or the appearance of influence, there is no justification for treating former high-level civilian employees any less restrictively than retired senior military officers.[35]

THE USER

Whereas the developer (the Director of Defense Research and Engineering) and the buyer (Assistant Secretary of Defense for Production and Logistics) have their counterparts throughout industry, the user, a concept that is possibly the only notion more elusive than "the firm military requirement," does not. Leonard Sullivan describes the user in vivid terms:

> Surely the User is that wise and dedicated career military man who establishes those firm military requirements; the man who spends his career with his life put on the line; the man who understands the subtleties of combat — and also of logistics support; the man who understands the risks of his mission and can keep the civilian infrastructure from jeopardizing our nation's real war-fighting capability.
> The User is, in short, the man who should bring you an affordable,

maintainable, appropriately ready, fully sustainable force posture, coupled to a realistic strategy based on honest threat assessments, and demonstrably interoperable with sister Services, and brother allies.

Based on these anticipated capabilities, the U.S. acquisition system is laced with Users. They comprise about one-third of the OSD staff (including USDRE) to assure realism in its actions. They are responsible for generating, reviewing, and endorsing requirements. They contribute to analytical studies rationalizing program decisions. They are the schools that train our operational forces and our most promising officers. They run most of the major program offices.

Users sit on the DSARC [DAB] in the form of the JCS. They provide operational flavor to the DRB [Defense Resources Board] in the form of the CINCs. They serve on the OT&E [Office of Test and Evaluation] staffs to assure complete testing before force introduction. They are the champions of supportability — for current systems as well as future systems.[36]

Reflecting the situation described by Mr. Sullivan, user experience is frequently cited as "essential" for a defense program manager. Indeed, officers from user organizations are frequently assigned as program managers for development and production programs; however, they usually have few or no industrial management skills. This problem is discussed at greater length in chapter 4, "Program Management."

How the Pentagon Works

Because of the scope and complexity of its responsibilities, the Pentagon must perform many difficult tasks. Some it does well, others not. It develops and procures high-technology methods that produce the most advanced ships, planes, and missiles in the world. It is most effective in making decisions and taking actions that neither require aggressive cost control nor threaten the roles of the military services.

In the absence of normal business incentives, senior defense officials adopt a variety of management styles. A few managers, military and civilian, come to the Pentagon with an understanding of its size and complexity and the ways in which any large bureaucracy resists change. The successful ones recognize the need to focus on only a few areas in which they wish to make improvements. They then implement their strategies in four steps.

1. They communicate ideas orally and in writing for a change in management policy to all concerned personnel throughout the particular area and institute a training program;
2. They gain support of the career military and civilian personnel who will continue to operate the department after the change is instituted;
3. At frequent intervals, they measure progress toward achieving the change; and
4. They try to adjust the system of rewards and penalties so that adherence to the improved procedures will be rewarded.

When reforms by senior civilians or military officers run counter to established priorities of a segment of the defense bureaucracy, they may be subverted in any of several ways. For example:

Directives establishing a new management policy are sent to field organizations, but the field organizations do not institute adequate training programs to develop the appropriate management skills.

Directives are sent to the field, but subordinate officials continue to reward individuals for following older management policies, not the new policy.

Those opposing a reform quietly solicit support from members of Congress, industry, industry associations, and military service associations, who then voice strong public opposition to the new policy.

Subordinate organizations create long-term study groups to analyze the impact of the new policy and to outline a comprehensive method of implementation. After several months, the reports are completed. Tens of hundreds of pages of evidence attest to the difficulty of implementing the new policy.

Richard Stubbing describes an example of a successful end run by the services to Congress. In 1977, President Carter chose *not* to build the B-1 bomber, though he did not prevent a small strategic bomber research program from continuing. With the help of Congress, the Air Force managed to direct additional funds to the B-1 contracting team (at Rockwell International) from 1977 to 1981 until the program could be restored. With the acquiescence of Defense Secretary Harold Brown, the Air Force added a modified version of the B-1 bomber to the list of aircraft being considered as cruise missile carriers. When, in a November 1979 budget meeting, President Carter learned of the tacit continuation of funding for the B-1 contractor, he reacted with dismay: "I hope I'm dreaming! Can't we get out of this?" The answer turned out to be no. Although the B-1 derivative was ultimately rejected as the cruise missile carrier, the funds from that program had proved adequate to sustain Rockwell's B-1 team through to the 1980 election.[37]

As noted in chapter 1, Defense Secretary Caspar Weinberger and his first Deputy Secretary, Frank Carlucci, issued a list of thirty-two management reforms (the Carlucci initiatives) designed to improve efficiency. The initiatives attempted to encourage realistic weapons pricing, economical (i.e., higher) rates of production, and cancellation of marginal programs rather than program stretch-outs or the reduction of funds for support functions. Even critics agreed that some progress was made. But Deputy Secretary Carlucci, acknowledged as a talented, dedicated manager, resigned from the Pentagon early in the Reagan administration to return to private industry. Subsequently, doubt spread about the extent of any lasting reform without Mr. Carlucci's leadership. A general officer who retired in the mid-1980s as one of a handful of senior officials with major control over weapons buying claimed that the initiatives were not enforced and were easy to ignore.

> We saw [them] more as a statement of aspirations, to which we could all subscribe, than as a radical new game plan. There were some pretty good things in the initiatives, but they tended to puff it and hype it too much. Not much really changed.

A high-level OSD official in the defense acquisition hierarchy described one of the tactics employed.

> The budget reviews are very frustrating. You spend hours fighting to get the military to drop some $400 million program you think is a waste, and then they [the military planners] put it back in at the next meeting, or next year. They know they'll outlast you.

In late 1986, a number of influential Pentagon officials described their approach to dealing with the Packard Commission recommendations calling for significant changes in managing the acquisition process. One flag officer in a senior procurement position said, "Everyone is expecting the big mirrors. Packard wants to see this and wants to see that. We will show it to him with big mirrors."

On June 8, 1986, approximately one week after the issuance of the

Packard Commission report, Deputy Defense Secretary William Taft appeared to have adopted another tactic. He stated that most of the Packard recommendations had already been implemented.

It is difficult within any bureaucracy to measure the effectiveness of specific management practices. It is particularly difficult in the Defense Department, which operates without the profit incentive and, even in peacetime, uses few of the standard business techniques for measuring effectiveness or efficiency. In most small and medium-sized commercial businesses, these qualities can be measured annually, and often monthly. In large commercial organizations, the effect of senior-level decisions may not be fully discernible for a number of years. But even there, cost effectiveness is measured regularly to analyze the impact of management decisions on long-term profits and the efficiency of continuing operations.

Former Army Under Secretary Norman Augustine describes the differences between managing in private industry and managing in the Defense Department, noting that industry places greater responsibility and accountability on individual managers.

> I believe the principal distinction between managing in government and in industry is that in the Government one operates principally by consensus and that there is relatively little discipline in the Government in preventing dissenting views from becoming counterproductive after a decision has been made.
>
> By and large in industry, once a decision is made either to do or not to do something, everyone gets behind it. In the Government that certainly has not been my observation.[38]

Representatives of firms that contract with more than one DOD buying organization repeatedly express amazement at the variety of interpretations these organizations apply to Pentagon policy statements. Managers at each level interpret directives to conform to their own management methods. Because many intermediate-level managers have limited experience in the acquisition process, it is not surprising that policy directives are not uniformly implemented.

Some senior defense appointees attempt no changes in the status quo during their terms of office. They read the letters and documents they receive every day, attend the numerous briefings scheduled within the Pentagon, and maintain a low profile. In 1987, one senior Pentagon official told us:

> I know there are many who say there are too many people in OSD. But I know that when I am in the office there is all this stuff coming through that I have to do. And every time I go away, I return to find all this stuff piled up that I must do.

Managers in large companies at times find themselves in similar situations. They occupy a position in a bureaucracy. Papers come in and papers go out. Soon the managers believe their role is a key one in achieving the goals of the organization. Sometimes it is; sometimes it is not. But the papers pile up until the position is abolished.

Many senior officials have been frustrated in their attempts to introduce change in the Pentagon. After serving as Deputy Defense Secretary for nearly two years, David Packard, one of the ablest Pentagon managers, commented on the difficulties he had experienced.

> Let's face it — the fact is that there has been bad management of many defense programs in the past. We spend billions of the taxpayers' dollars; sometimes we spend it badly. Part of this is due to basic uncertainties in the defense business. Some uncertainties will always exist. However, most of it has been due to bad management, both in the Department of Defense and in the defense industry. . . .
>
> Frankly, I am ashamed I have not been able to do very many of the things that need to be done to improve the situation I found here in January 1969. The most frustrating thing is that we know how we ought to manage — you, me, all of us — and we refuse to change based on what we know.[39]

Not everyone agreed with Mr. Packard. At the same meeting, an Assistant Secretary and a senior military officer voiced opposing opinions. Neither saw any outstanding problems in government procurement, certainly nothing to indicate that criticism of the department was anything more than an overreaction to "routine" problems of cost overruns and schedule delays.

Toward the end of the 1970s, Defense Secretary Harold Brown expressed puzzlement and some dismay over the political pressures and interservice rivalries that he felt thwarted his efforts to save money and improve DOD efficiency. Secretary Brown said that his key disappointment was his inability to induce a genuine effort to achieve cost efficiency within the department.

> I have found that efficiency with taxpayers' dollars is deprivation of expected economic gains to somebody — whether it's people in a city near a

base that efficiency says we should close, or the unhappiness of a civil servant who wants to have a bigger across-the-board raise in salary or unhappiness of a military service who does not want to see some of its activities consolidated with another service.[40]

Some senior DOD managers are from business firms where for years they managed successfully by making immediate decisions with a minimum of analysis. These people were often a major source of rewards and penalties for their employees, and many of them try to apply the same management style to their new activities in the Pentagon. Here, however, they control few of the rewards and penalties, and the size of defense operations makes formal analyses, detailed planning, and thorough follow-up mandatory. After these appointees have been in the department for a year or two, they become disheartened by their failure to effect change, usually without understanding the reasons for that failure.

One deterrent to better cost-control management is the constant military pressure on Pentagon decision makers to solve cost-overrun problems by petitioning Congress for more money. All senior military officers, understandably, want to strengthen their services in order to minimize chances of failure in the event of international conflict. Each believes that national security depends on acquiring more armed forces and more advanced weapons.

Another deterrent to improved cost control is the belief that development programs will cost a fixed amount, no matter what management policies are followed. Defense officials, both military and civilian, often treat the cost estimates prepared during the budget cycle each year as minimum amounts that must be approved in full if a program is to begin or continue. Often, the only method considered for cutting program costs is a reduction in the number of weapon systems produced. More efficient development or production is only rarely considered as an alternative. The remark of a senior official concerning a development program experiencing sizable cost increases is not uncommon: "The high cost of the program is simply a fact of life, and if we want the program, we'll have to live with it."

Senior military officers are rarely given incentives to trim the size of their organizations or to cancel or curtail programs that incur significant cost increases. Instead, they are motivated to work for increases in appropriations for new weapons and equipment. Former President Eisenhower took note of this preoccupation: "The military services, traditionally concerned with 100 percent security, are rarely satisfied with the amounts allocated to them out of an ever-generous budget."[41]

Given the military commitment to expanding programs, arguments for defense sufficiency must come from the Congress or from government officials who do not depend exclusively on the military hierarchy for information or political support. Civilians in charge of setting policy and priorities — beginning with Congress and proceeding from the Secretary of Defense to the service secretariats — should be prepared to distinguish between the military's single-minded dedication to their service and the nation's true defense needs, before making decisions.

More than thirty years ago President Eisenhower expressed frustration over service parochialism. In 1956 in a letter to a friend, Everett Hazlett, he described the problem of persuading the military services to see beyond their own goals.

> when each Service puts down its minimum requirements for its own military budget for the following year, and I add up the total, I find that they mount at a fantastic rate. There is seemingly no end to all this. Yet merely "getting tough" on my part is not an answer. I simply must find men who have the breadth of understanding and devotion to their country rather than to a single Service that will bring about better solutions than I get now.[42]

In addition to pressures from the military, high-ranking defense officials are subject to demands from congressmen and senators seeking to benefit their constituents or financial contributors. To avoid unwelcome congressional attention, many Secretaries and Assistant Secretaries avoid the public eye; they feel that taking a strong position on any controversial issue will subject them to unreasonable attack. Some choose to follow the advice given by a ranking staff member on a major congressional committee to a group of senior military and civilian defense personnel: "The fastest way to succeed in Washington is to avoid making decisions. That way, you do nothing that anyone can criticize."

Some members of Congress, by keeping track of DOD programs affecting their constituents, often act as unofficial lobbyists at the Pentagon for defense contractors within their districts. Some are partisans of one or more branches of the armed forces, and some are devoted to achieving more efficient use of defense appropriations. A number of defense officials are self-confident enough to receive inquiries and complaints from congressional members with equanimity. Others experience anxiety at the slightest hint of criticism. One Assistant Secretary was known to receive an unusually large number of telephone calls from members of Congress. No matter what the complaint, he attempted to comply by modifying the offending practice. His subordinates felt that the merits of the cases were rarely at issue.

THE CONCERN WITH IMAGE

Because the Defense Department depends on Congress for appropriations, most of its Under Secretaries and Assistant Secretaries are eager to project an image of managerial efficiency. When Congress or the press cite a DOD managerial problem, some officials blame it on a particular type of contract or the mistake of an earlier administration. A more common Pentagon response to congressional or media criticism of defense management is that the critic is the problem.

In the interest of counteracting sensationalistic journalism, the Pentagon sometimes exaggerates its own reports of cost reductions or improvements. It frequently reports cost reductions in weapon systems when only the quantity is reduced, even when the unit cost has increased. In 1983, *The Wall Street Journal* reported:

> In March, the Pentagon asserted it had cut $18 billion from the projected total cost of 53 major weapons programs. In fact, the reductions were phony. The Pentagon merely renamed seven submarines, and then claimed they were cut, and it took credit for cutting billions in jet fighter and cruise-missile costs that weren't really eliminated but just dropped from publicly released charts.[43]

Although some high-ranking officials concede that the DOD acquisition process does not function as efficiently as it should, they worry that the institution of new management policies will instigate congressional and public indictment of past policies. If program costs are reduced, according to this rationale, critics will complain that past program costs should have been lower too. Consequently, they are reluctant to "risk" reform.

There are many examples of this kind of reasoning. An Assistant Secretary vetoed a planned industrial engineering study of a program experiencing unexpected cost increases, saying to a senior officer of the buying organization: "If you conduct the study and the price comes out lower, people will say you've been doing a bad job. I don't believe that you have, do you?" The study was dropped.

Some Pentagon officials interpret criticisms of their programs as personal attacks. A senior Pentagon analyst prepared and submitted a management survey of the acquisition process of one military service to the service Secretary and one of his Assistant Secretaries. The report cited a number of serious problems: lack of trained civilian personnel, too-frequent turnover of military personnel, understaffing of program offices, and ineffective cost-control efforts from program office staffs. The commander of the service buying organization was outraged at the implication that the personnel in his command were not well-trained, well-supervised, and highly efficient administrators and managers. In an angry letter to the Assistant Secretary, he censured the report and insisted that the situation was completely under control.

> Many of the alleged deficiencies noted by [name] have been recognized previously and corrective actions have been initiated or accomplished. Certain findings and proposals of the report, I consider either unrealistic or beyond our control. . . . We can ill afford to expend our resources correcting false impressions.

During the next four years, however, a number of military and civilian personnel from the same buying organization stated informally that the problems cited in the report were still widespread in the command. During that four-year period there were repeated cost increases and failures in technical performance.[44]

REPORTING DEFENSE ACQUISITION INFORMATION
TO THE PENTAGON

Among the most serious problems in the acquisition process are the schedule delays and cost increases resulting from delays, which begin early in the process. The basic responsibility of the services for determining military requirements is diluted by a review process that provides many OSD staff members with an opportunity to challenge — and in some cases, to modify — aspects of the service-established requirements. The services sometimes respond by providing limited information to the OSD staff.[45]

The problem of incomplete, or sometimes distorted, information continues throughout the life of an acquisition program. An Air Force officer assigned to the program control division of a major development program described the following incident. His office had prepared for OSD a quarterly progress report that, when routed to the next higher management level, included information on fourteen serious problems. Between the program office and OSD, each management level (i.e., five levels, with three to five functional offices in each) evaluated it, earmarking certain funds for the program and eliminating all references to one or more of the fourteen problems. Three days later, when the report reached the Secretary of Defense, it indicated that the program was in excellent condition, with no significant problems. The officer who discussed the incident did not know whether the fourteen problems had actually been solved or whether their disclosure had simply been "postponed." In any event, there were obviously strong incentives at every management level to keep controversial information from reaching the Secretary of Defense.

Middle-level managers worry that if higher-level officials in the Defense Department or Congress know what is really happening in some programs, they will make the "wrong" decision; that is, they will reduce or cancel the programs. These managers are convinced that Pentagon and congressional officials have neither the background nor the training to understand the need for the funding levels required for the programs. Therefore, the information presented to higher-level managers invariably contains more positive evaluations than are contained in uncirculated reports prepared by managers closer to the programs — and these reports are likely to be optimistic in themselves.

The middle-level managers often regard high-ranking DOD officials in much the same way that management executives in private corporations regard their boards of directors. Like most corporate board members, most senior Pentagon officials accept management decisions at face value. In a thought-provoking study of boards of directors, Harvard Business School Professor Emeritus Myles Mace quoted a board member who explained why he never asked critical questions at board meetings:

> I, as an outside director, am unwilling to show my lack of grasp of understanding of the problem or to display my ignorance. To be able to challenge the management with a discerning question, you've got to know enough really to be on fairly sound ground. Part of the problem is that you don't want to look like an idiot. And it's very easy to look like an idiot, unless you spend enough time getting your facts in line, and, you know, understanding what you're talking about.[46]

Assistant Secretaries new to defense acquisition often find themselves in the same position, realizing that their knowledge of defense systems is limited. Development and production of large weapon and equipment systems are so complex that independent analysis by untrained outsiders is not feasible. An inexperienced Assistant Secretary faced with program decisions usually asks a few rudimentary questions and then approves the recommendations of his military or civilian staff.

In this context, as noted earlier, the nature of the working relationship between civilian appointees and military officers ranges from excellent to poor, depending on the capabilities and dedication of the military and civilian personnel involved. In most cases, newly appointed Pentagon Secretaries and Assistant Secretaries are eager to cultivate the good will of their military associates to facilitate the flow of information and ensure their cooperation. One must earn the right to challenge the status quo. One Assistant Secretary, who had yet to cultivate that good will, commented: "If you start asking probing questions around here, the sources of information soon begin to dry up. The attitude of the career personnel seems to be, 'What's the matter, don't you trust us?'"

At the same time, military officers often refer to so-called civilian control of the Defense Department when under attack from critics. In an address to an influential industry group, one senior flag officer stated: "Remember, we don't make national policy or military policy, we simply execute it." A 1970 *New York Times* article quoted Gen. Thomas S. Power, USAF (retired), former commander of the Strategic Air Command:

> Let us look at the Pentagon. At the top is a large group of civilians appointed by the President and the Secretary of Defense. These men are in complete charge of all military operations. They exercise this authority through the Joint Chiefs of Staff. . . . I do not think it is widely understood that there is not a single military man in this country who has any authority to do anything given to him by law by the people of this country. The authority is held entirely by civilians and is only delegated to the military at their discretion and subject to their veto. Keep this in mind when inclined to raise a fuss about too much military influence.[47]

In any complex decision-making process the individuals who most significantly affect the process are those who control the sources of information. In the Defense Department, as in other bureaucracies, several tactics are employed to affect the decision-making process. A standard practice is to present a top official with two solutions to a problem. The official believes he has the evidence on which to base an objective choice. Usually, however, the favored alternative is attractively presented, and the other is made to seem untenable. Another tactic is called decision briefing. The official is invited by the staff to a meeting attended by other interested principals. He is told that this is a decision briefing (as opposed to an information briefing, during which no decisions are made). The idea is to convince the official that he must make an immediate decision and then to present him with facts that support only the course of action favored by the military staff.

In one instance, a military officer was in the process of preparing a budget request for a major program. A briefing on the request was to be held in OSD. In his proposal, the officer also described a less costly alternative and provided an analysis of the impact of both budgets. When the advocates of the program learned that the briefing would include a description of the lower-cost alternative, they demanded its deletion, even though they agreed that the presentation was accurate. They argued that presenting an alternative would weaken the opportunity for the service to obtain the higher budget request. No alternative was discussed when the formal briefing was conducted.

A seasoned Pentagon manager will listen to a briefing, ask questions, and then, despite pressure for an immediate decision, confer with his staff and attempt to gather more information. A newcomer, on the other hand, might play the game as directed.

In 1987, a Pentagon official described the frequent occurrence of a similar tactic.

> On Tuesday a program comes to DSARC with a fixed-price contract. The parties have made firm offers, and the offers expire on Thursday. You can't tell them they should open it up and negotiate a new contract. It's a freight train, and it's impossible to stop.

In another useful game, called the-decision-has-already-been-made, the official is informed that events have taken the military staff by surprise, that he would surely have been informed earlier had his interest in the program been known, but at the moment a particular course of action is well under way, and any change would cost taxpayers millions of dollars.

Officials who must make decisions in these circumstances soon learn about these realities. One former Assistant Secretary commented, "It was my experience that adequate, reliable information usually did not exist for decision making on major issues." Three other Assistant Secretaries recalled that before arriving at the Pentagon, they believed that major defense decisions were based on careful analyses of all relevant facts. They were soon convinced, however, that decisions were more often based on information carefully screened before being presented to the nominal decision maker. Another Assistant Secretary concluded: "If the events presented as facts around here actually turned out to be facts, most of our problems would disappear." One official claimed to have learned that the only way to control the development of new programs was to enter the decision-making process long before the senior military officers had taken a strong position on individual programs. "Once a formal position is announced, it is very difficult to bring about any change without endangering your sources of information on future programs."

In every large organization, senior officials are seldom able to maintain constant contact with multiple sources of information. The Pentagon is no exception. Large corporations deal with this problem by creating semiautonomous divisions whose presidents are responsible for profit and loss and other measures of accomplishment. In the Pentagon, several factors hinder this approach: the variety and complexity of the work; the absence of profit and loss indicators; and limited measures of effectiveness and efficiency. In addition, the size and duration of major development and production programs leave lower-level managers room to make optimistic forecasts of time, costs, and technical performance. According to one program manager, "There is simply no need to lie; one only has to be optimistic."

THE GOVERNMENT-INDUSTRY RELATIONSHIP

In the defense business, as in commercial business, the buyers (defense officials) are the focus of pressure, both subtle and overt, from the sellers (defense contractors). The pressure is directed toward achieving financial support for various programs — planned or ongoing — under contract with industry. Industry executives visit military and civilian officials in the Pentagon several times a year. An Assistant Secretary may see representatives from the ten to twenty largest contractors for his service every few months. Pleasantries are exchanged, and the visitor mentions company progress on various programs. Sometimes a low-key sales talk is delivered: The service should buy additional quantities of a weapon system or should undertake a new development program to capitalize on technological advances or to preserve the firm's defense capabilities. Sometimes the contractor mentions problems his company is having with DOD contract administrators. Soon, the contractor's most senior executive is on a first-name basis with the Assistant Secretary. At the same time, the Assistant Secretary's military and civilian staff — some of whom are involved in contract negotiations with the visiting executive — address him as "Mr. Secretary" as a matter of protocol.

Many senior defense officials are on the regular guest lists for industry cocktail parties in Washington. Here they discuss development and production problems informally with senior representatives of major contractors. When the companies have complaints about program administration, they voice them to those at the highest level of the Pentagon. Officials from smaller contracting or subcontracting companies cannot afford these social contacts. When they do visit the Pentagon, they are often surprised at the "open door policy" of many generals, admirals, and civilian officials. Despite this, and because they do not have frequent social contact with senior officials, they feel they are treated with less deference than the larger contractors and that their grievances are given less attention.

When a senior DOD official visits a defense plant, the government program manager and the government plant representative are usually present for all formal meetings with senior contracting executives. Toward the end of the visit, however, the DOD official is often invited to a private meeting with one or more company executives. This custom is severely criticized by field procurement and program management personnel, knowing that matters relevant to their programs are often discussed. The exclusiveness of the private discussions suggests to them that senior defense officials are more sympathetic to industry executives than to those responsible for protecting government interests in the field. This attitude weakens the authority of conscientious government representatives who try to monitor contractor performance and administer contracts effectively.

After a year or more of experience with the cost increases and failures in technical performance that occur on major defense programs, Pentagon officials often express surprise and disappointment at the poor performance of many major defense contractors. An Assistant Secretary, formerly employed by a defense contractor, noted his own change in attitude after a year and a half in the Pentagon.

> One of the metamorphoses I have gone through down here is to change my view of the condition of American business. I came to this place thinking they were the greatest. Now I think that even among some of the giants, there are serious problems that need to be corrected.

Other officials have reached the same conclusion. A former service Secretary commented:

> I was very surprised at the poor contractual performance of many contractors and was equally surprised to see these firms by-pass the chain of command and come to the top of the organization seeking to have their case supported on the basis of their comments. Time after time, when they came to us with problems, I would look into the situation and then find that, if anything, the field personnel had been lenient in dealing with the contractor on the problem that had arisen.

Management personnel at all levels of the government often express uncertainty about the nature of the government-contractor relationship. This is not surprising, because Pentagon officials express so many divergent views. Some refer to the relationship as a partnership between government and industry. Others call it an adversarial relationship, in which two parties with some identical and some conflicting objectives conduct, at arm's length, ongoing negotiations of contracts, contract changes, and material acceptance criteria.

Many senior officials support the partnership theory. A recently retired flag officer, formerly in charge of purchasing for his service and now an industry consultant, stated: "The team approach instead of the adversary approach cannot be emphasized too much. We must get back to the team approach between the Defense Department and the defense industry."

The appropriate model for industry-government relations in the defense business has been a source of disagreement for more than fifty years. In the mid-1930s, a commission on military spending commented:

> any close association between munitions and supply companies on the one hand and the service departments on the other hand . . . constitutes an unhealthy alliance in that it brings into being a self-interested political power which operates in the name of patriotism and satisfies interests which are, in large part, purely selfish.[48]

A similar view was offered by Robert Anthony during his tenure as Assistant Secretary of Defense (Comptroller):

> I think it is softheaded to talk about a "partnership between Government and industry." We are partners when it comes to performance and delivery, but are not partners on price. On matters relating to price, we are on opposite sides of the fence, and we should face this frankly.

A former commander of one of the major buying organizations described the relationship as a partnership with a special twist:

> The relationship between the Defense Department and its contractors is a partnership in the same way that two people playing poker are partners.

In 1987, a committee of the American Bar Association, in a study of the role of the DOD contracting officer, described the business-government relationship.

> With all the current attention on contractor fraud, a reasonable expectation would be that the relationship between [DOD] contracting officers and contractors has deteriorated and is now strongly adversarial. This is not the condition found by the ABA committee. If by adversarial one means animosity and contentiousness accompanied by suspicion and mistrust, then the relationship between the two is not generally adversarial. If by adversarial one means a business relationship characterized by wariness and hard-nosed bargaining, accompanied by tenacious regard for the best interest of one's own side, that is a much closer description of the situation.[49]

The relationship in 1987 between government and industry in the defense business has deteriorated because of what each group sees as excessive oversight — by Congress, GAO, OSD, and the service headquarters staffs, depending on one's perspective. In the words of a former commander of the Air Force Systems Command,

> Reports are demanded, endless briefings are given, [and] the results are delays, more delays, and added costs with early planning becoming worthless. These all set the stage for disaster. We have a historic opportunity to make a real change, or do nothing and let the acquisition process slide into further decay.

In commenting on the government-industry relationship, Sen. David Pryor (D-AR), a member of the Senate Finance Committee, was even harsher.

> Defense contractors have always sought what they like to call a "cooperative" relationship with government. That kind of relationship exists in its purest form in the Soviet Union, where the two are inseparable and jointly bleed the Russian taxpayers white. Unfortunately, because of the absence of capitalistic competition, our own Defense Department can be considered one of the world's largest socialist economies.
>
> It also seems that a lot of contractors deserve an unfriendly attitude from government, since some of them have taken outrageous advantage whenever government has not been vigilant, critical and suspicious. Unfortunately, government has failed in many of those instances to protect its own interests against those who profess to want to be "cooperative."[50]

Conclusion

The Pentagon system for distributing responsibility and authority between civilian appointees and military officers seriously impedes the efficient and effective functioning of the weapons acquisition process. If sufficient defense capability is to be maintained efficiently and effectively, civilian control of defense activities must become a working reality. Civilian appointees control few of the incentives or penalties for personnel performance. They have only as much authority in the Defense Department as do the board of directors in a private corporation, often less. Qualified civilians must, in deed as well as in intent, control information channels and make the final decisions on defense priorities. Finally, to achieve stability within the department, it is imperative that Secretaries and Assistant Secretaries serve, at a minimum, four-year terms of office. Fundamental reform must begin both in Congress and in the Pentagon.

Knowledgeable military and civilian officials agree that the number of organizations and personnel in the review and approval process — from the buying command divisions, to commands, to service headquarters, to OSD, to OMB, and on to the Congress — must be greatly reduced. The problem is that no one in the current chain of command is prepared to recommend the elimination of his own job.

There is widespread agreement by these officials that the current track record of twelve-plus years to develop and field major weapon systems must be reduced. To accomplish this, the most crucial step is to streamline the organizational decision-making process.

During 1986, OSD revised its acquisition organization, creating the positions of an Under Secretary for Acquisition (USD(A)), acquisition executives, and program executive officers. Richard P. Godwin, a corporate executive was appointed USD(A) and given the charter to improve the way the Defense Department develops and produces weapon systems. One year later, Godwin resigned because he believed his attempts at reform failed to gain the necessary support from senior levels in the Army, Navy, Air Force, and the Office of the Secretary of Defense. In an interview with the *Washington Post,* Godwin stated:

> I can't make anything stick. . . . The thing I can't accept is to be ignored by the system.
>
> When problems occur and you've got these layers of bureaucracy, the information gets so levelized, normalized and truncated, you can't even recognize it. The service commands can protect the service secretaries from learning about it, and they can protect us. Meanwhile, you're in the soup, and you don't even know about it until 10 to 15 months later.
>
> You couldn't possibly do this in industry. You'd be broke by next week.[51]

As of this writing, it is still unclear whether the new defense organization will reduce the layers of management, increase them, or leave them unchanged.

Notes

1. Staff Report to the Senate Committee on Armed Services, "Defense Organization: The Need for Change," October 16, 1985, p. 22.
2. President's Blue Ribbon Commission on Defense Management, *A Quest for Excellence,* Final Report to the President, June 1986, p. 43.
3. "Organization," *Defense,* September-October 1986, pp. 6–7; this journal is produced by the DOD American Forces Information Services and distributed by the Government Printing Office. "Pay Structure of the Federal Civil Service," Office of Personnel Management, Office of Workforce Information, 1900 E. Street, N.W., Washington, D.C.
4. Rachel L. Jefferies, ed., *U.S. Government Manual, 1987–88* (Washington, D.C.: Government Printing Office, 1987), pp. 163–221.
5. Ibid., p. 116.
6. Russell Murray II, "Congressional Actions to Improve the Defense Acquisition

Process," paper prepared for the Defense Acquisition Study, Center for Strategic and International Studies, Georgetown University, February 19, 1986, p. 2.

7. Murray, "Congressional Actions to Improve the Defense Acquisition Process," p. 6.

8. Ibid., p. 2.

9. "Press vs. President: New Battle in Old War," *U.S. News & World Report,* March 22, 1982, p. 55.

10. U.S. Senate, hearing before the Subcommittee on Defense Acquisition Policy of the Committee on Armed Services, "Defense Procurement Process," January 30, 1985, pp. 36–37.

11. Ibid.

12. Staff Report to the Senate Committee on Armed Services, "Defense Organization," October 16, 1985, p. 534.

13. *Defense,* September-October 1986.

14. "Pay Structure of the Federal Civil Service" (see note 3).

15. Francis J. West, Jr., "Secretaries of Defense: Why Most Have Failed," *Naval War College Review,* March-April 1981, p. 91.

16. Richard A. Stubbing, *The Defense Game* (New York: Harper & Row, 1986), p. 261.

17. Charles DeBenedetti, *The Antiwar Movement in America, 1955–1975* (forthcoming). Excerpts from a letter to Everett E. Hazlett, from President Dwight D. Eisenhower, August 20, 1956, recording his thoughts on prevailing needs for reorganization of the top military command structure.

18. Alain C. Enthoven and K. Wayne Smith, *How Much Is Enough? Shaping the Defense Program, 1961–1969* (New York: Harper & Row, 1971), p. 266.

19. Interview on September 10, 1986, with Pentagon personnel responsible for policy guidance on contracting, manufacturing, and quality assurance.

20. Arnold F. Klick, "The Newly Created Office of Under Secretary of Defense, Acquisition," *National Defense,* January 1987, p. 31.

21. Ibid.

22. U.S. General Accounting Office, "Joint Major Systems Acquisition by the Military Services: An Elusive Strategy," GAO/NSIAD–84–22, December 23, 1983. See also *National Defense,* January 1987, p. 64.

23. Background Information, Senior Steering Group, Defense Acquisition Study, Center for Strategic and International Studies, Georgetown University, November 7-8, 1985, pp. 8.7 to 8.9.

24. Staff Report to the Senate Committee on Armed Services, "Defense Organization," October 16, 1985, pp. 533–534.

25. William D. Brown, Paul J. Kern, L. Kirk Lewis, and John G. Zeirdt, "Acquisition Management — The Role and the Reality," National Security Program Report, John F. Kennedy School of Government, Harvard University, June 1987, p. 61.

26. Ibid., p. 66.

27. *Defense News,* February 23, 1987, p. 15, and March 1, 1987, p. 10.

28. Leonard Sullivan, Jr., "Characterizing the Acquisition Process," paper prepared for the Defense Acquisition Study, Center for Strategic and International Studies, Georgetown University, January 1986, p. H-3.

29. Stubbing, *The Defense Game,* pp. 392, 394.
30. Department of Defense Instruction (DODI) 5000.2, "Major System Acquisition Procedures," March 12, 1986, pp. 2–3.
31. Klick, "The Newly Created Office . . . ," p. 31.
32. Comdr. Lawrence J. Korb, *Naval War College Review,* December 1971.
33. Sullivan, "Characterizing the Acquisition Process," pp. F-1 to F-3.
34. Blue Ribbon Defense Panel, Report to the President and the Secretary of Defense on the Department of Defense, July 1, 1970, p. 187.
35. Ibid.
36. Sullivan, "Characterizing the Acquisition Process," p. F-3.
37. Stubbing, *The Defense Game,* p. 102.
38. U.S. Senate, testimony of Norman Augustine, President of Martin Marietta and former Under Secretary of the Army, before the Task Force on Selected Defense Procurement Matters of the Committee on Armed Services, "Defense Procurement Process," September 20, 1984, Part 2, p. 148.
39. Keynote address by David Packard at the annual meeting of the Armed Forces Management Association, August 1970.
40. "Foes of Cost-saving Vex Pentagon Chief," *New York Times,* January 3, 1979.
41. Dwight David Eisenhower, *The White House Years,* volume II, *Waging Peace 1956–61* (Garden City: Doubleday, 1965), p. 615.
42. Dwight D. Eisenhower to Everett E. Hazlett, August 20, 1956, in DeBenedetti (forthcoming).
43. "Reagan Arms Buildup Lags in Its Second Year as Costs Keep Rising," *The Wall Street Journal,* July 6, 1983.
44. Comptroller General of the United States, "Acquisition of Major Weapon Systems," Report to the Congress, B-163058, March 18, 1971.
45. R. L. McDaniel, "An Assessment of Management Information Related to Weapon System Acquisition Decisions," Systems Planning Corporation, August 1979, p. 7.
46. Myles L. Mace, *Directors: Myth and Reality* (Boston: Division of Research, Harvard Business School, 1971), p. 53.
47. *New York Times,* May 23, 1970.
48. Report of the Special Senate Committee to Investigate the Munitions Industry. Sen. Gerald P. Nye (R-ND), Chairman, 1936. 74th Congress, 1st Session. Senate Committee Report No. 3. Cited in "Statements from Previous Defense Reform Commissioners," paper prepared for the President's Blue Ribbon Commission on Defense Management, *A Quest for Excellence,* June 1986.
49. Richard J. Bedner and John T. Jones, Jr., "The Role of the DOD Contracting Officer," Draft Report of the American Bar Association (ABA) Section of Public Contract Law, Ad Hoc Committee, John E. Cavanagh, Chairman, January 11, 1987, p. 120.
50. "Keeping Contractors at Arm's Length," *Military Logistics Forum,* July-August 1985, p. 60.
51. "Pentagon's Purchasing Chief to Quit," *Washington Post,* September 14, 1987.

4

PROGRAM MANAGEMENT

Program management in the Defense Department is a distinct departure from traditional military procurement methods, in which task-oriented management organizations worked on several weapon systems simultaneously. By the late 1950s, the services sought to streamline the procurement process, introducing ad hoc program management offices into the acquisition process. The practice has continued since that time.[1]

The key person in each military service program office is the program manager, most often a senior military officer, who is regarded as the means to strengthen the management and allocation of resources for the most crucial or most costly acquisition programs. Each program manager is assisted by a deputy program manager (either military or civilian) in interacting with industry and government personnel, including the division chiefs within the program office.

In 1987, there was a program office for each of approximately one hundred major defense acquisition programs. These offices draw upon various functional specialists in the buying commands, including those in contracting, engineering, logistics, cost and schedule, and quality control. The specialists support the program office (part time or full time) by preparing specifications, analyses, work statements, requests for proposals (RFPs), contracts, and other documents.[2]

The Federal Acquisition Regulation (FAR), Part 34, Major Systems Acquisition, requires that program managers prepare an acquisition strategy — an overall plan for satisfying the mission need. The plan covers a range of important issues during the life of a program, such as objectives, resources, milestones for completion, alternative technical approaches, types of contracts, testing and evaluation, and operations and maintenance.[3]

During the various phases of the acquisition process — concept exploration, demonstration and validation, full-scale development, and production — the program manager is expected to plan, monitor, and control the various government and contractor activities in the design, production, testing, deployment, and support of new systems.[4] The management techniques used have evolved over recent decades. On July 13, 1971, the Office of the Secretary of Defense (OSD) issued DOD Directive 5000.1 (subsequently revised every few years), outlining management responsibilities, principles, and objectives for the acquisition of major defense systems. Three years later, it was supplemented by the more explicit DOD Directive 5000.23 (November 26, 1974, revised December 1986), which states that successful management of major systems depends on experienced and competent personnel. It specifies that career opportunities be established to attract, develop, retain, and reward the outstanding military officers and civilian employees needed to manage defense acquisition programs.

The Program Manager

Program managers for major development or production programs are usually Army or Air Force colonels or Navy captains. For a few larger programs, they are flag officers (i.e., generals or admirals of one- to three-star rank). They are responsible for acquiring and fielding weapon systems, including all technical and business aspects of development and production programs.[5] They are assigned resources (money and people) to execute program decisions. Despite having overall acquisition responsibility, program managers seldom have authority to enter into contractual arrangements with industry to fulfill program objectives; such arrangements are the sole province of contracting officers (described later in this chapter).

Program managers are frequently on their first or second tour in the acquisition process and tend to come from the operational forces (i.e., combat operations, such as infantry, armor, aircraft, or ships). Those from the Air Force generally have several years' more acquisition experience than their Army or Navy counterparts. Few serve more than six to eight years in program management in any capacity, however.[6] A general officer offered a rationale for the nearly exclusive use of military officers as program managers.

> Military officers are trained more to sustain the pressure and are trained to get things done. But they often do not have the functional technical skills. The problem is that their tours of duty are limited to two to three years.

As the key figures in the acquisition process, program managers must oversee the efforts of their military services to acquire, deploy or operate, and support major weapon systems of proven capability within approved schedules and budgets. To fulfill these objectives, they are expected to

1. establish firm and realistic system and equipment specifications;
2. define organizational relationships and responsibilities;
3. identify high-risk areas;
4. select the best technical approaches;
5. explore schedule, cost, and technical performance trade-off decisions;
6. establish firm and realistic schedules and cost estimates;
7. formulate realistic logistics support and operational concepts; and
8. lay the groundwork for contracting for the program.

Gen. Henry A. Miley, USA (ret.), one of the most experienced and knowledgeable experts on the acquisition process, describes the program manager's role in the Army context, but his comments apply to the Navy and Air Force as well.

> the functions of the Army's project manager are *not* those classically associated with the term "manager." This stems from the fact that the Army does not develop or produce its weapons systems in house. The management of these functions is contracted for, with, or through prime contractors. Hence, the principal functions of the project manager are contracting for and/or monitoring and evaluating the technical performance of the contractor(s). The term "technical performance" is used here in the broadest sense to comprehend not only the performance and quality of hardware but also the contractor's management of resources [costs] and sub-contractors.
>
> . . . the Army is not completely satisfied that the project managers which OPMS [Officer Personnel Management System] (and its predecessor system) has produced over the last twenty or so years have uniformly achieved

the same level of success as its Combat Commander group. The Army's project managers have been on the "acquisition battlefield" continuously since 1962. Even though many weapons systems have been developed and deployed during that period, the Army's perception is that at least some of the programs were not as successful as they could have been. Further, there is a perception that the quality and performance of the project managers have been contributing factors. The accepted indicators of the less than reasonable success of the programs have been the highly publicized reports of system deficiencies, cost over-runs and delayed fielding.

According to the charter of the project manager, he is vested with total responsibility and authority for his project. In reality, he does not enjoy that authority and control. He cannot, unilaterally, make any substantive changes in schedule, cost, or performance characteristics of his system. Such decisions are made at levels above the project manager — AMC [Army Materiel Command], ASARC [Army Systems Acquisition Review Council], DSARC [Defense Systems Acquisition Review Council, now Defense Acquisition Board], and even by the Congress. Technical design decisions are made by the contractor(s). Hence the Army should recognize this real-world situation and reorient its perception (and charter) of the project manager to recognize his actual role. His fundamental responsibility is to continuously observe and evaluate the technical performance of the contractor(s) and the Army agencies which provide service and support. This spectrum comprehends design, development, procurement, production, training, testing, and field support. The word *technical is used here in its broadest sense to include not only the engineering aspects of his weapon system but also the contractor's management of resources [costs] and sub-contractors.* It should be crystal clear to all involved, and in the related documentation, that *the project manager's function is that of the wise buyer rather than the advocate.*[7] (emphasis added)

General Miley's statement describes a problem that has resisted correction for more than thirty-five years. It was also described in chapter IX of *Arming America.*

For the past two decades many in the Defense acquisition process have not recognized that business management skills are distinct from engineering and scientific skills. A general in one of the larger buying commands commented: "One of the causes of our current problems arises from the fact that we failed to recognize that a program manager must be a business manager and need not be an expert scientist or an expert engineer." In private industry the scientists and engineers who work on defense programs can usually count on the assistance of skilled financial and business analysts from within their own company. This support capability is rarely present in Defense Department program offices. Some Government program managers hire engineering or technical consultants from outside the Government on a part-time basis. In the area of business management, however, they are reluctant to request outside assistance because they feel this would call attention to their own lack of management capability.[8]

In 1987, an industry senior vice-president emphasized the importance of a program manager's skill in understanding and dealing with business management.

> Many government program managers do not understand contractors. Unless a program manager understands how a contractor operates and what incentives apply to contractor personnel, it is virtually impossible for him to do an effective job.

PROGRAM MANAGER AUTHORITY

Since 1980, the stated objective of DOD efforts has been, in the words of the 1986 Packard Commission, "controlled decentralization." Through this approach, senior-level commitment to reform was to be translated into results at the program office level. More specifically, program managers were to have both the responsibility *and* authority necessary to manage their programs. With this authority would come increased accountability for what was actually happening on their programs. The goal was a more streamlined, less time-consuming decision-making process with an increased ability to locate responsibility. Despite the stated objective of controlled decentralization, however, more than half the seventy-plus program managers responding to the Packard Commission survey reported that their authority ranged from marginally adequate to very inadequate.

The Packard Commission concluded that the senior-level commitment to change had not reached the program manager level. Moreover, it concluded that defense acquisition was encumbered by unproductive layers of management and by overstaffing. The commission recommended specific actions to reduce and clarify the lines of authority, to streamline the acquisition process.[9]

In his 1984 study, defense analyst Robert Magnan confirmed the limited authority of a program manager.

> A government program manager (PM), usually an Army or Air Force colonel or a Navy captain, theoretically has the authority and responsibility

of a top-level business executive over a program. His actual authority, however, falls considerably short of his designated authority.

Mr. Magnan asked, Why can't the program manager effectively exercise his authority? He suggested three main reasons: brief tenure, limited management ability or experience, and his position within his own command structure.[10]

In 1986, the Packard Commission came to similar conclusions:

> The program manager finds that, far from being the manager of the program, he is merely one of the participants who can influence it. An army of advocates for special interests descends on the program to ensure that it complies with various standards for military specifications, reliability, maintainability, operability, small and minority business utilization, and competition, to name a few. Each of these advocates can demand that the program manager take or refrain from taking some action, but none of them has any responsibility for the ultimate cost, schedule, or performance of the program.
>
> None of the purposes they advocate is undesirable in itself. In the aggregate, however, they leave the program manager no room to balance their many demands, some of which are in conflict with each other, and most of which are in conflict with the program's cost and schedule objectives. Even more importantly, they produce a diffusion of management responsibility, in which everyone is responsible, and no one is responsible.[11]

Program managers' minimal authority, in sharp contrast to their maximum responsibility, often impedes success. Our interviews with DOD program managers tend to reinforce the observations of the Packard Commission:

> The program manager has very little flexibility. He is given a program and resources. He does not have the flexibility to trade off among the parameters of technical performance, cost, and schedule. He can recommend changes. But he has very limited authority other than that to grant an exemption from some minor specifications and standards.
>
> *   *   *
>
> In DOD there is nobody really in charge as is a contractor's program manager. Instead, we have many interest groups that can influence the system. There are so many checks and balances that decisions are very slow. Many can say no and very, very few can say yes.

THE PROGRAM MANAGEMENT OFFICE

The program management office (PMO, or simply, program office) is assigned responsibility for R&D, evaluation, procurement, deployment, and effective overall management for one weapon system program. PMO specialist staffs, or divisions, such as the following, perform all program activities.

1. *The program control (or business management or program management) division* directs overall systems planning, programming, collection and analysis of cost and schedule data, performance reporting to higher levels in DOD, and financial management.
2. *The configuration management division* establishes and implements policies and procedures for configuration management: system equipment and facility identification specification, engineering change control, and performance reports on all such activities.
3. *The procurement/contracting and production division* manages all procurement and production activities and supervises the planning and execution of all contracts for research studies, engineering development, tests, and production.
4. *The systems engineering division* manages the total systems engineering function, including the integration of engineering systems and subsystems. This division is also responsible for the quality of the technical performance of the weapon system.
5. *The product assurance (or test and deployment) division* plans and coordinates the test programs for the weapon system.

Usually in the Air Force, although less frequently in the Army and Navy, PMO division chiefs are military officers. The remaining PMO staff is divided between military officers and civil service personnel generally of middle rank and grade, depending on who is available in the buying organization. The PMO staff may also include officers from other service organizations with a direct interest in the weapon system (e.g., the operational user organization, training organization, and logistics support organization) as well as part- or full-time participation by functional specialists (e.g., in fields of engineering, procurement, or cost and schedule) in the buying organization.

The Air Force F-16 aircraft system program office is an example of a self-contained PMO (i.e., a large defense program with its own cadre of full-time functional specialists). This PMO comprises approximately

300 people, with about 75 engineers, 30 testers, 25 logisticians, and 40 contracting specialists working together in a group of approximately 180 military and 120 civilian professionals. Over several years, this PMO has delivered 1,300 F-16 aircraft to the U.S. Air Force and to foreign countries, costing almost $70 billion.

For the Army's M-1 tank program, there were approximately 200 people assigned to its PMO. Military officers held senior positions, and career civil service personnel held most of the others. For the Army's DIVAD program, there were approximately 30 people assigned for the first two years, 60 for the second two, and 80 for the last two. Again, military officers held the senior positions and career civil servants the remainder.

In contrast to the self-contained PMO, there is a second type of PMO: one that uses a matrix system of management, drawing its personnel on an "as needed" basis from the permanent functional specialty offices (created to support a number of program offices) within the buying organization.[12] In the simplest form of the matrix organization, each member serves two supervisors through two chains of authority. For example, in addition to reporting to a program manager, an analyst assisting in price analysis reports along functional lines to a senior price analyst, who prepares his or her annual performance evaluation.

In the matrix organization, as in the self-contained PMO, the program manager supervises the development or production program, working with personnel in the functional and other military organizations and with industry contractors. Although he must coordinate all work of the government personnel assigned to the program, he has limited control of functional specialists, who work on essential tasks but are not a permanent part of the PMO staff. A matrix PMO may be staffed by as few as fifteen to twenty people, as is, for example, the Navy's F-14 (fighter aircraft) program office. Another ninety or more people who work on the F-14 program are part of the functional organizations within the Naval Air Systems Command. Unlike those in self-contained PMOs, they may also work on other programs concurrently. Time conflicts are negotiated by the appropriate program managers.

One program manager described his matrix program office in some detail.

> The office has a small core that includes engineering, laboratory, budgeting, logistics, contracting, production, testing, and data analysis. If I am putting together a request for proposal, I obtain additional functional

support from outside the program office. Program offices are seen as prima donnas by the functional people, and they view themselves as job shops. But it is very hard to fire a person. If you are dissatisfied with someone assigned to you by a functional office, what you do is to turn him back, so they give him to someone else.

Because the program manager in a matrix organization depends on specialists from many other DOD organizations, gaining their cooperation is crucial to the success of the program. If a program manager is unable to maintain a healthy working relationship with specialists, the program is in jeopardy. Some of the problems encountered in a matrix PMO are inherent.

The matrix matter, while appearing to be the way most systems commands are going, fosters more second guessing and review, especially when they [functional specialists] are not integral to my office. Why, I've got matrix support types telling me to coordinate or they won't do what they are supposed to. They don't report to me. I don't write their performance evaluations. I get their help when it's convenient to them. In a small PMO, you wait on their schedule.[13]

Most defense officials and contractors agree that the most appropriate type of management for a development or production program depends on several program characteristics. The greater the technical complexity, budget, concurrency, and importance of a program, the greater the need for a self-contained PMO with its more direct control of functional activities.

BRIEFINGS

Program managers point out that most of the major decisions affecting the progress of their programs are made at higher levels of the Defense Department — often within OSD. Their superiors are as dedicated and hard working as the program managers and are deeply interested in the progress of all programs within their jurisdiction. Understandably, they want to review and participate in all important decisions affecting their programs. As a result, program managers regularly receive instructions and requests for information from several sources, including higher-level organizations within the service acquiring the weapon system and the Office of the Secretary of Defense. They also hear from a variety of organizations with varying degrees of interest in the acquisition process:

1. the General Accounting Office (auditing agency that reports directly to the Congress);
2. the Defense Contract Administration Service (DCAS) (part of the Defense Logistics Agency [DLA], which reports to OSD);
3. the Defense Contract Audit Agency (DCAA) (which reports to OSD);
4. the DOD Inspector General;
5. the using command (e.g., Strategic Air Command, Tactical Air Command, or U.S. Army Europe);
6. the service training command;
7. the service logistics command; and
8. the House and Senate Defense Authorization and Appropriations committees.

Many of the organizations making demands on a program manager's time are staffed by military officers or civilians who could exercise significant influence on his career advancement. If he is interested in advancing his career, he must be responsive to their "special requests." Consequently, he often has limited time to devote to the more basic management tasks of evaluating progress, anticipating problems, considering alternatives, and conducting ongoing discussions and information exchanges with contractor personnel. As the program manager forwards information from contractors to higher DOD management levels, he may feel he lacks the status to give first priority to his own management responsibilities.

Professor Ralph Nash of George Washington University, an expert on the government procurement process, observed in early 1985:

> One of the interesting things you see when you look at what program managers do is that they spend more time answering questions from all the people around the department than they do running the program. That is backwards. They ought to be running the program.[14]

In 1983, the Defense Department received more than eighty-four thousand written inquiries from the Congress alone. Telephone inquiries were several times that number. Although they covered the entire range of defense activities, a significant portion pertained to defense acquisition programs, requiring answers from a program manager. During our interviews with Army, Navy, and Air Force program managers they repeatedly mentioned the time lost to giving reports and answering queries as their biggest problem. The questions are often budget questions, asking "what if" a certain amount of money were cut. To every question, no matter how small, theoretical, or remote, the program manager must give a careful and detailed answer.

Professor Nash summarized his views on the "briefing problem" in testimony before the Senate Armed Services Committee.

> Now, what does the environment look like from the point of view of the program manager and the contracting officer?
>
> Above them are a myriad of staff people reviewing, commenting on and ultimately approving their proposed actions. They are taking a lot of time in doing it. Around them are a growing number of auditors and investigators searching for fraud, waste and abuse.[15]

One of the hidden costs in the time and effort required to brief higher levels of management is the coordination and preparatory briefings that must take place along the way. According to Assistant Defense Secretary James Wade, "If you add another peg point on which the services and program managers have to respond by reporting to members of the department or Members of Congress, you will find 40 briefings and meetings getting ready for that."[16] In the opinion of program managers responding to the Packard Commission survey, DOD improvement programs of the 1980s had produced little or no reduction in time spent on briefings.

PROMOTING THE PROGRAM

There is an additional aspect of the program manager's role that significantly affects his performance. He must devote 30 to 50 percent (or more) of his time promoting and defending his program before upper levels of DOD and before Congress. He usually feels obliged to fight continually for a larger budget and a larger program or to protect his current funding. Such activity takes on particular significance when superiors are reassigned, at the time of annual budget hearings, or whenever competing demands for funds (from inside or outside the department) jeopardize the status of a program. This responsibility is interpreted in different ways by individual program managers and higher-level procurement managers. In 1987, a senior officer in one of the buying commands described the situation.

> In these times, I'm convinced there are many more programs under way than there are funds to carry them to completion. The program manager who sounds alarms or even just progresses at a conscientious rate will probably find he has insufficient funds to cover his program. However, the manager who drives his program forward the fastest (on paper) will get the money. The name of the game these days seems to be achieving high-spending rates to keep the money from being taken away (i.e., not available for reprogramming). The squeeze is on.

In examining the history and outcome of various major systems acquisitions, a GAO task force found a common thread in program advocacy. Development programs that lacked strong advocacy were much more likely to be canceled than those that had energetic and dedicated advocates. The task force concluded that without a continuous selling effort, the chances of a program proceeding through its complete acquisition cycle into production and deployment were significantly diminished, whereas with such effort, a program might survive long after it should have been terminated because of technical problems, inadequate capability, cost or schedule overruns, or similar reasons.[17]

In 1986, the Packard Commission confirmed, once again, that pressures, both internal and external to DOD, compelled program managers to spend most of their time defending or selling programs to upper levels of management. The commission concluded that, in effect, the program manager "is reduced to being a supplicant for, rather than a manager of, his program. The resulting huckster psychology does not condition the program manager to search for possible inconsistencies between performance and schedule on the one hand and authorized funding on the other. Predictably, there is a high incidence of cost overruns on major weapons systems programs."[18]

Program managers are well aware of the position they are in. They are the main advocates of any program and must convince higher levels of the value of the program.

> The program manager wants to keep the program alive. If the program manager is not the advocate, who will be? Most people are lined up against the program. The whole system is lined up to say no.

* * *

The program manager must be extremely optimistic in his role as program advocate.

A serious consequence of this, in addition to the time spent, is the change it brings about in the manager's relationship with the contractor. Because the manager needs the contractor's support, it is very difficult to maintain the arm's-length relationship between buyer and seller.

Program managers' selling activities are not confined to service leaders and the various staffs in OSD. They also must promote their program, repeatedly, to at least four congressional committees and numerous subcommittees and then promote it again for each fiscal year in which it is considered. In so doing, program managers are often either assisted or opposed by a variety of contractors, each advocating an individual view of the program on Capitol Hill. A similar dichotomy occurs when congressmen affirm an interest in greater program effectiveness and efficiency while also maintaining a pragmatic interest in their own constituencies. These two interests are frequently in conflict as congressmen exert pressure on specific programs through legislative oversight.

The demands on a program manager's time have not diminished over the years. In 1974, a program control division chief estimated that more than 60 percent of his time and 25 to 50 percent of that of his key personnel was spent preparing briefings and special studies. The situation is the same, or worse, in the late 1980s.

EVALUATING A PROGRAM MANAGER'S PERFORMANCE

Many factors beyond the control of a program manager affect program performance. The large number of organizations and people impinging on a program usually precludes measuring performance against schedules and budgets as an accurate indicator of a program manager's performance. Hence, performance is usually judged by the continuing existence of the program, the manager's adherence to traditional DOD management procedures, and loyalty to his service.

Dedicated, able program managers naturally want to impress their superiors and receive favorable annual performance evaluations. Because these senior officers serve for a relatively short period in each assignment, they are compelled to produce visible results of their efforts in the near term. Unfortunately, these results can be costly to a program in the long term. One colonel who had worked under three highly respected general officers over a five-year period pointed out that all of them had announced in staff meetings that they wanted to know what could be done tomorrow.

During our interviews it became clear that despite their limited training for the complex tasks assigned to them, military officers were highly motivated and worked unusually long hours. This motivation may stem from the military tradition of doing the best job possible with the available resources. Among program managers, esprit de corps is enhanced by each officer's belief that "his" program is vital to national defense. Managers' identification with their programs is so strong that there is virtually no chance they would recommend cutbacks based on unfavorable cost-benefit analyses. When they see the acquisition of a weapon system as essential to national survival, ordinary management concerns of cost increases often become secondary considerations.

The Contracting Officer

In negotiations with contractors, the program manager works closely with one or more contracting officers. By definition, a contracting officer is any person, military or civilian, formally assigned the authority to enter into and administer contracts in the name of the United States government.[19] This authority is based on legislation and is implemented in accordance with the Federal Acquisition Regulation (FAR). Contracting officers may be assigned full time to a program office or remain as part of a functional procurement organization and provide part-time support to several programs. Most have several responsibilities in addition to negotiating or administering contracts (e.g., preparing and maintaining contractor performance records), and their career advancement depends on their total performance record. Their involvement with a program begins on receipt of the purchase request and extends through issuance of an invitation for bid (IFB), a request for proposal (RFP), or a request for quotation (RFQ) through the end of the contract.[20]

Alan Beck, a professor at the Defense Systems Management College, notes that the authority to contract was granted to the service Secretaries by the Armed Services Procurement Act of 1947. Contracting authority within the services extends to designated heads of contracting activities (HCAs), usually commanders of major acquisition activities such as the Air Force Systems Command, the Naval Sea Systems Command, or the Army Materiel Command. Below HCA level, contracting authority, which is issued by a formal certification of appointment, often called a warrant, is held by those designated as contracting officers. Criteria for issuance of this warrant are general.

Contracting officers receive varying amounts of specialized training — ranging from a few weeks to several months — through a combination of formal schooling and on-the-job training. General courses in awarding and administering contracts and specific courses in contract law, pricing, and negotiation are available within DOD. Yet, to be effective in complex acquisitions, contracting officers need experience as well as training. Retirements in the late 1970s and early 1980s of the "old hands" who entered the work force immediately after the Second World War have reduced significantly this group of men with experience. Moreover, a 1986 American Bar Association survey of defense contracting officers found that they lacked confidence in the value of their training to prepare them for the rapid changes in the contracting environment or to compensate for their lack of experience. Contracting officers believed their limited training resulted from a need to have officers assigned as soon as possible.[21]

THE ROLE OF THE CONTRACTING OFFICER

There are two primary types of contracting officers:[22] procuring contracting officers (PCO) and administrative contracting officers (ACO).[23] The PCO directs overall procurement contracting efforts: negotiating contracts, signing the contractual documents, issuing orders to stop work or terminate the contract, and making final decisions on any contract disputes with the contractor. The contractor, in turn, can appeal a contracting officer's decision to the Board of Contract Appeals or the U.S. Claims Court.[24]

On small contracts, PCOs are the only contracting officers involved in the acquisition process, exercising complete control from solicitation planning to contractor award to final payment. On large contracts, PCOs focus on the formation and award of the contract, delegating selected postcontract-award administration duties to the ACO, whose duties commonly include arranging payments, negotiating changes, and monitoring contractor performance.[25] ACOs are assigned to the Defense Contract Administration Service (DCAS) or other contract administration activities such as Army, Navy, and Air Force plant representative offices.[26] (See chapter 7.)

During the past thirty years, the Defense Department has faced a continuing controversy over the specific roles of the program manager and the contracting officer and their relationship to each other and to other DOD units. Some attempts have been made to clarify the program manager's role and authority, including the creation of program charters that define responsibilities and reporting channels. The contracting officer's role has been debated extensively in research papers and studies, and alternate roles have been tried — without clear success.[27]

In practice, a contracting officer's relationship with a program manager varies so much from case to case that the fundamental question is what the ideal relationship should be. Indeed, in 1985, at a national conference of contracting officers held to resolve a number of issues, including the question of their roles, the participants were unable to reach an agreement.[28]

Frequently, PCOs are assigned to programs too late to be involved in acquisition strategy planning, and DOD policy is not clear on their role. The PCO role in such plans is only outlined in DOD policy, and in practice varies greatly among the services. For example, in planning the design or production competition, the role of the PCO may be advisory, joint, or primary. The participation of PCOs can also be complicated by their place in the hierarchy. The PCO often serves two masters — the program manager and the buying command's senior manager of procurement or contracting.[29]

In addition to the contracting function, contracting officers are specifically responsible for notifying industry of the proposed system acquisition; convening conferences for firms and sending them an advance copy of the RFP for comment; including in the RFP source-selection criteria consistent with the acquisition strategy; and sending the final RFP to all prospective contractors. It must describe the mission capability needed (not a specific system), and state that each offeror is free to propose its own technical approach, main design features, subsystems, and other features.[30]

Contracting officers play little or no role in reviewing statements of need or requirements that give rise to particular acquisition programs. The program managers' role in defining the military requirements is similarly unclear. They usually do *not* review statements of need or requirements to determine if design freedom and trade-offs between performance and cost are appropriate. Instead, they review them only to gain a more complete understanding of their program.[31]

Program managers normally take the lead in planning and executing the contracting strategy (i.e., selecting the types of contract, terms, and incentives). Although DOD policy is unclear on the contracting officer's role in planning the contracting strategy, it does give him a key role in its execution.[32]

Of concern to many in the Defense Department (as well as to those in the defense industry) is the changing role of the contracting officer, whose discretion and authority have been greatly diminished by recent legislative and administrative changes. For example, in every buying command, there is an increasing number of "advocates" — for competition, small business, specification control, small and disadvantaged business utilization — whose responsibilities overlap those of the contracting officer. In addition, in recent years DOD has expanded and strengthened the audit function so that it now plays one of the major roles in the negotiation and administration of contracts.[33] Jean A. Caffiaux, senior vice-president of the Electronic Industries Association, summarized the problems this has created.

> No businessman hires an auditor, a lawyer, or an engineer for the purpose of surrendering his business decisions to him. Commercial businesses conduct themselves efficiently because the decision makers can seek advice from experts but are free to discount their advice if it makes good business sense to do so and if they are not otherwise restrained by law.[34]

Although DOD regulations and contracts designate the PCO as the final authority in all contract proceedings, the program manager is usually the only official with the breadth of knowledge required to direct, coordinate, and control the numerous organizations involved in the program. This situation dilutes the contracting officer's authority, often making it difficult for him to manage contractor activities effectively.[35] In fact, trade-offs of time, cost, and technical performance are often made, without his knowledge, by agencies outside his jurisdiction, to the detriment of the management process.

Although the contracting officers' authority has decreased, their responsibilities have increased as procurement regulations and policies have introduced formal management techniques, mandatory and optional contract clauses, and contract reviews into the acquisition process. Contracts now cover a number of specialized contractor activities (e.g., data management, quality control, reliability, human engineering, systems engineering, and maintainability), and the contracting officer must ensure compliance with each provision. In fulfilling these duties, they deal with a large variety of people: contractor representatives, contract administrators, equipment specialists, government and industry financial managers, pricing specialists, small-business personnel, legal counselors, industrial mobilization representatives, quality assurance personnel, and management officials from several other levels of the DOD hierarchy. Again, contracting officers must have the program manager's approval for nonroutine administrative actions.

Many government and industry officials believe that the contracting officer is the only government agent authorized to direct contractor activity.[36] In fact, however, contractors usually receive advice and direction from a variety of DOD sources (including the program office, DCAS, DCAA, the using command, the buying command headquarters, and various representatives of OSD).

Contracting officers (as well as government program offices and contractors) also are visited by and receive information requests from a variety of inspectors whose task it is to monitor and evaluate adherence to procedural regulations, directives, and guidelines. These inspectors include representatives of DCAA, military service audit agencies, the DOD Inspector General's office, the Justice Department, the Securities and Exchange Commission, the GAO, the FBI, the Defense Investigative Service, any of several congressional committees, and special teams assembled by a senior DOD civilian or military officer to investigate a particular acquisition problem.

SUMMARY

An article in the weekly edition of the *Washington Post* described the problems of the program manager of the Army's $2.4-billion procurement of the new High Mobility Multipurpose Wheeled Vehicle (Hummer) program. The program manager's problems are typical.

> To plan Hummer's spare parts needs, he [Colonel Petrolino, the Hummer's program manager] calls AMCCOM (the Armament, Munitions, and Chemical Command). To talk about Hummer's role as missile carrier, he calls MICOM (the Missile Command). Before sending Hummers to Fort Lewis, he has to execute an MFA (Material Fielding Agreement) with FORSCOM (Forces Command).
>
> In recent months, Petrolino has spent three quarters of his time on the road, mostly in Washington. He briefed the Army's vice chief of staff three times, the undersecretary of the Army twice, three-star generals of the

Army staff twice, two-star generals on the same staff several times, AMC's deputy commanding general for research and development several times, the Army deputy undersecretary for research twice, not to mention Marine generals and TRADOC [Training and Doctrine Command] colonels, CECOM majors, and General Accounting Office auditors.

There are 43 Defense Department inspectors at the Misawaka plant [where the Hummer is manufactured], but they do not report to Petrolino. They report to an Army major who reports to a colonel who works for DCAS [the Defense Contract Administrative Service in Indianapolis], who reports to another colonel in Columbus, Ohio, who reports to the Defense Logistics Agency in Washington.

And then there is the inevitable paper. "Memos, messages, reports, plans, briefings, paper to support briefings," Petrolino says. "Weekly reports, weekly electronic mail, weekly significant action reports. Monthly program manager control system reports . . . reports on financial management obligations, quality reports, testing reports. . . . The more detail that Congress asks for, the more detail that every other layer of the system asks for. . . . It ripples down."

All of which frustrates an officer who commanded a maintenance battalion in West Germany with few superiors looking over his shoulder.

"I think this is a much harder job, an infinitely harder job, than being a troop commander," Petrolino says. "You control your destiny more there than you control it here."[37]

The Contractor's Program Management Office

Most defense firms find that a task-oriented, or functional, organization is the best environment for the professional development of their employees — their most important asset. Because defense contracts usually require information and guidance from several of these functional groups, many companies adopt a matrix program office structure to provide management direction on specific contracts and a clearly defined point of contact with the customer. The person heading this program office is called a program manager.

When government program managers deal with private industry, they usually exchange information and negotiate courses of action with their counterpart, the contractor program manager. But the industry approach provides an interesting contrast to that of the government. An industry program manager is expected to produce a profit for his company; and this requires industrial management skills as well as knowledge of the government acquisition process.

The organizational structure of an industry program office, though usually modeled on the government program office, varies according to program requirements. In general, the program manager is chosen from a management level appropriate to the size of the program. Small research or limited development programs performed in a narrow segment of the company are directed by middle-level functional managers. Larger programs, which draw on broad segments of the company, require larger program offices and managers of a more senior level, who have direct and immediate access to senior management.

An Army brigadier general program manager pointed out the crucial difference between the industry and government program managers.

> The contractor program manager, unlike his government counterpart, is the authority. If people recommend a strategy to him and he does not want to do it, then he does not do it. In industry, the organization is there to support the program manager.

Two reasons for the greater managerial autonomy of industry program managers are their longevity and expertise. The combination of their managerial skills, knowledge of the company — its people and its operating methods — and their experience with and knowledge of the government acquisition process elicits senior management trust in their judgment and ability to accomplish the job.

Because industry program managers and their staffs are assigned to programs for several years at a time, they are generally responsible for realizing the program's full profit and sales potential. Their duties include:

1. interpreting total contract requirements;
2. developing a plan for fulfilling program requirements within contract budget and schedule;
3. dividing the requirements into discrete work packages;
4. assigning the work packages to functional groups or to outside sources ("make or buy" decisions);
5. defining and assigning responsibility for interfaces between work packages;
6. determining the adequacy of resources assigned to each work package (in accordance with the overall program plan);
7. obtaining adequate funding from the government customer to accomplish the program plan;

8. maintaining continuous program surveillance (i.e., identifying budget or schedule problems and then notifying appropriate internal management levels of them);
9. satisfying the customer with and informing company management of program progress; and
10. providing liaison with the customer.

During our interviews, we learned that a company generally selects a program manager when it first decides to bid for a new development program. Throughout the development program, the industry program manager is the key person, and because his role is key to the company's financial health, he works under constant pressure. If he performs successfully, his promotion to a higher management level is ensured. If he is not successful, promotion channels close quickly.

THE CAREER OF AN INDUSTRY PROGRAM MANAGER

There is no single career path for industry program managers (most are trained in a technical specialty, business management, contract requirements, and negotiations with customers). Most spend years of uninterrupted assignment to the design and management of programs under government contract. An assignment as an industry program manager is generally considered a broadening experience for potential company executives. Most transfers involving program managers are lateral, that is, into and among the company's various program and functional departments. Although program management is considered a relatively high-risk route to general management, it is also a well-paid risk. Annual salaries for industry managers of major defense programs in 1987 began at figures above $100,000, usually two or more times the salaries of their government counterparts.

As a general rule, an industry program manager is evaluated in terms of customer satisfaction with the weapon system developed or produced in his program and his ability to contribute to the company's growth and profitability. His record in meeting the contract terms for schedule and cost is important, but secondary as long as he can persuade the customer to accept a schedule or budget change. Especially important is the manager's record in generating subsequent contracts. He continually attempts to expand the scope of the program by proposing and negotiating changes or by persuading a government agency to buy more production items. The need of the company for follow-on business is urgent because highly qualified program personnel do not like to mark time between government contracts. When government funds are expended, talented employees are idle and grow restless. If the period between programs lasts from three to six months, personnel may move to other firms, especially if promotions or lateral transfers are available. Companies make a great effort to avoid this.

When an industry program manager has exhausted all opportunities to attract follow-on programs, his responsibilities decrease considerably. This usually occurs between the middle of the development phase and the first phase of production. Work then becomes relatively routine, and the possibilities for contract changes or additions are significantly reduced. In some cases, management of remaining program performance is transferred to the manufacturing or production department. At other times, a less experienced program manager is assigned to the program.

In many major defense firms, as in many government program offices, a small group of specialists assists the program manager in directing the work performed in functional departments. This group includes a chief engineer and a director of program control, who usually remain with the program throughout its duration and are rewarded with pay increases commensurate with its sales and profit success. Other group members are drawn from the functional departments of the company and phase in and out of the program as needed. They include specialists in contracts, production, logistics, systems, technical support, data, and planning and control. Program support staffs range from fewer than ten to several hundred people, depending on the size of the program.

A program manager can have special problems as a result of sharing staff with other programs. For example, a program manager assigns a task to the manufacturing department, whose manager will then provide the necessary manpower. The program manager will direct and coordinate the overall program activity, but responsibility for the daily supervision and periodic performance appraisals lies with the manufacturing department manager. This division of authority, if not well managed, can be a serious impediment to the success of the program.

Some major contractors have therefore organized their program office as self-contained units, with each program manager comparable to the general manager of an independent company. Some firms even assign one or more separate buildings to major programs. According to industry managers, this organizational structure provides work incentives and a sense of participation not afforded by a matrix organization. Many industry program managers believe that a group of experts working closely together on one program perform better than a collection of specialists separated by discipline or function. When all participants share the goals of the program, there is less conflict and misspent energy. In addition, senior management has found that these relatively independent program management organizations are easier to monitor for contract performance.

INDUSTRY ENGINEERS WHO WORK ON DEFENSE PROGRAMS

Skilled engineers (in government as well as industry) are usually dedicated to their technical specialties. If they receive satisfactory salaries, their principal objectives are to work on challenging technical problems and to advance the state of the art. Because the program performance of one engineer, or an engineering task group, is usually integrated with the work of other engineering units, there is considerable intragroup discussion regarding technical activity. Industry executives believe that many engineers are often more sensitive to their colleagues' opinions than to their program goals. As they struggle with tasks that advance the state of the art, engineers working on defense programs feel particularly vulnerable. Not only must they develop new technical approaches in the development of a weapon system, but their solutions must also withstand the scrutiny of their peers. As such, it is often not enough that the equipment they design and construct meet program performance standards; it must also be more sophisticated, whether or not dictated by the contract requirements.

Industry managers welcome engineering achievements that will enhance the reputation of the company and attract new business. The technology developed on one defense contract may ensure large profits from subsequent defense and commercial ventures. Contractors use various incentives to encourage engineering advances. Employee appraisal systems (on which promotions and salary increases are based) usually give as much weight to technological achievement as to meeting cost and schedule requirements. Appraisals of a particular department sometimes consider the number of new patents developed by its engineers, who occasionally receive bonuses for these achievements.

Although engineers understandably prefer to pursue their technical objectives without constraints, budget and schedule requirements can impose limits. Engineers are expected to cooperate with the program manager, but their promotions are normally controlled by engineering supervisors, who share their quest for advancing the state of the art.

Because of the incentives described above, engineers understandably spend the funds available to them. Periodically, problems arise within programs when engineers exceed their budgets. When cost, schedule, and technical performance requirements are incompatible, program managers establish priorities, granting in most cases highest priority to technical performance. Given a choice of meeting cost or schedule requirements, program managers generally prefer to meet schedules. As one contractor explained: "Missing a schedule is one of the few justifications the government has for terminating a contract for default."

In parts of the country where there is considerable movement of technical personnel among firms, industry program managers are solicitous in their treatment of especially proficient engineers. The exercise of strict cost discipline can drive good engineers to rival companies. Rather than run that risk, managers concentrate on meeting technical and schedule needs and try to avoid conflicts over costs. This policy explains the need for company "management reserves," which account for 3 to 8 percent of contract costs. Funds must be allocated not only for the unforeseeable problems that arise in all development efforts but for the cost of professional curiosity and competitiveness as well. These factors provide major challenges to government program managers interested in maintaining control of program costs.

Although program managers, contracting officers, and their superiors in government and industry are dedicated to the success of their programs, the word *success* means something different to each one. Among government officials — ranging from the program office to the Secretary of Defense and from Congress to the executive branch — interpretations of weapon systems priorities vary widely and derive from divergent values and goals. In comparison, the primary goals of industry are relatively simple: maintaining customer satisfaction, realizing a profit, developing the professional skills of employees, and generating more business.

Notes

1. Comptroller General of the United States, "Action Required to Improve DOD Career Program for Procurement Personnel," Report to the Congress, August 13, 1970, p. 12.
2. U.S. General Accounting Office, "DOD Acquisition: Strengthening Capabilities of Key Personnel in Systems Acquisition," GAO/NSIAD–86–45, May 1986, p. 2.
3. U.S. General Accounting Office, GAO/NSIAD–86–45, May 1986, p. 20.

4. Alan W. Beck, "The Program Manager and the Contracting Officer: Shared Responsibility in Systems Acquisition," *Contract Management,* March 1985.

5. 10 U.S.C. 1621 and OMB Circular A-109, "Major Systems Acquisitions," para. 5.6, April 5, 1976, defines a major system as

> [T]hat combination of elements that will function together to produce the capabilities required to fulfill a mission need. The elements may include, for example, hardware, equipment, software, construction, or other improvements or real property. Major systems acquisition programs are those programs that (1) are directed at and critical to fulfilling an agency mission, (2) entail the allocation of relatively large resources, and (3) warrant special management attention. Additional criteria and relative dollar thresholds for the determination of agency programs to be considered major systems under the purview of this circular may be established at the discretion of the agency head.

See also Department of Defense Directive (DODD) 5000.1, "Major Systems Acquisitions," March 12, 1986.

6. Leonard Sullivan, Jr., "Characterizing the Acquisition Process," paper prepared for the Defense Acquisition Study, Center for Strategic and International Studies, Georgetown University, January 1986, p. E-4.

7. Gen. Henry A. Miley, letter to the Assistant Secretary of the Army, July 11, 1984; and U.S. Senate, testimony before the Task Force on Selected Defense Procurement Matters of the Committee on Armed Services, "Career Paths and Professional Development for Acquisition Managers in the Department of Defense," December 13, 1984, pp. 17–22.

8. J. Ronald Fox, *Arming America: How the U.S. Buys Weapons* (Boston: Division of Research, Harvard Business School, 1974), p. 199.

9. U.S. General Accounting Office, "Department of Defense's Defense Acquisition Improvement Program: A Status Report," GAO/NSIAD–86–148, July 1986, pp. 13–14.

10. Robert A. Magnan, "In Search of the 'End Game': A Comparison of U.S. and Foreign Weapons Acquisition Systems," a study conducted under the DCI Exceptional Intelligence Analyst Program, 1984, pp. 63–66.

11. President's Blue Ribbon Commission on Defense Management, *A Quest for Excellence,* Final Report to the President, June 1986, pp. 46–47.

12. Comptroller General of the United States, "Action Required to Improve DOD Career Program for Procurement Personnel," August 13, 1970, p. 12.

13. Wilbur D. Jones, Jr., "Reflections of a Department of Defense Program Manager," *Program Manager,* January-February 1986, pp. 30–54.

14. U.S. Senate, hearing before the Subcommittee on Defense Acquisition Policy of the Committee on Armed Services, "Defense Procurement Process," February 20, 1985, p. 19.

15. Ibid., pp. 18–19.

16. U.S. Senate, testimony of Dr. James P. Wade, Jr., before the Subcommittee on Defense Acquisition Policy of the Committee on Armed Services, "Implementation of the 1984 Defense Procurement Legislation," October 17 and 29, and November 7 and 13, 1985, p. 17.

17. U.S. General Accounting Office, "Can the United States Major Weapon Sys-

tems Acquisition Process Keep Pace with the Conventional Arms Threat Posed by the USSR?" GAO/PSAD/GP, May 27, 1980, pp. 56–57.

18. President's Blue Ribbon Commission on Defense Management, *A Quest for Excellence,* June 1986, p. 47.
19. Federal Acquisition Regulation 1–201.3.
20. John Holmes and E. J. Thigpen, Jr., *Principles of Contract Law* (Washington, D.C.: Federal Acquisition Institute), pp. I-2–13.
21. Richard J. Bednar and John T. Jones, Jr., "The Role of the DOD Contracting Officer," Draft Report of the American Bar Association (ABA) Section of Public Contract Law, Ad Hoc Committee, John E. Cavanagh, Chairman, January 11, 1987, p. 119.
22. The author is grateful to Paul G. Dembling, chairman of the American Bar Association Section of Public Contract Law, for information on the role of the DOD Contracting Officer.
23. Department of Defense Inspector General, "Work Measurement Systems and Engineered Labor Standards," June 26, 1986.
24. Alan W. Beck, "The Program Manager and the Contracting Officer."
25. Bednar and Jones, "The Role of the DOD Contracting Officer," pp. 46–47; and Federal Acquisition Regulation 42.100.
26. The Defense Contract Administration Service (DCAS), a component of the Defense Logistics Agency, was formed from the contract administration organizations of the three services, which previously administered DOD contracts. DCAS was created in order to improve management and reduce costs by eliminating duplicate administrative services. Other contract administration organizations include Army, Air Force, and Navy plant representatives' offices and foreign government organizations.
27. U.S. General Accounting Office, GAO/NSIAD–86–45, May 1986, pp. 18–19.
28. Ibid., p. 44.
29. Ibid., pp. 3–4.
30. See the September 1985 update of DOD Directive 4105.62, "Selection of Contractual Sources for Major Defense Systems."
31. U.S. General Accounting Office, GAO/NSIAD–86–45, May 1986, p. 34.
32. U.S. General Accounting Office, GAO/NSIAD–86–45, p. 19.
33. U.S. Senate, testimony of Karl Harr, President of Aerospace Industries Association, before the Subcommittee on Defense Acquisition Policy of the Committee on Armed Services, "Implementation of the 1984 Defense Procurement Legislation," October 17 and 29, and November 7 and 13, 1985, p. 377.
34. U.S. Senate, letter of Jean A. Caffiaux, Senior Vice-President of the Electronic Industries Association, to Sen. Dan Quayle, December 12, 1985, quoted in hearings before the Subcommittee on Defense Acquisition Policy of the Committee on Armed Services, "Implementation of the 1984 Defense Procurement Legislation," October 17 and 29, and November 7 and 13, 1985, p. 363.
35. Instructions of Gen. James Ferguson to Program Managers, Air Force Systems Command, January 24, 1970.
36. Aerospace Industries Association, "The Role of the Contracting Officer," July 1971.
37. *Washington Post,* June 3, 1985.

__ 5 _____

CAREERS IN ACQUISITION MANAGEMENT

This chapter describes the current practice with respect to DOD program management careers. It begins with a section on assignment practices, and then deals with career fields, training, and the revolving door.

Tenure of Program Managers

Most major defense programs are managed by a succession of military officers who rotate in and out of their assignments, with as many as five to nine in charge at different stages. Because many major programs extend ten years or more from initial development to initial production (with overlapping development and production stages), program managers rarely acquire the necessary knowledge and experience or have clear responsibility for either success or failure.[1]

In late 1986, an industry program manager of a large defense program described the problem of rapid turnover among government personnel.

> Army project managers stay two years, possibly three. The best end up staying the shortest time because they get promoted or assigned to a better job. There have been two military program managers and three deputy program managers on the Patriot program in the past three years. One of the deputy PMs was reassigned, and two retired to industry. On the Patriot program over a period of 20 years there have been nine government program managers.
>
> There is a lot of turbulence in the program when program managers change. Each government PM knows that he is not going to get his star

unless he does something different. Then, his next assignment is to run an Army base; this happens even to excellent program managers.

At the Naval Air Systems Command, there is the same turnover as in the Army. The program managers and the deputy program managers are usually pilots, and the turnover is every two to three years, same as in the Army.

The Packard Commission described program management turnover as a longstanding problem in managing the acquisition process. Indeed, frequent turnover has persisted for more than thirty years despite periodic statements from Pentagon officials, beginning in the late 1960s, that the problem had been solved.

In 1954, the House Committee on Government Operations conducted hearings on the organization and administration of military R&D programs. The subcommittee report zeroed in on the reasons for high turnover.

> It appears clear to the subcommittee that military personnel career requirements are basically different from those of scientists and other technical personnel, and that rotation is understandably necessary in order that military officers might familiarize themselves with a variety of military operations. The subcommittee recognizes the unique need for military rotation, but accelerated rotation programs which result in short tours of duty are both disturbing and harmful to the productivity of the research and development programs.
>
> At the commanding-officer level, short tours of duty might not in themselves be harmful if the officer is primarily fulfilling a military need for his having a variety of experiences. Difficulties do appear when an officer, fresh from the field and with limited technical experience, enters a research center with a view to reorganization based on limited technical qualifications.[2]

Two years later, in 1956, a study of the military services and weapon systems reached the same conclusion: "Project officers lack sufficient training, rank, and continuity of assignment."[3]

The problem of turnover again received attention in 1962, this time from Merton J. Peck and Frederic M. Scherer in their private research. They too found a high rate of turnover and evidence of its consequences.

> Since it usually takes one or two years for a person to obtain a thorough working knowledge of the technology and personalities involved in a com-

plex weapons program, rotation can interfere seriously with the smooth administration of programs. The rapid turnover of U.S. weapons project officers has been the subject of much criticism. Schlaifer, for example, found unduly short tours of duty a serious problem in the development of U.S. aircraft engines during the 1930s. More recently, the Robertson Committee concluded that the duty tours of aircraft weapons project officers should be lengthened beyond the 26- to 32-month average which prevailed during the early 1950s. Yet our case studies conducted during the late 1950s indicated that rapid turnover of project officers remained a problem.[4]

Before 1970, 80 percent of the program managers in the Army remained in their assignments for less than three years, and 60 percent for less than two years. The figures for the other services were similar. During 1970, however, each service made plans to assign program managers to minimum three-year tours and to schedule transfers to coincide with natural milestones within their programs. In the same year, the Army began a personnel development program for procurement managers, with more than fifty officers assigned to its design. After nearly a year, the senior officer on the project commented: "The improvement program itself has been hampered by the military rotation system taking officers out of their jobs in the program and moving them to another place, simply because the personnel branch noted that the time had come for a move."

In the late 1980s, military rotation and individual military career considerations caused program managers to be assigned to programs for an average period of only thirty months.[5] Frequent reassignment of managers not only produces unnecessary shifts in program emphasis but also leads to a loss of direction and momentum while the newly assigned program managers settle in and learn their jobs.[6]

In 1982, a panel of the American Defense Preparedness Association, a major defense industry association, reviewed the situation and concluded that

> qualified officers must spend enough time on the job to have their impact felt and to be accountable for the results. In spite of past efforts to ensure adequate tenure, the duration on many programs is still less than two years, and the turnover is often higher one or two levels below the program manager. Tenure should be at least three years in a position and should be based on or lead to other assignments within the same program. Assign-

ments should also relate to logical milestones in the program rather than to a calendar time or promotional reassignment.[7]

In July 1986, a survey by the U.S. General Accounting Office found that program managers averaged approximately twenty-seven months on a given program as either the program manager or deputy program manager, and their deputies thirty months (see table 5.1).[8]

These periods are still relatively short, considering that the typical major weapon system acquisition cycle spans more than a decade. According to an Assistant Secretary of Defense, short tenures can push managers to sacrifice quality for short-term results.[9]

TABLE 5.1. Tenure of Program and Deputy Program Managers

Current Position	As program manager	As deputy program manager	Combined
Program Manager			
Army	19.1	3.1	22.2
Navy	28.0	7.6	35.6
Air Force	19.3	3.8	23.1
Average[a]	22.4	5.0	27.4
Deputy Program Manager[b]			
Army	6.6	40.8	47.4
Navy	0.5	27.0	27.5
Air Force		23.9	23.9
Average[a]	0.6	29.5	30.1

[a] Averages are weighted to consider the different numbers of managers and programs in each service. They are based on seventy-seven program managers and seventy-five deputy program managers who provided tenure data.
[b] Between program managers, a deputy program manager may serve temporarily as program manager.
SOURCE: U.S. General Accounting Office, "DOD's Defense Acquisition Improvement Program," GAO/NSIAD–86–148, July 1986, p. 11.

In a Senate hearing held in March 1985, Gen. Lawrence Skantze, commander of the Air Force Systems Command, reported that the average tenure of program managers in his command was twenty-nine months. In his opinion, that was long enough for a program manager to understand the complex program environment.

> I think the Air Force program managers are able to develop a sufficient understanding of their programs in a matter of months. The 29 months

average tenure reflects the current average length our program managers are assigned to major programs, it does not reflect their total previous acquisition experience.[10]

In 1986, the General Accounting Office found that changes of program managers in the Navy were most often associated with retirement, which accounted for two-thirds of their turnover. By contrast, slightly less than one-half of Army and slightly less than one-fifth of Air Force program managers retired from their assignments, suggesting that further military career opportunities may be more attractive for Army and Air Force program managers.[11]

The early loss of program managers to retirement has prompted criticism of the current military retirement system. The view of B. B. Bray, executive director of the Federal Managers Association, is shared by many industry observers and by the Packard Commission.

The basic problem with the retiring military personnel is the fact that the military retirement program is 100 years old. The span of service is based on your physical attributes; really your ability to ride a horse across the plains fighting the Indians. With today's sophisticated, complex, electronic fighting gear, the military mind is of greater importance than ever before. The military officer goes out of active duty often at the height of his mental capabilities. Thus, you obviously have a terrific supply of manpower, womanpower, for use in our economy.[12]

If military personnel are leaving the armed services at the height of their careers, they are also leaving after extensive education and training in many areas, thanks in part to the high rate of turnover in the Army, Navy, and, to a much lesser extent, the Air Force. The 1970 report of the President's Blue Ribbon Defense Panel included a study of 174 military officers with an average service career of twenty-four years. The 174 officers had served in a total of 3,695 assignments, or an average of 21 per person.[13] The average officer had spent eight years in operational assignments, five years in military service schools and other educational institutions, and eleven years in a variety of staff assignments. Many DOD managers think there has been little change since then.

The rotation policy is obviously one factor preventing most officers from gaining the in-depth experience needed for their program management assignments. The services believe that rotation from one type of assignment to another at frequent intervals broadens the capabilities of their officers, qualifying them to hold any senior position. One Army lieutenant colonel commented, "The attitude is that they have to cycle you through everything fast. I've never had an assignment for longer than two years; this is partly motivated by the short military career."

Although frequent rotation may be useful in training combat commanders or those assigned to less technical military tasks, the increasingly sophisticated technical nature of defense acquisition makes the practice an anachronism in the 1980s. The use of rotation as an educational tool does not acknowledge that even the most capable officers assigned to program management offices need extensive training and apprenticeship. Both the officers and the programs to which they are assigned suffer when such training and experience are missing. As the President's Blue Ribbon Defense Panel observed in 1970:

> The system of rotation not only fails to provide management and leadership needed on the job but also has deficiencies in accomplishing its stated purpose — the development of the officer himself. Men are not developed by being observers; they must have responsibility to assure growth. From the point of view of the position to be filled, as well as the best interests of the officer himself, his job assignments should be of sufficient duration so that he can become thoroughly involved in the work and be fully responsible for results.[14]

This view is widely shared by industry managers as well. F. R. Sims, of LTV Aerospace and Defense Company, pointed out that the constant change in military personnel assigned to procuring agencies "limits long-term applications of lessons learned, introduces a heavy training and learning burden, and guarantees that management styles are constantly in a state of flux."[15]

A May 1986 GAO study of seventeen defense programs found that the tenure of program managers averaged nine months for three programs in the Army, fifteen months for five in the Air Force, and thirty-nine months for five in the Navy.[16] As the seventeen programs progressed, tenure for those then (August 1985) serving as program managers tended to increase — to an average of twenty-five months (Army) and thirty-one months (Air Force). Only in the Navy did tenure decrease — to an average of twenty-six months.

The study also found that the tenure of program managers replaced from January 1982 to August 1984 — for all programs and phases — was longest in the Navy, where it averaged 3.9 years, compared with 3.1

years in the Army and only 1.9 years in the Air Force. The relatively short tenure of Air Force program managers is consistent with the view expressed in testimony by General Skantze. He disagreed that fixed tours were needed, explaining that it is desirable to maintain the flexibility to change program managers based on program needs and the manager's performance. The GAO study found, however, that tenure in none of the services was connected with tangible results.[17]

Resistance to Change

In December 1970, the House Committee on Government Operations expressed doubts about the effectiveness of the attempts of the Defense Department to stabilize program manager assignments.

> Secretary Packard has referred to the need for drastic reorganization of the services, but he has not spelled out any details, and there is little indication that the services share his view of the problem or are prepared to institute such changes on their own.
>
> It is fair to ask whether the new call for expertise in program management squares with policy and practice regarding the rotation of military officers. The new goal is three-year tours of duty for program managers. It is difficult to see how three-year tours of duty for military officers will enable them to gain the degree of technical and managerial expertise that Mr. Packard emphasized so strongly. Development projects frequently are maintained for much longer periods. The concept of expertise that Admiral Rickover espouses, and Mr. Packard seems to endorse, is associated with rigorous technical training, career professionalism, and longer tenure than even a three-year tour of duty.[18]

In 1984, Norman Augustine, president and chief operating officer of Martin Marietta Corporation and former Under Secretary of the Army, stated during a Senate hearing:

> In other words, one program manager would stay through the entire development process. That may mean six or eight years normally. I realize that is in conflict with the current promotional scheme, particularly in the uniformed military.[20]

Mr. Augustine elaborated on this point during a House Armed Services Committee hearing in September 1986, stating that he would seriously consider that [the same people remain with the project through completion], and I would consider, in fact, at a minimum, staying with a project through a major milestone. . . . Maybe we need a new approach to career programs. Managing a major defense acquisition program is simply too important to be left to people who are going to be there for a couple of years and then leave.[19]

In a 1985 Senate hearing, Caleb Hurtt, a senior officer of the Martin Marietta Corporation, compared the early retirement of military program managers with a very different practice in industry.

It is true that that system [the military system] is different than our system. Very few of our people, in my opinion — and I am talking of the guy who is 45 — think of retirement at all. He is an awfully long way from it, so he does not think about it.[21]

A senior vice-president of another major defense contractor commented:

It is crazy to place military officers in the acquisition business for two to three years and then send them back to the mainstream. A military person must have the experience and understanding of how the system works. This is the number one priority. It is hard enough running these programs when you spend your entire career doing it.

Because of the military policy of relatively short assignments, performance incentives are geared to the success of short-term tasks. A management action with a short-term result will be recorded in the evaluation of the officer currently assigned to the task and considered in his annual performance rating. Maintaining progress, making no changes, and progressing efficiently toward long-term (eight- to twelve-year) program goals are seldom considered "rewarding" activities. They may lead to ultimate program success, but they seldom lead to outstanding performance ratings for the manager.

Personnel problems within the armed services are certainly not limited to program management. In other military areas, however, they are not as difficult to remedy. There is more than irony in a story by Kenneth Turan of the *Washington Post* (December 1969).

Rear Admiral James Calvert, superintendent of the Naval Academy, announced at yesterday's annual Army-Navy Luncheon at the Touchdown

Club that Coppedge, who has been athletic director since June 1968, will retire from the service in July to take the post as a civilian.

The admiral said the change to a civilian director is "absolutely essential, if the Naval Academy's program is to catch and overtake those on our schedule in football and 20 other sports." Navy takes a 1–8 record, its worst in more than 20 years, into the November 29 game with Army.

Admiral Calvert emphasized that "by constantly changing our athletic director every two or three years we have destroyed continuity, which is necessary to an effective athletic administration," and Coppedge agreed, saying "If you had a million-and-a-half dollar business, would you want to change bosses every three years for someone who didn't have any experience?"

Previously, the athletic director's post was simply another two- to three-year tour of duty for career Navy men. "Most directors come right from sea duty to this job," Coppedge said, "and it can take a full year to get to know the ropes. When I became director I barely knew the NCAA ground rules. How many people in the Navy do you think know about things like scheduling problems?"

Although the Naval Academy solved its rotation problems in the early 1970s, those responsible for defense acquisition did not. Defense program managers in the late 1980s still rotate their assignments, on average, every twenty-seven to thirty months.

Congressional Action

In October 1984, Congress passed legislation requiring a minimum four-year tour for program managers. In 1986, the Packard Commission supported that legislation.[22]

Two months after the four-year requirement became law (albeit with a stipulation allowing each service Secretary to waive the requirement), Sen. Dan Quayle (R-IN) of the Senate Armed Services Committee asked an Air Force spokesman, Maj. Gen. Richard Steere, for his assessment of the law. He replied:

> The purpose of the legislation is to promote stability in the DOD acquisition process. The primary effect will be to reduce personnel management flexibility regarding our key program managers, particularly with waiver authority at the Secretary level. As a practice, the Air Force always tried to make rotation dates for program managers coincide with major program milestones.[23]

General Steere's reference to the reduced "personnel management flexibility" apparently meant that the Air Force would not be able to rotate their officers as often as it had in the past. That, in fact, was the purpose of the law. Although the Air Force may have always tried to accommodate major program milestones, it did not always succeed and the high-turnover rates suggest that mandatory four-year assignments would help alleviate the problem.

At the same hearing, General Steere compared program management turnover rates in the Air Force and in industry to illustrate their similarity:

> AFSC [Air Force Systems Command] program manager tenure is averaging about 29 months. Industry program manager tenure is averaging about 36 months — based on a survey of SAR [largest programs] prime contractors conducted in May 84 by AFSC.[24]

Although industry representatives believe General Steere's figures for industry are low, there is an important difference between the two sectors that is not revealed in these statistics. When industry program managers leave a position, they are normally assigned to another government-contracted program or to a more senior position overseeing a group of those programs, in either case making use of the knowledge and skills they acquired. This is far less often the practice in DOD; it happens only occasionally in the Army and Navy, although more frequently in the Air Force. Unlike their industry counterparts, government program managers often return to combat operations assignments or retire. Whatever skills they gained are often lost to the Defense Department.

Although acknowledging some advantages to four-year tours, General Steere went on to cite the disadvantages.

> Tenure is a two-edged sword. While there are benefits from long tenure (e.g., corporate memory, historical basis for decisions, enhanced understanding of complex program environment), there are also benefits from limiting individual program management tenure. Mobility is important. It provides for fresh perspectives, innovative approaches to institutional problems, dynamic program leadership, and mitigates against stagnation, complacency, or the development of too close an identity between the program manager and his system.[25]

One could conclude that General Steere differs with the goal of the congressional legislation: to keep military officers in program management acquisition assignments for *years* so as to better understand and become expert in the intricacies of planning and controlling the schedule, cost, and technical performance of large industrial corporations performing work on major defense contracts.

Despite the congressional legislation, the resistance of senior military officers (many of whose views are well represented by General Steere) in each service raises doubts about whether the longstanding problem of the rate of turnover among program managers has been solved.

In November 1974, then Deputy Secretary of Defense William Clements wrote to each of the service Secretaries a memorandum introducing DOD Directive 5000.23, on systems acquisition management careers. He emphasized the importance of the directive by stating: "I can foresee no reason that a program manager's tour should be less than four years." Judging from the situation in the mid-1980s, a number of unforeseen reasons have frustrated Secretary Clements's goal.[26]

Career Fields

DOD Directive 5000.23, "System Acquisition Management Careers," is intended to provide the basic framework for program manager career development. Among other goals, the directive stated:

Career opportunities should be established to attract, develop, retain, and reward outstanding military officers and civilians employed in acquisition management.
Promotion opportunities for military officers should be equal to those of their contemporaries in operational and command positions.
The tenure of program manager assignments should be sufficient to ensure management continuity.[27]

DODD 5000.23 also stated that Army and Air Force colonels and Navy captains or civilians assigned as program managers should have previous program management or defense system acquisition experience, including one or more assignments to a program office. In addition, general or flag-rank officers and their civilian counterparts in the acquisition field should have "substantial" prior experience in program management or system acquisition, including experience at the lieutenant colonel or colonel (or equivalent) level.[28] In 1987, thirteen years after the directive was originally issued, many program managers and flag-rank officers assigned to the DOD acquisition process failed to meet these standards.

The DOD directive was an effort to implement recommendations made repeatedly by different groups. In 1969, a Defense Science Board task force concluded that a "major increase in the recognition, the status, and the opportunities in program management may be necessary to attract and retain a larger share of the most capable career officers" for system acquisition management.[29]

In 1970, the President's Blue Ribbon Defense Panel identified the status of program management as a weakness in defense acquisition.[30] In the same year, Deputy Defense Secretary David Packard, in a policy guidance memorandum, observed that "program management in the services will be improved only to the extent that capable people with the right kind of experience and training" are chosen as managers, and that "program managers must be given more recognition."[31]

In the late 1980s, the qualifications of program managers continued to be a topic of serious concern. Indeed, a May 1986 study by the General Accounting Office found that few defense program managers had the desired mix of experience (four years in a program office and eight years in acquisition) and training (the twenty-week Defense Systems Management College [DSMC] course) (see table 5.2).[32]

TABLE 5.2. DOD Program Managers

	Army (n = 13)	Navy (n = 10)	Air Force (n = 11)
Percentage with four years of program office experience	30.8	30.0	54.6
Median years of program office experience	4.1	1.2	4.1
Percentage with eight years of total acquisition experience	46.1	40.0	63.6
Median years of total acquisition experience	7.2	7.4	13.0
Percentage completing the DSMC program management course	66.6	30.0	18.2
Percentage with combined experience and training: four years of program office experience, eight years of total acquisition experience, and completion of the twenty-week DSMC program management course	15.4	0.0	36.4

SOURCE: U.S. General Accounting Office, "DOD Acquisition: Strengthening Capabilities of Key Personnel in Systems Acquisition," GAO/NSIAD–86–45, May 1986, p. 78.

The GAO study points to widely differing practices across the military services. For example, program manager acquisition experience in the Air Force exceeds that of the Army and Navy by significant amounts. Nonetheless, by 1987, the term *acquisition experience* had become a catch phrase used by many government officials. Unfortunately, however, the term as used throughout the Defense Department and Congress now includes almost any kind of logistics experience: maintenance, supply, purchasing, contracting, deployment, R&D management, and training related to one of the Army, Navy, and Air Force materiel commands. As a result, many of the officers with "acquisition experience" assigned to program management offices arrive with few skills in planning, oversight, and control of development and production programs performed under contract with large industrial firms. Consequently, the term misrepresents the qualifications needed to produce a competent manager of complex development and production programs.

In examining the program managers' backgrounds, GAO researchers found that although some possessed significant acquisition experience, few possessed the desired mix of training and experience.[33] The proportion of those with a combination of substantial program office experience (four years), eight years of total acquisition experience (even with the broad definition), and completion of the DSMC program management course was low: none from the Navy, only 15.4 percent from the Army, and 36.4 percent from the Air Force met these criteria.[34]

- The Air Force had the highest proportion of program managers with substantial program office experience, slightly more than one-half; the Army and Navy had less than one-third.
- The Air Force had the highest proportion with acquisition experience, nearly two-thirds; the Army and Navy had less than one-half.
- The Army had the highest proportion who had completed the DSMC program management course, two-thirds; the Navy had less than one-third and the Air Force less than one-fifth.[35]

Although completion of the DSMC twenty-week course and eight years of acquisition experience are useful preparation for a program manager, the officer faces powerful pressures for assignment rotation to acquire training as a generalist. This is more the case in the Army and Navy than in the Air Force. Continuing support for assigning generalists to key acquisition positions is attributable, in part, to a commonly

held view that assigning a combat arms officer to an acquisition assignment (often as program manager) is the best way for a military service to
develop a system that is "what the user wants." Unfortunately, it may
also be the best way of ensuring that acquisition managers will not have
the skills required for managing large development and production programs.

CAREER PATH DEVELOPMENT

In 1974, I reported in *Arming America* that the problem of attracting
and developing enough qualified military personnel to fill positions
within program offices was becoming more urgent year by year.

> Although Pentagon officials, such as Deputy Secretary Packard, began
> to make improvements in 1970 and 1971 in the training and assignment
> process for military officers, it is still doubtful whether their efforts will lead
> to significant changes in promotion and assignment policies. The most far-
> reaching reform would be the establishment of a clearly defined procure-
> ment career field within the military, with senior procurement managers
> controlling assignments and promotions. Anything short of this will not
> resolve the continuing crisis in procurement management.[36]

Between 1972 and 1974, Pentagon officials issued numerous statements about the need to establish clearly defined military career fields in
program management and procurement. Those initiatives were resisted,
however, by senior officers in personnel and combat arms units, who
were unconvinced of the need for a highly skilled and stable professional
force to manage the acquisition process. Senior combat arms officers
(who control military assignments and promotions) were also concerned that they would lose some of their most able officers to acquisition careers if they lost control of the assignment and promotion process.

During our interviews, many industry executives working on defense programs highlighted the need for a more effective DOD procurement management career field. The following statements from four industry managers are typical of the views expressed.

> Acquisition should be conducted by professionals who have only one
> career motivation — to be the best acquisition professional in the system —
> and who see only that profession as the means to promotion. Setting aside

a number of high-level military ranks for procurement assignments does not alone ensure the professional needs of acquisition.

* * *

There is a need for much more care in translating policies down through each organizational level within the Department of Defense. The military services need to do much more in terms of training their procurement personnel and in creating a clear procurement field. There needs to be a separate career ladder for procurement, and the career assignments need to be under the control of the people in charge of procurement.

* * *

There should be career progression ladders for procurement officers and program managers, separate from the career progression ladders for operational personnel. We see no advantage to the country in taking a good boat commander and making him a program manager.

* * *

You will find very few military officers who have had more than one assignment as a program manager. The promotion system usually doesn't give credit for having the same ticket punched twice.

A retired lieutenant general, formerly in charge of one of the buying commands, reflected on his experience:

> There is a widely held belief in the services that the weapons acquisition process is a "secondary specialty" that anyone can learn. In reality, we need to create a program management career and a professional program management organization — not half a career in acquisition and half a career in operational commands. I have really turned around on this point. I used to think that the fifty-fifty arrangement was the best one.

In March 1985, Senate Armed Services Committee (SASC) questioning of Gen. Richard Thompson, commander of the Army Materiel Command (AMC), revealed that two Army program managers had less than one year of "acquisition experience" at the time of appointment and that the prior experience level of eight other program managers (identified by the SASC) ranged from five months to three years. General Thompson went on to explain how the background of one program manager with less than a year's acquisition experience led to the Army's senior leadership to conclude that he could manage the Patriot Air Defense Missile System (a development and production program). The manager's qualifications consisted of a "strong tactical air defense background, his experience in Europe — where Patriot is being fielded — and his credentials as a systems analyst."[37]

It is difficult to understand how the Army considered this background satisfactory, because none of the experience entailed any significant involvement with contractors (where development and production work is actually performed), procurement, contracting, or day-to-day negotiations.

Referring to another Army program manager with less than a year's acquisition experience, General Thompson said that the "Army's senior leadership felt that he was eminently qualified for this important developmental position, having both the tactical intelligence background and solid data processing experience that is so necessary for the position." Again, the experience fell far short of qualifying a program manager for the complexities of procurement, contracting, and negotiating with contractors.[38]

One Air Force general in the acquisition field commented on the effects of the failure to establish a genuine career field, and thereby defined one of the most important benefits of a separate field.

> Why should Congress grant ultimate decision-making power to a program manager who is inferior to his counterpart in industry? Up-or-out policy in the military means that the really crusty types get out early. Without a designated career field, Congress will never trust the military pseudomanager with total autonomy.

In November 1983, Mr. Packard made specific recommendations to the Senate Armed Services Committee.

> I believe that each service should be restructured to have two clearly defined and separate career paths for the development of officers. One should be to train men and women as commanders of military forces. The other would be to train men and women as managers in procurement.
>
> At the present time, officers often rotate back and forth from military assignments to procurement and almost without exception, project managers are not allowed to stay with that program long enough to actually see it to completion.[39]

Many factors contribute to problems of schedule, cost, and technical performance in the DOD acquisition process, but most actions to maintain cost and resolve other problems must be implemented by the government program manager. Until the Defense Department heeds Mr.

Packard's advice, Congress has little reason to expect improvements in DOD's management of the acquisition process.

ACQUISITION CAREER SHOULD BE COMPARABLE
TO OPERATIONAL CAREER

The military chiefs of staff of the Army, Navy, and Air Force, though highly able, dedicated officers, usually have no training or experience in running large industrial R&D and production programs. Most chiefs of staff share the mistaken belief that the weapons acquisition process can be managed by military officer generalists, whose primary training and experience have been in military field operations with no more than one or, at best, two assignments to one of the materiel commands. It is obvious that a procurement officer or program manager cannot become a wing commander without years of extensive flight training and experience. Yet it is often assumed that a pilot can become a competent procurement or program manager with little or no industrial management training.

Some spark of hope shines in the creation by the Air Force in the 1980s of attractive career opportunities in program management; the Army and Navy soon followed suit (these are described below). Unfortunately, many of the officers for whom these opportunities are intended view them with skepticism. This is not the first time acquisition career improvements have been promised. Every two or three years for the past fifteen years, senior DOD officials have announced that the program manager career development problem has been solved. Then, once the announcement has been made, critics of the process are accused of attacking a problem of the past.[40]

Because contract negotiation and management of multi-hundred-million-dollar programs are so complex and the risk of mediocre performance, or even failure, in these tasks by inexperienced military officers is so high, many officers avoid repetitive assignments in procurement and program management. Consequently, a number of otherwise excellent senior officers fall far short of the demanding requirements of DOD program management.

The efforts made by the Air Force in the early 1980s to improve career opportunities were later reinforced. In 1986, the General Accounting Office announced that a triservice panel of acquisition experts had emphasized the necessity of substantial acquisition skills — technical, management, and leadership — to produce a highly qualified program manager.[41] The GAO triservice panel and other experts believed that the typical career path used to prepare officers for command in operational fields provided a useful model for developing career programs to prepare program managers. It includes a minimum of eight to eleven years of experience, specialized training, and professional military education in intermediate and senior service colleges, all of which enable progress to command at the colonel or captain rank. For example, the career path to command of an infantry brigade includes a minimum of eight, but more likely eleven, years of experience with the troops plus eleven months of specialized training. The GAO experts believed that, given the complexity of the acquisition business, the military services should be willing to devote at least as much time to developing program managers.[42]

The career development paths in fields of combat operations are similar in the three services (see tables 5.3 to 5.5).

Although program management offices often attract outstanding individuals, operations command experience is a far more certain, and therefore popular, career path to flag officer positions. The senior combat arms officers who control the military personnel system, in practice, have given lower priority to most defense buying organizations for assignment of qualified personnel. In the mid-1980s, 48 percent of the approximately twelve thousand officers assigned to the Air Force Sys-

TABLE 5.3.   U.S. Army: Career Path to Command of Infantry Brigade

Grade	Target position	Years with troops (at each grade)	Specialized training	Professional military education
LT	Platoon leader	2 to 3	Basic (5 mos.)	
CAP	Company commander	2 to 3	Advanced (6 mos.)	Combined arms and services school (2 mos.)
MAJ	Battalion executive officer	2 to 3		Command and general staff college (11 mos.)
LTC	Battalion commander	2		Senior service college (11 mos.)

SOURCE: U.S. General Accounting Office, "DOD Acquisition: Strengthening Capabilities of Key Personnel in Systems Acquisition," GAO/NSIAD–86–45, May 1986, p. 73.

TABLE 5.4.   U.S. Navy: Career Path to Major Sea Command for Surface Warfare
Officer

Grade	Target position	Years with troops (at each grade)	Specialized training	Professional military education
ENS/LTJG	Division officer	2½ to 4	Basic (6 mos.)	
LT	Department head	3	Department head course (6 mos.)	
LCDR	Executive or commanding officer	3		Junior service college (11 mos.)
CDR	Ship commanding officer	2 to 3		Senior service college (11 mos.)

SOURCE: U.S. General Accounting Office, "DOD Acquisition: Strengthening Capabilities of
Key Personnel in Systems Acquisition," GAO/NSIAD–86–45, May 1986, p. 73.

TABLE 5.5.   U.S. Air Force: Career Path to Wing Commander

Grade	Target position	Years with troops (at each grade)	Specialized training	Professional military education
LT	Copilot/pilot	3	Undergraduate flying training (12 mos.)	
CAPT	Aircraft commander/ instructor pilot/flight examiner	6½	Initial crew training (6 mos.)	Squadron officers school (2 mos.)
MAJ	Flight commander/ operations officer	4		Intermediate service college (10 mos.)
LTC	Squadron commander wing staff	4		Senior service college (10 mos.)

SOURCE: U.S. General Accounting Office, "DOD Acquisition: Strengthening Capabilities of
Key Personnel in Systems Acquisition," GAO/NSIAD–86–45, May 1986, p. 73.

tems Command were lieutenants.[43] By the end of 1987, it was unlikely that the military services would assign to the increasingly responsible positions in buying commands sufficient numbers of officers in the 0-3 through 0-5 ranks (captain, major, lieutenant commander, commander, lieutenant colonel).

In sum, until recent years the military personnel system in the Army, Navy, and, to a lesser extent, Air Force has largely ignored the reality that an effective and efficient acquisition program requires advanced program management skills, based on extensive practical training and years of program management experience. In the 1980s, there were signs of progress, particularly in the Air Force. Clearly, the key to developing highly skilled program managers lies, as it does in industry, in the development of a stable acquisition career path. It is essential that the path progress from procurement and technical assignments to program office assignments at several levels, ranging from the deputy division chief or deputy program manager for a smaller program to full responsibility for a major program. With each assignment extended to three years or more, considerable dedication by the individual to the system acquisition field is required.

A process for identifying those more suited to program management is also necessary. As they move upward, these people can then be more thoroughly trained and assigned. Such a selection process is used successfully in industry.

A former commander of a military service buying command recommended to us that a corps of prospective program managers and their staffs be established in each service. The corps would consist of officers who, by virtue of their education and skills, are "experts" in development, procurement, production, and wholesale logistics support of weapon systems. These officers would apply for entry to the corps after a few (four to six) years of service, during which they would have acquired a hardware orientation (artillery, missiles, combat vehicles, aircraft, ships, etc.), and would be selected on the basis of their performance and skills and the needs of the service. After entering the corps, they would broaden their expertise in several aspects of weapon systems acquisition. This would mean assignments to buying commands and laboratories, program management offices, or the service headquarters staff, or advanced management education courses and tours with industry.

Although I support creating a corps of military professionals to manage the acquisition process, I see a danger in a corps with a charter so broad that its officers and their superiors believe they need expertise in military deployment, supply, and maintenance as well as in negotiating with contractors and overseeing development and production programs in contractor plants. As a first priority, program managers and their staffs must have the training and experience necessary to accomplish the complex job of controlling the schedule, cost, and technical performance of million-dollar contracts. If the Defense Department waits until officers are well into their careers before they enter such a program and it then defines a broad array of assignments in supply, maintenance, procurement, contracting, and deployment, the officers are unlikely to become expert before retirement in the specific tasks required to be well-qualified program managers.

The DOD Authorization Act of 1986 took a small step toward creating a more rigorous acquisition career program by calling for DOD regulations requiring experience and training for those assigned to manage major programs. The regulations would require that, at a minimum, program managers complete the DSMC twenty-week introductory program management course (or a comparable course) and have at least eight years of experience in the acquisition, support, and maintenance of weapon systems, including two years at a procurement command. (Time spent at DSMC or pursuing graduate education in a technical or management field can be counted as part of the eight-year requirement.)

The authorization act is important for introducing minimum qualifications for program managers, but these standards are considerably less stringent than those recommended by the standards panels and other sources. In particular, a wide range of experience not directly related to managing acquisition programs can satisfy the eight-year requirement. Indeed, to attain the goal of a highly qualified cadre of program managers, the Packard Commission concluded that the military services should establish qualifications more demanding than those set by the 1986 act.[44]

By 1987, each of the services had established an acquisition career program for its officers. These include the Army's Materiel Acquisition Management (MAM) program, the Navy's Weapon Systems Acquisition Management (WSAM) and Material Professional (MP) programs, and detailed career planning regulations for Air Force technical personnel and program managers.[45]

THE ARMY ACQUISITION CAREER FIELD

The Army's program for developing acquisition managers, including program managers, is the Materiel Acquisition Management program.

Initiated in 1983, MAM was intended to ensure that officers with the appropriate background and interest be assigned to acquisition positions and that they obtain specialized training. In 1986, the General Accounting Office described the three-phase program as follows:

> MAM operates within the framework of the Army's Officer Personnel Management System, a system based on the concept of dual specialty development. Under the current system, officers entering the Army are assigned to a combat arms branch (e.g., infantry, aviation), combat support branch (e.g., Signal Corps), or combat services support branch (e.g., Ordnance, Transportation Corps). Officers also select an initial specialty generally associated with their branch, such as infantry or missile materiel management. By completion of their eighth year, the officers must also designate an additional specialty or functional area. Additional specialties include most of the 26 initial specialties and 12 other specialties not available to officers on initial entry into the Army. The latter includes such acquisition-related specialties as research and development and procurement. Starting about the sixth to eighth year, and for the remainder of their careers, officers generally alternate between assignments in their initial (branch) specialty and those in their additional specialty.
>
> MAM consists of three phases. The first, called the user/support development phase, is the officers' first six to eight years of service, spent in the initial branch. . . . This phase provides experience with the type of systems and equipment that officers may eventually develop and acquire.
>
> The second phase, known as the MAM development phase, begins after formal entry into MAM and runs from about the officers' sixth to eighth year of service to the sixteenth year. During this phase, MAM officers attend the nine-week MAM training course at the Army Logistics Management Center and complete their first acquisition assignment. Following an assignment in their branch, officers also attend the DSMC Program Management Course and complete a second MAM assignment.
>
> The third phase, known as the certified manager phase, commences at approximately the sixteenth year of service. After selection for promotion to lieutenant colonel, officers are evaluated for certification as Materiel Acquisition Managers by a central board. Certification requirements for the mature MAM program [sic] include completing two acquisition assignments and the MAM and DSMC training courses. As certified acquisition managers, the officers could be considered for appointment as program managers of major programs, as well as other acquisition positions of significant responsibility.
>
> MAM certification is not a prerequisite for appointment as a program manager. Selection criteria depend on the specific position but generally include command, program office and headquarters experience, DSMC

training, and senior service college. Selections are made by a central board.[46]

Army officers normally enter the materiel acquisition management program between their sixth to eighth year of service (see chart 5.1). By their sixteenth year, they should complete the materiel acquisition management course, the DSMC program management course, and two (three-year) acquisition assignments. The certified manager phase begins at approximately the sixteenth year and lasts throughout the remainder of an officer's career. (Officers are eligible for retirement after twenty years.)

Army Maj. Gen. David W. Stallings, of the Army Materiel Command, explained the MAM dual career program to the Senate Armed Services Committee. "The program manager must be able to participate in meaningful, constructive dialog with military officers in the qualitative requirements [user] area."[47]

Gen. Henry A. Miley (ret.), former commander of AMC, in responding to General Stallings, expressed a different view:

> I don't think you have to fight inside a tank to experience what a tanker feels. . . .
>
> My vintage has always disagreed with the idea you had to serve half your time in the fighting forces to be a good procurement officer. I still disagree with that. . . .
>
> If you are going to produce good procurement officers, you have to let them work at procurement full time and see a light at the top.
>
> They have to see that the generals that are in the procurement business came out of the corps they are serving in and not Joe, the combat arms guy, moving in at the two- and three-star level and cutting off their chances of promotion.[48]

Also commenting on General Stallings's view, a retired Army major general formerly assigned to AMC said: "The Army has the view that you've got to be able to charge up and down hills and go to war. So they get rid of program managers at fifty years old (or earlier). It's no surprise that there is little on-the-job experience in managing the acquisition process."

A deputy commander of AMC recently expressed his rationale for opposing alternate operational assignments.

CHART 5.1. Typical Army Career Path for MAM Officer

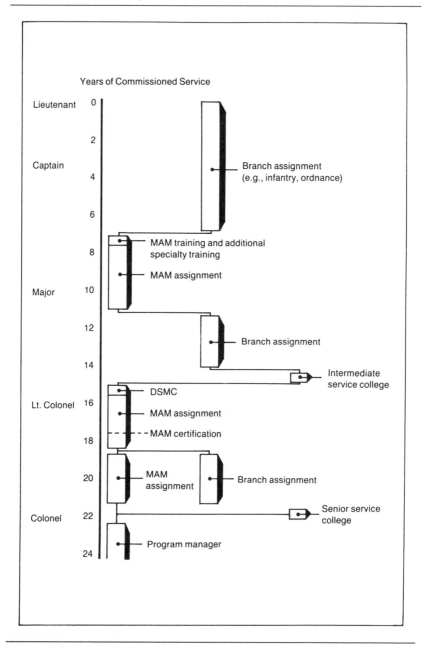

SOURCE: U.S. General Accounting Office, "DOD Acquisition: Strengthening Capabilities of Key Personnel in Systems Acquisition," GAO/NSIAD–86–45, May 1986, p. 90.

The normal path to general officer is company commander, brigade commander, battalion staff officer, battalion commander. I do not believe there is sufficient time for a man to have a full career as a program manager and as an operational combat commander.

Despite the moderate change promised by the new MAM program, it was not unanimously well received by the Army officer hierarchy. They were concerned that MAM would increasingly remove officers from troop leadership, affecting their qualifications for battalion command, which are closely related to promotion. (In 1985, 94.4 percent of the lieutenant colonel candidates with battalion command experience were promoted to colonel [first time considered], compared with an Armywide promotion rate to colonel of 53.4 percent.)[49] The unrest surrounding the MAM program raised serious questions about the chances for achieving even the modest goals of the program.

In 1986, the Army selected seventeen officers for assignment as program managers. Although three-quarters of these officers had commanded a battalion and all had acquired master's degrees, only slightly more than half (55 percent) had previously been assigned to a program office. Further, only one-half had taken the DSMC twenty-week program manager course. Nonetheless, the qualifications and training of these program manager designees represented an improvement over the 1970s.

THE NAVY ACQUISITION CAREER FIELD

In March 1985, the *Washington Post* quoted Adm. James Watkins, Chief of Naval Operations, in an unusually candid criticism of the Navy's management of the acquisition process.

> "It was almost impossible for naval officers in uniform to come up to an acceptable level of business management in the modern industrial world," he said. "We simply were naive, not well prepared, and we didn't stick to it long enough. . . ."[50]

Admiral Watkins was not the only officer concerned about management and acquisition career programs. It was this awareness that led the Navy to introduce two programs in recent years: the Weapon Systems Acquisition Management (WSAM) program (instituted in 1975) and the Material Professional (MP) program (instituted in 1985).[51]

WSAM, covering officer development from grades of ensign to captain, was created "to identify, monitor, and improve the use of personnel with acquisition-related experience and education. Like the Army's MAM program, WSAM has no one specialty; it is a system comprising officers from several specialties."[52] It is less structured than MAM and requires less experience for designation as a fully qualified manager.

To be designated a program manager, naval officers at the lieutenant commander grade or above must have a technical or business education background and one two-year tour in an acquisition position. They generally enter the WSAM program at the grade of lieutenant commander or commander (see charts 5.2 and 5.3). Officers do not enter the MP program until they reach the grade of commander or captain and above.[53]

In 1984, Assistant Secretary of the Navy Everett Pyatt expressed to the Senate Armed Services Committee his commitment that the Navy "acquisition program . . . have experienced and highly skilled people performing program management and contracting functions. Without competent managers, other cost reduction initiatives cannot be implemented."[54] Five months later, when the MP program was announced, Secretary Pyatt supported it strongly.

> This Material Professional program will provide select officers with the education, experience, and the career incentives required to make our acquisition managers capable, skilled business professionals with the warfare background necessary to properly manage weapon systems acquisition.[55]

MP program officers are drawn from the unrestricted line (those eligible for command at sea), the restricted line (those in engineering duty and aeronautical engineering duty specialties), and the Supply Corps. Once selected for the program, they are assigned to MP-designated positions for the remainder of their careers. Assignment of an MP officer to a nonprogram position or a nonprogram officer to an MP position requires a waiver recommended by the Chief of Naval Operations and approved by the Secretary of the Navy.

In 1986, the GAO study of acquisition personnel found:

> Navy unrestricted line officers spend a considerable portion of their first 20 years at sea or in specialized training, usually about twelve to fourteen years. This leaves limited time available for development of a

CHART 5.2.   Typical Navy Career Path for Restricted Line (Surface Warfare) Officer

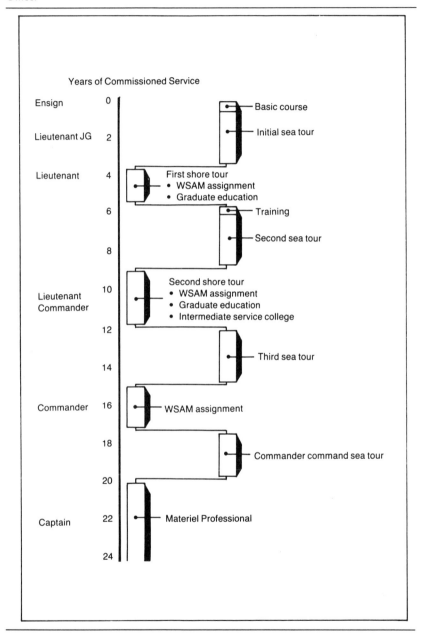

SOURCE: U.S. General Accounting Office, "DOD Acquisition: Strengthening Capabilities of Key Personnel in Systems Acquisition," GAO/NSIAD–86–45, May 1986, p. 96.

CHART 5.3. Typical Navy Career Path for Restricted Line (Aeronautical Engineering Duty) Officer

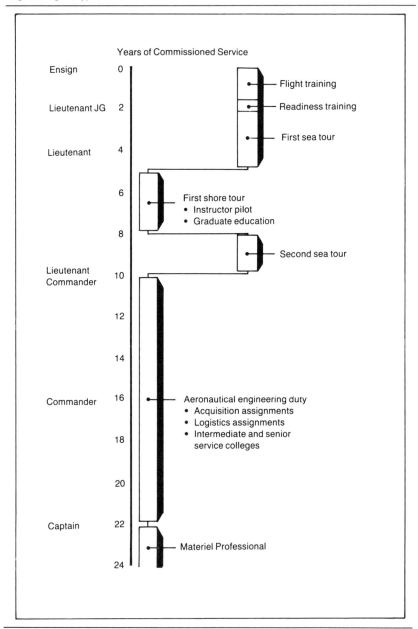

SOURCE: U.S. General Accounting Office, "DOD Acquisition: Strengthening Capabilities of Key Personnel in Systems Acquisition," GAO/NSIAD–86–45, May 1986, p. 97.

WSAM [acquisition] subspecialty. . . . Unrestricted line officers typically serve in their first acquisition assignment at the grade of lieutenant or lieutenant commander. As commanders, they are likely to have a second acquisition assignment, and possibly a third assignment as a senior commander. Thus, by the time unrestricted line officers reach the grade of captain, they are likely to have approximately four to seven years of acquisition experience.

The Navy career pattern for restricted line officers more closely resembles the desired career pattern. Officers spend the first part of their career in the unrestricted line. Officers typically transfer into the engineering duty community after completing their first or second sea tour. Aviation officers typically transfer into the aeronautical engineering duty community at the rank of lieutenant commander, usually after nine to twelve years of service. These officers spend the remainder of their careers in engineering positions and thus have the opportunity to gain a substantial number of years of acquisition experience.

Navy Supply Corps officers alternate between sea and shore assignments, typically spending about six to eight years at sea during their first 20 years of service. They are primarily concerned with the financial management and contracting aspects of acquisition and have little opportunity to gain experience in technical positions. Supply Corps officers are thus only considered for program manager positions for programs in the production phase.[56]

The General Accounting Office found that unrestricted line officers qualified in the WSAM program (as of November 1984) had an average of 4.3 years of acquisition experience. In contrast, restricted line officers qualified in the WSAM program had an average of 7.2 years and Supply Corps officers, 7.4 years.[57]

The Navy created the MP program to attract and develop excellent senior officers to manage systems acquisition, logistics, and support. The program seeks to achieve this objective by providing a path to flag rank for officers in material management. Nonetheless, it is worth noting that the program does not significantly alter the career path of officers, thus providing little increase in the time available for unrestricted line officers to obtain acquisition experience.[58]

Moreover, in 1987, the extent to which the new Navy program would produce a significant improvement remained uncertain. As before, restricted line and Supply Corps officers would have repeated assignments in their specialty, except that they were likely to be designated material professionals upon promotion to captain. Unrestricted line officers would, as before, spend most of their first twenty years in operational assignments and be evaluated for the MP program upon promotion to commander.[59] Selected commanders would be expected to complete their command assignments, thus becoming available for their *first* material professional assignment at about their twentieth to twenty-first year of service.[60]

As of September 1985, 44 percent of the program managers for the major Navy programs were restricted line officers and 41 percent unrestricted; none was from the Supply Corps. (The remaining major program managers were civilians, Marine Corps officers, and Medical Corps officers.)[61]

Despite the best intentions of Navy management, one cannot help being skeptical of the chances for the success of such programs. Military officers are not selected for the MP program until their sixteenth year or later, leaving four years or less until qualifying for retirement, at 50 percent pay. Their first assignment in the MP program does not occur until after they are eligible for retirement.

Further, in 1985, Adm. Steven A. White, then chief of Naval Material, requested that Congress *not* prescribe specific education, experience, and grade levels for the acquisition force.

> Finally, I would recommend that any legislation on the subject emphasize the intent and general desires of the Congress. It would be a mistake to deprive the Service Secretaries of the flexibility they need to tailor their programs in terms of education, experience, and grade levels.[62]

Unfortunately, the Navy's program for officers' acquisition careers sounds a great deal like "business as usual." In 1984, Adm. Joseph Sansone, the Navy's senior expert on contracts and acquisition business management, stated that the first tour for an officer is initially afloat and lasts for two or three years.

> Then we bring the officer ashore and we start the selective process into the acquisition contracting officer program. This occurs at the Lieutenant JG level. They will stay in that until they complete their training. Then they will go to another tour, usually afloat. Then they will come back to a shore tour in acquisition and will continue to serve in acquisition tours with about a 50–50 split to start with, and then it will take on a little more imbalance in terms of acquisition vis-à-vis operational. . . .
>
> We have opted with the concept in the Navy that the operational training and experience that our officers receive afloat is very important to their ability to adequately manage a very highly complex and technical program.

So, the operational experience is a real supplement to his ability to manage a program to deliver a new weapon system to the fleet on time, under cost, and to really serve the need of the user.[63]

Although it is clear that operational assignments enrich the program manager, more than four to six years of this enrichment occurs at the expense of understanding the acquisition process and contractor incentives and practices. In sum, many Navy material "professionals" will be merely half-time experts, introduced relatively late in their careers to the complex tasks of managing programs with contractors and formulating actions to deal with their full-time industry counterparts with far more industrial program management experience.

Any significant improvement in the problems described by Chief of Naval Operations Watkins will require a major change in Navy practice and attitude. In 1987, it was unclear whether the new program would lead to that change or to a continuation of the status quo.

A GAO discussion with senior Navy officials revealed a reason for the Navy's commitment to using acquisition assignments as alternate shore duty. In exploring with them the possibility of an all-civilian defense acquisition agency, the General Accounting Office was told that removing the military from the buying commands would adversely affect officers in key leadership positions because it would significantly reduce the number of available shore duty billets. Loss of these billets would increase the likelihood that Navy officers and enlisted personnel would spend more time at sea, which could damage morale.[64]

Similarly, in early 1987, the Chief of Naval Operations placed a limit on the number of women in the Navy, since they were occupying shore duty billets that had traditionally been used as rotational assignments for men in operational billets at sea. The limit was subsequently rescinded by Defense Secretary Caspar Weinberger.[65]

THE AIR FORCE ACQUISITION CAREER FIELD

The Air Force is generally recognized as having the best record of the three services for acquisition training and career development, although the record is far less attractive for rated than for nonrated officers. Rated officers (pilots and navigators) constitute about one-quarter or less of those in acquisition management, although they account for about one-half of the major program manager positions.[66]

According to the General Accounting Office, for the Air Force to receive an appropriate return on training and for officers to qualify for aviation incentive pay, rated officers must spend at least nine to eleven years on flying duty. Typically, rated officers who are eventually assigned to acquisition have spent their first nine years on flying duty. They then rotate into the Air Force Systems Command (AFSC) for a three-year acquisition assignment, often followed by attendance at an intermediate service college, and then a return to flying duty for an additional three years. After their fifteenth to sixteenth year, they are likely to return to AFSC and spend the remainder of their careers in acquisition management. By their twenty-first to twenty-second year of service, these rated officers can be considered for program manager positions on major programs. By that time, they are likely to have approximately seven years of acquisition experience.

Those selected are then transferred to the program management career field. Requirements (often waived) for this field, as stated in Air Force regulations, include an undergraduate degree in engineering, a physical science, or math; completion of the DSMC twenty-week introductory program management course; and full qualification in a research and development career field, usually meaning eighteen months to four years of experience in either acquisition program management, engineering development, or a scientific career field. Air Force regulations also identify as desirable an advanced degree in management and completion of a training assignment with industry (Education with Industry program).[67]

In summary, Air Force rated officers often receive only one three-year acquisition assignment, broadly defined, before their fifteenth year of service, and have repeated acquisition assignments beginning in their fifteenth to sixteenth year (see chart 5.4). Nonrated officers can enter the acquisition field directly or transfer into it after an initial assignment in an operational command. They receive repeated assignments in acquisition management, often including positions in a program office and staff assignments at headquarters (see chart 5.5).

The career paths of eleven recently appointed Air Force program managers cited in the GAO sample deviated significantly from the desired pattern. Four lacked operational experience. Three lacked program office experience. Four lacked headquarters experience. One officer's experience was almost exclusively in headquarters; another's was exclusively in testing. One entered the acquisition field as a colonel. Fewer than half attended the DSMC program management course. Rated officers had less acquisition experience than nonrated officers; only one of the five rated officers in the GAO sample had as much as eight years.[68]

CHART 5.4.   Typical Air Force Career Path for Rated Officer

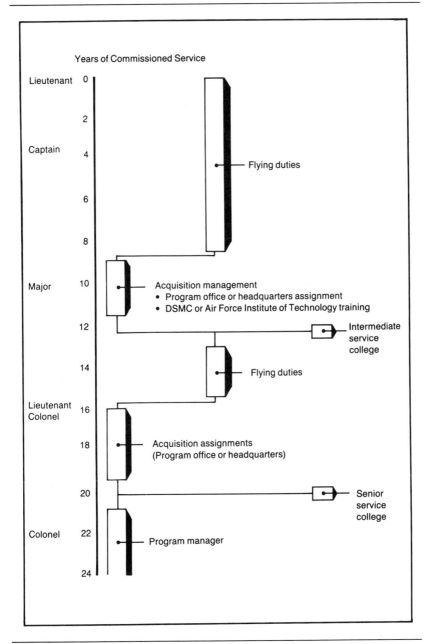

Years of Commissioned Service

Lieutenant	0
	2
Captain	4

Flying duties

	6
	8
Major	10

Acquisition management
• Program office or headquarters assignment
• DSMC or Air Force Institute of Technology training

| | 12 |

Intermediate service college

| | 14 |

Flying duties

| Lieutenant Colonel | 16 |
| | 18 |

Acquisition assignments
(Program office or headquarters)

| | 20 |

Senior service college

| Colonel | 22 |

Program manager

| | 24 |

Source: U.S. General Accounting Office, "DOD Acquisition: Strengthening Capabilities of Key Personnel in Systems Acquisitions," GAO/NSIAD–86–45, May 1986, p. 85.

CHART 5.5.   Typical Air Force Career Path for Nonrated Officer

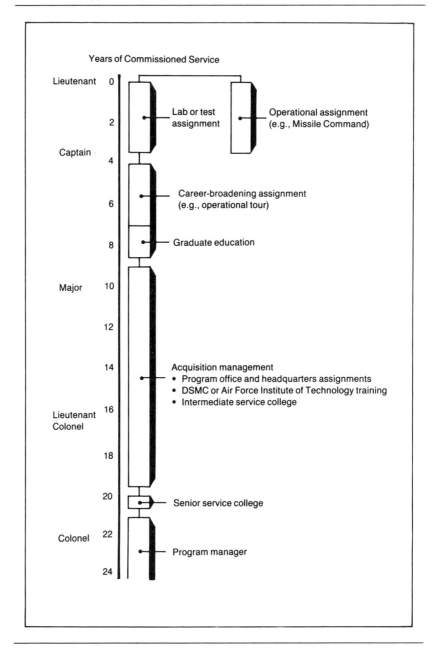

SOURCE: U.S. General Accounting Office, "DOD Acquisition: Strengthening Capabilities of Key Personnel in Systems Acquisition," GAO/NSIAD–86–45, May 1986, p. 84.

In 1986, one Air Force officer explained the practice of assigning rated officers with limited acquisition training to program management positions.

> In times of peace, we still must be prepared for war. Today it takes many years to train and provide flight experience to a new officer in order to gain a fully mission-ready pilot. Thus, the "rated supplement" was formed. This system takes pilots and navigators out of airplanes (especially if there are far too many rated officers for the available aircraft) and tries to utilize them in other jobs in the service. On the one hand, the system may save money and morale (as opposed to having these people do nothing, or simply firing them). On the other hand, given the need to manage effectively multimillion-dollar acquisition programs, it may be less expensive to hire or train experts in acquisition and let the rated officers remain in overmanned assignments.

In the 1970s, a typical pilot spent the first five or six years after his commission on flying status and another three years working toward a master's degree. Eight or more years out of a possible twenty were spent in nonprocurement activity. During the remaining twelve years, alternate three-year tours were usually spent on operational assignments. The typical pilot had five years remaining for on-the-job training in program management. The situation has not changed markedly since then.

In 1985, Air Force Gen. Lawrence Skantze presented his views on the desired program manager career preparation to the Senate Armed Services Committee.

> As an example of the way in which this [the Air Force acquisition career] system works, I would like to discuss the career of General Selectee Ronald W. Yates, currently the System Program Director for the F-16 fighter. I do this because I believe General Yates *reflects the success of our approach*. (emphasis added)
>
> After graduating from high school in Nashville, TN, in 1956, he earned a bachelor of science degree in military science from the U.S. Air Force Academy.
>
> As a second lieutenant, Ron received pilot training and was then assigned, in 1964, as an F-102 pilot at Clark Air Base in the Philippines. While there, Ron flew 100 combat missions in Southeast Asia.
>
> Upon his return to the United States in 1966, he was assigned as a student at the Aerospace Research Test Pilot School at Edwards Air Force Base, CA. He remained there as a test pilot and chief of the Aerospace

Research Pilot Branch until December 1970. During this time, he earned a master of science degree in systems management from the University of Southern California.

From 1971 to 1973, he was assigned to Headquarters, Air Force Systems Command, as the assistant director of senior officer assignments [military personnel].

From there he was selected [at age 36] to attend the Defense Systems Management College. Upon graduation [from the twenty-week program], he was assigned as director of development flight test for the A-10 weapon systems program office at Wright Patterson Air Force Base, OH.

Upon graduation from the Industrial College of the Armed Forces [a one-year assignment] in June 1977, he was assigned to Headquarters, U.S. Air Force, as the F-16 program element monitor, Office of the Deputy Chief of Staff for Research and Development.

In March 1979, Ron returned to Wright Patterson Air Force Base, where he served successively as deputy F-15 system program director, the F-15 program director, the commander of the 4950th Test Wing, and the aeronautical systems division deputy for tactical systems [all in less than four years].

General Yates assumed his present duties in August 1983.[69]

Based on the record, General Yates is indeed an outstanding officer with remarkable credentials. But his preparation for the tasks of over-seeing, negotiating, and controlling the activities of large industrial development and production firms is seriously deficient. Instead of reflecting the success of the Air Force approach, the General Yates example demonstrates the substantial risks the Defense Department takes by the way it manages its large programs. From General Skantze's description, it appears that General Yates had little experience in dealing with contracts or contractors before he was assigned responsibility for one of the Air Force's largest programs with industry. He apparently had little training or experience with financial reports and cost estimating, the problems and opportunities associated with contractor profit policy and other incentives, independent R&D costs, cost and schedule planning and control systems, or make-or-buy decisions.

Indeed, Senator Bingaman was dissatisfied with the General Yates example. He replied to General Skantze:

> As I see your example here, General, about Major General Yates, he obviously has had a great deal of experience, and a good deal of it in acquisition. But it strikes me that he jumped all over the place. You had him

as program manager for a couple of years, then off to do something else, then back, then off. I was asking the earlier witness about accountability in the system.

If a person is not allowed to stay as program manager, or required to stay as program manager of a particular program for some period of time, how can you hold anybody accountable for anything in this program manager situation?[70]

The Air Force view of the importance of acquisition compared to combat operations as a career field for outstanding officers remains clouded. In early 1987, a major general holding a senior management position in Air Force acquisition management explained the Air Force policy:

> We [the Air Force] put our best people in our product line, and our product line is our operational forces, not the acquisition field. Our job is to fly and fight and win, and that is in the operational commands.

Despite the drawbacks cited above, the fact remains that in the past fifteen years the Air Force has made more progress than the Army or Navy toward improving the training and experience of nonrated officers it assigns to acquisition positions. And if it continues to improve its training and career programs by attracting and retaining outstanding acquisition officers, the Air Force will have taken an important step toward achieving better control of its acquisition programs.

THE OUTLOOK FOR DEFENSE ACQUISITION CAREER FIELDS

If the Defense Department is not successful in establishing more comprehensive and attractive acquisition career programs, Congress would be well advised to impose more specific requirements on the services and, if that fails, introduce a markedly different approach to managing the acquisition process. The French system is often cited as a successful alternative to the U.S. approach. The French have two completely different military organizations: combat arms and armament. The combat arms group, under their counterpart to the U.S. Joint Chiefs of Staff, has little or nothing to do with procurement, and few of its members hold nonoperational management positions. They retire at about the same age as U.S. military officers, because, as one defense analyst commented, "they don't need fifty-year-old company commanders or sixty-year-old fighter pilots any more than we do." A few of the more talented can move from the combat arms branch to the Armament Directorate, which is responsible for the acquisition process, but none can move the other way. Officers in the Armament Directorate spend their entire careers at the job, passing through progressively more responsible positions. Many, if not most, are graduates of the Ecole Polytechnique, one of the finest technical schools in the world. They are not forced to retire at a relatively early age and therefore can remain for their entire career. Further, anyone who negotiates contracts with a firm is prohibited from working for that firm for five years. The French government enforces this rule and has imposed severe penalties on offenders.[71]

In reflecting on the recent performance of the military services, it is evident that each military service should have attractive career fields dedicated to procurement and program management, similar to the Army's Corps of Engineers or the French Armament Directorate, with assignments dedicated exclusively to the acquisition process.

In 1986, the Packard Commission concluded:

> DOD must be able to attract and retain the caliber of people necessary for a quality acquisition program. Significant improvements should be made in the senior-level appointment system. The Secretary of Defense should have increased authority to establish flexible personnel management policies necessary to improve defense acquisition. An alternative personnel management system should be established to include senior acquisition personnel and contracting officers as well as scientists and engineers.
>
> Our study convinces us that lasting progress in the performance of the acquisition system *demands dramatic improvements* in our management of acquisition personnel at all levels within DOD.[72] (emphasis added)

In December 1985, Assistant Defense Secretary James Wade, then the Pentagon's top acquisition official, came to similar conclusions and suggested the establishment of a professional defense purchasing corps as one of the several ways to streamline procurement (see chapter 6). In a forty-two-page study criticizing the buying practices of the military, Dr. Wade said, "We do not need more people, but we do need superior, better-qualified people [in acquisition]. To attract these people, we need changes in pay structures, rotational programs, and training, and more flexible personnel procedures."[73]

In the 1980s each of the services has taken steps to plan improvements in the acquisition work force. Although these steps should be recognized and commended, at least two dangers persist. First, the career programs described in the plans may be considered "sufficient" instead of merely one step toward the goal of creating a core of professional acquisition managers. Second, the plans may not be translated into practice, or translated in form only, with little actual change occurring.

Nevertheless, some progress has been made.

The Military Promotion System

The promotion system is a major incentive in the careers of military officers. With the absence of bonuses or differential pay within rank for varying degrees of performance, promotion is virtually the only formal reward available within the military services. As one Air Force officer commented:

> The promotion system is incredibly important to us as human beings, regardless of desire to become a flag officer. When you consider the reward system in the service, you quickly realize that promotion is *the* fundamental bottom line reward that the system structurally provides. In addition, you realize that even the "early" promotions come slower than true "fast track" advancement rates in industry. All officers are paid the same amount. Ribbons and plaques are nice, but they lose meaning when many are awarded and they don't result in the greater rewards of early promotion. Promotion is the recognition by the service that the individual is performing at least an adequate job (up to the rank of lieutenant colonel). Promotion rates to major are about 80 percent and to lieutenant colonel, about 70 percent. Thus, if officers are not promoted to these ranks, they are told that they're in the bottom 20th or 30th percentile.
>
> The greatest reward that the system can give an officer is an "early" promotion. If an officer is promoted ahead of his or her contemporaries by one to three years, it means that that officer has gained recognition as being in the 95th percentile. An early promotion, in a behavior-based evaluation system, confers a "halo effect" upon an individual in future assignments. Additionally, it is virtually impossible to reach the rank of general or admiral without an early promotion to major or lieutenant colonel. An officer maintaining peak mobility will advance in rank every two to four years (from second lieutenant/ensign to general/admiral).

The Secretary of each service has nominal responsibility for military promotions. He appoints the selection board that reviews officers' records, instructs the board on promotion policy, and approves promotion lists that are forwarded to the President. In fact, however, the military chief of staff of each service directs the promotion process, although he is not specifically mentioned in the directives designating responsibility in this area. Rarely does a civilian Secretary interfere with the military promotion system. When Secretary of the Navy John Lehman did so in the mid-1980s, senior military officers were outraged, and an admiral serving as head of the Navy selection board resigned in protest. Most doubted that Secretary Lehman's exercise of his responsibilities in this regard would have any lasting impact on the Navy's promotion system.

Before a selection board is appointed, the chief of staff makes a number of recommendations to the service Secretary regarding the board policies. In cases involving promotions to the higher ranks, the chief of staff may personally meet with the board to provide specific instructions. In considering officers for promotion, priority is almost always given to men with operational command experience. Experience in fields requiring technical competence or management skills or both (e.g., program management, procurement, intelligence, communications, and electronic data processing) has rarely been an asset.[74] As a result, officers often regard an assignment in one of these areas as a liability in the development of their careers, leading many officers to avoid assignments to the acquisition process.

PROMOTION OPPORTUNITIES FOR PROCUREMENT OFFICERS

In the early 1970s, I met with a group of twenty officers attending the Industrial College of the Armed Forces. When discussing the need for outstanding officers in procurement and program management, one officer said: "I can see the value in what you say, but the problem is we can't get to be general officers by doing it. We have to have a command to get promoted." Most of the other officers held the same view, which seemed to have sound basis in fact. In May 1971, a service Secretary instructed his selection board to promote to the rank of brigadier general five colonels who met specific criteria in the field of procurement. When the promotion list was distributed, it contained the names of four officers who supposedly met these criteria. Not one of them had had any experience in the procurement of major weapon systems. The closest any had come was an assignment in determining procurement requirements and a few brief assignments in the purchase of conventional products. Upon further inquiry, I learned that several colonels with extensive acquisition experience had been passed over for promotion.

One or more of the following reasons was given: he had not been to Vietnam; he had not attended a senior service school; he did not have command experience in field operational units. Although senior Pentagon officials had stated for twenty years that procurement and program management experience would be a major factor in promotions, there had been little evidence to support these pronouncements.

Fifteen years after these interviews, the perception had not changed. At the systems commands (Army, Navy, and Air Force) visited by the General Accounting Office for its 1986 report on DOD acquisition, program managers generally thought that promotion opportunities were not as favorable in acquisition as in operational fields. An exception to this were Air Force program managers, who perceived that promotion opportunities in acquisition were available up to the rank of colonel but not for the rank of general officer. According to the GAO study, however, promotion statistics seemed to contradict this perception.

> Promotion rates for officers in acquisition management programs exceeded service averages. For example, for promotion to colonel/captain, the average (first time considered) rate of promotion for those in the Army's acquisition management program was 64.4 percent for 1983 to 1985, compared with the Army [overall] average of 48.5 percent. For the Navy, the (in zone) promotion rate for officers in the weapon systems acquisition management program was 69.1 percent over the past 3 years, compared with a Navy [overall] average of 59.7 percent. Similarly, the average Air Force (first time considered) rate for those in acquisition/program management career fields was 51.6 percent in 1982 to 1984, compared with the Air Force [overall] average of 43.5 percent.
>
> Available statistics also suggest a healthy picture for promotion to general officer/flag rank. The average promotion rate for Air Force officers in the program management career field for 1983 to 1985 was 1.7 percent, compared with the Air Force [overall] average of 1.5 percent. For the Navy the average for officers in the weapon systems acquisition management program was 5.3 percent over the past 3 years, compared with the Navy [overall] average of 4.4 percent. Comparable statistics were not available for the Army, but it is noteworthy that the number of officers promoted to general officer, who were or had previously served as program managers, increased sharply from three in 1983 to three in 1984 to eight in 1985.[75]

Other data in the same study suggest a different picture. For officers in the Army's Materiel Acquisition Management program considered for promotion to colonel in 1985, the selection rate was higher among those with *less* acquisition experience. In the Navy, of the eight program managers from previous operational assignments (unrestricted line) promoted to flag rank in fiscal years 1983–1985, all but one had a previous major command at sea as a captain, confirming, according to Navy officials, that promotion had been based on success in operational specialties. Moreover, at the various systems commands the General Accounting Office visited, DOD program managers generally believed that promotion opportunities in acquisition were not as numerous as in operational fields. Further, they often perceived that command-equivalent program manager positions were not valued as highly as command of operational units.[76]

The GAO report concluded, "The picture is thus confused." It pointed out that military officers perceive promotion opportunities in the acquisition field as *not* equivalent to those in military operations. That military officers' perceptions differ from some of the facts could mean that these officers are not yet well informed about the promotion system. Or, it could mean that the statistics are based on a broad interpretation of procurement and acquisition assignments.

During our Pentagon interviews, we were told that in 1985, the Army headquarters staff had indicated that it had promoted five colonels to brigadier general in the "97 series" (procurement officer career field). Senior Pentagon acquisition officials recognized only two and asked the Army's deputy chief of staff for personnel to identify the others. As it happened, the three remaining officers (allegedly promoted from the procurement field) had listed procurement as their secondary specialty; they had never had a major assignment in procurement. Such a situation tends to distort the facts, thereby undermining any efforts to change traditional perceptions of the promotion opportunities available to officers in procurement and program management.

GAO discussions in 1986 with thirty-four DOD program managers and their assistants made clear that to attract outstanding officers to the acquisition field, there must be promotion opportunities at least comparable to those available in military operations. The GAO panel believed that "adequate promotion opportunities were needed to attract and retain promising personnel to acquisition." Further, they believed that "promotion opportunities should be equivalent to those in operational fields."[77] To make promotion comparable to typical military career fields, some panel members believed that general officer and flag-rank positions involving acquisition management should be reserved for those in acquisition career fields.[78]

The promotion boards in the Army, Navy, and Air Force are always looking for marks of distinction among the candidate officers. For this reason, senior acquisition officers have for several years lobbied their services to treat certain assignments in procurement and program management as command equivalents. Using the Army as an example, it is easy to understand a bias toward operational assignments. In 1987, the assignment and promotion of Army MAM officers was vested in the deputy chief of staff for personnel (DCSPER), not in the commanding general of the Army Materiel Command. Chairmen of the Army promotion boards are senior combat arms officers, as are the majority of the board members, most of whom have a limited knowledge of acquisition management or the requirements of the job.

In 1985, Gen. Richard Thompson, AMC commander, acknowledged during testimony at a Senate Armed Services Committee hearing the importance of command assignments. Sen. John Glenn (D-OH) had suggested that assignments to operational command positions improve chances of promotion. General Thompson responded:

> I think you have described it very well, sir. We have always had a mindset that says you have to command and you have to go out, and, as you say, get certain jobs if you are going to aspire to the higher level.

In elaborating on his description of the Army's promotion system, General Thompson added: "And, of course, in the Army at least, to be promoted you have to be a generalist."[79]

Obviously, such a policy poses serious problems for the defense acquisition process, where individuals need to invest years learning the many skills required to be an effective program manager, business manager, or procurement officer.

A few months earlier, in another SASC hearing dealing with the same subject, Sen. Jeff Bingaman (D-NM) inquired:

> Let me ask General Stallings [AMC]. It is my understanding that in the Army today if an officer wants to get a star, he had better stay in an operational command. Is that accurate? You can do it the other way, but your chances are generally reduced. Is that correct?

General Stallings responded:

> Historically the key to success in the Army has been in command positions. . . . I think we have made a good movement toward recognizing the importance of our project managers and saying to those folks that you

are equal to our command positions. . . . I have some statistics here that there were three Army general officers that came out of procurement programs, out of 40, on a recent promotion list.[80]

In March 1985, General Thompson reported to the Senate Armed Services Committee:

> At the grade of lieutenant colonel [0-5], there are currently 28 command positions which are available to most qualified procurement officers.
>
> At the colonel level [0-6], 28 commands are also available to most qualified procurement officers, representing a significant increase since 1981.[81]

The twenty-eight command positions in procurement at the 0-5 and 0-6 levels can serve as an important incentive for current and prospective procurement officers. But to be effective, these positions must be used as rewards for outstanding acquisition performance and regarded as equal to combat arms command assignments in practice as well as in theory.

In 1987, the Army announced the selection of fifty-six colonels for promotion to the rank of brigadier general. Following the historic pattern uninspiring to officers assigned to the acquisition process, the promotion list included none from six officer specialties, three of which were Procurement, Comptroller, and Finance Corps (there are twenty-eight officer specialties). Only three officers with R&D specialty codes were selected, two of whom were program managers.[82]

EVALUATING PROGRAM MANAGERS FOR PROMOTION

Senior military officers prepare comprehensive evaluations annually on each officer within their jurisdiction, and more frequently if an officer changes assignment. Over the years, these evaluations have evolved to the point where they must be written in superlatives, not in realistic comparisons, simply to enable the candidate to maintain parity with peers.

An Air Force officer described one way the promotion system affected the acquisition process.

> A very strong de facto mentoring system exists in the services. The main differentiating factor in military Effectiveness Reports is the rank of the officer signing the bottom-line endorsement of the report. An officer's

commander can decide to request or not request a lieutenant general or full general endorsement, without having to answer to anyone. Thus, the commander can "punish" a subordinate without actually having to take any real action. On the other hand, a general officer has quite a lot of power to help individuals whom he judges (by whatever means) worthy. Many times, one will find that officers who garner early promotions have worked directly for a general officer or have worked as his aide. In fact, there is a saying that "to become a general, you must have been a general's aide. . . ."

Keeping the [promotion system] in mind, think about the likelihood of an officer passing on unfavorable information about a program, once a higher-level officer has publicized his support for the system. Picture a man who has been in the service for 15 or more years. He has moved numerous times, he has rationalized many of the system's policies and requirements. He believes in the promotion and rank system and very much wants (and feels he deserves) the next promotion. It will be very, very, very hard for him even to think of being "disloyal" (and thus enduring subtle and effective punishment) by bringing up questions about a weapons system to individuals outside a close-knit group that he trusts.

Senior officers learn about their newly assigned officers or about prospective candidates for promotion by reading between the lines on their annual Effectiveness Reports. The specific areas selected by supervisors for comment, together with the comments left unsaid, signify the real performance evaluation. Although ratings are often far higher than logically possible (e.g., in one survey, 85 percent of the colonels being evaluated were rated among the "top 12 percent" of the colonels), military services place considerable weight on these reports. By the time an officer reaches the rank of lieutenant colonel or colonel, he knows that even one report that is less than outstanding will be sufficient to destroy his chances for promotion.

Other factors that bear on a program manager's evaluation were expressed by an Air Force officer describing the promotion process.

When thinking about the military promotion system, you need to realize the power of the commander and the critical nature of each Effectiveness Report. *Each* Effectiveness Report has significant bearing on whether the individual will receive the next promotion, at least "on time." I know of individuals who were passed over for promotion to lieutenant colonel or major, and the nonselection, they believe, was based upon having had when they were lieutenants an overall rating of less than "1" on the Effectiveness Report scale of one to six [one = highest; six = lowest].

The person writing your Effectiveness Report (i.e., the program manager's boss) can quickly, inexpensively, and effectively end the program manager's career with one unenthusiastic report.

In the acquisition process, the boss's job is to build the program and to make sure it continues to receive funding. Thus, the "loyal" subordinate's job is just the same. In addition, even if the program manager is a high-ranking flag officer, he seeks either higher rank or a future "consulting" job, if not a direct job, with the contractor.

Assignment to program management offices can lack status for some military officers because there are few, if any, standards by which to evaluate the effectiveness and efficiency of program management techniques and program managers. In August 1971, Dr. John Foster, the Pentagon's senior officer for research and development, made a prediction during an address to the Armed Forces Management Association.

> Those project managers who do well will be easily identified and will be rewarded just as an outstanding ship's captain or brigade or wing commander is rewarded. Poor performance will be equally conspicuous, and the poor manager will be relieved [of his assignment] just as he would if he did poorly while leading troops in the field.[83]

Sixteen years later, in 1987, some progress has been made toward creating command-equivalent positions for program management and procurement assignments, but most military officers doubted that these positions were considered comparable to operational commands. Dr. Foster's goal is a laudable one, though yet to be achieved.

PROSPECTS FOR ACQUISITION PROMOTION OPPORTUNITIES

In the executive and legislative branches of government there is considerable resistance to compelling the military services to increase promotion opportunities in procurement and acquisition management. In February 1985, Sen. Dan Quayle (R-IN) asked a senior Air Force general his view on the notion of Congress designating top management posts, such as specific flag and general officer positions, for program managers. The general responded: "In my view, this is a function best left to the services."[84]

Again, in March 1985, in testimony before the same Senate committee, General Thompson referred to the Army's promotion system and requested continued "flexibility" — presumably flexibility to promote combat arms officers at a rate in excess of that for acquisition officers.

In regard to the proposed criteria for promotion to brigadier general positions within the services' materiel commands, the Army shares your concern that officers in the materiel acquisition field should receive recognition for their accomplishments. Last year we promoted three colonels to general officer who had served primarily as PMs. I expect this trend to continue in the future. I do not believe, however, that we should approach our appointments of our general officers by using a "cookie cutter" approach. Doing so may not allow the proper balance of different experiences desired in these positions, such as acquisition, logistical, and user.[85]

But there are signs that the situation will yet improve. Senator Quayle asked General Thompson, "What incentives are needed to retain these experienced officers?" General Thompson responded:

The Army identified the need for additional incentives in 1983 and set forth a series of initiatives for military procurement officers which includes an increased opportunity for advanced schooling and a clear progression pattern for advancement to the general officer ranks. Key procurement positions at the grades of lieutenant colonel and colonel have been redesignated as command positions. This number has increased from 3 to 58 over the last two years. Because command experience greatly enhances an officer's career, the number of procurement officers selected for senior service college and promoted to general officer should continue to improve. Since 1983, six additional general officer billets have been designated for procurement officers.[86]

In the Navy, Assistant Secretary Everett Pyatt testified about promotion opportunities for procurement officers in that service.

We have set aside roughly 80 flag officer billets that can be filled only by people who have been through this professional [material professional] career. . . .

The long-term key is career incentives — there must be opportunities for these deserving individuals to rise to the top of the acquisition management field.[87]

It is clear that public statements by senior military officers and civilians point to increased promotion opportunities for program managers and other acquisition officers. Increased promotion opportunities for acquisition officers, however, are likely to mean decreased opportunities for others. Hence, there is little doubt that any genuine improvement will require consistent, strong support from all who agree that change is needed, whether they be senior military officers, the service Secretaries, or members of Congress. The outcome remains unclear.

Training

In his first annual message to Congress, President Andrew Jackson wrote, "The duties of all public officers are, or at least admit of being made so plain and simple that men of intelligence may readily qualify themselves for their performance."[88]

Although the "plain and simple" approach might have been effective in the 1830s, it has proved far from satisfactory for government program managers in the 1970s and 1980s. The complexities of carrying out the development and production of multibillion-dollar weapon systems programs require managers with highly developed skills in planning, evaluating, negotiating, overseeing, and controlling the industrial firms that perform the work.

In its 1986 study of defense acquisition, the General Accounting Office found that many program managers were simply not equipped to undertake the intricate problems of weapons procurement. The report concluded, "Qualified program managers require appropriate experience, training and education, and many do not have it." By contrast, industry program managers are well trained and experienced for the day-to-day negotiations and program administration, often leaving their DOD counterparts far behind.[89]

The General Accounting Office also found, in an earlier study, that program managers failed to treat the budget process with the interest they believed it should receive. "The program managers look at money as a dirty medium, and they feel uncomfortable dealing with it. They tend to ignore the budget and only get involved with it when they have to."[90]

Congressional testimony confirmed the existence of serious training problems. During the September 1984 Senate Armed Services Committee hearings on the defense procurement process, Sen. Jeff Bingaman (D-NM) asked Norman Augustine, president and chief operating officer of Martin Marietta Corporation and former Under Secretary of the Army, "In your view, do the people we put in positions of managing these programs have the necessary training and qualifications to do these jobs?" Mr. Augustine responded:

I would say that in many cases they truthfully don't. We do much better than we did 10 years ago, but it is not uncommon for someone who has been commanding a ship at sea or a division or squadron to suddenly be placed in a position where they have the job of overseeing the work of an industrial giant.

It is pretty tough to be equipped to do that when one comes out of a military operating force. It would be much the same as taking somebody like myself and putting them in charge of an air wing; it would be a terrible mistake.

I think we would need much more training for these people before we put them on the firing line.[91]

The appraisals by the General Accounting Office and by Mr. Augustine were reinforced by other respected industry spokesmen. Karl Harr, then president of the Aerospace Industries Association, observed:

You cannot underestimate the importance of the quality of the people in the process, obviously. We would agree . . . anything that can be done [to improve the quality] will be helpful. . . .

Sure, one of the ways to improve performance is to upgrade quality, but much more practical I suppose, in the immediate area is to make sure they get trained. Training is a function of time, organization.[92]

Another industry spokesman, Roy Anderson, then chief executive officer of Lockheed Corporation, commented:

In addition, more can be done, in my opinion, to train and attract more qualified military personnel into the procurement process. The services must realize the vast amount of dollars that must be expended and prudently managed to carry out their missions. I believe some sort of business education should be offered in the military academies, and a career in procurement elevated as a factor for promotion, equivalent to strictly military paths including potential for flag positions.[93]

These observations on the inadequacy of acquisition training were virtually the same as those I heard fifteen years earlier when I asked ten presidents and vice-presidents from companies with major defense and space contracts to comment on the government personnel who managed their programs.

In the 1970s and 1980s, most military officers have had extensive academic education and general service training. In addition to a bachelor's degree, each officer acquires more education by assignment at midcareer to the Command and Staff College, or its equivalent, for a year. Many officers have the opportunity to earn a master's degree, which requires one or two years. Other officers earn a master's degree through evening programs. Then, at the lieutenant colonel or commander level, officers are sent to the War College for approximately one year.

Many officers now believe they need a master's degree just to be competitive for promotion. As suggested by one Air Force officer, "A number of marginal master's programs are endured because they serve the purpose of getting a ticket punched." Some military officers told us that they believe the heavy emphasis on academic degrees is also seen as a means to help qualify them for jobs in the civilian economy after military retirement.

But academic master's degrees rarely develop the negotiating skills or provide a familiarity with the aggressive business tactics employed in the defense acquisition process. Academic training is no substitute for experience in negotiating solutions to day-to-day problems; evaluating contractor schedule, cost, and technical performance; motivating government and industry personnel; and dealing with an array of unanticipated problems in the day-to-day management of complex industrial development programs.

Although extensive practical training and on-the-job experience are considered essential for military combat organizations, their importance for excellence in acquisition management is less widely recognized. Much of the acquisition training available to government program managers is confined to introductory descriptions of types of contracts, procedures, regulations, reporting systems, and related topics. Little or no time is spent practicing implementation, using these tools, or in testing the reasonableness and validity of the data employed.

The limited training in industrial management and the acquisition process is acknowledged, but it has not produced an outcry from senior military officials. One former Assistant Secretary of a military service explained, "There is a great deal of defensiveness in the military services. Senior military officers often state: 'We have the ability to manage.' 'We have enough training,' when in fact the training is far from sufficient to deal with the problems that arise in the acquisition process." This attitude, often prompted by a "can do" attitude and loyalty to colleagues, reappears in congressional testimony. For example, a flag officer commander of one of the buying commands stated:

> I believe this command [AFSC] has "top notch" management resources to meet our responsibilities. AFSC has been particularly sensitive to building and maintaining the highest quality professional skills in our pro-

gram managers. For example, of the 59 officers identified as fully qualified program managers and assigned to direct control of their program, all have bachelor's degrees, 90 percent have master's degrees, and 20 percent have their doctorates. Seventy-five percent of these managers have completed one or more DSMC training courses.[94]

Once again, the focus is on bachelor's and master's degrees and, in this case, on doctorates instead of the practical skills military officers need for dealing with the situations they will confront as program managers.

Not all acquisition managers who seek further training are able to take advantage of what exists. A first lieutenant who had worked in a program office for eighteen months told us that he had been unable to persuade his supervisor to send him to one of the short (one- to three-week) training programs, despite his lack of experience in program management. The workload in the organization was so heavy that it was not possible for the program manager to spare anyone for school. Several program managers said that they usually sent only those people whose loss would have the least harmful effect on productivity. Obviously, this meant that the person most eager and qualified for training was often the least likely to receive it. The problem was outlined by a civil servant enrolled in the twenty-week DSMC program management course.

> Supervisors in the field fear that if they give up a man for twenty weeks to attend a school, government personnel specialists may conclude that the man is not needed. If the man's position is not filled during his twenty-week absence, personnel specialists will ask why the position cannot be given up permanently. If the position is filled by another civil servant for the twenty-week period, the man attending school is concerned that he may lose his position to his replacement.

THE DEFENSE SYSTEMS MANAGEMENT COLLEGE (DSMC)

In the spring of 1971, I participated with a group of senior Pentagon officials in establishing a twenty-week training program, called the Defense Systems Management School, for military and civilian personnel working in program offices. In the late 1970s, the faculty and staff changed the name to Defense Systems Management College (DSMC).

DSMC was established to provide professional education in program management and defense systems acquisition management. The directive from the Deputy Secretary of Defense gave the school three missions:

to prepare selected military officers and civilian personnel for assignments in program management career fields;

to conduct research and special studies in program management and defense systems acquisition management; and

to assemble and disseminate information relative to program management and defense systems acquisition management.[95]

DSMC was not intended to be an academic institution. It was intended to offer practical courses to help students acquire knowledge and skills in the operation of defense program management and procurement: the problems encountered, the options for dealing with these problems, and the methods of selecting from among the options. Originally designed for middle managers (0-3, 0-4, GS-12, GS-13), the goal of the school was to increase their ability to manage a defense systems acquisition program successfully. The curriculum committee was concerned that the school not develop a theoretical focus. A danger was seen in the term *college,* leading the school to evolve into an academic organization in which the faculty would devote the short time available for classroom sessions to more theoretical topics such as theories of motivation, personal assessment, typology, and interpersonal behavior. By the 1980s, courses on each of these topics had been suggested by the faculty — and even offered at times. Although such courses can have intrinsic value, they are necessarily of low priority in a practical program manager course condensed into twenty weeks.

The twenty-week duration grew out of a 138-day DOD-imposed restriction on the length of temporary duty assignments. Anything longer would be classified as a permanent change of duty and thus entail housing and moving expenses. Indeed, DSMC has been under continuing pressure over the years to *shorten* rather than lengthen the course, because the twenty weeks has been seen as a great sacrifice from so-called permanent (two- to three-year) assignments. In the late 1980s, the course was indeed becoming shorter. In response to pressure from senior DOD officers, the DSMC faculty and administration developed a schedule permitting students to spend only fourteen weeks at the DSMC campus, preceded by six weeks of preparation at DSMC or another location.

Given the limited time available in a twenty-week course, the DSMC faculty and staff have made commendable progress in designing and teaching a set of introductory courses. The curriculum is designed to train students in planning, organizing, directing, and controlling acquisition programs from the conceptual stages through production and fielding of the system and equipment. Fundamental knowledge of acquisition management methods is emphasized, as are the qualities of judgment (including common sense) and initiative. In addition to developing skill and confidence through the presentation of individual and team reports, the curriculum provides students with an introduction to effective operation of a program office.

The severe time constraints under which the DSMC operates, however, are readily apparent in the time allotted to each of the following selected topics covered in the course.

Hours	Selected Topics
4	Parametric Cost Analysis (with Introduction to Cost/Quantity Relationships and Improvement Functions)
2	Case I: Parametric Cost Estimating
3	Cost Proposal Estimation
1	Preparation of the RFP
3	Proposal Evaluation
1	Types of Contracts
1	Cost Incentives
1	Methods of Contracting
1	Award Fee Contracting
1	Source Selection
1	Negotiation Preparation
1	Government Profit Policy
1	Contract Modifications
1	Constructive Changes
3	Understanding Financial Reporting of DOD Contractors
3	Financial Analysis of DOD Contractors
2	Cost Principles in DOD Contracting
1	Introduction to Overhead and General and Administrative Rates
1	Principles of Cost Control Systems
2	Cost Control Terminology
1	Development of Cost Performance Baseline
2	Review of Cost/Schedule Control Systems Criteria (C/SCSC) and Earned Value Techniques
1	C/SCSC Implementation and Surveillance
2	Financial Reporting to the Government[96]

Three hours are devoted to cost management in the defense industry. The "desired learning outcome" specifies that "each student taking this three-hour required topic should gain a very significant amount of knowledge:

Become aware of how defense contractors develop their sales forecasts and appreciate the risks inherent in such forecasts.

Understand the relationship between forward pricing rates, billing rates and end-of-year actual rates.

Have knowledge of the financial impact that a change in contract volume has on indirect cost rates.

Become familiar with how materials, labor and indirect costs are accumulated under a typical job order cost-accounting system used by defense contractors.

Become aware of how budgets, standards and variance analysis are used for controlling defense contracting operations and activities.

Understand the reasons for the importance of cost accounting standards in the defense industry."[97]

One hour is allocated to multiple-incentive contracts. By the end each student should be able to

Explain the policy on use of performance incentives;

Explain how to structure noncost incentives;

Explain the role of the program management office team in structuring performance incentives;

Explain and compute final payments when given essential contract terms and final cost.[98]

After one hour devoted to principles of cost-control systems, each student should be able to

Define the purpose and nature of control systems;

Describe how control systems and techniques can be designed to improve the quality of managerial control;

Describe the process of control;

Understand past problems associated with cost-performance reporting.[99]

Several days, or even weeks, could usefully be spent on an introductory course on *each* of these topics. The pressure on the faculty to crowd vast amounts of material into twenty weeks is immense, often leading to cursory treatment of many important and complicated topics and precluding the development of skills in applying or using the knowledge.

Although there is little time for students to study outside the classroom, the course curriculum does reserve thirty hours within the twenty weeks for electives, enabling students to devote some time to topics in which they are particularly interested.

THE DSMC FACULTY

Since its creation in 1971, DSMC has experienced difficulties in attracting and retaining well-qualified civilians or military officers to its faculty. Assignment of military officers is normally a two- to three-year tour. Civilian faculty, recruited from GS-13 civil service employees for GS-14 faculty positions, are initially assigned for three-year periods, which can be extended to five years and possibly seven. But the average civilian tour has been three years; only 5 to 10 percent have remained for five years. A problem in attracting civilians is that they must resign a career civil service position to assume a faculty position at DSMC. Then within three to seven years they are out of work. Consequently, many of the faculty spend much of their third year looking for a job. It is no surprise that the school has difficulty recruiting faculty skilled at teaching as well as in the practical substance of program management.

During our interviews, we learned that one Army officer, a DSMC faculty candidate, had spent a year assigned to a contractor plant, had then been assigned to a program management office, and had subsequently moved to a personnel office. The DSMC administration had encouraged him to join the faculty. He had refused, saying "it would be suicide" for him. He believed that he had a chance to be a battalion commander, a position that would count much more favorably in his next promotion review.[100] A brigadier general currently assigned to the acquisition process expressed the same view.

Despite the problems posed by a twenty-week course limit and difficulties in attracting faculty, senior military officers responsible for the acquisition process do not see the need to take action. In testimony before the Senate Armed Services Committee in 1984, senior Army,

Navy, and Air Force officers expressed their satisfaction with the current arrangement.

Gen. Richard Thompson, Commander, Army Materiel Command

> The Defense Systems Management College is doing a great job. . . . We believe the approved five year plan is adequate to meet Army needs.[101]

Adm. Steven A. White, Commander, Navy Material Command

> The Defense Systems Management College is performing well in the preparation of officer and civilian personnel for material acquisition assignments. . . . In view of recent actions at the school, I do not see a need for any further extensive expansions at this time.[102]

Gen. Lawrence Skantze, Commander, Air Force Systems Command

> DSMC is doing an excellent job. It is an *essential* element in the careers of our program managers; . . . At this time I do not feel we need to expand our training program.[103] (emphasis added)

The comment from the Air Force is particularly interesting considering that less than 20 percent of the Air Force program managers interviewed in the 1986 GAO study had attended DSMC. If indeed DSMC is an "essential element," then a significant number of Air Force program managers may lack the required training.[104]

THE FUTURE OF ACQUISITION TRAINING

Congressional hearings on the acquisition process, beginning in 1984, along with the 1986 Packard Commission Report citing serious deficiencies in program manager qualifications, have increased the attention paid to the training and experience of people assigned to acquisition positions. In March 1985, Adm. James Watkins, Chief of Naval Operations, said, "The Navy plans to require training in weapons technology and financial management for 100 procurement-related posts that currently are open to officers from various backgrounds." Admiral Watkins added that procurement officers lacking such training will be replaced by officers holding the new classification of "material professional." The replacements will be made when current procurement officers leave their posts under a normal rotation system.[105]

Army Assistant Secretary Jay Scully commented on the training of program managers.

> The Army has developed and submitted to OSD a separate budget for mandatory procurement training and, as part of a DOD Task Group, has initiated action to establish centralized (OSD) funding for mandatory training. . . .
>
> We have developed and implemented a program to send both military and civilian employees to Training with Industry for approximately a one-year period and are sending outstanding civilians to senior-level schools.[106]

In 1987, military and civilian incumbents of senior defense positions indicated that some improvement in training would take place. But as one senior military officer commented, "Training is a long-term solution, and very few have the long-term view." By 1989, present Pentagon officials are likely to be long gone from their influential positions. It remains to be seen whether their successors will have the same commitments.

Assuring adequate training of government acquisition managers will require a major change in current practice. Minimal formal training will need to include at least a year of intensive study and practice in the acquisition process. In addition to the introductory courses now offered by DSMC, students will need several months of practical exercises and discussions dealing with the dilemmas and decisions encountered by program managers and their staffs. These courses will need to be taught by a faculty skilled in guiding student discussions (versus imparting theory or dispensing information) and sufficiently familiar with the acquisition process so that prepackaged lectures are unnecessary — indeed, inappropriate.

The Revolving Door

Army and Air Force colonels and Navy captains usually retire if they are not promoted to general or admiral within three to four years. (Very few — fewer than 5 percent — are promoted.) Such officers are usually in their midforties; many have children in college, elderly parents, home mortgages, and other large expenses. Retiring from military service after twenty years and accepting a job with the defense industry, or with a firm advising the defense industry, means that they can usually increase their total income (including retirement pay) by 50 percent or more.

Under current legislation, defense contractors are required to report on retired military officers and civilian defense officials who join their company. The Council on Economic Priorities (CEP), a private organization based in New York, has compiled the data from these reports.[107]

Between 1971 and 1979, according to the council, 1,455 or more officers above the rank of colonel went to work for defense contractors. They were joined by 335 civilian DOD and 31 NASA employees of equivalent rank (GS-15 or higher). (The NASA figures cover only the period between 1975 and 1979.) At the same time, there was also a smaller amount of traffic in the other direction, with 223 company officials who went to work for DOD and 47 for NASA. Boeing led the list with 398 changes, Northrop was second with 360, Lockheed was third with 321, and General Dynamics was fourth with 239.[108]

Although it is unfair to impute unprofessional conduct to military officers who accept jobs with defense contractors, many critics argue that the need for a postretirement job ten to fifteen years before normal retirement at age sixty-five is a strong temptation to treat contractors sympathetically before retirement. These critics suggest there is little incentive for program managers and contracting officers to adopt a probing attitude toward contractors' claims involving cost and performance.[109]

Based on my interviews in government and industry, along with my experience with DOD over several years, overt favoritism to a contractor in contract negotiations or claims settlements is rare. Nonetheless, the loss of a military officer or civilian to a firm with which the person's government office has been contractually involved has the appearance of conflict of interest and often creates a demoralizing effect on the remaining staff, who continue the negotiations. (Negotiations occur throughout the life of a development or production program and do not end with the signing of the initial contract.)

The General Accounting Office reported that more than 30,000 people with the rank of Army major or above or with comparable civilian pay grades (GS-13 or above) had left the Defense Department in 1983 and 1984. More than 6,000 of these later held industrial security clearances and, based on a GAO study, approximately 5,700 were thought to be working for companies contracting with DOD, although not necessarily those involved with their former office.[110]

The General Accounting Office mailed questionnaires to a stratified sample of the former DOD officials with industrial security clearances and obtained 658 replies. Even though the responses were anonymous, the agency suggested that because some of the questions concerned "a sensitive issue dealing with potential postemployment conflict of interest," some respondents might not have fully reported their involvement with military programs.[111]

Approximately one-fifth of the respondents currently worked on the same projects that they had worked on while employed by the Defense Department, and more than half of those said that they spent most of their time on such projects.[112]

The report showed that nearly three-fourths of those surveyed had had some degree of responsibility, while at DOD, that they viewed as affecting industry contractors. Forty percent thought their responsibilities of this kind were substantial. About 26 percent had had DOD responsibilities involving contractors for whom they subsequently worked.[113]

Eighty-two percent continued to have work-related contact with current Pentagon officials while employed by contractors, and 45 percent said they continued to do business with officials with whom they had worked while employed by DOD.[114]

Most of the respondents said they saw nothing wrong with the situation. Sixty-one percent called the movement of people from DOD to its contractors "extremely advantageous" for the government. Only 3 percent thought it disadvantageous.[115] At the same time, 36 percent thought it would be good for DOD if a pending proposal restricting postgovernment employment were made law. Forty-three percent thought the legislation would not be good for DOD.[116]

Some of the moves from government to industry can easily create the impression that there is a symbiotic relationship between a government program office and a contractor. For example, three program managers assigned to the Maverick program subsequently worked for its contractor. In the words of a manager from the Air Force contract management division of the Air Force Systems Command, "It appears that these people can get a high-paying job with the company if they take it easy on [the company]. I don't see why I shouldn't be doing that."[117]

One major general, a former commander of a buying command, commented:

> Many of the program managers who got along well with their contrac-
> tors have obtained good jobs after they retired. A second career is waiting
> there for them.

Sen. Jeff Bingaman (D-NM), speaking to Gen. Lawrence Skantze at a 1984 Senate hearing, indicated that a major defense contractor had hired an Under Secretary of Defense who had been in charge of weapons development and later became a company vice-president, a lieutenant colonel who had headed the test program associated with the company's product, three defense program managers who had been associated with the company's product, two DOD auditors who had been in charge of monitoring the company's contracts, and a colonel who had been in charge of contract administration at the company's plant.[118]

These situations are not unusual. The Packard Commission survey of military program managers found that almost one in four (24 per-cent) said they had considered (during the year preceding the survey) a definite offer of employment in the private sector. It is not at all clear, however, how many of these offers were made by contractors with whom they were then working.

As one senior officer of a major defense contractor — a former DOD official — told us:

> Hardly a day goes by that I do not receive a call from a colonel or
> lieutenant colonel looking for a job in industry. The answer to this problem
> may be to build a truly professional career civil service to run the show. I'm
> not sure you can do that. Today, civil service pay is poor.

Obviously, there is a problem here. Contractors should have the right to offer jobs to government officials being encouraged (for what-ever reason) to retire. Retiring government officials should have the right to accept jobs where they can make a contribution and earn more money. At the same time, there needs to be a way of accomplishing this without creating the appearance, or the reality, of a conflict of interest. Increasingly restrictive laws are likely to accomplish little more than unfairly penalizing retiring government personnel.

Although there is a law prohibiting former military officers from selling products or services to their former services, it has been easy in the past to avoid the law by designating them consultants or technical advisers rather than sales employees. In fact, most contractor officials performing key sales roles are not formally assigned to marketing or selling positions. Instead, they are assigned to research, engineering, product development, program control — any of a wide variety of positions throughout the contractor organization. Richard Stubbing, former defense specialist at the Office of Management and Budget, described the problem.

> In fact, almost anyone can be placed in a nonmarketing position involving direct sales to the government. The imparting of inside information on programs and people, plus the informal "old-boy network" with former colleagues — many of whom will soon be leaving DOD and looking for lucrative industry positions — will go on, no matter what we call the individual's position. Thus the revolving door remains wide open.[119]

In mid-1985, a senior-level Pentagon procurement policy official resigned while being investigated on charges that she had solicited business from several defense contractors for her planned private consulting firm. According to the Pentagon report, the official, and her deputy, began in spring 1985 to develop plans to leave the Defense Department and establish a consulting firm. She contacted twenty-five major defense contractors and two law firms through phone calls and letters, informing them of her plans and, in some cases, enclosing a draft contract. It was at that point that she resigned, while under investigation.[120]

There is a positive side to having retired military officers and civil servants working for defense contractors. There is nothing inherently unethical about military officers or government civilians retiring and accepting employment in the defense industry. Indeed, it is only reasonable that talented professionals who have performed their duties conscientiously and have acquired skills in managing large defense programs find subsequent employment where their skills can best be used — the defense industry. To do otherwise could deprive the country of their acquired defense acquisition skills. Further, employment outside the defense industry could deprive these officials of a standard of living difficult to regain in commercial fields, where they have had no experience. Finally, there is little doubt that the exchange of personnel smooths the contracting process and helps communicate to industry important technical and administrative concerns of the government.

The problem is a particularly difficult one because the military retirement system necessitates early retirement, leaving people with few options but to find a job in the private sector. One Air Force officer appropriately asks:

> Where are the negotiators or program managers going to work when they retire? A lieutenant colonel will be required to retire after 25 years in service at age 47 and receive a pension of about $25,000 per year. These are certainly generous benefits; however, what does this individual do to make up the other $20,000 to $25,000 that he had been earning?

Critics see the movement of retired military officers to the defense industry solely as a case of favoritism and a narrowing of perspective in which private and government interests converge to impair objectivity.[121] It is easy for an outside observer to conclude that those responsible for procurement relationships with defense suppliers are under tacit but substantial pressure to play the game, to cooperate, not to rock the boat.[122]

In one of the more persuasive statements criticizing the revolving door, an experienced official with the Air Force Systems Command told the House Armed Services Committee:

> Most of our people are basically honest and straightforward. The biggest problem of our military officials is that the "up or out" system forces them out into the private sector job market at a young age. They have college-age kids and need the extra income to continue to acquire their personal amenities and to support their families at a comfortable level. . . .
>
> I, and many of my coworkers, have observed that when a manager is ready to retire, he doesn't just retire and go to work for the contractor. There is planning involved. The process begins two or three years prior to the separation from Government service, and the manager becomes increasingly soft on the contractor.
>
> To get the job, he must know someone in the contractor's hierarchy, he must do things which the contractor likes, and he must prove his worthiness for his new job.
>
> Consciously or unconsciously, the thought of future security begins to affect him. He begins to think more about his future employer than his current one. Loyalties become confused. . . .
>
> There are many and complex reasons for the problems in the procurement system, but the revolving door is one of the key contributors.
>
> A boss who is seeking postretirement employment is more likely to reward those who do not discover problems than those who do.
>
> When your promotion and bonuses are based on not finding anything

wrong, you learn to find nothing wrong, and you finally become conditioned to believing that there is nothing wrong.

The flow of high-level government personnel from the government to the contractors has a lasting impact on the working-level people. When their commander or supervisor suddenly goes over to the other side of the table and becomes a manager for the contractor, the first reaction is one of outrage and anger. We don't know if we have been working for the contractor or the government. . . .

When we found out that our former commander of the [deleted] command had become a consultant to Pratt and Whitney, one of our employees commented to the effect that, "They make us read all these regulations and fill out all those forms and make us attend all those conflict-of-interest briefings, when the big people can get away with anything they want."

When they are our bosses, they terrorize us by saying that if we do some little thing, it will be a conflict of interest. Meanwhile, they themselves have been negotiating a job with the contractor. . . .[123]

Irrespective of the view one holds on the revolving door, it is clear that the Defense Department places military officers in a difficult position when it effectively requires retirement at a relatively young age, immediately after having held positions of evaluating, controlling, and negotiating with the contractor firms that are the officers' most likely source of postretirement employment.

Instead of sponsoring ever more restrictive legislation, the Defense Department and the Congress need to take prompt action to provide the opportunities and the incentives for military officers and civilians to remain with the government acquisition process for a full career. Both the government and the people involved would derive substantial benefit from the increased experience, more finely honed skills, and greater independence from contractors. In the absence of such reform, it is difficult to see how most military officers and government civilians can be expected to maintain the appearance, as well as the reality, of being effective evaluators, controllers, and overseers of firms they will soon approach as prospective employers.

Notes

1. Glenn Pascall, *The Trillion Dollar Budget* (Seattle: University of Washington Press, 1985), pp. 147–148.

2. U.S. House of Representatives, Committee on Government Operations, Hearing on the Organization and Administration of Military Research and Development Programs, 1954.

3. U.S. Department of Defense, Ad Hoc Study Group (Robertson Panel), *Manned Aircraft Weapon Systems: A More Vigorous Project Management,* vol. V, August 1956.

4. M. J. Peck and F. M. Scherer, *The Weapons Acquisition Process: An Economic Analysis* (Boston: Division of Research, Harvard Business School, 1962), pp. 93–94.

5. Robert A. Magnan, "In Search of the 'End Game': A Comparison of U.S. and Foreign Weapons Acquisition Systems," a study conducted under the DCI Exceptional Intelligence Analyst Program, 1984, pp. 63–66.

6. Edmund S. Dews, Giles K. Smith, Allen Barbour, Elwyn Harris, and Michael Hesse, "Acquisition Policy Effectiveness: Department of Defense Experience in the 1970s," RAND Report R-2516-DR&E, October 1979, pp. 15–17.

7. American Defense Preparedness Association Panel on the Acquisition Management Career Field, Chicago, Illinois, July 1982.

8. U.S. General Accounting Office, "Department of Defense's Defense Acquisition Improvement Program: A Status Report," GAO/NSIAD–86–148, July 1986, p. 11.

9. Ibid.

10. U.S. Senate, hearing before the Subcommittee on Defense Acquisition Policy of the Committee on Armed Services, "Improving the Professionalism of the Defense Acquisition Work Force," March 11, 1985, pp. 56–57.

11. U.S. General Accounting Office, "DOD Acquisition: Strengthening Capabilities of Key Personnel in Systems Acquisition," GAO/NSIAD–86–45, May 1986, p. 80.

12. U.S. House of Representatives, joint hearing of the Subcommittee on Seapower and Strategic and Critical Materials and the Subcommittee on Investigations of the Committee on Armed Services, "Revolving Door, H.R. 272, Defense Production Act Amendments of 1985," April 18, 1985, p. 130.

13. Blue Ribbon Defense Panel, Report to the President and the Secretary of Defense on the Department of Defense, July 1, 1970, p. 137.

14. Ibid.

15. F. R. Sims, Manager of Program Management, LTV Aerospace and Defense Company, Vought Missiles and Advanced Programs Division, "Defense Contracts — Why Do They Cost So Much?" unpublished paper, July 19, 1985.

16. U.S. General Accounting Office, "DOD Acquisition: Strengthening Capabilities of Key Personnel in Systems Acquisition," GAO/NSIAD–86–45, May 1986, pp. 79–80. In the remaining Army and Navy and two Air Force programs, the first program manager had not been replaced.

17. U.S. General Accounting Office, GAO/NSIAD–86–45, May 1986, pp. 79–80.

18. U.S. House of Representatives, Committee on Government Operations, "Policy Changes in Weapons Systems Procurement," December 10, 1970.

19. U.S. House of Representatives, Committee on Armed Services, "Defense Procurement Procedures," February 12, 1982, p. 24.

20. U.S. Senate, hearing before the Task Force on Selected Defense Procurement Matters of the Committee on Armed Services, "Defense Procurement Process," September 20, 1984.

21. U.S. Senate Committee on Armed Services, hearing, March 11, 1985, p. 16.

22. President's Blue Ribbon Commission on Defense Management, *A Quest for Excellence,* Final Report to the President, June 1986, p. 67.

23. U.S. Senate, testimony of Maj. Gen. Richard Steere, AFSC, DCS/Systems, before the Task Force on Selected Defense Procurement Matters of the Committee on Armed Services, "Career Paths and Professional Development for Acquisition Managers in the Department of Defense," December 13, 1984, pp. 38–41.

24. Ibid.

25. Ibid.

26. Ibid.

27. Department of Defense Directive (DODD) 5000.23, "System Acquisition Management Careers," December 1986; originally issued November 26, 1974.

28. U.S. General Accounting Office, "DOD Acquisition: Strengthening Capabilities of Key Personnel in Systems Acquisition," GAO/NSIAD–86–45, May 1986, p. 68.

29. Defense Science Board Task Force on Research and Development Management, *Final Report on Systems Acquisition,* Washington, D.C., September 11, 1969.

30. Blue Ribbon Defense Panel, Report to the President and the Secretary of Defense on the Department of Defense, July 1, 1970.

31. David Packard, "Policy Guidance on Major Weapon System Acquisition," memorandum, Department of Defense, May 1970; and Dews et al., "Acquisition Policy Effectiveness," RAND Report R-2516-DR&E, October 1979, p. 11.

32. U.S. General Accounting Office, GAO/NSIAD–86–45, May 1986, p. 78.

33. Ibid., pp. 75–77. Acquisition experience was defined as any involvement in the development of the system, from requirements determination through production and deployment, including supply and maintenance.

34. A 1987 study by Air Force officers found a different figure for the Air Force personnel: 45 percent. William D. Brown, Paul J. Kern, L. Kirk Lewis, and John G. Zeirdt, "Acquisition Management — The Role and the Reality," National Security Program Report, John F. Kennedy School of Government, Harvard University, June 1987, pp. 112–117.

35. Ibid.

36. J. Ronald Fox, *Arming America: How the U.S. Buys Weapons* (Boston: Division of Research, Harvard Business School, Harvard University, 1974), p. 201.

37. U.S. Senate, hearing before the Subcommittee on Defense Acquisition Policy of the Committee on Armed Services, "Improving the Professionalism of the Defense Acquisition Work Force," March 11, 1985, pp. 65–66.

38. Ibid.

39. U.S. Senate, hearing before the Task Force on Selected Defense Procurement Matters of the Committee on Armed Services, "Career Paths and Professional

Development for Acquisition Managers in the Department of Defense," December 13, 1984, pp. 27–28.

40. J. Ronald Fox, "Revamping the Business of National Defense," *Harvard Business Review,* September-October 1984, pp. 63–64.
41. U.S. General Accounting Office, GAO/NSIAD–86–45, May 1986, pp. 70–71.
42. Ibid., p. 72.
43. Brown et al., "Acquisition Management," pp. 66–67. See also *Commander's Fact Book* (Los Angeles: Air Force Systems Command, Space Division, September 1986), pp. 21–23.
44. President's Blue Ribbon Commission on Defense Management, *A Quest for Excellence,* June 1986, p. 106.
45. Ibid., p. 67.
46. U.S. General Accounting Office, GAO/NSIAD–86–45, May 1986, pp. 88–91.
47. U.S. Senate Committee on Armed Services, hearing, December 13, 1984, pp. 10–11.
48. Ibid., p. 29.
49. U.S. General Accounting Office, GAO/NSIAD–86–45, May 1986, p. 94.
50. "Navy Pushes Business Skills," *Washington Post,* March 15, 1985, p. A1.
51. U.S. General Accounting Office, GAO/NSIAD–86–45, May 1986, pp. 94–102.
52. Ibid., pp. 94–95.
53. Ibid., p. 101.
54. U.S. Senate, testimony of Everett Pyatt, Assistant Secretary of the Navy (Shipbuilding and Logistics), hearing before the Task Force on Selected Defense Procurement Matters of the Committee on Armed Services, "Reducing the Cost of Weapon Systems Acquisition," December 18, 1984, p. 7.
55. Everett Pyatt, Assistant Secretary of the Navy (Shipbuilding and Logistics), in a memorandum for the Under Secretary of Defense (Research and Engineering), May 30, 1985.
56. U.S. General Accounting Office, GAO/NSIAD–86–45, May 1986, p. 98.
57. These figures are subject to error but are the best available; they should thus be viewed as indicative of trends rather than as precise measures of acquisition experience.
58. U.S. General Accounting Office, GAO/NSIAD–86–45, May 1986, pp. 98–99.
59. Ibid.
60. Ibid., p. 101.
61. Ibid.
62. U.S. Senate Committee on Armed Services, hearing, March 11, 1985, p. 30.
63. U.S. Senate Committee on Armed Services, hearing, December 13, 1984, pp. 26–32.
64. U.S. General Accounting Office, "A Perspective on the Potential Impact of a Centralized Civilian Acquisition Agency (CCAA)," B-224853, November 1986, p. 30.

65. "Weinberger Orders Navy to Reverse Course on Women," *Washington Post,* February 4, 1987.
66. U.S. General Accounting Office, GAO/NSIAD–86–45, May 1986, p. 86.
67. Ibid., pp. 84–86.
68. Ibid., p. 87.
69. U.S. Senate Committee on Armed Services, hearing, March 11, 1985, pp. 32–34.
70. Ibid., p. 39.
71. Thomas S. Amlie, Assistant for Technical Systems, Office of the Assistant Secretary of the Air Force (Financial Management), memorandum to A. Ernest Fitzgerald, March 2, 1984.
72. President's Blue Ribbon Commission on Defense, *A Quest for Excellence,* June 1986, pp. 65–66.
73. Robert S. Greenberger, "Pentagon Official Urges Setting Up Purchasing Corps," *The Wall Street Journal,* December 6, 1985.
74. U.S. General Accounting Office, GAO/NSIAD–86–45, May 1986, p. 79. For additional information on this topic, see the President's Blue Ribbon Commission on Defense Management, *A Quest for Excellence,* June 1986; or the Blue Ribbon Defense Panel, Report to the President and the Secretary of Defense on the Department of Defense, July 1, 1970, p. 140.
75. U.S. General Accounting Office, GAO/NSIAD–86–45, May 1986, p. 80.
76. Ibid., p. 81.
77. Ibid., p. 75.
78. Ibid., p. 81.
79. U.S. Senate Committee on Armed Services, hearing, March 11, 1985, pp. 44–46.
80. U.S. Senate Committee on Armed Services, hearing, December 13, 1984, pp. 26–32.
81. U.S. Senate Committee on Armed Services, hearing, March 11, 1985, pp. 17–18.
82. Department of the Army News Release, "Army selects 56 officers for promotion to brigadier general," July 21, 1987.
83. Dr. John Foster, Director, Defense Research and Engineering, Address to the Armed Forces Management Association, August 19, 1971.
84. U.S. Senate, hearing before the Subcommittee on Defense Acquisition Policy of the Committee on Armed Services, "Defense Procurement Process," February 20, 1985, Part 4, p. 35.
85. U.S. Senate Committee on Armed Services, hearing, March 11, 1985, p. 22.
86. Ibid., p. 66.
87. U.S. Senate Committee on Armed Services, hearing, December 18, 1984, pp. 4, 7.
88. "Most Federal Workers Need Only Be Competent," *The Wall Street Journal,* May 21, 1986.
89. U.S. General Accounting Office, GAO/NSIAD–86–45, May 1986; and *Washington Post,* June 12, 1986.
90. U.S. General Accounting Office, "Can the United States Major Weapon Sys-

tems Acquisition Process Keep Pace with the Conventional Arms Threat Posed by the USSR?" GAO/PSAD/GP, May 27, 1980, p. 41.

91. U.S. Senate, hearings before the Task Force on Selected Defense Procurement Matters of the Committee on Armed Services, "Defense Procurement Process," September 20, 1984, Part 2, pp. 163–164.

92. U.S. Senate, hearings before the Subcommittee on Defense Acquisition Policy of the Committee on Armed Services, "Implementation of the 1984 Defense Procurement Legislation," October 17 and 29, November 7 and 13, 1985, p. 353.

93. U.S. Senate, hearings before the Subcommittee on Defense Acquisition Policy of the Committee on Armed Services, "Defense Procurement Process," January 30, 1985, Part 3, p. 36.

94. U.S. Senate, hearing before the Task Force on Selected Defense Procurement Matters of the Committee on Armed Services, "Defense Procurement Process," September 13, 1984, Part 1, p. 139. DSMC offers several one- to three-week courses in addition to the twenty-week program management course.

95. David D. Acker, "The Maturing of the DOD Acquisition Process," *Defense Systems Management Review,* Summer 1980, pp. 37–38.

96. Defense Systems Management College Course Book, PMC 86–1, Fort Belvoir, Virginia, March 1986.

97. Ibid.

98. Ibid.

99. Ibid.

100. Interview with faculty and administrators at the Defense Systems Management College, October 6, 1986.

101. U.S. Senate Committee on Armed Services, hearing, September 13, 1984, Part 1, p. 137.

102. Ibid.

103. Ibid.

104. U.S. General Accounting Office, GAO/NSIAD–86–45, May 1986, p. 78.

105. "Navy to Upgrade Procurement Careers as a Way to Combat Contractor Abuses," *The Wall Street Journal,* March 15, 1985.

106. U.S. Senate Committee on Armed Services, hearings, October 17 and 29, and November 7 and 13, 1985, pp. 220–221.

107. Leon S. Reed, *Military Maneuvers* (New York: Council on Economic Priorities, 1975), plus periodic updates. Also Gordon Adams, *The Iron Triangle* (New York: Council on Economic Priorities, 1981).

108. Adams, *The Iron Triangle,* and James Fallows, *National Defense* (New York: Random House, 1981), p. 65.

109. "Critics See Key Flaws in Arms Cost Controls," *New York Times,* May 18, 1985.

110. U.S. General Accounting Office, "DOD Revolving Door: Relationships between Work at DOD and Post-DOD Employment," GAO/NSIAD–86–180BR, July 1986. See also "Pentagon-to-Contractor Job Shift Is Profiled," *New York Times,* August 31, 1986, p. 37.

111. U.S. General Accounting Office, GAO/NSIAD–86–180BR, July 1986, p. 2.

112. Ibid., pp. 12, 14.
113. Ibid., pp. 12–13.
114. Ibid., pp. 15–16.
115. Ibid., p. 17.
116. Ibid., p. 18.
117. U.S. House of Representatives, testimony of Ompal Chauhan, Contract Management Division, Air Force Systems Command, before the joint hearing of the Subcommittee on Seapower and Strategic and Critical Materials and the Subcommittee on Investigations of the Committee on Armed Services, "Revolving Door, H.R. 272, Defense Production Act Amendments of 1985," April 18, 1985, p. 157.
118. U.S. Senate Committee on Armed Services, hearing, September 13, 1984, Part 1, p. 114.
119. Richard A. Stubbing, *The Defense Game* (New York: Harper & Row, 1986), p. 178.
120. "Pentagon Official Quits during Probe of Her Conduct," *Los Angeles Times,* August 20, 1985, p. 6.
121. "Former Officials' Impact on Defense Purchasing," *Boston Globe,* January 17, 1984, p. 10.
122. Seymour Melman, *Profits without Production* (New York: Alfred A. Knopf, 1983), p. 221.
123. U.S. House of Representatives Committee on Armed Services, hearing, April 18, 1985, pp. 134–136.

6

CIVIL SERVANTS IN THE
DEFENSE ACQUISITION WORK FORCE

Although military officers usually manage major acquisition programs, the importance of civil service personnel should not be underestimated. As 89 percent of the procurement work force, they far outnumber military personnel in defense procurement organizations and are the only source of continuity in program management offices and in the various functional support offices in the military services (e.g., procurement, engineering, and the comptroller's office). It is difficult, however, to attract and retain qualified civil servants to careers in defense acquisition. Not surprisingly, civil servants are often reluctant to join an organization in which military officers occupy most of the senior positions. Further, because most supervisory jobs must be filled by military officers of a specific rank, positions remain vacant until the appropriate officer is found. The conclusions of a 1970 GAO report apply to the late 1980s as well:

> In many cases the situation inhibits the professional development of civilians because of the lack of suitable opportunities. It also requires civilians to work under the supervision of personnel who do not have adequate training or experience in procurement, which encourages "treadmill" performance, or premature separation from government service, by well-qualified civilians.[1]

Few civilians actually manage major defense programs. In 1986, none served as a program manager on a major Army program, four served on major Navy programs, and one on an Air Force program.

They are more commonly found managing smaller programs — 35 percent in the Air Force, 25 percent in the Navy, and 21 percent in the Army — but these are generally lower-grade positions. Civilians more often serve as deputy program managers on both major and smaller programs.

GAO analysts, together with current and former military service officials, identified several reasons for the difficulties encountered in establishing viable civilian career programs leading to senior program management and procurement positions.

The civil service system is considerably less flexible than the military system, making it difficult to control or influence the career path of civilians;

civilians are narrowly developed in a functional specialty because of difficulties in assigning them to positions outside their functional specialty;

it is considerably more difficult to remove a civilian from a program due to performance problems than a military officer, and it is also difficult to geographically relocate civilians;

military PMs are preferred because they bring a user perspective to the PMO and have more credibility with their counterparts in operational commands.[2]

In 1985, Navy spokesman Adm. Steven A. White described to the Senate Armed Services Committee the Navy's approach to program management positions. He pointed out that in major programs, 4 of 46 program managers were civilians, and in smaller programs, 79 of almost 400 were civilians. Admiral White went on to explain the disparity.

> We now want to use that [smaller program] as a training ground to get them into the larger programs. . . . In the past, we have not nurtured the civilians in what I would say in the military would be a career path. We have started that in the last two years, specifically, a mobility program, where we take our senior civilian grades and move them to places to gain experience, so they will someday be major program managers.[3]

Gen. Lawrence Skantze reported that only two or three of the thirty-three major Air Force programs had civilian program managers. He attributed this small number to the reluctance of civilians to move and to their lack of military knowledge and experience.

Gen. Henry A. Miley, USA (ret.), former AMC commander, described to us the reluctance of the military services to assign civilians to program management positions. He pointed out that there was a general consensus among senior officers in the Army, Navy, and Air Force that for mainline weapon systems — aircraft, ships, submarines, artillery, tanks — military program managers, with their specialized knowledge and experience, are preferred. There was also a consensus, however, that secondary and support programs — for such systems as radar, avionics, computer-based logistics support hardware, possibly even missiles — could be effectively managed by qualified civilians. He added that senior military officers believed that military program managers were more acceptable to and comfortable working with the using commands (e.g., the Strategic Air Command, U.S. Army European Command, and the Pacific Fleet Command).

To complicate the problem, it is worth noting that civil service employees working in program offices do not have the same job security as their counterparts in functional offices. Although they may remain within the procurement field, they must find new jobs when the program ends, sometimes at another location, sometimes at a lower salary. There is greater security — and more opportunity for professional development and advancement — in functional staff positions.

Many civil servants working in program offices have been government employees for most of their careers, often in low-grade purchasing activities. Contractors describe many of them as "tired men" who have worked their way up through the civil service grades. When a senior civil service position becomes vacant, those next in grade in the same specialty compete to fill it and thus advance in grade. A military program manager commented: "It does not take these individuals long to tell you about their rights and privileges and the difficulty you would have in removing them from the system."

The 1970 GAO report discussed the demoralizing effect of the present program management system on civil service personnel, a discussion that still applies.

> There is also the matter of satisfying what is sometimes referred to as a person's ego needs, contrasted with his financial needs. It is generally established that today, once a person's most fundamental financial needs have been met, he develops other needs which must be satisfied. In the procurement field it is difficult for civilians to satisfy such needs, because many of the higher status positions are filled by military officers. A combination of

factors (e.g., limited training compared with that provided for the military profession, limited promotion, and limited responsibility) is demoralizing to civilians and makes it difficult to encourage their professional development in the procurement field.[4]

A highly regarded civil service procurement specialist, who had resisted the pattern of low productivity exhibited by many of his colleagues, commented: "People who stay in one of these jobs for a long time may start out performing at an adequate or even an above-adequate level. But after a while, 'the blues' set in, and they become rigid in their ways and resistant to new ideas."

The problem of attracting and retaining qualified civilian procurement personnel has been well known throughout the Defense Department since before 1970. Air Force Assistant Secretary Philip Whittaker, addressing the National Contract Management Association in 1970, discussed the problem:

> We are faced with a very serious problem of attracting capable young college graduates with the promise of rewarding careers in the contracting field, training them, improving their professional standing, and then retaining them in the face of manpower reductions. As a matter of fact, one of the major concerns of many of us who work for the military departments is that these very demanding and crucially important procurement jobs are being filled with an ever-aging and thinning core of experienced personnel.[5]

From all reports, the situation is worse in 1987 than it was in 1970.

The federal classification and compensation system of the civil service has remained largely unchanged since the passage of the Classification Act of 1923, although during intervening years the size of the federal work force and the nature of many of its tasks have changed dramatically. Throughout the mid-1980s, there has been widespread agreement that the civil service system frequently inhibits effective recruitment, retention, and management of federal civilian employees. This is especially true for those in occupations for which there is strong private-sector demand, such as scientists, computer specialists, engineers, and contract specialists.[6]

In 1983, the National Academy of Public Administration conducted a study on the effectiveness of the procurement work force. The study concluded that the civil service work force was "overloaded, untrained, and inexperienced" and recommended that the government make the work force more professional through improved personnel management.[7] Although there are many highly able civil servants, there are many others of marginal ability for whom the federal government is the employer of last resort. It is very difficult to retain the former and even more difficult to remove the latter. Any manager in the acquisition process, and any recommendations for improvement, must take into account both groups of civil servants.

Civil Service Acquisition Specialists

Because of the size and complexity of major weapon development and production programs, program managers and contracting officers cannot by themselves plan and control their programs and award and administer contracts.[8] Typically, then, they are supported by teams of specialists who perform such functions as planning, budgeting, contract negotiation, contract administration, small purchases, price analysis, production surveillance, configuration management, quality assurance, and financial analysis.[9]

Nearly 25,000 members of the Defense Department acquisition work force specialize in the awarding and administration of contracts. Approximately 12 percent, or 3,000, of these contract specialists are military officers. Eighty-eight percent are civilians, who deal with an extensive, complex body of regulations encompassing materials and operations management, contract law, cost analysis, negotiation techniques, and industrial management. It is surprising, therefore, that only half of the DOD civilian contract specialists have college degrees, many of which are not business related.* Of the 22,000 civil servants, 84 percent are in the lower civil service grades (GS-5 to GS-12).[10]

At present, more than 75 percent of procurement civil servants above the grade GS-12 are assigned to headquarters of buying organizations or staff positions within DOD. More than half of the remaining 25 percent are assigned to routine activities involving small and medium-sized purchases. More complex procurement tasks, such as measuring progress in development programs and negotiating complex contract changes, require the kinds of skills that few civil service personnel have.

A 1987 American Bar Association (ABA) report pointed out that

---

*Of the civil service contract specialists with a college degree (50 percent), less than one-third have a degree in a field relevant to acquisition (i.e., business, data processing, engineering, law, mathematics, physical science, or public administration).

civil servants who perform these specialties may work directly under the supervision of the program manager or contracting officer, or, as is nearly universal in large acquisition organizations, they may report through separate functional lines of authority, providing direct support to the program manager or contracting officer. In addition to this direct support, the contracting officer works with auditors, lawyers, engineers, program managers, aquisition planners, and competition advocates. These people usually do not work directly under the supervision of the contracting officer, but the contracting officer must effectively direct them.[11]

A principal specialist supporting the contracting officer is the contract specialist (contract administrator or contract negotiator). Employees in this category are typically GS-1102-series civil servants.[12] Usually, three to ten contract specialists work directly for a contracting officer. They do most of the routine work, including processing correspondence, initiating and responding to inquiries, drafting contractual documents, and most other day-to-day duties nominally assigned to the contracting officer.[13]

A second significant member of the contracting officer's support team is the price analyst (also GS-1102 series). People in this category perform the important tasks of examining cost and pricing data, historical prices, audit reports, technical evaluations, and projections to determine whether contractor-proposed costs and prices are reasonable.[14] Usually, a price analyst does not work directly for a particular contracting officer. Instead, a team of price analysts supports a number of contracting officers, responding to individual requests and coordinating information from other technical and audit agencies.[15]

A third member of the support team is the industrial specialist (GS-1150 series). The primary functions of those in this category are to analyze and monitor the capability and output of manufacturing facilities. The ABA report stated that, generally, industrial specialists do not work directly for individual contracting officers; they are usually part of the contracting activity, responding to specific requests for assistance and providing routine reports of their monitoring activities. Through their analyses, industrial specialists enable contracting officers to make decisions on matters such as contractor responsibility and delivery schedules. In their monitoring role, they provide the contracting officer with feedback from the manufacturing plant, regularly contacting a contractor's employees to monitor production progress and discuss problems.[16]

A fourth important supporter is the quality assurance representative (QAR), more commonly known as inspector. On some government contracts, the inspector is appointed from or by the requiring organization. For example, he or she might be the contracting officer's representative (COR) or the representative of the agency or command for which the purchase is being made, that is, the user of the goods or services. On larger contracts, however, the contracting officer has the support of a team of inspectors. The ABA report noted that these people are more than mere inspectors.[17] Those assigned to the procuring contracting officer's (PCO) organization obtain technical specifications from the requiring organization, recommend to the PCO what quality assurance provisions should be incorporated into the contract, and coordinate with the administrative contracting officer (ACO) on matters of quality surveillance.[18] The quality assurance personnel at the ACO's organization also monitor the contractor to ensure that it is maintaining required quality control and that the product delivered meets the contract requirements.[19]

Classification and Training of Civil Service Acquisition Jobs

Selection of DOD contracting officers has never been based on specific experience or educational and training criteria: Federal Acquisition Regulation (FAR) 1.603-2 provides no more than general guidelines. It does not specify *what* training courses should be completed, *what* specialized knowledge is needed for various kinds of procurement, *what* particular educational backgrounds should be required, and so forth. Indeed, the regulation is so broad that it effectively encourages people with little training or experience to become contracting officers.[20]

In addition, little emphasis is placed on providing contracting officers with specialized (program office or product) experience.[21] In a 1986 study of 141 DOD contracting officers, the General Accounting Office found that only 2 had previous experience in a program office and only 28 had as much as six months of experience as contract administrators or price analysts.[22]

The military services differ on the criteria for appointing contracting officers. The Air Force requires an interview by a contracting review board. Air Force Systems Command product divisions and centers often include a question-and-answer session on contracting matters as part of the interview process. How such sessions are conducted and the thoroughness of the reviews, however, vary from one command to another. The Army and the Navy do not have any formal, uniform contracting officer selection criteria or procedures.

By the mid-1980s, many senior defense officials began acknowledging the need for better training of civilian as well as military acquisition managers. Yet there are significant barriers to implementing the changes required to achieve better civilian training. For example, the federal Office of Personnel Management (OPM) classifies job series as professional, administrative, technical, clerical, or other.[23] To qualify for the professional series, an occupation must require the completion of certain college-level work specific to it. Thus, OPM defines a professional position as one in which successful performance requires a base of knowledge that is acquired, not through on-the-job training, but only through a course of study in a specified discipline.

Because of this requirement, OPM does not classify as professional many functions ordinarily considered professional in the generic sense. For example, it classifies contract specialists (including contracting officers), budget examiners, program analysts, and management analysts as administrators.[24] *Contract specialist* covers a broad spectrum — from contracting personnel who purchase spare parts, commercial items, and services, to those involved in major weapon systems acquisition.

In 1986, both the General Accounting Office and the Packard Commission strongly recommended that the entire GS-1102 series be reclassified as professional. They argued that the procurement profession was a complex one involving a major portion of the federal budget and that it required knowledge and skills in various areas, including cost and price analysis, contract law and procurement legislation, mathematics, forecasting, and the economic climate.

Not easily persuaded, OPM argued that specific educational requirements are not necessary to enter or be promoted within the procurement field. Therefore, the 1102 series remains administrative. (It should be noted that OPM did not focus exclusively on major system contracting personnel, who are a relatively small part of the series.)

In response, the General Accounting Office suggested, as an alternative, that because major weapon systems are complex and contracting for them requires a high level of skill, a separate civil service job classification system for contracting officers be considered. The GAO believed that professional status would signal to outsiders the high level of skill needed to become a contracting officer and this, in turn, would increase the desirability of this career.[25]

Navy and Air Force senior management subsequently endorsed this view. According to Air Force managers, this minimum educational level is necessary because contracting officers are required to ensure compliance with laws and regulations and to understand the effect of competition, the marketplace, analytical models, computer technology, and business strategies. The GAO panel also pointed out that new cost-accounting standards and legislative and regulatory requirements have increased the complexity of contracting tasks, reinforcing the need for a strong background in accounting and business.[26]

The Packard Commission leveled broad criticism at both the civil service and the OPM classification system. The commission cited the rigid pay grades and seniority-based promotion standards as disincentives to continued employment (i.e., for those civil servants with above-average ability). Higher pay and better opportunities in private industry lure the best college graduates and the brightest trainees away from government, particularly in such highly competitive fields as science, engineering, and contracting.[27]

In testimony before the Senate Armed Services Committee in November 1985, Assistant Secretary of Defense James Wade commented on the problems in the current civil service system.

> My initial areas of concern include the civil service restriction not allowing DOD to require college degrees for acquisition personnel except for engineers and lawyers; roadblocks to training and testing requirements as prerequisites for advancement to higher levels of responsibility; greater flexibility to transfer and remove people performing inadequately on their jobs; establishing higher salary levels for a professional Defense Acquisition Corps; and recruiting employees based on qualifications of the individual rather than qualifications of the vacant position.[28]

Former defense acquisition official Dr. Jacques Gansler expressed similar views and highlighted the need for an alternative to the current civil service system.

> An extremely important means to improve the acquisition work force within the government would be to establish an alternative personnel management system that would provide greater flexibility with respect to status, pay and qualifications of civilian employees. The so-called "China Lake experiment" [described below], in which recruitment and retention of key civilians was correlated with pay incentive, and advancement based on performance, is an example of one such program. In addition, greatly

increased educational and training opportunities must be offered to the government's acquisition community. In the Department of Defense the Defense Systems Management College has been filling a narrow portion of this need in recent years; but its quality (in terms of greater professionalism) and its scope need to be significantly enhanced, and complemented by comparable programs.[29]

In 1986, Deputy Defense Secretary William Taft directed the services and the Defense Management, Education, and Training Board to establish experience prerequisites and training requirements for civilian procurement personnel. In 1987, however, many in the Defense Department remained unconvinced about how effective these would be when put into practice.[30]

Plans to make significant improvements in the careers of civilians assigned to the acquisition process are not new. In the mid-1960s, the Defense Department initiated a program intended to upgrade the skills of those already in procurement management: the Civilian Career Program for Procurement Personnel. In 1970, the General Accounting Office reported that a majority of military and civilian procurement personnel had not attended procurement courses the Department of Defense had designated as mandatory for their grade levels. The program failed to produce skilled procurement managers because of a lack of senior-level insistence on enrollment.[31]

Choosing qualified people to attend training courses is frequently difficult. One procurement supervisor explained: "We face the problem of having so few qualified people that we send our deadbeats to school, where they often do not work and are not assigned grades. As such, there is no measure of performance included in their records."

Only 20 to 52 percent of the civilian contract and procurement specialists in the Army and Navy have a college education (see table 6.1). The Air Force percentage is somewhat higher, ranging from 46 to 78 percent. The percentage of the civil service industrial specialists with a college education is even lower, ranging from 9 to 44 percent in the Army and Navy and from 27 to 66 percent in the Air Force. Approximately half the college degrees are in business.[32]

In general, the education level for procurement civilians is so low that one is tempted to suspect errors in compiling the data. Other statistics, however, indicate that civilians in other government logistics positions have even less education. In fact, the average education level for civilians in defense contracting (GS-1102) *exceeds* (by a wide mar-

TABLE 6.1.   Education Level of DOD Acquisition Civilians (Percent College Graduate by Service and Grade)

Contracts and Procurement (GS-1102)	GS9–12 Middle Level	GS13 + Upper Level
Army	38%	52%
Navy	20%	50%
Air Force	46%	78%

Industry Specialist (GS-1150)	GS9–12 Middle Level	GS13 + Upper Level
Army	17%	44%
Navy	9%	18%
Air Force	27%	66%

SOURCE: Office of Federal Procurement Policy, Report on the Acquisition Work Force through Fiscal Year 1982, October 1983.

gin) that of the defense logistics work force as a whole, including general business and industry (GS-1101), property disposal (GS-1104), and industry specialist (GS-1150).

In addition to those currently in place with a low education level, only 50 percent of those newly hired in the contracts and procurement specialties (GS-1102) are college graduates. Among industrial specialists (GS-1150), only 35 percent are college graduates.[33]

It is clear that defense contract specialists are less qualified, on average, than their industry counterparts. The relatively low level of experience among those in DOD (approximately 40 percent report five years or less) highlights the need for high-quality training in contracting.[34]

The DOD Civilian Career Program for Acquisition Personnel (DOD Manual 1430.10-M-1) and the procurement intern programs call for general contracting experience and training (e.g., contract negotiations and price and cost analysis for contracting officers). In a 1984 review of the training records of 1,551 intermediate- and senior-level contracting personnel, however, the DOD Inspector General found that 67 percent of these people had not received the mandatory training prescribed by the manual.[35] As in the case of military program managers, training requirements are, in effect, frequently waived. Contradictory training policies, a shortage of training resources, and the high rate of turnover of experienced personnel are cited as causes of the problem.[36]

Assignment problems inherent in the low educational level of civil service personnel are compounded by rigid civil service rules of tenure. According to the General Counsel of the Civil Service Commission, it is relatively easy to remove an incompetent worker from a job, requiring that one merely document the charge of incompetence. In the opinion of military and civilian supervisors who have attempted such action, however, removal of a civil servant for cause is so lengthy and difficult a task that it is best avoided in all but extreme cases. One general officer worked with a civil servant who was so unproductive that the officer was determined to have him fired. After one year of documenting numerous instances of incompetence, the general officer was successful. In looking back, however, he felt that he had made a mistake. Instead of spending so much time on the case, he felt it would have been better to assign the man to a position in which he could do the least harm. Other military and civilian supervisors indicated that many have come to the same conclusion.

The difference between the point of view of the Civil Service Commission and that of field supervisors hinges on the interpretation of the term *incompetent*. It may be relatively easy to remove an individual who is flagrantly incompetent. When employees merely coast — that is, do the least possible work within the job definition — their incompetence is more difficult to document. Supervisors in field offices and in the Pentagon usually find it easier to render such people harmless by working around them.

In 1986, the Packard Commission survey of civil service personnel discovered that a significant group (55 percent) of contract specialists would leave their current jobs if offered comparable ones in other federal agencies or in private industry. The survey also found that contract specialists who had taken college-level business courses were more interested in seeking new employment than those without such education. This difference was only slight if the new employment was with another federal agency (42 percent with college courses, 36 percent without). The difference increased significantly when the lure was private enterprise (44 percent with college courses, 20 percent without).

More than half (52 percent) of the government contract specialists considered industry program business managers more qualified than their government counterparts.[37] Many in industry hold the same view. In early 1987, an industry vice-president commented on the deteriorating condition of the civil service acquisition work force.

In the past three years, the quality of the civil service has fallen sharply due to early retirement, scared personnel, and few young people being developed.

A recently retired lieutenant general, former commander of a buying command, observed:

Good people are leaving in droves. There is much less psychic income today, and this is the problem throughout the acquisition process. Industry hires these people away. Also, at the secretariat level, there are very few experienced people.

To attract, develop, and retain a truly professional work force, all three services either have been updating or are in the process of establishing career programs for civilian contracting personnel. These programs encompass all contracting specialties and other civilian fields related to acquisition (e.g., GS-1102 and GS-1150 grade series).[38]

The new Acquisition Civilian Career Enhancement Program of the Air Force employs career advisory boards composed of major command management and functional and personnel specialists. Program elements include general training and development, career-broadening courses, career-planning assistance, recruitment, and training in the use of management information systems.

The Army also has instituted a new program, called the Logistics and Acquisition Management Program, to supplement its contracting career management program. Its goal is to develop career civilians by planning their development from intern to senior executive level, providing a managerial training curriculum, providing a multidisciplinary understanding, and providing a blend of assignments and schooling. One of the fears associated with this program, however, is that it will be so broad in scope that it will fail to provide the necessary specialization for managers in the acquisition process.

The Navy's program provides rotational assignments through an internship program. In addition, through their education programs, the Navy (as do the other services) pays the tuition for job-related courses and awards fellowships for graduate study in contracting.[39]

The extent to which these programs are successful will depend on the availability of personnel (with some spared for training) and the commitment of senior DOD managers to create a genuinely professional acquisition work force.

The Civil Service Personnel Evaluation System

Each civil service employee is evaluated annually by a supervisor. The rating systems are so general and restricted, however, that evaluations reveal little about a person's job performance.

Theoretically, each civil service rating must, by governmentwide regulation, be placed in one of five categories: "superior," "excellent," "fully acceptable," "minimally acceptable," and "unacceptable." In practice, supervisors admit that the vast majority of individuals receive "superior" and "excellent" reports: far more than deserve them. This exaggeration is usually justified as a means of promoting morale or inspiring a person to perform better in the following year. Such a practice effectively undermines the power of the pay system to reward outstanding performance and to penalize substandard performance. "Unacceptable" has been determined in semijudicial hearings to be such a low standard that very rarely can a government employee fail to make a case that he or she exceeds the standard. Hence, supervisors do not usually find it sensible to avoid awarding a pay increase or, worse yet, to engage in the lengthy semijudicial procedure required — often without success — to remove a civil service employee. One high-level supervisor at one of the buying divisions told us that he had never seen an "unacceptable" rating for any of the three hundred civil servants he reviewed. In the most recent evaluations, he observed only one of the three hundred was rated "minimally acceptable." Consequently, although highly qualified civil servants receive less pay than their industry counterparts, many civil servants receive pay equal to or higher than what they could earn in industry."[40]

The China Lake Demonstration Project

In 1980, under the provisions of the Civil Service Reform Act of 1978, OPM authorized the Navy to conduct a five-year demonstration of an alternative personnel system. This project, designed to allow management to reward individual performance and to compete in the open labor market for highly qualified personnel, was conducted at the Naval Weapons Center at China Lake, California, and at the Naval Ocean Systems Center in San Diego. In 1984, it was extended for a second five-year period.

The China Lake project included full-time personnel in science and engineering, and senior professional, administrative, and technical specialists at both naval facilities. At the San Diego facility, it also included clerical personnel, to ensure a comprehensive basis for evaluating its performance and potential.

Within each functional group, five new general personnel classification pay bands replaced the eighteen-grade civil service schedule. Initially each employee was assigned to a classification pay band on the basis of attained professional expertise. Thereafter, each employee was ranked competitively within the pay band on the basis of performance. Unlike the standard civil service system, length of service and veterans' preference were secondary considerations. The higher an employee's performance rating, the better his or her chance of advancement — and of retention in the event of personnel cutbacks (see table 6.2).

Each pay band was matched with a broad range of compensation, applicable at different levels of expertise, which allowed line managers significant flexibility in making initial salary offers more competitive with local market conditions. Compensation was linked to performance rather than length of time in the grade level. Thus, it was possible to reward deserving employees with higher pay without promotion to a higher pay band. Moreover, both naval facilities established funds to draw upon for cash awards as an additional means of recognizing superior performance. End-of-year performance bonuses also provided tangible incentives, making it possible to reward especially deserving employees without permanently increasing their pay.

According to the Packard Commission, the China Lake demonstration project had the following results for its initial five-year period:

Improved ability to attract highly qualified personnel to entry-level positions;

Dramatically reduced separation rates for scientists and engineers — from 8.1 percent in 1979 to 4.2 percent in 1983;

Improved employee morale through greater potential for advancement and professional growth; and

Reduced personnel management costs and streamlined administration, including the reduction of paper work by 50 to 80 percent.[41]

The China Lake project pointed the way to substantial improvement over the current civil service system for the scientists, engineers, technical specialists, managers, and senior professionals involved. What remained unclear was whether Congress and OPM would adopt such a

TABLE 6.2.   Classification/Pay Band Example* (Classification Group: Scientists, Engineers and Senior Staff)

Current System	Navy Personnel System Demonstration Project	Pay Range (in thousands)
GS-5 6 7 8	I Entry Level	$14.4 to 25.7
9 10 11	II Advanced Training	21.8 to 34.3
12 13	III Journeyman	31.6 to 48.9
14 15	IV Senior Specialists, Supervisors & Managers	44.4 to 67.9
16 17 18	V Professional Exceptional	61.3 to 72.3 (pay ceiling set by Congress)

*Other classification groups, such as technician, technical specialist, administrative specialist, and clerical, have similarly designed pay bands.

SOURCE: President's Blue Ribbon Commission on Defense Management, *A Quest for Excellence,* Final Report to the President, June 1986, Appendix, p. 158, figure J-1.

system. In 1987, the administration reintroduced legislation on this topic — after Congress failed to pass it the year before. Even assuming successful congressional action, each military service has a different idea about how to implement the plan. Many observers concluded that seven years for an experiment was long enough, especially considering its success.

A Civilian Acquisition Corps

To remedy the problem in the current DOD approach to the acquisition work force, a growing number of people both inside and outside the department have come to believe that a civilian acquisition corps may be desirable. In 1985, Assistant Secretary of Defense James Wade indicated the direction of the desired change.

> We lack a cadre of seasoned, well-rounded, technically oriented acquisition professionals. These people are the key to improving the DOD systems acquisition process. While no amount of reorganization will, by itself, solve these problems, a system which results in clearly defined lines of authority, responsibility, and accountability — and manned by experienced, high-tech-oriented professionals dedicated to making the system work — has a far better chance of success.
>
> A true service corps with dedicated professionals is a necessity. Management of the corps, in the main, must be by civilians rather than military personnel who rotate out after a number of years. Experience and ability must be key determinants for advancement, as well as more discipline in carrying out the objectives of the Office of the Secretary of Defense. Military personnel would be included in the corps in jobs they qualify for by education and experience.[42]

Dr. Wade described a model of a new acquisition corps. The Defense Department would

> establish a special "professional service" or elite "Acquisition Corps" along the lines of the Foreign Service, based on education, experience, and examination. This Corps must be highly professional with required degrees in science, engineering, business, financial management, or other related disciplines. This heightens DOD's ability to lead the way in high-technology research, development testing, and manufacturing. The Acquisition Corps would have as an aim the goal of a total professional career.
>
> The "Corps" would include *all acquisition-related personnel.* . . .
>
> Corps members would work for their respective service or agency, but would be easily transferred to another service or agency, depending on need. Transfer would be determined at the Secretary of Defense level.
>
> The "Acquisition Corps" would be civilian managed and have a professional orientation. Military officers would occupy key positions for which they qualify.
>
> In order to attract such a professional work force, a special salary scale should be established by legislation for this "Acquisition Corps," somewhat like the alternative personnel management system being proposed for scientists and engineers. In exchange for higher compensation, personnel in the "Acquisition Corps" would be subject to certain employment risks, such as demotion, salary cuts, removal, and rotation.
>
> [DOD would] establish a bonus system for the Acquisition Corps based on achievement, i.e., attaining and maintaining professional certifica-

tion, holding contracting officer warrants, retaining selected critical skills in the government.

[DOD would] establish a new, and modify the existing, award system to ensure adequate and timely recognition of significant contributions to the acquisition and logistics process.

[DOD would] establish an umbrella defense acquisition university encompassing all the existing acquisition-related Defense schools. The University should include separate colleges of specialization such as contracting and acquisition, logistics, quality, program management, systems engineering, production and manufacturing, all offering accredited degrees. All students should participate in a core acquisition and contracting curriculum to ensure a common understanding of mission roles and responsibilities.[43]

In late 1986, the General Accounting Office conducted a survey of current and former government officials to obtain their views on a civilian acquisition corps, identifying the potential advantages and disadvantages.

Potential Advantages

Create a better trained corps of acquisition professionals. Reduce the acquisition work force and administrative layering.

Reduce unnecessary turnover in rotational assignments of key personnel, thereby providing continuity to a weapons program.

Reduce the logistics and supportability requirements by promoting the development of more common weapons systems and components.

Increase the early coordination and collaboration among the services in the requirements formulation phase of a weapon program.

Establish more uniform implementation of procurement policy among the services, as well as with multidivisional defense contractors.

Improve relations with the Congress by providing a single organization that could foster more uniformity and accountability.

Potential Disadvantages

Reduce the military's influence in providing their perspective on combat tactics and operations.

Create difficulties in finding sufficient numbers of technically knowledgeable personnel at the government pay rates.

Make it more difficult to dismiss or reassign marginally qualified civilians in leadership positions [i.e., by substituting civil servants for military officers].

Complicate and delay decision making rather than streamline the process by adding another layer of review.

Leave unresolved the (1) problem of what weapon systems to buy, which can be a more difficult question than how to buy; and (2) problems associated with program funding instabilities.

Increase the number of government personnel because the services may have to retain a variety of staff to monitor the agency.

Create a management challenge because of the large size of the agency.[44]

Six months before the proposal by Dr. Wade, the concept of a civilian acquisition corps was promoted by Sen. William Roth (R-DE), Chairman of the Senate Committee on Governmental Affairs. Writing in the *Washington Post,* he proposed a centralized Defense Procurement Agency.

The agency would be staffed by a highly trained, well-paid cadre of civilian procurement and systems management professionals similar to the diplomats in the U.S. Foreign Service and the medical specialists in the Public Health Service.[45]

The employees in Senator Roth's civilian acquisition corps would be evaluated, and bonuses and promotions based, on their "ability to procure major weapons at the lowest possible cost." In addition, the senator proposed that "these procurement professionals would be unable to accept employment from a major defense contractor for five years. . . . This would put our military back in the business of planning war strategy and defining equipment needs, and civilians in the business of business, translating the hardware needs of the military into high-quality, low-cost products."[46]

Because of strong opposition from the services, the proposal for a civilian acquisition corps has never had a full hearing. Many senior military officers believe that a central defense procurement agency would interfere with the freedom of the Army, Navy, and Air Force to develop separate weapons and equipment programs. Although that fear has some foundation, it is highly unlikely that an acquisition agency would be assigned responsibility for decisions regarding which weapons to develop and produce.

Former Assistant Secretary of Defense Leonard Sullivan also supported the concept of a civilian acquisition corps.

The notion that this is "just another job" for the military generalist is offensive — and repeatedly disproved.

There are, of course, some very good officers whose carefully screened leadership qualities produce some fine program managers. The trouble is, of course, that they come to the job late in their careers, and generally leave early to go on to better assignments in the military hierarchy. And so they should. They cannot avoid being less than fully experienced, or more than transients in their acquisition jobs — unless acquisition becomes a career-long specialty. . . . A professional corps of acquisition personnel must be developed whose work is respected and who can aspire eventually to top-level jobs.[47]

A senior vice-president of a major defense contractor commented that the "all-civilian corps has some appeal, where you could train people from the ground up and gradually give them more and more authority and responsibility."

Congressional staff member Donna Martin, testifying before the House Armed Services Committee, stated:

> We think it would be fair to allow and encourage a civilian procurement corps to continue their careers until retirement while the military tackles the tasks for which it was designed. Again, the military should define the mission and the need for a weapon; the civilian procurement corps, trained in business practices and management, would translate those military needs into principles for negotiation with the contractor to produce the desired equipment. A civilian procurement specialist who is recognized and rewarded for exercising sound business judgment, getting the best product at the lowest price and who could remain in his position until normal retirement age, would have less incentive for getting cozy with the contractor than the military officer who is not trained to deal with the sophisticated tactics of the corporation representative. That military official is now subject to the pressure of having to find employment when he is forced out of the military at the peak of his productive years. At that point, his major concern is to keep that weapon program going and its budget funded with a minimum of fuss.[48]

Many of Ms. Martin's points are persuasive. Nonetheless, although the civil service contains a number of highly motivated people, it also has many employees who perform on a marginal level. In my view, Ms. Martin's proposal may give too little consideration to the difficulties of motivating the average civil servant to apply the time and effort comparable to that applied by military officers. Unless the civilian acquisition corps employs a radically improved civil service without tenure rights, any benefits from establishing such a corps are likely to be far outweighed by the problems of removing marginally effective performers.

As senior civilians and military officers in the Defense Department are quick to note, once you experience the pain of trying to remove a marginally capable civil servant, you never try again.

After considering the strengths and weaknesses of the proposed civilian acquisition corps, I concluded that the disadvantages outweigh the advantages. Regardless of the disadvantages in the current military and civilian controlled acquisition process, military participation brings a sense of esprit and dedication to long hours and hard work that is essential to retain.

Before adopting a civilian corps, the Army, Navy, and Air Force should make one more attempt to create comprehensive career programs for acquisition professionals in which both military officers and civilians have proper training, career progression dedicated to acquisition management, genuine authority, and attractive pay and promotion opportunities, thereby freeing military officers from the need to seek combat arms assignments or postretirement positions at a relatively early age.

If the Army, Navy, and Air Force fail to implement these career programs in the near term, Congress should impose them. Failing this, the Defense Department should establish a separate acquisition service staffed by military and civilian personnel, along the lines of the French Armament Directorate. Career assignments and promotion opportunities should be independent of the Army, Navy, or Air Force.

In the event that the Defense Department is unable in the near term to implement one of these alternatives, Congress should then, and only then, create a civilian acquisition corps with a personnel system without tenure, offering pay and benefits comparable to industry.

Notes

1. Comptroller General of the United States, "Action Required to Improve DOD Career Program for Procurement Personnel," Report to the Congress, August 13, 1970, p. 46.
2. U.S. General Accounting Office, "DOD Acquisition: Strengthening Capabilities of Key Personnel in Systems Acquisition," GAO/NSIAD–86–45, p. 103.
3. U.S. Senate, hearing before the Subcommittee on Defense Acquisition Policy of the Committee on Armed Services, "Improving the Professionalism of the Defense Acquisition Work Force," March 11, 1985, pp. 40–42.
4. Comptroller General of the United States, "Action Required to Improve DOD Career Program for Procurement Personnel," August 13, 1970, p. 46.

5. Air Force Assistant Secretary Philip Whittaker, Address to the National Contract Management Association, Washington, D.C., October 30, 1970.
6. President's Blue Ribbon Commission on Defense Management, *A Quest for Excellence,* Final Report to the President, June 1986, pp. 157–158.
7. Report by a Panel of the National Academy of Public Administration, "Revitalizing Federal Management: Managers and Their Overburdened Systems," November 1983, p. 34.
8. The following paragraphs draw heavily from American Bar Association (ABA) Report prepared by Richard J. Bednar and John T. Jones, Jr., "The Role of the DOD Contracting Officer," American Bar Association (ABA) Section of Public Contract Law, Ad Hoc Committee, John E. Cavanagh, Chairman, January 11, 1987.
9. Ibid., p. 2.
10. "Data on the Acquisition Work Force, Fiscal Year 1986," Federal Acquisition Personnel Information System, General Services Administration, May 1987.
11. Bednar and Jones, "The Role of the DOD Contracting Officer," p. 43.
12. GS-1102, *Contracting Series,* TS-71 (December 1983), cited in Bednar and Jones, p. 50.
13. Bednar and Jones, p. 50.
14. Ibid., p. 51.
15. Ibid.
16. Federal Acquisition Regulation 42.11 and Defense Federal Acquisition Regulation 42.11, cited in Bednar and Jones, p. 52.
17. Federal Acquisition Regulation part 46 and Defense Federal Acquisition Regulation part 46, cited in Bednar and Jones, p. 52.
18. Federal Acquisition Regulation 46.103, cited in Bednar and Jones, p. 52.
19. Bednar and Jones, p. 52.
20. U.S. General Accounting Office, GAO/NSIAD–86–45, May 1986, p. 110.
21. Ibid., pp. 116–117.
22. Ibid., p. 116.
23. 5 U.S.C. 3308 (1982).
24. U.S. General Accounting Office, GAO/NSIAD–86–45, May 1986, p. 121.
25. Ibid., pp. 120–121.
26. Ibid., p. 116.
27. President's Blue Ribbon Commission on Defense Management, *A Quest for Excellence,* p. 67.
28. U.S. Senate, hearing before the Subcommittee on Defense Acquisition Policy of the Committee on Armed Services, "Implementation of the 1984 Defense Procurement Legislation," October 17 and 29, and November 7 and 13, 1985, p. 31. Dr. James P. Wade, Jr., Assistant Secretary of Defense (Acquisition and Logistics), accompanied by Mrs. Eleanor Spector, Deputy Assistant Secretary of Defense for Procurement.
29. Jacques S. Gansler, "Strengthening Government Acquisition Management through Selected Use of Experienced Industrial Managers," paper prepared for the Procurement Round Table, Washington, D.C., June 11, 1987.
30. U.S. General Accounting Office, GAO/NSIAD–86–45, May 1986, p. 119.

31. Comptroller General of the United States, "Action Required to Improve DOD Career Program for Procurement Personnel," August 13, 1970, p. 14.
32. President's Blue Ribbon Commission on Defense Management, *A Quest for Excellence,* p. 171.
33. Mike Miller, Federal Acquisition Institute, "The Acquisition Work Force, Fiscal Year 1983," August 1984; and "Data on the Acquisition Work Force, Fiscal Year 1986" (see note 11).
34. President's Blue Ribbon Commission on Defense Management, *A Quest for Excellence,* p. 167.
35. Office of the Inspector General, Department of Defense, IG Audit Report 84-047, February 14, 1984.
36. U.S. General Accounting Office, GAO/NSIAD–86–45, May 1986, p. 114.
37. President's Blue Ribbon Commission on Defense Management, *A Quest for Excellence,* pp. 174, 178.
38. U.S. General Accounting Office, GAO/NSIAD–86–45, May 1986, p. 110.
39. Ibid., pp. 111–112.
40. "Most Federal Workers Need Only Be Competent," *The Wall Street Journal,* May 21, 1986.
41. President's Blue Ribbon Commission on Defense Management, *A Quest for Excellence,* pp. 68, 157–158.
42. James P. Wade, Jr., Assistant Secretary of Defense (Acquisitions and Logistics), "DOD Acquisition Improvements — The Challenges Ahead," November 5, 1985, pp. 7–10.
43. Ibid.
44. U.S. General Accounting Office, "A Perspective on the Potential Impact of a Centralized Civilian Acquisition Agency (CCAA)," B-224853, November 1986, p. 11.
45. *Washington Post,* May 20, 1984.
46. Ibid.
47. Leonard Sullivan, Jr., "Characterizing the Acquisition Process," paper prepared for the Defense Acquisition Study, Center for Strategic and International Studies, Georgetown University, January 1986, pp. H-9, H-10.
48. U.S. House of Representatives, testimony of Donna Martin, Committee on Armed Services, April 18, 1985, pp. 63–64.

—7

GOVERNMENT REPRESENTATIVES
AT CONTRACTOR PLANTS

The size and complexity of Defense Department contracts necessitates a full-time government presence at major contractor facilities. Until the early 1960s, each military service maintained its own group of contract administration specialists to represent program office interests on the shop floor. The Office of the Secretary of Defense (OSD) created, in 1963, the Defense Contract Administration Service (DCAS) to consolidate these plant representative offices. At the time, OSD considered a single contract management organization desirable to eliminate duplication of effort, thereby lowering overall contract administration costs, and to increase the uniformity and quality of contract administration services. Staffed by approximately 18,400 civilian and 320 military personnel (in 1987), the agency administers contracts through nine regional offices across the country. Each office is headed by an Army or Air Force colonel, Navy captain, or a flag officer (the position usually rotates among the three services), who reports directly to the director of the Defense Logistics Agency (DLA), headquartered in Cameron Station, Alexandria, Virginia. In fiscal year 1986, DCAS worked with more than 28,000 contractors throughout the United States in the course of administering more than 407,000 prime contracts worth $262 billion.

DCAS Regional Organization

The DCAS provides services through one of two types of field offices in the nine regions. The first is called a Defense Contract Administration

Service Plant Representative Office (DCASPRO). Located in contractor plants where either the volume or the complexity of work requires continuous oversight, DCASPROs provide full-time, extensive administrative services. In 1986, forty-eight DCASPROs were in operation, unevenly distributed among the nine regions because of the random location of major defense plants. The second type of field office, designated a Defense Contract Administration Service Management Area (DCASMA), provides administrative services on a less frequent basis to smaller plants performing contracted work of insufficient volume or complexity to warrant constant DCAS attention. In 1986, thirty-nine DCASMAs operated in the nine regions.

Although Defense Department policy stipulates that DCAS administer contracts at all defense contractor plants, the Army, Navy, or Air Force can request from OSD cognizance (assignment) of a specific contractor plant. If the request is granted, that service normally assumes responsibility for administering the contracts of the other services at that plant as well. In general, to obtain cognizance, a service must receive a majority of the output of the plant or place a high priority on its contracted work or both. Cognizance can be temporary. For instance, after a program matures, a service might decide that DCAS can and should be in charge.

In addition to the DCASPROs mentioned above, in 1986 there were forty-three plant representative offices under cognizance of the services: twenty-five Air Force (AFPROs), fifteen Navy (NAVPROs), and three Army (ARPROs). This large number underscores the limited success of previous efforts to consolidate DOD contract administration services. In fact, the consensus among government managers we interviewed was that a full consolidation would never occur, for two reasons. First, the initiators and supporters of the effort have long since retired from public service. Second, the services are extremely reluctant, for reasons discussed below, to withdraw from this traditional field of influence.

In practice, military service rivalries and internal DOD politics often determine the assignment of plant cognizance to either DCAS or a particular service, for the simple reason that cognizance affords the exercise of considerable contracting authority and, by extension, program control. For example, in the case of a joint-service program, cognizance assigned to one service will result in its having more control over the progress and direction of the program than the other services. Understandably, from the perspective of the other services, this is an unsatisfactory arrangement. Similarly, the service assigned cognizance at a plant performing separate work for each service could, at least theoretically, give priority to its own program at the expense of that of the other services. Therefore, it is no coincidence that the military services usually request cognizance over contractors involved in the largest or most expensive programs of a service, as evidenced by the Air Force Contract Management Division administration in fiscal year 1984 — mostly through its AFPROs — of a total of 26,506 contracts with a face value of $120.4 billion.

Gradually, the services are beginning to prefer the impartial treatment by DCAS as an alternative to losing cognizance over a plant or program to a rival. This broader view, however, has been slow in coming. For the most part, the division of contract administration duties among DCAS and the services has changed little in the past decade, and few expect it to change significantly in the foreseeable future. A few DCAS officials are encouraged by the increasing reluctance of OSD in the last few years to reassign cognizance from DCAS to one of the services. These same officials, however, are quick to point out that this could change with the next presidential administration. The bottom line remains that since the inception of DCAS more than two decades ago, four organizations, instead of three, now administer DOD contracts.

Contract Administration

In order to understand fully the role of the cognizant contract administration office (CAO) in the acquisition process — be it a DCASPRO, DCASMA, AFPRO, NAVPRO, or ARPRO — it is necessary to examine in detail the many aspects of contract administration. Together, subsection 42.3 of the Federal Acquisition Regulation (FAR) and the Defense Acquisition Regulation (DAR) list seventy-four functions, or tasks, that collectively define contract administration. The following list summarizes the major functions:

Review and evaluate contractors' proposals and, when negotiation will be accomplished by the [procuring] contracting officer, furnish comments and recommendations to that officer.
Perform preaward surveys.
Negotiate forward pricing [overhead] rate agreements; establish final indirect cost [overhead] rates and billing rates.

Conduct postaward orientation conferences.

Review contractor's compensation structure and insurance plans.

Determine the allowability of costs suspended or disapproved, as required, and direct the suspension or disapproval of costs when there is reason to believe they should be suspended or disapproved.

Determine the adequacy of the contractor's disclosure statements.

Determine the contractor's compliance with cost accounting standards.

Negotiate prices and execute supplemental agreements for spare parts and other items.

Review and approve or disapprove the contractor's requests for payments under the progress payments clause.

Make payments on assigned contracts.

Ensure timely notification by the contractor of any anticipated overrun or underrun of the estimated cost under cost-reimbursement contracts.

Negotiate and execute contractual documents for settlement of partial and complete contract terminations for convenience and for settlement of cancellation charges under multiyear contracts.

Perform property administration.

Perform necessary screening, redistribution, and disposal of contractor inventory.

Evaluate the contractor's requests for government-owned facilities and for changes to existing facilities and provide recommendations to the [procuring] contracting officer.

Advise and assist contractors regarding their priorities and allocation responsibilities.

Monitor contactor's industrial labor relations and apprise the [procuring] contracting officer of actual or potential labor disputes.

Review and evaluate preservation, packaging, and packing.

Ensure contractor compliance with applicable safety standards.

Review and evaluate for technical adequacy the contractor's logistics support, maintenance, and modification programs.

Perform engineering analyses of contractor cost proposals.

Review and analyze contractor-proposed engineering and design studies and submit comments and recommendations to the [procuring] contracting office.

Review engineering change proposals for need, technical adequacy of design, producibility, and impact on quality, reliability, schedule, and cost; submit comments to the [procuring] contracting office.

Assist in evaluating and make recommendations for acceptance or rejection of waivers and deviations.

Monitor the contractor's value engineering program.

Review, approve or disapprove, and maintain surveillance of the contractor's purchasing system.

Consent to the placement of subcontracts.

Perform industrial readiness and mobilization, production planning, field surveys, and schedule negotiations.

When authorized by the [procuring] contracting office, negotiate and execute supplemental agreements incorporating contractor's proposals resulting from change orders.

Monitor the contractor's financial condition and advise the [procuring] contracting officer when it jeopardizes contract performance.

Perform production support, surveillance, and status reporting, including timely reporting of potential and actual slippages in contract delivery schedules.

Ensure contractor compliance with contractual quality assurance requirements.

Report to the [procuring] contracting office any inadequacy noted in specifications.

Perform engineering surveillance to assess compliance with contractual terms for schedule, cost, and technical performance in the areas of design, development, and production.

Evaluate for adequacy and perform surveillance of contractor engineering efforts and management systems that relate to design, development, production, engineering changes, subcontractors, tests, reliability and maintainability, configuration management, and data control systems.

Perform postaward surveillance of contractor's progress toward demonstration of cost/schedule control systems to meet the cost/schedule control system criteria, provide assistance in the review and acceptance of contractor's cost/schedule control systems, and perform postacceptance surveillance to ensure continuing operation of contractor's accepted systems.

Monitor the contractor's costs as prescribed under Subpart 42.70 [Indirect Cost Rates].

As the list indicates, contract administration covers a broad assortment of critically important and complicated tasks, many of which seem only casually related. The role of a CAO in the acquisition process becomes clearer, however, if one considers the seventy-four functions to constitute not just one overall contract administration service but three separate though connecting services: contract definition, contract management, and contract performance monitoring.

The first service, contract definition, generally involves analyzing and reviewing contractor cost proposals and management systems before the negotiation and award of a contract. CAOs give advice and make recommendations to the buying command's source selection team to assist it in establishing negotiating positions with each competing bidder. Examples of support include price analyses and technical evaluations of proposals and preaward surveys to assess performance capability of bidding contractors.

Once a contractor is selected and a contract signed, the CAO provides the second service, contract management, which involves the execution of the contract until completion. The buying command's procuring contracting officer (PCO) delegates to the CAO the administrative and (selected) negotiating functions. Examples of these functions include establishment of interim billing rates; review, approval, and payment of progress payments; pricing and negotiation of spare parts and change orders; and the annual resolution of final indirect cost (overhead) rates.

The third service, contract performance monitoring, involves measuring and comparing the contractor's performance with the terms of the contract. CAOs report variances and discrepancies directly to the program office. Examples of these functions include monitoring of indirect costs; ensuring compliance with quality assurance requirements; review of purchasing and cost-estimating systems; evaluation and surveillance of management systems, including cost and schedule control systems; engineering surveillance to assess compliance with contractual terms during the stages of design, development, and production; and production surveillance and reporting of potential and actual delays in delivery schedules.

Conspicuously absent from the list of contract administration functions is the audit of a contractor's financial records, which is the responsibility and primary function of the Defense Contract Audit Agency (DCAA), a separate DOD agency under the direction and control of the Assistant Secretary of Defense (Comptroller). The DCAA mission is to

> perform all necessary contract audits for the Department of Defense and provide accounting and financial advisory services regarding contracts and subcontracts to all Department of Defense components responsible for procurement and contract administration. These services will be provided

in connection with negotiation, administration, and settlement of contracts and subcontracts.[1]

According to the Defense Department, the "primary objective of DCAA audits is to determine the reasonableness, allowability and allocability of proposed or claimed contract costs."[2] As a result, approximately half of the audits pertain to contractor cost proposals. Their findings and recommendations are reviewed by contracting officers when negotiating or modifying contracts and establishing indirect cost and billing rates. In addition, DCAA auditors often attend and participate in contract administration meetings between contractor and plant representative personnel, especially when complex financial issues are discussed. Without a constant flow of audits, financial and accounting information, and advice from DCAA, the ability of a CAO to perform many of its contract administration functions properly would be greatly diminished.

In addition to the original seventy-four functions, government plant representative offices serve as hosts to visitors from DLA, OSD, any of dozens of interested organizations within a military service, GAO, congressional committees, or any other part of the government. Plant representative personnel work closely with the contractor to plan itineraries for several hundred to several thousand visitors per year, usually accompanying them on arrival at the plant. Typically, because of the geographic remoteness and therefore absence of most DOD program managers, CAO personnel brief visitors on specific programs. For high-ranking military officers, this briefing is often invaluable, for it provides them with an opportunity to learn the details of a program, formulate intelligent questions, and establish an appropriate government attitude vis-à-vis the contractor.

Subsection 42.402 of the FAR requires government visitors to inform the cognizant CAO fully "of any agreements reached with the contractor or other results of the visit that may affect the CAO." This requirement exists in part to prevent an extremely counterproductive practice described in *Arming America*:

visiting government officials provide informal "guidance" to contractors without the knowledge of the government program manager or the DCAS plant resident personnel. This guidance may or may not be consistent with management decisions made by the government program office or the plant representative.[3]

Although this practice still occurs, DCASPRO personnel we interviewed were more concerned about the enormous amount of time and resources spent on plant visits. The commanding officer of one large DCASPRO informed us that in fiscal years 1985 and 1986, respectively, 6,010 and 7,480 government and nongovernment personnel visited his contractor. This is equivalent to about 623 visitors per month in fiscal year 1986; by comparison, there was an average of 300 winter visitors and 150 summer visitors per month in fiscal year 1972 to a comparable contractor.[4] The DCASPRO commanding officer estimated that a quarter of his time was devoted to visitors. A DCASPRO division chief we interviewed commented:

> I don't think these visitors realize the impact they have on an operation. Work often stops in order to prepare for some of them. The worst thing they do is ask casual questions. Little do they know that this sets off a whole string of events; guys going around looking for answers to marginal questions. This takes a lot of time and man hours. We assign one man to find this stuff and prepare it on vugraphs so that the next time around, if he asks the question again, we're ready for him. Nine out of ten times the graphs are never needed.

The DCASPRO Organization at a Contractor Plant

The size of a DCASPRO can range from thirty to more than two hundred employees.* Its commanding officer's rank varies with its size so that rank is commensurate with responsibility. Therefore, the commanding officer of a medium-sized DCASPRO is usually an Army or Air Force lieutenant colonel or a Navy commander. (It is not uncommon in DCASPROs for civil service personnel to outnumber military officers by as much as forty to one.) As in government program offices, the internal organization varies from one case to the next. Usually, DCASPROs comprise two major divisions: contract management and quality assurance, both reporting directly to the office of the commander.

The contract management division is divided into the following branches (the exact number is determined by the size of the DCASPRO): contract operations, production and industrial re-

---

*Because DOD policy states that contract administration is the primary responsibility of DCAS (unless a service specifically requests and is subsequently assigned cognizance), I have focused on the DCAS organization, with DCASPROs serving as the generic CAO.

sources, systems and engineering, property management, and financial services. The quality assurance division normally contains two branches: operations and operations support. As a rule, civil service personnel serve as division and branch chiefs.

In fiscal year 1986, the largest DCASPRO was headed by a colonel and staffed by approximately 210 civilian and 5 military personnel. Approximately half of the civilians were assigned to contract management and the other half to quality assurance. In addition, DCAA had 75 resident personnel at the plant. This DCASPRO administered 3,709 prime contracts worth $18.1 billion; performed production surveillance on 2,368 contracts and engineering surveillance on 67 contracts; processed 1,160 proposals; completed 855 negotiations; settled 980 pricing cases; and performed 262 technical evaluations of cost proposals. In its official literature, the DCASPRO defines its mission as follows:

Monitor contractor performance to facilitate efficient operations, compliance with contract terms, and fulfillment of Government procurement objectives.

Increase the potential for contractor competition by enforcing timely deliveries of data, identification of compatible items and processes, and reducing or eliminating obstacles to competition.

Provide the best possible support to customer Program Manager and activities through effective, efficient contract administration.

Ensure only quality products are shipped to the Government.[5]

Contract Administration Problems: Past and Present

Government plant representatives have a unique opportunity, primarily because of location, to become intimately familiar with a contractor's production operations, estimating techniques, reporting systems, and personnel. They therefore often possess — or have immediate access to — valuable program-specific knowledge generally unavailable to either the PCO or program manager. Because of this advantage, plant representatives are assigned major responsibility for keeping the government program office informed about contractors' day-to-day activities and the extent to which these activities do and do not conform to the terms of a contract. Over time, it has become standard practice to refer to plant representatives as the "eyes and ears" of the program office or the "first line of defense" in the government's ongoing effort to avoid cost increases, schedule delays, and poor quality. The DCAS regional and DCASPRO managers we interviewed enthusiastically agreed with this.

Since its inception, however, DCAS has been plagued by a number of problems that many believe have undermined, to varying degrees, its ability to fulfill its mission. Critics point to the history of cost-schedule-performance difficulties in the Defense Department as evidence that government plant representatives are often incapable of managing an increasingly sophisticated contracting environment.

In the past, investigators analyzing the efficacy of DCAS have asked one fundamental question: What factors impair the service capabilities of DCAS? In *Arming America* I identified deficiencies in three areas: the quality of DCAS assistance and the recruiting, training, and staffing of its personnel; the objectivity and integrity of DCASPRO personnel; and the DCASPRO and program office working relationship. In the discussion below, each area is reexamined to determine what progress has been made since the early 1970s and what shortcomings remain. From this analysis, one can then determine the nature — or even necessity — of changes required to meet future contracting demands and challenges.

DCAS ASSISTANCE AND PERSONNEL

In the 1970s, both industry and government program managers complained that civilian DCAS personnel were often inadequately trained, inexperienced, and generally apathetic. They attributed these problems partly to ill-defined career opportunities, which often made if difficult for DCAS to recruit and retain highly qualified college graduates. In short, the personnel management problems DCAS experienced were nearly identical to those experienced throughout DOD in the late 1960s and early 1970s.

In addition, many of the same problems found earlier with program managers arise with military officers serving at DCASPROs, DCASMAs, and the nine DCAS regional offices: frequent turnover and lack of pertinent skills. Senior and junior officers alike commonly viewed DCAS as a dead-end assignment.

Today, because of the well-known, and often significant, disparity in wages between the public and private sectors, DCAS is having even greater difficulty recruiting and retaining high-caliber civilian personnel. For instance, the senior negotiator assigned to a DCASPRO, the corporate administrative contracting officer (CACO; GS-14, one billet per DCASPRO), is likely to earn approximately $50,000, or one-third to one-half the income of his or her counterpart in industry. Similarly, negotiators supervised by the CACO, the administrative contracting officers (ACOs; GS-12), earn on average $37,000, or half the income of many of their counterparts in industry. Unquestionably, noncompetitive government compensation levels have become a major obstacle, preventing the creation of a stable, highly qualified, and well-motivated civilian DCAS work force. Without exception, in all interviews where we attempted to draw comparisons between government and industry contract administrators and negotiators, DCAS managers tactfully reminded us of a fact of government life that defined their professional world: "If the government wants a contracting work force comparable to industry's, it will have to pay for it; without competitive compensation levels, our job is to do the best we can with what we have."

Prospective contract administrators and quality assurance personnel enter the Defense Contract Intern Development Program, established by DLA in the early 1980s. (Earlier training programs did exist, but on a less structured basis.) Designed to attract high-caliber personnel and standardize training requirements, the intern program mixes two years of on-the-job training in a DCASPRO or DCASMA or both with course-related work.

Throughout the 1980s, the majority of interns were DCAS personnel previously employed in various lower-level clerical, technical, and administrative positions. The ratio of interns recruited internally to those recruited from the private sector can be approximated from a Federal Acquisition Institute study, which reported that in fiscal year 1987, of the 2,776 people hired in the GS-1102 (contracts and procurement) career field, only 31 percent were nongovernment applicants.[6] Despite the complexity and importance of the work, a college education is not required, for reasons discussed earlier.

Unfortunately, the high percentage of interns recruited from within DCAS is clear evidence of just how difficult it has become for the government, given the current disparity in wages, to attract talented private-sector personnel to its GS-1102 positions. In addition, many DCAS managers are wary of attempts to upgrade the series from an administrative to a professional classification, thereby establishing specific educational requirements for the job, unless the wage disparity is reduced. One CACO commented:

> Do you know where we get a good many of our ACOs — our negotiators? From the secretarial pool. In this DCASPRO, we're big on

upward mobility — we've got to be. You spot the good ones early on, bring them up, and protect them. They are a scarce resource.

I've got seven ACOs working for me; three, maybe four, have [college] degrees. On average, they've got about two years of experience.

Establishing educational requirements is fine in the long term. But in the short and medium term, if you're going to put that secretarial pool off-limits, there goes one source of ACOs.

In our society, where self-worth is often determined by salary, these ACOs sit across the negotiating table from people making twice as much. This has an impact on them, makes them feel inferior. It's not good.

Understandably, most of the problems concerning the staffing of military personnel in program offices are shared by DCAS. Civilian DCAS personnel complain that because of high turnover of commanding officers, which occurs, on average, every two years, leadership is marginal. The officers claim they bring a "can do" attitude and independent spirit that would be lacking without them. Almost without exception, the military officers we interviewed believe their presence in DCAS offices is essential to deal with the bureaucracy and remind the contractor — on a daily basis — of their "responsibilities to the operational forces."

Despite this perception, many of these officers were uncomfortable when asked how they viewed a DCAS assignment, even as a commanding officer. This officer's comments were typical.

I had the opportunity to command a DCASPRO. I chose otherwise. It's not that their mission is unimportant, but that contract administration is on the tail end of the acquisition process. The program office makes all the critical program-specific decisions — so that's where the action is, that's where the fun is to be had.

There's another reason why officers may avoid DCAS in particular. There is this sense that you are leaving your service by going there, that the time is spent running in place while your peers are advancing their careers within your service. And the services are reluctant to let their promising officers go to DCAS — to leave the service, so to speak — as if by assigning them there they'll lose control of them. Rather than send them to DCAS to get contract administration experience, they'll simply assign them to an AFPRO, NAVPRO, or ARPRO.

Realistically, we cannot expect the longstanding perception of DCAS as a less-than-desirable assignment (an enduring perception for more than twenty years, according to our research) to change any faster than the military's perception of the overall acquisition career field itself. Although it is becoming more common to hear of DCAS commanding officers assigned to choice acquisition billets in the later years of their career, most officers still consider such occurrences the exceptions to the rule. Although an increasing number of senior officers (who, because of their own experience, recognize the value of early exposure to contract administration principles) are encouraging junior officers to accept DCASPRO assignments, one senses that these recommendations are often accompanied by observations that more promising promotion opportunities lie elsewhere.

Other factors strongly suggest that the reluctance to seek or accept an assignment to a DCASPRO may be fully justified. A DCASPRO — at least on paper — would appear to be the ideal place for a junior officer interested in acquisition to learn the basics of contracting and industrial operations, but just the opposite appears to be true. A CACO explained why.

> Who's going to train these officers in contracting? The ACOs with too much to do and only two years of experience? I don't think so. I include one officer in my daily activities because I like him, because he's a good man with an interest in this business. I don't have to do this, but I do. If you want to send officers here to really learn about contracting, you'll have to change the way the civilians around here think. Right now we don't train them, and we don't really consider it one of our jobs.

The comments of a DCASPRO division chief were equally discouraging.

> When a Navy lieutenant or an Army or Air Force captain reports for duty at a DCASPRO, you want to try to assign him responsibilities commensurate with his rank. Yet many of them have no real schooling or experience in budgeting, accounting, or any other business discipline. As a result, they can't manage my people. What am I supposed to do with them? The best we can do is make them our liaison with other military offices, but that doesn't involve them too deeply in the details of contracting and manufacturing.

According to industry and government acquisition managers whom we interviewed, the quality of DCAS assistance varies widely across functions and regions. For example, there was general agreement that DCASPROs were strongest in the functional areas of contract management, price analysis, and quality assurance, and weakest in the areas of engineering support, and schedule and cost monitoring. Most managers believed this unevenness was largely the result of the personnel availability and management practices. In other words, they considered poor service a function of insufficient numbers, inadequate qualifications, or the inappropriate management of DCAS personnel.

Between fiscal years 1979 and 1983, although the defense dollars obligated per annum rose 118 percent and the number of contracts increased by 50 percent, the GS-1102 work force expanded by only 30 percent.[7] For DCAS, this burgeoning workload resulted in a further increase in the already substantial number of contracts assigned to each ACO. Consequently, there was even less time for ACOs to devote to individual programs; additional time spent on one set of contracts was invariably at the expense of another.

The manager of a major program explained how personnel availability determined the quality of service his program received from DCAS.

> My DCASPRO happens to be in a region with a small contracting base. As a result, the services I receive are good. I mean, the region has time to support my DCASPRO, and so forth. Now, if my plant were in the Los Angeles region, for instance, I know I'd never get the service I'm getting right now. There is too much for those people to do, and too few people. So, from a program manager's point of view, a lot of luck is involved: if his plant happens to be in a region with fewer contractors, the chances are he'll get better contract support than if it were sitting near L.A. No doubt about it, quality varies widely across regions.
>
> Now I've never looked into it, but I'd like to know how DLA decides their manning requirements for the different DCAS regions. DCAS takes a lot of pride in the fact that when they take over a plant representative office [from a service], they cut the number of people, claiming to be able to do the same type of job with fewer people. Well, it just isn't so. My gut feeling is that DCAS is taking longer and longer every year to do the things you'd like them to do, because their people are spread too thin.

Others had similar misgivings about the adequacy of DCAS staffing. One senior DCASPRO manager commented:

> It's common knowledge that whenever DCAS moves into a plant representative office, they cut the number of billets, and when an AFPRO, for example, takes over from DCAS or another service, they increase the number of existing billets. It's pretty much standard practice, back and forth, back and forth. DCAS brags about this, but in fact the quality of our

service isn't comparable. Before I came to DCAS, I worked in Air Force contract management, and they invest the resources in their plant representative offices.

When we asked why a typical DCASPRO is better at some functions than at others, a DCASPRO manager volunteered these thoughts.

> You want to know why our engineering support is not up to par? It's because we can't get engineers. Period. And those we do get are often the wrong kind. I mean, we're getting civil engineers, and what we need are mechanical and electrical engineers. Often times, because they're civil engineers, we can't even use them as witnesses — their testimony is considered invalid.
>
> In this DCASPRO, the best engineer we have, believe it or not, is a man who retired from our contractor. He retired at 60, and he's got a company pension, of course, and now he works for us. A number of them do. There's nothing wrong with this, but it's a sad comment on how bad things have gotten.
>
> Why the shortage of engineers? Money. Also, the greater the number of contractors in an area, the more opportunity there is for good engineers to work for them instead of us.
>
> On the subject of schedule monitoring, this is done by our Industrial Specialists. At least in this DCASPRO, few of these people have degrees, and their professionalism could be far better. Again, it's a question of salary.

Two additional factors that contribute to the variability of DCAS assistance are program size and the management outlook of the DCASPRO commanding officer. As a rule, the larger a program's funding and the higher its priority within DOD, the better support it is likely to receive in the field.

During the course of our interviews, it became apparent that most managers were extremely reluctant to blame the unevenness of DCAS assistance directly on the contributions of the average employee, preferring instead to focus on the process-related deficiencies discussed above. When asked to characterize DCAS employees, managers were usually noncommittal. For example, managers said that DCAS employees are like any other employees, that is, some are excellent, and others are so-so; the quality of personnel covers the entire spectrum. At least to some degree, this reluctance was in deference to the thousands of dedicated and experienced DCAS personnel who collectively provide high-quality service, despite the disadvantages of low salary and an often limited education. In large measure, these public servants' efforts explain an apparent contradiction between the recent hiring difficulties of DCAS and the general satisfaction of most program management officials with the quality of DCAS assistance. Many DCAS managers, however, are deeply troubled about the long-term effects of noncompetitive government salaries on their organization. According to a senior DCASPRO official,

> In many cases, we're still doing a credible job without an influx of highly talented new people because senior people are carrying the ball.
>
> When I entered government service back in the midsixties, contract administration was an acceptable thing to do. Back then, the money and pension seemed good, and President Kennedy made government service respectable. A lot of good people came into government, and the pension was a major reason why many of them stayed. You know, you work for so many years and you become reluctant to forgo accumulated pension benefits for a job with a better salary.
>
> Anyway, right now this group — myself included — is getting close to retirement. Who's going to take our place? The government can always fill a billet, that's never been a problem. The challenge is to fill the billet with somebody who's good. The fact is, right now this organization has less depth than it requires. I don't know what's going to happen in the future.

Indeed, the ability of DCAS to manage tomorrow's sophisticated contracting environment effectively remains highly questionable, unless it can recruit, train, and retain high-quality people. Congress and OSD must recognize and correct the handicap of noncompetitive government compensation, which directly affects turnover rates, experience levels, education levels, personnel availability, and competence. In the long term, improving the quality of DCAS services and the caliber of DCAS employees are inseparable issues.

OBJECTIVITY AND INTEGRITY OF DCASPRO PERSONNEL

In the early 1970s, it became clear that DCASPRO personnel often lost, to varying degrees, their objectivity and, therefore, professional integrity if assigned to one contractor plant for a long period of time. The problem is referred to as "going native," or becoming "contractor oriented." In *Arming America* I characterized the problem as follows:

There is an additional problem at plant representative offices, however — the result of the longevity of civilian officials' service at one plant. One of the primary reasons for assigning government personnel to a contractor's plant is to strengthen cost control and quality of work being performed. When personnel have been assigned to the same DCAS plant office for a number of years, these goals may be neglected. At any defense plant, programs come and go; military personnel come and go; government program offices come and go. But the civilian personnel in the DCAS plant offices and the senior executives in the plant remain on the scene.[8]

A management consultant to the defense and aerospace industry and an expert in contract negotiation explained the dilemma.

This [problem of friendship] is not intended to suggest that a buyer, whether a government buyer or one employed in private industry, is making under-the-table deals or that there is anything ethically wrong in the relationship. It is just that, in many cases, familiarity may not breed contempt, but may breed friendship which prevents the buyer from doing the most effective job at the negotiation table.[9]

Since the early 1970s, the Defense Department has revised existing policy and promulgated new initiatives in an effort to discourage further the loss of objectivity. Additionally, Congress has passed, in successive years, increasingly restrictive "revolving door" legislation in an effort to address this problem. Overall, these policies and legislative initiatives have successfully addressed conflict of interest in its most overt forms, and each year progress is made toward a constructive set of disincentives.

One must realize, however, that the government neither controls the views of its employees nor directs every decision and judgment made by DCASPRO personnel. Therefore, it may never be possible to solve completely a behavioral problem — traced to an intangible such as "friendship" — by legislative or regulatory fiat. Nor will it be possible to determine when a negotiator fails to do "the most effective" job possible. The most the government can do is provide its employees with the right combination of incentives and disincentives to reinforce objectivity. Identification with the contractor may never be eliminated — merely minimized.

Although DLA employees are forbidden by its standards of conduct to lose their "complete independence or impartiality," enforcement of this particular standard is nearly impossible — for obvious reasons.

Nevertheless, DCAS has shown a willingness to enforce strictly any standard if violations can be clearly documented. In one region we visited, the counselors discussed their role in the prosecution of a GS-12 and five other DCASMA employees for accepting race track tickets from a contractor. Price of each ticket: $7.00. The DLA message is clear: if counselors can document a violation, however small, sanctions will follow.

Because of the difficulties inherent in administrative enforcement of ethical standards, government officials in both the legislative and executive branches have made repeated attempts over the years simply to preempt the problem by establishing a rotational program for plant representatives. Initial opposition to the program was based on the grounds that it poses an undue inconvenience for personnel chosen for rotation and reinforces the belief that dishonesty is simply a function of time. Nevertheless, in November 1975 and February 1976, the Deputy Assistant Secretary of Defense for Installations and Logistics issued two memoranda, both titled "Mobility of Field Contract Administration Personnel," which required the establishment of rotational programs for plant representatives having a "continuous association" with defense contractors. DOD Directive 1400.24, "Civilian Mobility Programs," and DLA Regulation 1404.13, "Rotation of Contract Administration Services Personnel Assigned to Contractor Plants," followed.

Section II of the DLA regulation defines the intent of rotation.

> There are several advantages associated with the rotation of contract administration services personnel assigned to contractor plants. Knowledge gained at multiple locations provides the depth and breadth of experience needed for career progression, while familiarity with several contractors' products, systems, technical processes and procedures enhances professionalism and perspective. Additionally, rotation of in-plant key personnel helps remove any concern which may exist that government representatives in sensitive and demanding positions may be influenced by events or circumstances resulting from a continuing association with a defense contractor.

The rotation program is applicable only to "supervisors, senior specialists, and single-person residents in quality assurance, contract administration, or production who are stationed at a contractor's plant." Those selected generally rotate "to a position in a different plant or to a position not located in a contractor plant, after being assigned for five continuous years in the same contractor plant." Exceptions to a scheduled rotation are allowed, however, for a number of reasons, including personal hardship, expected retirement within twelve months, possession of a critical or rare specialty, and avoidance of serious program disruptions. Exceptions must be justified, documented, and reviewed annually to ensure continued applicability. Reassignment to a former plant is allowed only after a lapse of two years. DCASMA personnel, because of their less intensive involvement with any single contractor, are exempt from rotation; to ensure objectivity, key supervisors are simply assigned responsibility for a different set of contractors within their management area.

In practice, the policy of rotation, as implemented, affects the personal lives and careers of a surprisingly small number of DCAS personnel. In fiscal year 1986, a major DCAS region containing nine DCASPROs, four DCASMAs, more than 3,000 contractors, and approximately 1,800 contract administration and quality assurance personnel identified only 114 positions for rotation. Of the 114, 37 were filled by people who qualified for rotation, having spent more than five years in their assignments. The commanding officer of the region granted twenty-two waivers, leaving only 15 people to be rotated — a number equivalent to less than 1 percent of the 1,800-member regional work force — and 13 percent of the supervisors assigned to rotational billets. Only 15 of the 76 single-person quality assurance positions in the region were designated as rotational.

Unfortunately, the rotation program has its drawbacks. Most rotated personnel are financially penalized if their reassignment requires a move from their current residence. A DCASPRO official related the experience of a recently rotated colleague.

> His transfer to this DCASPRO was difficult, to say the least. Before his reassignment to this part of the country he had a reasonable mortgage on a nice house, and his wife stayed at home with the kids. He moved up here and got less of a home for literally twice the money. And he had trouble qualifying for the new mortgage because of his salary. In the end, his wife had to go back to work. Sure, the government covers the moving expenses and standard fees, but that's about it. There's no compensation for the cost-of-living differences between parts of this country.
>
> You know, we don't make a lot of money to begin with. He'll never tell you this himself, but the transfer was — and still is — a real financial hardship for his family. It will take years for them to recover.

Another substantial drawback attributable to rotation involves the systematic loss of supervisory-level managers with contractor-specific knowledge. Once assigned to a DCASPRO, DCAS supervisors often require two, possibly three, years to become familiar with a contractor's personnel, products, organizational and financial structure, business practices, and costing and management information systems.* In such situations, they can spend approximately one-half of a five-year assignment learning, instead of managing, a process. Moreover, because each contractor is unique, detailed knowledge of one is seldom applicable to another, thus requiring a significant amount of relearning with each transfer. The larger the contractor, the longer it will take for a supervisor to regain self-confidence and the ability to be effective.

THE DCASPRO-PROGRAM OFFICE WORKING RELATIONSHIP

At least in theory, few would question the logic, importance, or desirability of establishing a close — almost symbiotic — working relationship between the managers of a manufacturing program and their supervisors on the shop floor. In defense contracting, however, the standard working relationship is unclear and often coincidental. It has been this way at least since the 1970s.

> The relationship between the government program office and the DCAS plant representative office ranges from close cooperation to arm's-length negotiation. Difficulties occur because the program manager reports to superiors within his military service, while the senior official of the DCAS plant office reports to superiors within the DCAS regions . . . and then to the head of the Defense Supply [now Logistics] Agency. It is only at the level of the Office of the Secretary of Defense that there is a single focal point for both the program office and the DCAS plant representative.
>
> The government program offices and DCAS plant offices usually work closely together. But in a significant number of instances, government program managers work directly with contractors without including representatives from the local DCAS office. On the other hand, a senior officer of one military service told us that he knew of many cases where there was a much closer relationship between the contractor and the DCAS plant representative than between the plant representative and the government program manager.[10]

---

*The figure of two to three years is an estimate based on interviews with a variety of industry and government acquisition managers. If accurate by only 50 percent, it is nonetheless a substantial period of time, which does not speak well of the current practice of rotating military officers, on average, in and out of DCAS every two years.

In 1982, the Special Panel on Defense Procurement Procedures of the House Armed Services Committee reaffirmed most of the findings in *Arming America* regarding the DCASPRO-program office working relationship, concluding that contract administration within DOD was structurally flawed.

> The panel believes that the present decentralized approach to contract management within DOD does little to encourage consistent contract administration and management procedures. The panel feels that effective cost growth control appears to be hampered by ambiguous lines of authority for cost reporting and fragmented areas of responsibility for cost control.
>
> The Government's representatives at the contracting facility constitute the "first line of defense" in the fight against cost growth. General Charles Drenz, U.S. Army, Deputy Director of DCAS, in response to a question concerning plant representatives, agreed that because plant representatives are stationed at the contractor's facility, they should be able to detect cost growth rather quickly. General Drenz added, however, that on some occasions the contractor will inform the program manager of cost growth before notifying the plant representative.
>
> The record reflects that although most of the DOD [DCAS] and military departments' plant representatives understood their lines of reporting authority and functional responsibilities, there was sufficient ambiguity, specifically concerning the reporting channels, to merit review by the Defense Department. In fact, in one case, it was not clear if the plant representative should be reporting cost growth information to the program manager or to his DCAS supervisior.[11]

For our purposes, the detailed findings of these earlier analyses are less important than an appreciation for the common thread that runs through each: the multiple contracting organizations of the Defense Department often fail to communicate, coordinate, and use their combined resources to achieve predetermined program cost, schedule, and performance criteria. This is still true in the late 1980s.

The program management officials we interviewed thought the congressional panel, by focusing on ambiguous reporting channels, had identified a symptom, not a cause, of poor coordination between plant representatives and program offices. In fact, these managers pointed out that intersecting reporting channels alone provide few clues about organizational effectiveness.

Typically, reporting channels and procedures are clearly defined — and carefully respected — by the program and plant representative offices when applied to specific and detailed contractual matters. As discussed earlier, the procuring contracting officer (PCO) delegates contract administration functions to the ACO at the time of signing the contract.

In practice, not all functions performed by plant representative personnel are of pressing concern to a government program manager, and vice versa. Therefore, it is unlikely that the Defense Department will ever fully develop a much coveted "single voice" with which to address the contractor. As one DCASPRO commanding officer explained, "The PMO is normally involved with the more macro program-related issues and only infrequently becomes involved in the more micro functions (such as the preservation, packaging, and packing of end items). We do just the opposite; our DCASPRO is always involved in the small details." In short, the kind of problem or the proximity of desired information and expertise will determine if the plant representative is notified or not when the program office and contractor communicate with each other. Expediency is another factor that must be considered.

Memoranda of agreement (MOAs) are often used on major programs to clarify reporting channels and requirements between program and plant representative offices. Normally initiated, as appropriate, by the program office, they are renewed yearly and tailored to address the needs arising from individual contracts and the variety of organizational structures across buying commands, PMOs, and plant representative offices. Individual buying commands provide their own MOA guidance. Issues frequently addressed include quality assurance personnel, reporting and surveillance on the contractor performance monitoring system, authority for engineering change orders, and assignment of technical representatives from the program office to the plant representative office.

Rather than attribute lapses of government contracting teamwork to reporting channels and deficiencies in the current organizational structure, these same program office officials believe the problem is simply a lack of requisite management skill, especially among their peers. As one program manager said, "People tend to forget the basic lessons taught in Management 101." A senior officer attached to a buying command saw the issue in more complex terms.

> Contract administration does have an identity crisis, no doubt about it. Program officials often have a difficult time coming to terms with the extent to which government plant representatives fit into the program.

They have second-hand, i.e., contractor-derived, information; they are not included in major program decisions. Contract administrators plainly have a second-hand status in programs.

On the other hand, DCAS is in the business of providing a service. They are anxious to do a job and they have resources. They are there to assist — and they want to help — the program office, which needs all the help it can get in order to successfully complete the contract.

The essential management challenge is how to successfully match the service — DCAS — with the need — the program office. How do we make each organization aware of the others' needs and capabilities? How do we bridge the communications chasm that often exists? How do we establish the spirit of the relationship?

In general, program managers are more likely to underuse DCAS if they do not fully appreciate the value of a close working relationship with their plant representatives or the scope of available contract administration services. Because this failing is so common, it is worth considering how an officer with extensive program management experience characterized the usefulness of DCAS.

> On the most simplistic level, contract administrators are the doers of the small program-related tasks that have got to be done on a daily basis to keep the program going. You know, work involving the 74 functions. Because of their location, they collect information and coordinate contractor-specific administrative details for the program office, which is often located many miles away.
>
> On another level, however, contract management services represent a set of levers, or tools, for us to influence the behavior of the contractor. For instance, possibly the two most valuable levers available to a program manager are progress payments and preaward surveys — both of which are plant representative functions. Believe me, you get the contractor's undivided attention rather quickly when you direct — or threaten to direct — the plant representatives to alter progress payments in response to unsatisfactory contract performance. Similarly, if a contractor believes marginal performance on one job will definitely result in a less-than-favorable preaward survey prior to another job, he's likely to be more responsive to your current needs.

Many people we interviewed made suggestions to improve the DCASPRO-program office working relationship. Without exception, they considered a major reorganization neither a realistic nor a desirable option. Instead, they focused on concrete ways to better exploit existing contracting mechanisms and procedures to achieve a higher level of coordination among government contracting resources. Below are three of their suggestions.

First, reinvigorate the underlying spirit of the MOA. The original purpose of the MOA was to facilitate coordination between program and plant representative offices on complex programs in two ways: by documenting the division of labor on individual contracts and by creating — in the process — a spirit of cooperation and teamwork between the two parties. Over the years, however, the spirit has largely dissipated, and the typical MOA has degenerated into an inch-thick document whose text is commonly derided as "pro forma legal jargon." In most cases, program offices consider the MOA merely one more document to prepare and subsequently forget. In short, compiling the paper work has become an end in itself. Managers who recognize the value of the MOA as a coordinating tool would like to see it become a more practical guide to individual program needs, and the best way to accomplish this would be to reduce standardized clauses to a minimum.

Second, redirect emphasis of the postaward conference. The purpose of this conference, attended by program office, plant representative, and contractor personnel, is to assign or clarify program-specific duties and responsibilities immediately after the award of a contract. Too often, however, the government parties emphasize the coordination of activities between themselves and the contractor, giving less attention to coordination between one another. One program official observed:

> The requirement for the government people to coordinate their activities exists on paper. However, as in the case of the MOA, the spirit of teamwork is often missing at these meetings. The program office is always concerned about marketing and selling its program. Yet it ought to be aware that establishing close ties with its plant representative office, or offices, is equally important.

The important point is that the postaward conference should be three-way rather than two-way.

Third, integrate the advantages of DCASPRO locations into contractor performance measurement systems. Contractor performance measurement systems correlate costs incurred with progress achieved to anticipate and identify possible cost increases and schedule delays. In general, plant representatives involved in these systems have not taken full advantage of their location at contractor facilities. For example, involvement beyond data verification is usually limited to the submission of monthly analyses of system data that are then compared against similar analyses performed by program office personnel. Because DOD guidelines require both analyses to be prepared in similar fashion, more often than not the plant representative analysis adds little to what program office personnel already know.

Instead of merely accepting these analyses, some program officials have developed ways to use plant representatives' skills in a more meaningful way. The program manager of a major high-technology system described an effective approach to using the DCASPRO to identify the significance of variances in performance measurement reports.

> Sure, we get a monthly analysis from our DCASPRO, but it typically doesn't tell us anything that we don't already know. I look at it, but that's about it.
>
> Doing these analyses, however, is not where our DCASPRO adds value to the performance measurement system. You see, every month I also get about a 20-page variance report from the measurement system crammed with individual variances. You know, a component is held up due to this or that problem at a plant — that sort of thing. Well, I read through these variances very carefully, and I decide which ones I'll worry about. Then I get on the phone with the DCASPRO people, and I ask them if they'd mind investigating the variances I'm worried about. They come back and tell me if we've got a problem or not. And if we do, they can tell me what's being done about it or what I need to do.
>
> I definitely utilize DCAS as my eyes and ears in the plant. Of course, my people could chase these variances down, but why not use the DCASPRO people? That's why they're there.

A DCASPRO division chief fully supported this approach.

> Most of the MOAs we have contain a clause that requires us to do "special variance analysis as required," or something to that effect. We're asked to do that on a number of contracts, but it wouldn't be accurate to say that we're doing it on all of them.
>
> Right now, a number of program offices are set up to receive the performance measurement system data directly from the contractor right into their office. They have it analyzed by the time the print shop can even finish printing the data that we eventually receive. By the time we do our

analysis and send it to them, they've moved on to something else. The time lag simply reduces our ability to participate.

But variance analysis is a smart way to use our resources. Look at it this way. I've got two engineers doing performance measurement system analysis at one of our plants with over 7,000 employees. This plant is doing a couple of hundred million dollars worth of work. Instead of expecting these two engineers to identify, within a broad monthly report, those program areas of greatest concern to the program office, the program office is essentially focusing the efforts of these two people on issues of real consequence to them. It's one way to get the most out of limited manpower resources.

This interdependence of contracting resources reflects the kind of cooperative relationship intended when performance measurement systems were developed in the 1960s. For such productive relationships to become the norm, however, program and plant representative officials will have to reduce the bureaucratic barriers between their organizations, recognizing that they are both on the same team and working toward common objectives.

During the past three decades, changes in the defense contracting environment have not diminished — to the slightest degree — the potential value of plant representatives to the overall contracting effort of the government. If anything, the need to locate skilled, dedicated, and resourceful government personnel at major contractor facilities has increased as the cost and complexity of major weapon systems have escalated. Rather than question the basic usefulness of plant representatives, this chapter identified shortcomings in personnel availability, management practices, and contracting teamwork that often reduce the contribution of these essential employees to a level below current needs.

At issue is whether the cost increases, schedule delays, and performance difficulties of the past three decades are considered serious enough to warrant a reallocation of resources to increase the qualifications and capabilities of government personnel who deal with contractors on a daily basis. In our view, the problems became serious enough long ago. We cannot state this too strongly: Government oversight of defense contractors cannot be expected to improve significantly until a degree of parity, in competence and professionalism, is established between contractor personnel and government plant representatives.

Notes

1. Department of Defense Directive (DODD) 5105.36, "Defense Contract Audit Agency," June 8, 1978.
2. U.S. Senate, hearing before the Subcommittee on Defense Acquisition Policy of the Committee on Armed Services, "Audit Practices in the Department of Defense," March 12, 1985, p. 101.
3. J. Ronald Fox, *Arming America: How the U.S. Buys Weapons* (Boston: Division of Research, Harvard Business School, 1974), pp. 221–222.
4. Ibid., p. 222.
5. DCASPRO, Raytheon Corporation, Lexington, Mass.
6. Mike Miller, Federal Acquisition Institute, "The Acquisition Work Force, Fiscal Year 1983," August 1984, p. 10.
7. Ibid., p. 2.
8. Fox, *Arming America,* pp. 217–218.
9. Ibid., p. 219.
10. Ibid., p. 217.
11. Report of the House Armed Services Committee, Special Panel on Defense Procurement Procedures, *Defense Procurement Procedures,* February 12, 1982, pp. 22–23.

──8────────────────────

CONCLUSIONS

> I have concluded that in the defense acquisition process minor cosmetic changes are not of much use. We are far beyond that point. I think we need to address very fundamental, tough issues.
>
> — Norman Augustine, chief operating officer of the Martin Marietta Corporation and former Under Secretary of the Army.

During the past fifteen years, numerous attempts to reform the acquisition process have fallen far short of their goals.[1] Nevertheless, I conclude that the alarming federal deficit, the continuing need for a strong defense, and a growing awareness of the need to deal more effectively with the high cost of defense may provide a conducive environment for major improvements in cost control and overall program management.

Concern over high costs and cost increases in the acquisition process is not new. In the past three decades, hundreds of studies and articles have cited numerous instances of unexpected cost increases and inappropriate charges to the government. An abundance of improvement recommendations exists. Yet government officials continue to express surprise when costs increase dramatically over initial estimates.

Every Secretary of Defense has made a commitment to efficient management of the defense acquisition process. Indeed, each has taken specific steps to identify problems and to initiate improvements, which, in a few cases, have had lasting effect. All too often, however, they have fallen far short of their goal.

Fifteen years ago, I wrote, in *Arming America:*

> The current relationships between Congress and the Defense Department, among governmental defense agencies, and between government and industry, effectively prevent the [acquisition] system from functioning to its best advantage.[2]

In 1988, the same statement applies, and, in my view as well as that of many in the Defense Department and the defense industry, the situation is worse in 1988 than it was in 1973 or in 1960.

The Unusual Defense Marketplace

The U.S. economic system is built on the concept of free enterprise regulated by competition. The marketplace is the testing ground for products and methods of production and management. A well-managed firm will prosper, and a poorly managed one will fail. Lower costs mean higher profits. Investors take risks that, if successful, will be rewarded by higher profits.

Many defense acquisition problems are rooted in the mistaken belief that the defense industry fits naturally into the free market model. Most Americans believe that the defense industry, as part of private industry, is equipped to handle any kind of development or production program. They also by and large distrust government "interference" in private enterprise. Government and industry defense managers capitalize on these attitudes, going to great lengths to preserve the myth that large defense programs are developed and produced through the free enterprise system. It bears repeating: Neither the defense industry nor defense programs are governed by the free market; defense acquisition programs rarely offer incentives resembling those of the commercial marketplace.

In the defense industry, most of the major producers depend heavily on the Defense Department for business. They develop a large group of engineers, draftsmen, scientists, technicians, production workers, and managers to maintain their capability for defense work and to increase their chances of selection for the next contract. Few, if any, commercial projects would enable a firm to support such a large and varied work force. On many large defense programs, the federal government also supplies a very significant part of the working capital and investment. Once a weapon system contract has been signed, a firm faces little chance of cancellation for default because the large number of government and industry managers involved makes it difficult to ascribe responsibility. The firm is further protected because contract cancellation would lengthen the acquisition schedule and risk cancellation of the entire program by OSD or the Congress.

The Relationship between Government and Industry

The relationship between a government program office and its major contractor is necessarily a close one. Government and industry program managers must work together to solve complex technical problems, and, on finding solutions, they must initiate contract changes in the work being performed. In this environment, both government and industry must recognize that on development programs and most large production programs, a contract mechanism, by itself, is an ineffective substitute for rigorous day-to-day evaluations and negotiations. A government manager is not simply a partner with private industry but an independent manager charged with supervising the use of public funds — that is, a wise buyer.

Defense contractors, motivated by a commitment to a strong defense program as well as economic gain, have three important objectives: achieving the technical performance objectives of a program, meeting payrolls, and satisfying stockholders. Therefore, industry managers must continually strive to obtain additional contracts that will engage their R&D and production work force.

Meanwhile, the Defense Department program managers and contracting officers are responsible for monitoring three areas of contractor activity: technical performance, delivery schedules, and program costs. If the acquisition process is to run smoothly and efficiently, it should be structured so that contractors have a reasonable opportunity to earn returns comparable to commercial returns for comparable risk, without undermining government program objectives. When contractors perform well, government managers should be empowered to recognize that performance and to reward it with attractive profits and improved opportunities for future defense business. On the other hand, when contract terms are not complied with, defense program managers and plant representatives must be sufficiently trained, experienced, and motivated to identify and report inadequate performance to higher echelons of the Defense Department, and to search for and implement corrective actions. Government officials at all levels of the Defense Department — and Congress — must be prepared to support this kind of responsible management.

Present statutes and regulations concerning the defense acquisition process have evolved over the years in a piecemeal fashion, with little attention paid to developing a coherent package. Congress and DOD need to undertake a major review of laws and regulations, with the goal of removing inconsistencies and reducing the number of governmental organizations, including congressional committees and subcommittees, overseeing and directing the acquisition process. Laws and regulations concerning defense acquisition should be not only comprehensible but also well organized; those too complex to be understood by the people applying them are ineffective. Unfortunately, many of the existing laws and regulations are not readily understood, even by lawyers. Those responsible under the law for performing certain duties must know exactly what their obligations are, and should be able to understand them by reading the relevant statute or regulation. Standards for performance, for example, should be explicit and lines of authority should be short, direct, and easily understood.[3]

Some government managers deal with contractors as adversaries, failing to appreciate the need for the informal cooperation so necessary between buyer and seller in managing any large development program — especially a major weapon system under conditions of technical uncertainties and changing requirements. In an adversarial relationship, these managers at times inappropriately attempt to enforce fixed-price contracts for engineering development work when cost-reimbursement contracts would be far more appropriate. Or they treat cost-reimbursement contracts as if they were fixed-price contracts, trying to enforce rigid task statements when the work inherently requires flexibility.

Other government managers see themselves as no more than partners with industry, apparently unaware of the mixed motives inherent in the buyer-seller relationship. They share the industry goal of producing a technically excellent program, but they sometimes lose sight of their role in conducting arm's-length buyer-seller negotiations on programs where changes occur weekly, sometimes daily. These managers often erroneously assert, "We know how much the program should cost because that's how much the contractor spent." They are proud, as they should be, of the technical excellence of their products. But unlike their peers in commercial business, they incur no penalty for programs exceeding their original budgets.

The challenge of managing the defense acquisition process effectively and efficiently requires a delicate balance between the adversarial role and the pure partnership role — a balance that produces what I refer to as the wise buyer. Achieving that balance requires years of training and experience to learn to cope with the complexities of the process, the day-to-day negotiations, and the marketing tactics within government, within industry, and between government and industry. What is needed is not an adversarial relationship characterized by animosity, suspicion, and mistrust but (paraphrasing an ABA report) a business relationship — partnership, perhaps — characterized by rigorous bargaining, accompanied by tenacious regard for the best interests of one's own side.[4]

Differing Perceptions of Defense Acquisition

In reflecting on my interviews with people directly involved in the defense acquisition process, one fact stands out: government and industry managers have widely differing perceptions of the current condition of the process. Some describe it as poorly managed and plagued by serious problems; others see it as well managed, with few problems. The differing perceptions do *not* reflect the conventional dichotomies of military versus civilian or government versus industry. Rather, they reflect managers' dissimilar views of the government role in managing the defense acquisition process.

Many people — in both government and industry — describe the job of government program management primarily as one of promoting a program, preparing progress reports and briefings, negotiating with officials at the Pentagon and various military commands, and resolving engineering conflicts between these organizations and contractors. The responsibility for cost control belongs solely to the contractor. I call this the liaison manager view; it is based on the belief that the defense business is part of the free enterprise system and therefore regulated by competition in the marketplace.

Others describe the government role as one of planning and making key decisions associated with rigorous oversight of, negotiation with, and control of the industrial firms that perform the development and production work. The responsibility for cost control belongs to the government program manager and the plant representative, as well as the contractor. Significant cost reductions are often possible, depending on government managers' abilities to establish and implement challenging productivity and cost incentives, formal and informal, throughout the life of a program. I call this the active manager view; it is based on the belief that the competitive forces of the marketplace do not, by themselves, produce the desired cost, schedule, and technical performance on large defense programs.

Those who hold the liaison manager view believe there is no need for government program managers to have years of training and experience in industrial management and methods of cost control. If the job of the program manager is limited to promoting the program, preparing progress reports, and performing technical liaison, then experience as a pilot, tank commander, ship captain, or engineer and possibly fourteen to twenty weeks at the Defense Systems Management College may be sufficient. But for those who hold the active manager view, military experience and twenty weeks of training — or even two or three years of training and experience — are insufficient for a manager of a large, complex program.

Not surprisingly, those of the liaison manager view consider the government acquisition job a reasonable *alternate* assignment, or "shore duty," for combat arms officers until reassignment to their primary duties in operational units. Proponents of the active manager view, however, consider the defense acquisition process too complex, too costly, and too important to national security to serve as an alternate assignment. I strongly agree with the active manager view.

People holding the liaison view often talk about the cost-control aspects of managing programs, but fail to understand that the planning and control of large industrial development and production programs are achieved neither by proclamation nor by good intentions. They are achieved only by performing difficult analyses and trade-offs, engaging in day-to-day negotiations, and making often-difficult judgments. The skills needed for these tasks require years of intensive formal and on-the-job training and experience.

Annual Congressional Authorizations and Appropriations

A fundamental issue in the management of defense programs is the need for greater funding stability and more effective long-range defense planning. The year-by-year congressional review process encourages continual selling to the Congress by the Defense Department and its contractors, and limits greatly the effect of any long-range planning. In addition, this process, as it now exists, lends itself to the most flagrant abuse. The long-term effects of short-term proposals are seldom analyzed or understood. Members of the Congress, as elected legislators, may not be present to evaluate programs begun with their approval. Thus, there may be no accountability from contractors, defense program managers and their superiors, and Congress itself.

As noted earlier, communication between the Defense Department and the Congress and between ascending levels within DOD is intended far more to obtain approval of a current budget request than to inform. Information is often proffered or withheld depending on whether it serves a narrow cause, that is, to protect a program, to increase a budget, to obtain more programs, or all three.

Members of the House of Representatives have many goals, not the least of which is reelection. Many act as if their every vote is measured by its effect on the electorate, because there is never a long enough time between biennial elections to cease campaigning. (Surely it is time to increase the term of House members to four years.)

Although senators are not always under the same reelection pressure, neither are they free from pressure to provide federally funded benefits for their constituents. Most voters are, by necessity, interested in steady employment and adequate wages, and they expect their representatives in Congress to work to ensure such stability. Members of Congress are seldom rewarded for looking beyond local needs to a national goal that most of their constituents do not understand, especially if that goal produces a loss of local jobs.

No change in congressional procedure will improve the acquisition process, however, if Congress is unwilling to demand accountability from defense officials. As long as senior military and civilian officials believe that Congress will routinely provide funds for almost all new and ongoing programs, there is little hope for improvements. It is essential that members of Congress make clear to the Defense Department that the federal budget is not a bottomless pit of funds.

Congressional reform must include an elimination of the redundancy among the reviews by the Budget, Appropriations, Governmental Affairs, Government Operations, Joint Economic, Armed Services, and other committees, most of which are time consuming and chaotic. Congress needs a simple line of authority for authorizing programs, appropriating funds, and overseeing the defense acquisition process.[5] In addition to clarifying the line of authority, Congress must limit the number of hearings that frequently result in detailed and nearly incomprehensible rules and regulations of questionable merit.

A more reasonable process is this: Congress would authorize and appropriate funds biennially, using the alternate years to oversee the acquisition process. Congressional oversight could then focus on overall defense policy, the quality of DOD management, the reasonableness of plans for major development and production programs, and the progress made in accomplishing earlier plans.[6]

Organizational Structure

The Packard Commission (1986) recognized the problem posed by the proliferation of governmental organizations influencing (or controlling) parts of the defense acquisition process. The commission attempted to correct this problem by recommending the establishment of acquisition executives (AEs) and program executive officers (PEOs) — an organizational change the Defense Department subsequently adopted. There is a widespread belief, however, that the layers of DOD managers (e.g., hardware and functional specialists, small-business, and other single-interest advocates with power to slow or stop programs) are unaffected by the reorganization and remain a major impediment to improving effectiveness.[7]

Regardless of the particular management structure adopted, it should contain four elements:

1. A single well-defined procurement chain of authority within DOD,
2. A program manager with clear authority over the horizontal layers of interested parties (e.g., the user, functional specialists, advocates of competition, small business, and other socioeconomic programs),
3. A single well-defined monitoring and auditing authority, and
4. A single, well-defined channel for congressional inquiry and oversight.[8]

To address the problem of excessive numbers of governmental organizations influencing the acquisition process, the Defense Department should identify each by name, define in unambiguous language an appropriate (and inappropriate) role in the acquisition process, and then follow up to ensure that proliferation does not occur.

Civilian Appointees in Senior Acquisition Positions

At the very top of the acquisition community are the presidential appointees, who fill the key positions in the various DOD secretariats that provide management and oversight of acquisition activities. Here, financial divestiture requirements and ambiguous conflict-of-interest legislation serve as significant — and growing — disincentives for experienced industry executives. That appointees are expected to take reductions — often significant ones — in their compensation only worsens the situation. As Dr. Jacques Gansler has pointed out, most of the conflict-of-interest legislation written in recent years — including that passed at the end of the 1986 congressional session — was intended primarily for civilian and military career personnel *leaving* the government for private industry. The intent is to deter government employees from setting themselves up for positions in private industry subsequent to government employment, or from benefiting a prospective employer through actions taken while employed by the government. Instead, the legislation serves as a deterrent to experienced, responsible industry managers accepting selected Defense Department acquisition positions.[9]

To maintain the important separation between military and civilian control of the acquisition process, Congress should find ways to attract dedicated, experienced industry managers to senior positions in the Pentagon. For example, Congress should pass legislation to enable appointees to limit or postpone the tax liability resulting from the present financial divestiture rules. I agree with Russell Murray that it may well be in the government's best interest to encourage reasonable perquisites as at least partial compensation for the reduced pay and more demanding aspects of DOD employment.[10]

At the same time, the administration should exercise more care in selecting candidates for senior DOD positions: What qualifications do candidates have? Do they understand the operation of the Defense Department? Do they understand the business operations of defense contractors? Do they have a clear understanding of the goals of effectiveness *and* efficiency? Do they have a plan for carrying out the proposed job? Do they have reasonable ideas for effecting change in the vast DOD bureaucracy? Why are they agreeable to the sizable pay reduction so often associated with government service? Is the presidential appointment being used by a defeated legislator or loyal party member simply as a steppingstone to the private sector?

Fortunately, as Dr. Gansler has pointed out, there are a limited number of critical acquisition positions — perhaps two dozen available to political appointees — throughout the federal government. Therefore, it is all the more reasonable that the executive branch and the Senate exercise great care in appointing people to these positions.[11]

Reexamining the Program Manager Concept

The program manager concept works well in industry. Why does it usually experience serious problems in government? Consider the unique characteristics of industry program managers, who usually report to the company president.

1. They have genuine decision-making authority regarding personnel assignment, promotions, technical matters, and budgets.
2. They have years of training and experience in the operations of the industry relevant to the program (e.g., development and production of missiles, aircraft, tanks, ships, and guidance systems).
3. They understand the roles performed and the tactics employed within government, within industry, and between government and industry.

Lacking the training, experience, and stature of their private-sector counterparts, DOD program managers encounter another serious obstacle to performing their jobs. Namely, they are required to respond to (indeed, often placate) many people capable of influencing their career: people in the buying command, the using command, the service headquarters staff, the service secretariat, OSD, and the Congress. Within these groups there are diverse elements: some who support the program, some who oppose it, and some who are undecided. The people representing one or more of these groups change every few months, as assignments change. These management groups have voracious appetites for data from program managers: How much will it cost to reduce the aircraft by two hundred pounds? What is the consequence of reducing the budget by $300 million? How much can we save by reducing the production rate by 50 percent? What will be the impact of replacing the radar? What caused the delay? What will it take to regain the lost schedule? How much can we save by introducing competition for the next production contract?

It is time to reexamine the current method of manning and operating program offices if DOD is to manage the acquisition process more effectively and efficiently. The current job descriptions portray program managers as supermen who

cut through the red tape laid by several hundred "interested" government managers;

always obtain budget approvals from the service headquarters, OSD, and the Congress;

work as partners with industry in solving technical problems;

obtain reliable data from which to determine independently the schedule, cost, and technical performance status of a program; and

provide incentives for industry to perform expeditiously at the lowest reasonable cost.

All this is to be accomplished by an underpaid and inexperienced staff operating within a procurement system that rewards higher costs and penalizes lower costs.

Although there is a pressing need for the Defense Department to adopt the active manager role, the current approach to program management is fundamentally flawed. After nearly thirty years, we know that an Army or Air Force colonel or Navy captain (0-6) can rarely orchestrate and control a giant contractor and a series of government organizations headed by people significantly his senior. If DOD is to perform the role of the wise buyer, a two-star or three-star commodity commander (e.g., NAVAIR, MICOM, ASD, or ESD) must serve as active program manager; lower-ranking senior military officers and civilians, well trained and experienced in the acquisition process, will be needed to gather and analyze data and implement program decisions. The commodity commanders must be highly skilled in the acquisition process and business management, and committed to effective *and* efficient performance; there is too much at stake for on-the-job training in these positions.

Program Advocates

Army, Navy, and Air Force officers understandably consider the acquisition of new and more advanced arms a primary goal. Inherent in the military ethos — and appropriately so — is the assumption that the United States is in constant potential danger from foreign enemies. Accordingly, service men and women may be called upon at any time to defend their country. Military leaders follow a code of responsibility to ensure that their services are prepared to fight and to win. This code was unequivocally expressed by Gen. Douglas MacArthur in a 1962 address to West Point cadets.

> Yours is the profession of arms, the will to win, the sure knowledge that in war there is no substitute for victory. That if you lose, the nation will be destroyed, that the very obsession of your public service must be duty, honor, country.[12]

Many DOD officials, inculcated in this code, find their dual roles in the acquisition process often in conflict. They are promoters of particular programs as well as guardians of public funds. On most defense programs there are always more demands for technical features than there are funds to achieve them, requiring the program manager to promote the program, postpone identification of problems, and seek additional funds. DOD officials, when performing that role, are often perceived as defensive, less than candid, promoters and liaison officers rather than prudent buyers. On the other hand, a guardian of public funds must seek early identification of problems; establish challenging schedule, cost, and technical performance goals; and conduct ongoing negotiations with contractors, maintaining options to reward or penalize performance.

These conflicting roles apply to government program managers, plant representatives, contracting officers, service Secretaries, Assistant Secretaries, and all others in positions of leadership within the Defense Department. The problem is compounded by the prevailing practice of linking promotion (for a military officer) or military cooperation (for a civilian Secretary or Assistant Secretary) with success as a program advocate. During the past two decades, effective management performance — cost and schedule control and rigorous contract administration — have seldom been rewarded. Indeed, if good management results in exposing problems in a program to public or congressional criticism, a defense manager is likely to be criticized by his superiors.

In this environment, industry managers often receive conflicting signals from the various management levels of the Defense Department. The official message contractors hear is to control costs. Unofficially, it often is to spend every available dollar and try to obtain more. Further, because defense contract profits are negotiated largely as a percentage of costs, contractors have only one way to earn profits comparable to those in the commercial marketplace: increase sales and keep investment at a minimum. Once a company has committed a major portion of its resources to defense development and production programs, it is locked in a life-and-death struggle for ever-larger programs and more contracts. Industry, too, begins to dispense information to serve its own needs, thus often finding itself allied with its customer, the Defense Department. The role of program advocate is important to the service, the Defense Department, and the nation, but it should be performed by the service headquarters and by the using command, not by the government program manager and his superiors in the acquisition organization. Failure to separate these functions places acquisition managers in the untenable position of carrying responsibility for three different roles — chief salesman, evaluator, and negotiator — roles that have proven to be incompatible for any one person to perform.

The Need for Acquisition Careers

For decades, many have observed that most government program managers and their staffs are intelligent, hard working, and dedicated. I agree with that observation. I add that program managers, along with most other defense managers, genuinely want to acquire advanced weapon systems that meet performance standards at reasonable costs. But in practice, too few government managers know much about contractor financial incentives or controlling costs, schedules, and technical performance in large industrial firms. As a result, government managers rarely make the difficult decisions required to create and reward lean industrial organizations that resist the expanding desires of functional managers in government and industry.

In reflecting on my discussions with government and industry managers, I conclude that people assigned to key acquisition positions — at every level in the Defense Department, from program managers to appointees in the Office of the Secretary of Defense — are often seriously unprepared for their jobs. One of the conclusions from studying the acquisition process is that managing it requires specific knowledge and skills well beyond those of many recent Assistant Secretaries, senior military officers, program managers, and congressional staff members. There has always been an implicit assumption within the Defense Department that people with little or no advanced training and experience in the management of large industrial programs could function effectively at any management level. This assumption has been a key factor leading to the disappointing results of virtually every improvement program in the past twenty-seven years. If the complex defense acquisition process is to be managed more effectively and efficiently, the Defense Department must develop better trained and more experienced acquisition managers and support staffs to manage the complex, continuing negotiations between one part of government and another and between government and large industrial firms. There is no realistic alternative to providing clear acquisition career paths for these people — both military and civilian — with genuine promotion opportunities comparable to those available in operational career fields. Short of these steps, the department can expect another decade or more of studies and recommendations for improvements, with little accomplished in the way of lasting change.

The term *acquisition,* as the Defense Department uses it to define military and civilian career fields, is so broad that it no longer defines a specialty. In fact, the term now refers to almost any function that has to do with a weapon system or a piece of equipment. If a primary objective is to improve the schedule, cost, and technical performance of major acquisition programs, the specialty should be defined as procurement, contracting, production, and R&D management — fields with substantial ongoing interactions with industrial firms. As in industry, the development of highly qualified program managers requires focused career paths, progressing from technical work to assignments at laboratories, program offices, and plant representative offices, to full program management responsibility for small programs, and ultimately for large programs. There is no time left to become expert in a military operational specialty as well.

It seems only reasonable that the heads of the Army, Navy, and Air Force acquisition organizations should be among the most qualified acquisition managers available, based on many years of training and practical experience. When selected for these positions, they should have sole responsibility for materiel acquisition *and* personnel recruitment, selection, and assignments. To separate these responsibilities is to recreate the problems of the past three decades.

Program managers' careers should follow a path similar to those of Army brigade commanders, Air Force wing commanders, and Navy wing and ship commanders. Not only do operations jobs have well-defined career paths that include training and practical experience, but they are centrally managed by formal career development systems to ensure that all supervisors are fully aware of the career requirements.[13]

As late as 1987, there was insufficient attention to career development for most military officers and civilians assigned to defense acquisition. The Air Force has developed a promising acquisition career program (for nonrated officers) that serves as an example of what needs to be done. The Navy uses a centralized approach through their Weapon Systems Acquisition Management (WSAM) and Material Professional (MP) programs, but they fall far short of the goal, from a career development perspective, for unrestricted line officers. The 1983 Army Materiel Acquisition Management (MAM) program lacks central control and authority and provides too little training and practical experience too late in Army careers.[14]

Although the twenty-week Defense Systems Management College course is an important first step in training program managers and their staffs, much more needs to be done to train potential managers to be capable of achieving an acceptable level of performance. The current policy of limiting this training to 138 days, because of regulations for moving-expense reimbursement, must be changed. Compared with the multibillion dollars involved in the acquisition programs and the opportunities for savings, moving expenses are trivial.

Future program managers should be required to complete a minimum of one full year of formal training in which they study hundreds of examples of the dilemmas both they and contracting officers will encounter. They should analyze these dilemmas and discuss the strengths and weaknesses of the alternatives available for dealing with them. Instructors skilled in conducting the practical training — those comfortable with discussion sessions requiring practical knowledge of the field — will require attractive compensation. The training program should develop the "wise buyer" skills needed to resolve the multitude of complex day-to-day problems in major R&D and production programs. The emphasis should be on making analyses and decisions, using simulation exercises, case studies, role playing, and other techniques. An internship in a program management office would ideally precede *and* follow the one-year practical training program; carefully chosen program managers would serve as supervisors.

Civil Service Personnel

Government civil service and military positions in acquisition have few similarities. Just as few military program managers remain in one job long enough to develop the required management expertise, so too many civil servants remain for so long that they resist innovation and change.

Inadequate professional management training is a serious handicap for civil service personnel. Those who devote their careers to program management and procurement need a comprehensive training program. But there should be an effective screening process for selecting candidates for these demanding positions; only those with the requisite talent and motivation should be accepted. In addition, a personnel board, comprising senior military and civilian acquisition officials, should review applicants for all major positions and be authorized and motivated to remove civil servants whose performance is marginal or inadequate. The board should also have the authority to provide significant financial rewards for outstanding performance. New senior executive service (SES) positions should be established to encourage ambitious and talented people to remain in the acquisition field.

There are several precedents for changing civil service rules for promotion and tenure. The National Security Council, the Central Intelligence Agency, and the Congress operate with personnel systems far less rigid than the civil service system imposed on the Defense Department by Congress. None of them is hampered by tenure regulations or unrealistic restrictions on the number of authorized senior positions.

Civil service acquisition managers face significant barriers at all levels. For example, there have been repeated and strong recommendations (again, from the Packard Commission) to require that the Office of Personnel Management (OPM) categorize selected civilian procurement positions as "professional" (in contrast to the current categorization of "administrative"). The distinction here involves the education, training, and experience to be required of candidates for these positions. But OPM has so far resisted this recommendation. Similarly, in civilian engineering and technical management positions, rigid pay scales and seniority-based promotion standards of the civil service serve as disincentives to continued employment by highly qualified people throughout the government acquisition system. Thus, Congress should establish an alternative personnel management system for key acquisition personnel that would provide greater flexibility in status, pay, and qualifications of civilian employees, particularly at the senior level. The successful China Lake project, in which key civilians received pay incentives and promotions based on performance, is worth emulating.[15]

David Packard summarized the current state of the civil service in a July 1987 letter to President Reagan.

Personnel policy is the keystone of virtually all of these reforms. With able people operating them, even second-rate organizational structures and procedures can be made to work; and without able people, even first-rate ones will fail. Last year an effort was made to obtain a government-wide reform of the Civil Service system. That effort failed. This year we would urge in the strongest possible terms that specific legislation be proposed to ensure that senior civilian acquisition personnel in the Department of Defense — scientists, engineers, contracting officers and the like — can be promoted, paid, and educated adequately. The present system does not even allow for educational criteria for contracting officers. We pointed out last year how the Navy's China Lake experiment had thoroughly tested and pointed the way to a new system for senior career civilians in acquisition.[16]

Civil service personnel, who rarely have opportunities similar to those of military officers for supervisory positions, are often given routine tasks demanding minimal commitment. This situation is a waste of talent of outstanding civil servants but no more than appropriate for many whose performance is mediocre or inadequate. Unless the civil service and OPM can establish higher personnel standards and revise regulations to enable quick removal of mediocre performers, defense acquisition programs will appeal primarily to those satisfied with the present low level of responsibility.

The Revolving Door

Prudent military officers, encouraged by the military retirement system, often leave the service between ages forty-five and fifty-five for positions in private industry, where their knowledge and skills can be usefully employed. Despite the urgent need in the government for well-qualified, knowledgeable acquisition managers, there are at present few incentives for talented officers to remain in the military service longer than twenty to twenty-five years. The defense industry, on the other hand, provides compelling incentives: rewarding salaries and career status.

The goal of obtaining a job in industry can easily have a subtle effect on a person's performance while in government service. Industry positions are offered, understandably, to those who have demonstrated an appreciation of the particular problems and commitments of industry. Unfortunately, government and industry goals regarding costs are rarely identical. To address these differences, acquisition careers must be designed to attract officers to remain five to ten years longer than at present.

If, as has been the case for nearly three decades, the military promotion system will not provide attractive promotion opportunities to flag rank, then the Defense Department should provide other incentives, such as additional pay. If an extra $15,000 per year were paid to selected military officers (at the rank of 0-6 and above) and career regulations permitted them to remain in the acquisition field, incentives to retire and join the defense industry would be greatly minimized. The extra cost would be negligible compared with the benefit of retaining experienced senior managers.

If an incentive pay plan were adopted, there would need to be a group of senior acquisition officials to determine the eligibility of those choosing an acquisition career. Otherwise, program management could become a haven for officers not qualified to enter the competitive world of private industry. Selection for these financial incentives could offset, at least partially, the lack of promotion opportunities in the acquisition field.

Such a proposal is not without precedent. Military officers on flight status and submarine duty as well as medical and dental officers and other specially trained officers currently receive incentive pay. Indeed, Sweden's government acquisition agency addresses the problem of attracting and retaining senior people — military and civilian — by a special law that allows a salary increase for crucial acquisition positions. Thus, a Swedish colonel serving as a program manager can receive a significantly higher salary than other colonels and even the director general of the agency. This incentive provides prestige and draws highly qualified, experienced people to senior acquisition positions.[17]

A second alternative for enhancing the acquisition career field would involve the establishment of a separate military service for acquisition managers, which has been done with considerable success in France. The service would need to include elite managers dedicated to and capable of achieving the goals of the acquisition process. Applicants would face an aggressive screening program to remove those who do not meet the high standards of the service. Advancement would be based strictly on management ability and performance. Only senior acquisition officers, with no interference from combat arms officers, would control assignments and promotions. In addition, the service would need a sufficient number of colonel or captain and general or admiral positions to reward officers for outstanding performance.

Were there a more attractive government career in acquisition management, it would then be possible to minimize the conflicts associated with widespread military retirements to industry while preserving the rights of officers to full-length careers. The basic goal of any legislative remedy must be restoring the integrity of our military procurement system.

Incentives

The Defense Department customarily does business with an inverted system of rewards and penalties. Contractors are often rewarded for higher than planned program costs with increased sales, contributions to overhead, and profits. The system also encourages government managers to place a far higher priority on gaining congressional approval to begin a new weapon program or obtain additional funding for an ongoing program than on controlling costs for existing programs.[18] The acquisition cost problems of the 1980s are not aberrations; they are the result of many government and industry participants reacting in accord with the distorted rewards and penalties inherent in the acquisition process.[19]

New contract forms, better planning, control and reporting systems, improved cost-estimating systems, and change control systems are unlikely to be effective unless government managers are skilled in the implementation and use of these techniques and are rewarded, along with the contractors, for their effective implementation.

Encouragement is not enough; improvements in management require significant changes in the system of rewards and penalties. Reluctance to establish more appropriate incentives has been a serious deficiency in most DOD improvement programs during the past three decades.[20] As defense analyst Richard Stubbing has observed, contractors should be rewarded with higher profits for complying with schedules, satisfying promised performance standards, and delivering goods and services at or below contracted cost. Conversely, penalties, in the form of reduced profits, should be imposed for late delivery, substandard work, and cost overruns. Prospects for obtaining future contracts should be closely linked to performance on existing contracts.[21]

Equally fundamental changes should be made in the incentives applicable to government program managers. Government program managers should be rewarded for effective use of formal and informal analysis and control techniques; early identification of problems affecting cost, schedule, and technical performance; and success in achieving program objectives and maintaining control of program costs. At present, managers who handle crises effectively are given high performance ratings. Often, however, timely action could have corrected problems before the crisis. Because preventive action requires day-to-day attention to management detail over a period of years, inexperienced supervisors controlling rewards are unlikely to appreciate the work of a good manager. As a result, there is often little motivation to exercise rigorous, systematic control.

One effective way of measuring management performance is by evaluating a manager's use of contingency funds. Such funds, which could be held in reserve by senior defense officials, would be available only on request. Program managers who find it necessary to apply for contingency funding would be rated negatively, unless able to prove just cause. (Just cause could include the decision to expand an R&D program to reduce production or support costs.) Those able to remain within budget would be rated positively.

Many in government and industry *want* to improve the acquisition process. But it is unrealistic to expect any lasting improvement if an appropriate system of incentives and disincentives is not established and enforced. For example:

Unless changes are made in the contractor source selection process, which makes optimistically low cost estimates a significant advantage in competing for a contract, it is useless to discuss realistic contractor proposals. The source selection process must give far more weight to realistic cost estimates and the contractor's record of past performance.

Unless changes are made in the current profit system that demands higher costs as a prerequisite for higher profits, it is futile to expect lower costs. Because profits are largely based on cost, there is little economic motivation for contractors to reduce direct or indirect costs. The profit system needs a major overhaul to relate profit more to contract performance than to the level of costs.[22]

Unless changes are made in the current military personnel system that makes short-term assignments necessary for military officers to acquire the number and variety of assignments required for promotion, any significant reduction in personnel turnover in defense program offices is unlikely.

Unless changes are made in the current OSD and congressional practice of routinely accepting program stretch-outs as a tactic for funding new programs, it is unrealistic to advocate economical production rates.

Unless changes are made in the current DOD practice of waiving training requirements and offering only short training courses, which limit coverage to introductory rather than in-depth treatment of important subjects, it is unrealistic to expect improved training for acquisition managers.

Unless changes are made in military careers that currently provide few opportunities beyond age forty-five or fifty, it is unrealistic to expect military officers not to seek a second career in the defense industry. In addressing this problem, DOD needs to listen to lieutenant colonels and colonels and Navy commanders and captains to learn their views on the advantages and disadvantages of the acquisition career field.

Without genuine promotion opportunities for those who make the difficult decisions associated with successful negotiating and wise buying, it is unrealistic to expect to retain in government service experienced program managers able to do much more than promote their programs, prepare progress reports, and conduct briefings.

Incentives and disincentives are clearly key factors in improved defense acquisition management. In the commercial sector, rewards accrue to those who manage effectively and efficiently the resources assigned to them, and who demonstrate high profitability. In the government sector, because there are no profit and loss statements by which to measure efficiency, the benefits from improved management are difficult to measure. Unfortunately, efforts to improve efficiency often generate political opposition from those who benefit from the existing inefficient practices.[23]

Retrospective

Why is the system so resistant to change? What will be required to ensure that five years from now the Congress, the Pentagon, the press, the public, and the defense industry are not once again discussing and responding to the same problems? Some say there is little reason to change. The problem of the 1980s, in the view of some defense officials, is that the Defense Department has been unable to obligate funds fast enough. In 1985, the department held a number of meetings on the topic of improving "program execution." The interpretation of that phrase, however, was not "improving the efficiency of the acquisition process." Rather, it meant finding ways to obligate funds more quickly.[24]

Former Defense Secretary Robert McNamara described the vicious circle associated with changing the acquisition process.

> Neither political party can afford to challenge the military-industrial complex until the public understands the economic, social, and, indeed, military damage that the present system can do. But the public is not likely to grasp the danger unless the system is challenged vigorously, repeatedly, and credibly.[25]

Reform is not simply, as many believe, a matter of spending less money; it requires that funds be spent wisely. Efficient managers do not cut costs arbitrarily; they demand and vigorously enforce an effective expenditure of resources.

The enduring problems in the defense acquisition process cannot be attributed to a lack of ideas for reform. In the past three decades, there have been numerous ideas, many of them well conceived. What is missing is a willingness to make lasting improvements in military and civilian careers and in the reward and penalty systems. Few members of Congress or the public understand the counterproductive incentives inherent in the present procurement and personnel systems.

The immediate effect of improved efficiency would probably be a smaller job force for both industry and the Defense Department. This is not attractive to Congress or to defense contractors, and certainly not to the men and women — voters — who depend on the defense industry for their jobs.

If reform is to be achieved, DOD managers must be persuaded that their organizations will benefit from improved management. Reform is unlikely to occur until external pressures — from Congress or the public — make it clear that the answer to cost growth is not simply appropriating more federal funds.

Reform may be stalled until forced by an intolerable federal deficit, increased funding requirements of the Social Security system, or the needs of other domestic programs in areas such as health, education, and environmental protection. For without a sustained sense of urgency, any imperatives for reform are unlikely to be successful.

During a 1985 hearing of the Senate Armed Services Committee, Prof. Ralph Nash, after suggesting improvements in acquisition management, offered his appraisal of the likelihood of change.

> Let me close by saying I have no illusions. None of the things I have suggested can be accomplished. The Pentagon is fully staffed with experts on why significant changes are impossible.
>
> Some of my suggestions might even take legislation, and nobody would suggest that. The key ingredient that is missing is management will.
>
> I wish you luck in your task, but I feel the best you will get is more studies of the problem.[26]

"Quick fixes" during the past three decades have usually been counterproductive or have led nowhere. Frequently, the easy solution one year would be an attempt to improve cost estimates and next year to control contract changes or contractor overhead costs. In the following year, efforts would be made to increase the proportion of fixed-price contracts or impose new reporting requirements on contractors. Because the goals shift from year to year, and are not related to a comprehensive plan, fresh problems are likely to appear in the areas not receiving attention, prompting managers either to suppress them or impose short-term solutions.

There will be no lasting improvements in the defense acquisition process until military commanders, beginning with the chiefs of staff, are convinced that the high cost of weapons and equipment is a serious problem that must be solved. The mandate to change must come from the top; only then will there be changes in the daily activities of defense managers.

The Need for Extended Follow-up Action

A persistent problem associated with previous attempts at improvement has been the failure of management to take vigorous action to ensure implementation of the best recommendations. As noted in a 1981 Navy acquisition study, "It is common practice for one level of management to direct a lower level to implement a set of suggestions, and then walk away."[27] Consequently, much activity is directed toward launching public relations campaigns to prove implementation instead of monitoring implementation efforts and following up to ensure that lasting change occurs.

Gilbert W. Fitzhugh, chairman of the President's 1970 blue ribbon defense panel, noted that when studies are completed and committee members depart, those who remain to assess and implement recommendations are those whose "toes have been stepped on" in the findings. There is, not unexpectedly, a noticeable lack of support. Those responsible for implementation need an advocate remaining on the scene to lend support to the findings with understanding and conviction.[28] The report of the 1986 Packard Commission has encountered the same problem. In early 1987, a Pentagon official told us:

> The official word is, the Packard Commission recommendations have already been implemented. Have they been completed? No. It will take as long as the next reorganization to implement them.

It is clear that the military and civilian leadership will need to be unambiguous in declaring the steps to be taken to improve management of the acquisition process and persistent in the follow-up to ensure that the changes take place.

Prospective

Because of the immense size of the defense acquisition budget, any changes or improvements in the process have the potential for achieving significant savings. Estimates range from $10 billion to $40 billion per year, without reducing the output of weapons and equipment.[29] In light of the opportunities to be gained from stabilizing funding, reducing contract changes, and adjusting the cost incentives for government and industry managers, I believe potential savings are closer to the upper end of that range — $40 billion per year.

After receiving the National Security Industrial Association's (NSIA) Forrestal Award for dedicated public service, then Deputy Defense Secretary David Packard offered, in a message prophetic of the 1986 Packard Commission report, a solution to the cost problems of the acquisition process.

> What is the solution? We are going to have to stop this problem of people playing games with each other. Games that will destroy us if we do not bring them to a halt.
> Let's take the case of the F-14. The only sensible course is to hold the

contractor to his contract. Although some companies may be forced to suffer financially because of this concept, it will not be a major disaster to the country. It will be a major disaster to the country if we cannot get the military-industrial complex to play the game straight. Until and unless we can stop this attitude, we are going to continue to waste the taxpayers' dollars — get less defense for the dollars we spend.

Quite simply it means the Army, the Navy, the Air Force and the Marines must put the welfare of America ahead of the welfare of their respective services in peacetime as well as in war. It means the great industrial corporations that forge the seams of our military strength must put the long-term gains of America ahead of the short-term gains of their respective organizations. It means that Congress should address America's security policy, stay out of day-to-day administrative problems, and discourage game-playing between the services and the business community.[30]

In 1971, after nearly three years of sustained effort to reform the defense acquisition process, Mr. Packard left the Pentagon, disappointed at the bureaucracy's successful resistance to change.

It may well be that the imperative for reform in the acquisition process must come from a coalition of ordinary voters who want their tax revenues used to solve domestic problems as well as to ensure national defense, a Congress alert to the need for vigorous and balanced control of defense activity, and a military establishment patriotic about national defense needs instead of parochial concerns. Such an alliance could bring stability and efficiency to a system long in trouble. Failure to act now guarantees a continuation of the past problems: increased defense spending, reduced defense capability, and increased risks of a major financial crisis for the country.

There is little likelihood that the costs of major programs will stabilize or decrease unless skilled government managers, at all levels, have a strong commitment to the changes required to accomplish that objective. Minor adjustments or corrections to the present acquisition process simply will not accomplish this vital job, nor will major reorganizations that seek to increase the decision-making authority of managers who lack the training and experience to manage the acquisition process efficiently.

Finally, the instrument of change must be a strong Secretary of Defense and an acquisition executive, chosen for industrial experience, knowledge of the acquisition process, and commitment to achieve an efficient as well as an effective acquisition process.

Notes

1. This is the view of many well-known figures. See, for example, U.S. Senate, testimony of Norman Augustine, President of Martin Marietta and former Under Secretary of the Army, hearing before the Task Force on Selected Defense Procurement Matters of the Committee on Armed Services, "Defense Procurement Process," September 20, 1984, Part 2, p. 149. Don Fuqua, retired congressman from Florida and current President of the Aerospace Industries Association, stated: "If anything, the situation is getting worse." Cited in "Pentagon Seen Changing Little in Arms-Buying," *New York Times,* July 15, 1987, p. 1.
2. J. Ronald Fox, *Arming America: How the U.S. Buys Weapons* (Boston: Division of Research, Harvard Business School, 1974), p. 449.
3. John C. Yoder and Jan Horbaly, "Department of Defense Procurement Alternatives," paper prepared for the Defense Acquisition Study, Center for Strategic and International Studies, Georgetown University, March 17, 1986, pp. 15–17.
4. Richard J. Bednar and John T. Jones, Jr., "The Role of the DOD Contracting Officer," Draft Report of the American Bar Association (ABA) Section of Public Contract Law, Ad Hoc Committee, John E. Cavanagh, Chairman, January 11, 1987, p. 120.
5. Richard A. Stubbing, *The Defense Game* (New York: Harper & Row, 1986), pp. 410–412.
6. William D. Brown, Paul J. Kern, L. Kirk Lewis, and John G. Zeirdt, "Acquisition Management — The Role and the Reality," National Security Program Report, John F. Kennedy School of Government, Harvard University, June 1987, p. 160.
7. Ibid., p. 156.
8. U.S. Senate, testimony of John D. Rittenhouse, Executive Vice-President, RCA Aerospace and Defense (representing the Electronic Industries Association), hearing before the Subcommittee on Defense Acquisition Policy of the Committee on Armed Services, "Implementation of the 1984 Defense Procurement Legislation," November 7, 1985, p. 234.
9. Jacques S. Gansler, "Strengthening Government Acquisition Management through Selected Use of Experienced Industrial Managers," paper prepared for the Procurement Round Table, June 11, 1987.
10. Russell Murray II, "Congressional Actions to Improve the Defense Acquisition Process," paper prepared for the Defense Acquisition Study, Center for Strategic and International Studies, Georgetown University, February 19, 1986, p. 2.
11. Gansler, "Strengthening Government Acquisition Management."
12. Gen. Douglas MacArthur, Address to West Point cadets, May 12, 1962.
13. Brown et al., "Acquisition Management," p. 153.
14. Ibid.
15. Gansler, "Strengthening Government Acquisition Management," pp. 2–3.
16. David Packard, letter to the President of the United States, July 10, 1987.
17. Gansler, "Strengthening Government Acquisition Management," p. 4.

18. Charles Mohr, "Critics See Key Flaw in Arms Cost Controls," *New York Times,* May 18, 1985, p. 1.

19. Arthur E. Fitzgerald, Deputy for Management Systems, Office of the Assistant Secretary of the Air Force, quoted in the *New York Times,* May 18, 1985, p. 8.

20. *Boston Globe,* July 27, 1986, pp. 73–74. The reluctance of members of the Packard Commission to recommend new incentives was most clearly seen at a press conference on July 2, 1986, at which Mr. Packard, presenting the final report, said that waste and fraud in defense industries should be rooted out by "self-discipline," not by government regulation.

21. Stubbing, *The Defense Game,* p. 416.

22. U.S. Senate, testimony of Lt. Gen. James Stansberry, USAF (Retired) (formerly commander, Electronics Systems Division, Air Force Systems Command), before the Subcommittee on Defense Acquisition Policy of the Committee on Armed Services, "Defense Procurement Process," February 20, 1985, p. 20.

23. Stubbing, *The Defense Game,* p. 58.

24. Mohr, "Critics See Key Flaws in Arms Cost Controls," *New York Times,* May 18, 1985.

25. *Los Angeles Times,* July 10, 1983, cited in Glenn Pascall, *The Trillion Dollar Budget* (Seattle: University of Washington Press, 1985), p. 172.

26. U.S. Senate, testimony of Professor Ralph C. Nash, Jr., professor of law, George Washington University, before the Subcommittee on Defense Acquisition Policy of the Committee on Armed Services, "Defense Procurement Process," February 20, 1985, p. 21.

27. Joseph F. Grosson, Joseph Augusta, John C. McKeown, and Lt. Comdr. Edwin Wicklander, "Completed Acquisition Cost Study Depicts an Iceberg of Knowns and Unknowns," *Program Manager,* May-June 1981, pp. 10–13.

28. U.S. Senate, testimony of Gilbert W. Fitzhugh, Chairman of the President's 1970 Blue Ribbon Defense Panel, before the Committee on Armed Services.

29. For example, President's Private Sector Survey on Cost Control (known as the Grace Commission), Summary Report, January 15, 1984; James Morrison, "Business Executives for National Security, Washington, D.C.," *Newsweek,* March 24, 1986; Jacques S. Gansler, "Program Instability: Causes, Costs, and Cures," paper prepared for the Defense Acquisition Study, Center for Strategic and International Studies, Georgetown University, March 1, 1986; Kim R. Holmes, Policy Analyst, "How to Save Money at the Pentagon While Improving the Nation's Defense," Heritage Foundation Background Paper; Robert Foelber, "Cutting the High Cost of Weapons," Heritage Foundation, Washington, D.C., March 16, 1982.

30. David Packard, Address to the National Security Industrial Association Forrestal Awards for dedicated public service, Los Angeles, CA, March 9, 1972.

APPENDIX

Excerpts from thirty-two reports (some paraphrased) of cost increases, inappropriate charges, and other problems associated with the defense acquisition process.

February 1983

A team led by five retired Air Force generals asked Air Force Secretary Verne Orr to study that service's procurement policies.

The generals asserted that "if we continue to do business as usual," the Air Force will be unable to buy as many planes and missiles as it plans, even if Congress votes every penny President Reagan requests. Costs of major weapon systems, the generals found, are continuing to rise far more rapidly than can be accounted for by simple price inflation.

The Air Force, say the generals, often grossly underestimates the cost of weapons, orders more than it can pay for, then juggles the production programs in a manner that plays havoc with efficiency. Also, it has a habit of "entertaining full-scale development with immature technology." Their conclusion: The Air Force should cancel some weapons-buying programs and concentrate on those it considers top priority.[1]

September 1983

Significant cost growth has resulted in decreases in the number of the Army's *AH-64 helicopters* to be procured.

The cost of the *Army Helicopter Improvement Program* has more than doubled; additional increases can be anticipated because its capabilities have not been demonstrated and because of program uncertainties.

The cost of the Army's *Patriot* air defense missile program has nearly doubled in the last two and one-half years, and the causes are still present, making further cost increases likely. Available funding may not be sufficient to maintain the planned procurement schedule.

The estimated cost of the Navy's *DDG-51 destroyer* has increased to the point where the Chief of Naval Operations has said the design proposed is not affordable and is not a lower-cost alternative to the CG-47, as the Navy had intended.

The Air Force's *Antisatellite weapon system* was envisioned as a relatively inexpensive (about $3.6 billion), quick way to meet mission requirements, but it has become more complex and costly than originally envisioned, potentially costing tens of billions of dollars.

The Army's *Extended Range and Wasp Wide-Area Antiarmor Munitions* will cost $6.3 billion more than initially expected.

The Air Force's *Advanced Medium-Range Air-to-Air Missile* acquisition cost has more than tripled since concept validation began three and one-half years ago; this does not include some known elements that could add significantly to the costs.[2]

June 1984

The cost of a single *MX missile* increased from $57.4 million in 1982 to $102.6 million in 1983, a 79 percent boost in a single year. Congress's General Accounting Office estimates that the current five-year defense plan as a whole will cost $173 billion to $324 billion more than the administration's budget projections.[3]

August 1984

The total cost of 32 major weapon systems is running much higher than the Pentagon had anticipated just eight months ago.

But an internal Pentagon budget document by Franklin C. Spinney (Office of the Secretary of Defense), dated June 6, 1984, indicates that the problem still exists. Some examples cited in the memo:

The expected cost of each of the Army's *Pershing nuclear missiles,* now being deployed in Western Europe, has shot up by 82 percent since January. As a result, the Pentagon now plans to cut back by 72 percent the number it had planned to produce in fiscal 1986.

The *DIVAD air-defense system* will cost 24 percent more than predicted last January, causing an 18 percent production cutback.

The Air Force's *Advanced Medium-Range Air-to-Air Missile (AMRAAM)* program will cost 400 percent more than had been predicted just eight months ago, and the Pentagon now plans to buy 91 percent fewer of them next year.

The Navy's *MK48 torpedo* program will overrun expected costs next year by 220 percent, forcing a 15 percent cutback in fiscal 1986.[4]

February 1985

Retired Air Force General James Stansberry testified before the Senate Armed Services Committee: "The systems acquisition process functions in an environment that almost guarantees high costs. The system is overregulated, chokes on its own paper, is characterized by lack of decision and commitment, vacillation and change, inefficient production rates, and little motivation to modernize and reduce costs. In fact, given our institutional processes, it's remarkable we do as well as we in fact do."[5]

March 1985

According to testimony before the Oversight and Investigations Subcommittee of the House Energy and Commerce Committee, General Dynamics billed the Government for an $18,000 country club admissions fee, and the charge of boarding a company executive's dog at a kennel.[6]

March 1985

Senator Dan Quayle: Very briefly, how widespread is procurement fraud, from your vantage point?

Joseph Sherick, DOD Inspector General: Well, I would say this: I do not think it is rampant, but I think it is significant. . . . I would say there are about 1,000 cases under way at any one time.

Senator Quayle: Is there any one particular area of fraud that is somewhat common?

Sherick: Our priorities are placed this way: One, product substitution. This is where people sell us shoddy material, junk. . . .

The second priority is cost mischarging. This occurs when the contractor gets up against the wall. He has cost-type government contracts and fixed-price commercial contracts. He sees that costs are overrunning on his commercial contracts, and he arbitrarily tells his people: Put your labor against the government contracts.

Our third area of priority is defective pricing. The contractor says: "We will sell you material and equipment at the lowest price we charge our best customers." He does not; he hikes the prices.[7]

April 1985

The Defense Department disclosed that its 84 largest weapon projects will cost $25.1 billion more than was estimated three months ago. . . .

The costs of the Army's *Patriot air defense missile* program were increased by $842.5 million, reflecting higher production costs.

The *Advanced Medium-Range Air-to-Air Missile* was estimated to cost $1.7 billion more than the last report indicated.

The Navy's decision to increase the number of *A-6E aircraft* it buys and upgrade the aircraft's design has added $3.5 billion to the estimated cost of this program.

Engineering changes in the *Tomahawk missile,* produced by General Dynamics Corporation, have boosted cost estimates by $774 million.[8]

April 1985

A federal grand jury indicted General Electric for allegedly defrauding the United States of $800,000 in nonreimbursable cost overruns, and the Pentagon has suspended GE from new defense contracts. Separately, the Secretary of the Air Force has just demanded that United Technologies and GE return millions of dollars of "unearned profits" from defense contracts, and the House Armed Services Committee has announced its intention to "audit" seven major defense contractors.[9]

May 1985

General Electric Company admitted that it illegally claimed more than $800,000 in cost overruns on a Minuteman Missile contract over three years and was fined $1 million, the maximum, by a federal judge in Philadelphia. . . . Last year government business accounted for one-fifth of GE's sales of nearly $28 billion. GE at first denied wrongdoing, but the admission by a former manager that he ordered the illegal claims and forged time cards forced the company to change its plea.

Because GE had agreed in one contract to a fixed price for part of the work, some of the added costs could not legally be passed along to the Pentagon, and the company faced possible losses. To cut down on the red ink, GE managers decided to shift the overruns to different contracts under which the Government would pay the added costs. Their method: falsify workers' time cards without their knowledge.[10]

May 1985

During the military buildup of the early 1980s, the Congressional Budget Office found that the budget for *aircraft* increased by 75 percent, but the number of planes bought increased by less than 9 percent. The budget for *missiles* increased by 91 percent but purchased only 6 percent more missiles. The Pentagon bought 30 percent more *tanks,* but spent 147 percent more to do it.[11]

July 1985

On April 24, 1985, DOD Inspector General Joseph H. Sherick testified before Congress that he had 45 of DOD's top 100 contractors under investigation for possible criminal activities, investigating them on 93 allegations of wrongdoing. General Dynamics Corporation was being investigated for overcharging, receiving kickbacks from subcontractors, and six other charges. Litton Industries, Inc. was being investigated for kickbacks, bribery, and four other allegations, ranging from bid rigging to false claims. Nine of the top ten DOD contractors were on the list of contractors under investigation.[12]

Contractors and 1985 Awards	Allegations
McDonnell Douglas $7.7 billion	Cost mischarges
Rockwell International $6.2 billion	Cost and labor mischarges
General Dynamics $6.0 billion	Cost and labor mischarges, subcontractor kickbacks, product substitution, security compromises, defective pricing, cost duplication, false claims
Lockheed $5.0 billion	Labor mischarges
Boeing $4.6 billion	Cost and labor mischarges, supply accountability
General Electric $4.5 billion	False claims, defective pricing, labor mischarges, product substitution
United Technologies $3.2 billion	Gratuities, subcontractor kickbacks, cost mischarges, bribery, defective pricing
Raytheon $3.1 billion	Labor mischarges, product substitution
Litton Industries $2.4 billion	Bribery, subcontractor kickbacks, labor and cost mischarges, false claims, bid rigging
Grumman $2.4 billion	Cost mischarges
Martin Marietta $2.3 billion	Subcontractor kickbacks, cost mischarges
Westinghouse $1.9 billion	Cost mischarges
Sperry $1.6 billion	Labor and cost mischarges, defective pricing
Honeywell $1.4 billion	Diversion of government property, bid rigging
Ford Motor $1.1 billion	Defective pricing, labor mischarges, falsification of performance records
Eaton $1.1 billion	Conflict of interest, gratuities, cost mischarges
TRW $1.0 billion	Defective pricing, cost mischarges
Texas Instruments $1.0 billion	Product substitution

July 1985

The Army, formally disclosing a federal criminal investigation and allegations of overcharging, said yesterday that it is slashing in half monthly contract payments to Bell Helicopter Textron, Inc.

The decision, announced by Army Secretary John O. Marsh, Jr., will cut monthly payments the firm now receives from about $13 million to $6.5 million for contracts covering a number of Army helicopters.[13]

September 1985

In May 1984, Sperry Corporation pleaded guilty to criminal charges of falsifying $325,000 in payment requests submitted to the Air Force for work on the MX missile.[14]

September 1985

The Army's DIVAD program was canceled after $1.8 billion was spent on it. Joseph Sherick, the Pentagon's inspector general, stated, "The DIVAD program is an example of the failure of the process."[15]

October 1985

Rockwell International Corporation has agreed to plead guilty to criminal charges of submitting false bills and to pay $1.5 million in fines and penalties to settle allegations of overcharges on military contracts, federal investigators said. . . .

These sources said the company has agreed to plead guilty to felony charges involving about $300,000 in false labor bills. . . .

The proposed settlement calls for the company to pay the maximum $200,000 in criminal fines for the false bills, sources said. The rest of the money would consist of civil penalties and payments to reimburse the government for the cost of the investigation.[16]

December 1985

The Defense Logistics Agency's (DLA) General Counsel charged that there is a lack of integrity in defense contracting. The problem, in his view, is not just media hype or a few small businesses.

The DLA's General Counsel also charged that American business has become sloppy. He stated that it has long been unlawful to lie to the government, to cheat, and to misrepresent; yet, he pointed out that too many defense corporations have done just that by mischarging costs, and even making false certifications of metal content in products provided to the government. Too often, in the past, when these incidents were discovered, the usual industry response has been an offer to replace the defective product, or refund the amount improperly charged. This practice of waiting to get caught and then attempting to dismiss the case with some payback arrangement does little to encourage doing it right the first time. DLA's fraud program is aimed at changing this attitude and restoring integrity to defense contracting, from the beginning.

He said that frequently the comment is made that we (DLA) are talking about conditions that existed a couple of years ago. In the General Counsel's view this is not correct. He states, "we *have* a problem — not just *had*." The number of fraud cases opened has grown over the past ten years, from an average of 25 percent per year to 600 percent in 1985. Product substitution cases account for almost two-thirds of the total case load. Cost mischarging cases have also increased from less than 5 percent, in 1982, to almost 25 percent in 1985. He acknowledged that 15 percent of fraud cases involve DLA people accepting bribes and gratuities from industry. In 1984 there were 216 cases of debarment. In the first six months of 1985 the number of debarments had jumped to 516 cases.[17]

December 1985

General Dynamics Corporation and four present or former executives were indicted yesterday [by a federal grand jury in Los Angeles] for trying to defraud the government on the development of an ill-fated Army weapon.

The defendants were charged with trying to hide excess costs on a contract to develop the DIVAD antiaircraft gun by illegally shifting excess costs to two other General Dynamics accounts also paid for by the Defense Department. Justice Department officials said the overcharge amounted to $7.5 million on the $40-million Army contract, which was to build two prototypes of the gun.[18]

December 1985

Fred Newton, Acting Director of the Defense Contract Audit Agency (DCAA), states that industry minimizes the cost problems. Newton states that industry would have Defense believe there are no significant problems, that the problems identified are merely incidents of waste arising from unintentional errors.

Newton says DCAA has a different perspective on the problem. In DCAA's view there is a significant amount of plain unadulterated fraud in defense contracts. Too many excuses are being offered by industry. Rather than recognizing the reality of the situation, industry just isn't doing enough to install strong systems of internal control to prevent fraud. Finally, if the taxpayers' interests are to be protected, Newton feels that strong, aggressive government action is necessary.

Newton pointed out that the number of fraud cases are increasing:

- In 1982 DCAA made 39 fraud referrals.
- In 1983 the number had risen to 60.
- In 1984 126 fraud referrals were made.

And in 1985, up to 10 December, the number had increased to 199. Newton challenged anyone who felt that 199 incidents of fraud in one year was insignificant to just ask a taxpayer.

Newton found that the incidents are not simple errors. Several examples were given to support this conclusion.

Contractors were charging for work never performed, and making false statements, including personal loans, vacation trips, clothing and other charges in overhead.[19]

1986

As David Packard explained soon after leaving his post as Deputy Defense Secretary in 1972, "I am convinced, after spending three years in the Pentagon, that the industry is grossly overstaffed and very inefficient by any sound managerial standards."[20]

And industry performance has certainly not improved since then. Returning as chairman of the 1985–86 Presidential Commission examining defense management, he concluded that the situation had gotten much worse.[21]

February 1986

At $2.36 million a copy, for example, the *M-1 tank* now costs 45 percent more than projected in 1981.

The *Bradley fighting vehicle* will cost 64 percent more.

The *F/A-18 fighter attack aircraft* now costs $33 million apiece, a 58 percent increase over 1981.

Some experts note that the prices of the Air Force's *F-15s* and *F-16s* have jumped 50 percent beyond inflation in the last four years.[22]

March 1986

Numerous studies — by the GAO and others — have shown that during its lifetime, the average defense program's cost grows by between 50 and 100 percent — depending upon how inflation and quantity changes are accounted for. This program cost growth is generally accompanied by an average program delivery slippage in the range of 30 percent.[23]

April 1986

Navy Secretary John Lehman characterized the corporate philosophy of one of the top five defense contractors as "catch us if you can." The Pentagon's chief spokesman [Michael Burch] described the company's actions as "nauseating."[24]

June 1986

TRW Inc. is under criminal investigation by the Defense Department for alleged "substantial overcharges" to the government on defense contracts, the Justice Department disclosed.[25]

July 1986

The Packard Commission talks about the need for ethical improvement all around, but clearly it thinks the gravest waste and abuse come from a system that necessarily inflates costs, destroys motivation, and takes three times as long as it should to build new weapon systems.[26]

July 1986

Litton Industries Inc. said it agreed to pay about $15 million in restitution and penalties after pleading guilty to defrauding the Pentagon of $6.3 million in funds for military-electronics contracts. . . . The fraud involved 45 contracts awarded between 1975 and 1984 at a division of the company's Litton Systems Inc. unit in Springfield, Pa., outside Philadelphia. . . .

The former Vice-President of Finance and Administration of the division was charged with submitting false cost and pricing data to the military, in part by inflating prices for materials, charging the military twice for certain raw materials, and failing to disclose rebates from vendors. According to the U.S. Attorney's office, the fraudulent practices became known around the division as "chicken fat."

The case isn't the first time Litton has run up against Pentagon procurement rules. Last year (1985), Litton's Springfield division paid $160,000 to settle a civil suit that alleged Litton overcharged the Army more than $300,000 on helicopter navigation instruments between 1979 and 1981.[27]

July 1986

A congressional study, released by Republican Senators Charles Grassley and Nancy Kassebaum and Representatives Denny Smith and Tom Tauke, described a pattern of cost growth. The Reagan administration bought 23 percent more ships in its first four years than the Carter administration did, but it spent 48 percent more to buy them. Under Reagan, the Army has bought 40 percent more helicopters — but paid over 150 percent more for them. Spending for Air Force and Navy airplanes rose by 75 percent, but the numbers of planes purchased fell by 12 percent.[28]

Of the *Advanced Medium-Range Air-to-Air Missile,* known as the

AMRAAM, the report said that to meet the initial deployment date of 1989, "the Air Force plans to begin low-rate production of an interim design missile that does not fully meet performance requirements. Full-rate production is scheduled before the completed design is fully tested.

"This increases the risk that missiles will be produced that do not fully meet requirements and require costly modifications," said the GAO report.

"It is noteworthy that the practice of manufacturing and testing concurrently was responsible for the present problems in the electronic countermeasures of the B-1 bomber," the group said.[29]

August 1986

The Pentagon has accused the Lockheed Corp. of inflating its production contract for the C-5B cargo plane by as much as $500 million by improperly withholding financial information from the Air Force during negotiations. . . .

According to the Pentagon statement, the heart of the case revolves around Lockheed's alleged failure to share with Air Force procurement agents the company's bargaining goals and objectives prior to negotiating a new union agreement in 1983.

Lockheed was the nation's sixth largest defense contractor in fiscal 1985, the last year for which figures are available. It received Pentagon contracts valued at $5.1 billion that year.[30]

June 1987

Northrop was cited in government audits for having excess inventory at its plant, allegedly because it was ordering duplicate parts through six fictitious businesses that it set up, using $2 million of "petty cash," according to Air Force testimony in the matter.

Separately, Air Force investigators have subpoenaed 80 boxloads of missile parts that were reportedly put into the garbage dumpster and then removed by a former manager of Northrop's electronics division in Hawthorne, California.

Industrywide rumors of cost overruns surround the Stealth bomber program. The growth in costs for the bombers has led the chairman of the House Armed Services Committee to introduce legislation opening the $35.6-billion project to competition.[31]

June 1987

Avco Corporation admitted overcharging the Pentagon $1.5 million in labor costs at its Wilmington, Mass. plant. The company pleaded guilty in U.S. District Court in Boston to 22 counts of making false statements and agreed to pay $4.6 million in fines and damages.

Officials said the case is the largest instance of labor overcharging prosecuted by the Justice Department. Avco works on the MX missile, antiarmor munitions and military satellites. . . .

According to court documents, the complex scheme involved shifting extra labor charges, which normally would not be reimbursed, to an account for overhead expenses, which was reimbursed.

The grand jury heard testimony that an Avco budget official admitted that cost overruns were "buried" in the overhead account, the court documents said.

Court documents also indicated that Avco supervisors testified before the grand jury that they filled in employee time cards according to predetermined budgets rather than the actual tasks performed. Supervisors said they were encouraged to use overhead accounts when the budgeted hours were in danger of becoming exhausted.[32]

Notes

1. Walter Isaacson, "Clashes and Compromises," cited by Neil MacNeil and Bruce W. Nelan, *Time,* February 14, 1983, p. 14.
2. U.S. General Accounting Office, "Weapon Systems Overview: A Summary of Recent [June 1982 to June 1983] GAO Reports, Observations and Recommendations on Major Weapon Systems," GAO/NSIAD–83–7, September 30, 1983, p. 15.
3. "Pentagon Bogs Down in Its War on Waste," *U.S. News & World Report,* June 4, 1984, p. 73.
4. "Report Says Costs Plague Pentagon," *Boston Globe,* August 17, 1984.
5. U.S. Senate, testimony of Lt. Gen. James Stansberry, USAF (retired), before the Subcommittee on Defense Acquisition Policy of the Committee on Armed Services, "Defense Procurement Process," February 20, 1985, p. 10.
6. "Getting Tough?" *Time,* March 18, 1985, p. 27.
7. U.S. Senate, testimony of Joseph Sherick, DOD Inspector General, hearing before the Committee on Armed Services, "Audit Practices in the Department of Defense," March 12, 1985, p. 40.
8. *The Wall Street Journal,* April 10, 1985.
9. "Three-ring Circus," *The Wall Street Journal,* April 9, 1985, editorial.
10. "Scandal Rocks General Electric," *Time,* May 27, 1985, p. 60; and "Mea Culpa, Says General Electric," *Business Week,* May 27, 1985, p. 46.

11. Bill Keller, "As Arms Buildup Eases, U.S. Tries to Take Stock," *New York Times,* May 14, 1985.
12. "Stepping up the Attack on Contract Abuse," *Business Week,* July 1, 1985, p. 24.
13. "Army Contractor Probed," *Washington Post,* July 20, 1985.
14. "McDonnell Douglas's F-15 Jet Pricing Is Being Probed by a U.S. Grand Jury," *The Wall Street Journal,* September 24, 1985.
15. "After a Big Gun Comes Up a Dud . . ." *U.S. News & World Report,* September 8, 1985, p. 11.
16. "Rockwell Is to Admit to Padding Costs of Labor on Defense Jobs, Sources Say," *The Wall Street Journal,* October 29, 1985.
17. Karl Kabeiseman, Defense Logistics Agency General Counsel, in remarks to defense contractors at a meeting of the American Defense Preparedness Association, Washington, D.C., December 10, 1985.
18. "NASA Chief Indicted over Weapon Contract," *San Francisco Chronicle,* December 3, 1985.
19. Fred Newton, Acting Director of DCAA (in December 1985). He made a strong indictment of the defense industry at an industry meeting on December 10, 1985.
20. *Aerospace Daily,* December 13, 1972.
21. Richard A. Stubbing, *The Defense Game* (New York: Harper & Row, 1986), p. 217.
22. *Newsweek,* February 3, 1986, p. 18.
23. Jacques S. Gansler, "Program Instability: Causes, Costs, and Cures," paper prepared for the Defense Acquisition Study, Center for Strategic and International Studies, Georgetown University, March 1, 1986.
24. *The Wall Street Journal,* April 29, 1986.
25. "Pentagon Runs Criminal Probe of TRW, Inc.," *The Wall Street Journal,* June 24, 1986.
26. *The Wall Street Journal,* July 7, 1986.
27. "Litton Pleads Guilty to Defrauding U.S. on Pentagon Work, Will Pay $15 Million," *The Wall Street Journal,* July 16, 1986.
28. James Fallows, "The Spend-up," *Atlantic,* July 1986, p. 7.
29. "GAO Study Finds Fault with Missile," *Boston Globe,* March 29, 1987.
30. *Albany Times Union,* August 29, 1986.
31. *The Wall Street Journal,* June 22, 1987, and *Los Angeles Times,* June 13, 1987.
32. *Boston Globe,* June 24, 1987.

INDEX

A

Acheson, Dean, 98, 101

Acker, David D., 12, 17, 53, 54, 56, 99, 244

Acquisition: concept exploration phase, 24, 25; demonstration and validation phase, 24, 25; experience in, 189; full-scale development phase, 24, 26; participants in process, 18–19; production and initial deployment, 24, 27; stages in process, 22–29

Acquisition executive (AE), 50, 119, 147, 306

Adams, Gordon, 48, 55, 56, 57, 244

Addabbo, Joseph P. (D-NY), 34, 92

Administrative contracting officer (ACO), 165–167

Aegis Cruiser, 33

AEI *Memorandum,* 52

Aerospace Industries Association, 176, 225, 324

Aircraft: AH-64 Apache Helicopter, 49, 80; A-7D, 18; Black Hawk Helicopter, 66; B-1 bomber, 49, 92, 131–132; C-5A cargo plane, 31, 43, 49; C-5B, 18; C-17 cargo plane, 18, 66; F-15, 17, 66; F-14 fighter, 158, 322–323; F-14A (Tomcat), 40, 43; F-111, 18; F-16, 33, 158; P-3, 31; UH-60A Helicopter, 33

Air Force: acquisition career field, 207–213; acquisition organization, 121, 123; Contract Management Division, 273; Logistics Command (AFLC), 119; Systems Command (AFSC), 119, 121, 145, 180, 186, 194–196, 208, 226–227, 235, 238, 253, 325

Allen, Richard, 109

American Bar Association (ABA), 53, 145, 149, 176, 251–253, 268, 303, 324

American Defense Preparedness Association (ADPA), 52, 179

Amlie, Thomas S., 243

Anderson, Roy, 111, 225

Anthony, Robert, 145

A-109 (OMB Circular), 46, 47, 175

Appropriations hearings. *See* Congress

Armed Forces Journal, 53

Armed Forces Management Association (AFMA), 222

Armed Services Procurement Regulation (ASPR), 17

Arming America, 190, 241, 280, 297, 299–300, 324

Army: acquisition career field, 197–201; acquisition organization, 121–123; Helicopter Improvement Program, 328; Materiel Command (AMC), 119, 121, 168, 191, 199, 219

Art, Robert J., 16, 53, 57

Aspin, Les (D-WI), 35, 63, 88

ASPR. *See* Armed Services Procurement Regulation